Australian Wine Vintages

Twenty First Edition

2004

Robin Bradley

Hunter Agencies

First Edition	Nov. 1979
Second Edition	Nov. 1981
Third Edition	Sept. 1983
Fourth Edition	Aug. 1985
Revised	Dec. 1986
Fifth Edition	Sept. 1987

First Five Editions Published
Under The Title:
Australian Wine Vintages

Sixth Edition	Aug. 1988
Seventh Edition	Aug. 1989
Eighth Edition	Aug. 1990
Ninth Edition	Aug. 1991
Tenth Edition	Aug. 1992
Eleventh Edition	Aug. 1993
Twelfth Edition	Aug. 1994
Thirteenth Edition	Aug. 1995
Fourteenth Edition	Aug. 1996
Fifteenth Edition	Aug. 1997
Sixteenth Edition	Aug. 1998
Seventeenth Edition	Aug. 1999
Eighteenth Edition	Aug. 2000
Nineteenth Edition	Aug. 2001
Twentieth Edition	Aug. 2002
Twenty First Edition	Aug. 2003

National Library of Australia
ISBN 0 9577280 4 2

Produced by
Phoenix Offset Hong Kong

Film separations by
Eastern Studios Graphics Australia

Published by Hunter Agencies
Telephone 61 3 5368 6770

Preface to the 21st edition

It is certainly more a tribute to the quality and reputation of Australian wine than to the Gold Book that Australian Wine Vintages is now being widely distributed throughout the USA. This 21st edition now has over 1500 wines from 350 makers in its 14,300 entries - a massive growth from the slim volume which constituted the first edition.

My usual few idle observations:

No new Gold Star wines have emerged for this edition, although the Reserve Pinot Noir of the Curlewis Winery - only three vintages to date - looks certain to receive this ultimate accolade in the near future. A sublime Pinot! I look forward to a few subsequent vintages. Dare I say - it is very French.

The trend toward Stelvin closures is growing apace. The romantic in us may regret the possible gradual demise of the cork, but I am afraid that encounters with tainted wines from bad corks are growing at about the same rate as is the appearance of Stelvin closures. This is sad for the traditionalists (of whom I am one) but probably a good thing for wine. But what shall I do with my corkscrew collection?

More and more Verdelhos are being seen - a pleasant circumstance for me, as I enjoy being beguiled by this unpretentious but entirely charming variety. The wine is short-lived, it is true, but then again so is the far less agreeable Sauvignon Blanc (mercifully often ameliorated by marriage to the much more worthy Semillon).

The role of Merlot seems very undecided in Australia: it is often blended with Cabernet(s), sometimes almost apologetically as if the result were a lesser wine; sometimes used to add complexity and finesse in some of our best wines; and sometimes bottled as a varietal, which can be either a lightweight quaffer or (unfortunately very rarely) a big, dark and convincing red. One hopes that a dedicated Merlot-loving maker will one day produce a Chateau Petrus lookalike. But think back just a few years to the early days of Australian Pinot Noir - it varied between a dismissable strawberry cordial, and a tight, teeth-gritting, Shiraz-pressings-enhanced plonk, with the occasional very good wine. Perhaps Merlot will one day be treated with dignity. Time will tell.

And now a grump. A rather serious one. The romance, the beauty, the essence of wine is a vineyard, a winery and a winemaker all combining to create a bottled thing of beauty, of individuality, of vinous pleasure. Enter the "big companies". They make some very good wines, but from what? From where? Instead of estate grown, made and bottled wines, we have "Labels."

Their marketing people invent a label with a name found by committee to be saleable, and away we go. But, where is the "Grange Vineyard"? Where is the "Yattarna Vineyard"? To stop picking on Penfolds, where is the "Jacobs Creek Vineyard"? The "Bin 65 Chardonnay Vineyard"? No such place. Do the grapes come from a vineyard, or nearby, or from the same area, or from the same State, or from the same country? (In fairness, to date, I think they come from the same country.) Please, can we have attribution, and the wines may earn more respect. (And well done, the small makers.)

WineBase for Windows: Now generally accepted as the world's best cellar management software, WineBase has the good sense to include the Gold Book data as standard. To acquire a copy, contact Almost Vertical Software on +61 3 9580 2100, or visit their Web page at **www.winebase.com.au**

And talking of Web pages, if you have difficulty obtaining a further copy of this book, come to www.gold-book.com/orderidx.htm. Readers in the USA and Canada can go to **www.gold-book.us** to find out where they can obtain copies.

How to use this book.

Wines are listed alphabetically by each maker's "short name", that is, the name by which the wine is commonly known to the consumer. Most wines listed are accompanied by reduced-scale versions of the current labels.

STAR RANKINGS: Each winestyle (label) listed is ranked out of a maximum of five stars. This ranking is my own, but is applied as honestly as I can manage, suppressing as best I can any prejudices, so that the star ranking reflects some of the earned respect for the particular label over the years of its production. If you disagree with my star ranking you are exhorted to ignore it and apply your own.

A few wines of supreme quality are given "Gold Star" highlighting. In their best years these wines are among the world's greatest.

At the other extreme, there are no "one star" wines in this book. It now seems wine-writers' convention that one star means undrinkable, (which should really be "no star"). But if I stay out of step with my colleagues it would be unfair to recipients of a one star ranking.

So what do these rankings mean? As a very broad and indeed oversimplified guide, something like this:

★	not applicable - see the previous paragraph
★★	basic, agreeable drinking
★★★	average to good quality
★★★★	very fine wines
★★★★★	the continent's best
★★★★★ (gold)	among the great wines of the world

VINTAGE RATINGS: These are out of seven, and are for the most part the makers' ratings. It is very important to understand that these ratings merely compare the specific wine being rated with itself in other years. A rating of "7" does not mean a perfect wine, merely that the winemaker has no higher quality aspirations for the label than are represented by that particular year's example.

BEST YEAR TO DRINK: By far the most useful entry in the book, this is intended to identify the particular year when, in the winemaker's opinion, you will derive the greatest pleasure from drinking the wine. I have sometimes been criticized for citing a particular year rather than a range of years over which the wine should be drinking well. But were I to ask winemakers for such a range instead of a year, I know that some drinking recommendations would come in as "now until 2030". This would be confusing, messy in print and completely wrong anyway.

There's a useful rule of thumb in considering wine development - that a wine improves for a third of its life, remains on a plateau for another third, and spends the remaining third declining gracefully into eventual feebleness.

The "Best Year to Drink" recommendation is an attempt to identify the middle of the plateau phase, not the extreme limit of the wine's longevity.

PRIOR: The word "Prior" does NOT mean that the wine is undrinkable, merely that the ideal time to have consumed the average bottle is prior to today. Some well-cellared bottles can still be superb.

CURRENT INTRINSIC VALUE: This is an arbitrarily derived estimate of value - not a price, nor yet a price recommendation. The formula applied to achieve these values allows for improvement in the bottle, inflation and the rating for the particular year compared with the average rating for the label, and effectively establishes a value to you the consumer, provided that -

(a) You feel that the current normal retail price is a fair one for the average wine of the series.

(b) The actual bottle under consideration has been cellared adequately (particularly important if the wine is of some age).

The formula ignores discounting, State pricing variations, star rankings and "rarity values". It does however continue annually to increase the value of a wine throughout its "drink now" life - a token acknowledgment that most wine-lovers will value more highly an older wine still drinking well than a mature but younger wine drinking just as well.

You will notice that no values are attempted for "Prior" wines. Again, this does not mean that all such wines are valueless, but that the relevant values cannot be established by a rigid formula (as bottle to bottle variation becomes extreme in the last third of a wine's life).

The entry "N/R" means that the wine of that year has not been released as yet.

Wine Regions of AUSTRALIA

by Ken Tripp July 1993

Western Australia

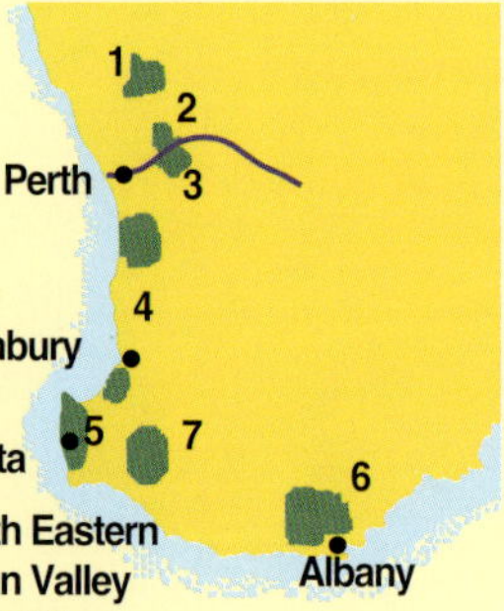

1. North Eastern
2. Swan Valley
3. Perth Hils
4. South-West Coastal
5. Margaret River
6. Mt Barker-Frankland
7. Pemberton

South Australia

1. Clare Valley, Wate
2. Barossa Valley
3. Riverland
4. Adelaide Plains
5. McClaren Vale
6. Langhorne Creek
7. Padthaway
8. Coonawarra
9. Adelaide Hills
10. Eden Valley

Brisbane
New South Wales
1. Hastings Valley
2. Upper Hunter Valley
3. Mudgee
4. Hunter Valley
5. Camden
6. Cowra
7. Murrumbidgee
8. Canberra
Sydney
Canberra
ura
Melbourne
Victoria
1. Murray River
2. North East
3. Goulburn Valley
4. Central Victoria
5. Pyrenees
6. Great Western
7. Yarra Valley
8. Mornington Peninsula
9. Geelong
10. Gippsland
11. The Lakes
12. Rutherglen
13. Macedon
smania
ipers River
amar Valley
entral East Coast
oal River Valley
erwent Valley
uon Valley
Launceston
Hobart
Verticle Software

Blank page precedes
Page 1 of Wine Listing!

__Alkoomi__ is an extreme quality Frankland River (Western Australia) producer of long-lived wines with admirably intense flavours. Winemaker: Michael Staniford.

ALKOOMI BLACKBUTT (BORDEAUX BLEND) ★★★★★

1994	6	2004	$74.00
1995	6	2005	$72.00
1996	6	2006	$70.00
1997	5	2006	$56.00
1998	6	2010	$66.00
1999	7	2013	$74.00
2000	5	2010	$52.00

ALKOOMI CABERNET SAUVIGNON ★★★★★

before 1983		Prior	
1983	7	Now	$54.00
1984	6	Now	$44.00
1985	6	Now	$43.00
1986	6	Now	$42.00
1987	7	Now	$47.00
1988	6	Now	$39.00
1989	5	Now	$32.00
1990	6	Now	$37.00
1991	5	Now	$30.00
1992	5	Now	$29.00
1993	5	Now	$28.00
1994	6	Now	$33.00
1995	6	2005	$32.00
1996	6	2005	$31.00
1997	4	2005	$20.00
1998	6	2008	$29.00
1999	7	2012	$33.00
2000	4	2006	$18.50
2001	6	2011	$27.00

ALKOOMI CHARDONNAY ★★★★

before 1996		Prior	
1996	6	Now	$30.00
1997	5	Now	$24.00
1998	6	Now	$28.00
1999	7	2006	$32.00
2000	6	2006	$26.00
2001	6	2007	$26.00

ALKOOMI RIESLING ★★★

before 1986		Prior	
1986	6	Now	$33.00
1987	5	Now	$27.00
1988	7	Now	$37.00
1989	5	Now	$25.00
1990	6	Now	$29.00

1991	6	Now	$29.00
1992	6	Now	$28.00
1993	7	Now	$31.00
1994	6	Now	$26.00
1995	6	Now	$25.00
1996	6	2004	$25.00
1997	7	2006	$28.00
1998	5	2006	$19.50
1999	7	2010	$26.00
2000	5	2007	$18.50
2001	6	2007	$21.00
2002	6	2008	$21.00

ALKOOMI SAUVIGNON BLANC
★★★★

1997	6	Now	$23.00
1998	5	Now	$19.00
1999	7	Now	$26.00
2000	6	2004	$21.00
2001	6	2005	$21.00
2002	7	2006	$23.00

ALKOOMI SHIRAZ ★★★★

1994	5	Now	$24.00
1995	6	2007	$27.00
1996	5	Now	$22.00
1997	5	2004	$21.00
1998	5	2005	$21.00
1999	6	2012	$24.00
2000	5	2010	$20.00
2001	6	2011	$23.00

ALKOOMI WANDOO (SEMILLON)
★★★★★

1997	5	2005	$31.00
1998	5	2007	$30.00
1999	7	2009	$41.00
2000	5	2009	$29.00

***Allandale** is a small Pokolbin area maker, producing a range of reliable wines including an admirable Chardonnay. Winemakers: Bill Sneddon and Peter Orr.*

ALLANDALE CHARDONNAY ★★★★★

before 1994		Prior	
1994	6	Now	$20.00
1995	5	Now	$16.50
1996	7	Now	$23.00
1997	6	Now	$19.00
1998	7	Now	$21.00
1999	6	Now	$18.00
2000	6	Now	$17.50

ALLANDALE MATTHEW SHIRAZ

★★★★

before 1987		Prior	
1987	6	Now	$40.00
1988	5	Prior	
1989	Not made		
1990	3	Prior	
1991	6	Now	$36.00
1992	Not made		
1993	5	Now	$28.00
1994	4	Now	$22.00
1995	6	Now	$32.00
1996	6	Now	$31.00
1997	5	Now	$25.00
1998	6	2004	$29.00
1999	6	2005	$28.00
2000	7	2007	$32.00

***All Saints Estate** is the label resulting from the amalgamation of St Leonards, whose white wines have always been remarkable achievements for the area, with Wahgunyah's (North East Victoria) oldest winery. St Leonards is listed seperately. If there is a better Durif made anywhere in the world, I am yet to taste it. Winemaker: Peter Brown.*

ALL SAINTS ESTATE CABERNET SAUVIGNON

★★★★

before 1990		Prior	
1990	7	Now	$30.00
1991	6	Prior	
1992	7	Prior	
1993	5	Now	$20.00
1994	5	Now	$19.50
1995	5	Now	$19.00
1996	7	2004	$25.00
1997	6	2005	$21.00
1998	7	2008	$24.00
1999	6	2007	$20.00
2000	6	2007	$19.50

ALL SAINTS ESTATE CARLYLE CHARDONNAY

★★★

1992	6	Prior	
1993	Not made		
1994	Not made		
1995	Not made		
1996	5	Now	$22.00
1997	7	Now	$30.00
1998	7	Now	$29.00
1999	6	Now	$24.00
2000	6	2004	$24.00
2001	6	2005	$23.00

ALL SAINTS ESTATE CARLYLE RUBY CABERNET ★★★★

1996	6	2008	$28.00
1997	6	2009	$27.00
1998	7	2010	$31.00
1999	6	2008	$25.00
2000	6	2009	$25.00

ALL SAINTS ESTATE CARLYLE SHIRAZ ★★★★★

1994	6	Now	$40.00
1995	7	2005	$45.00
1996	7	2008	$44.00
1997	6	2007	$36.00
1998	7	2010	$41.00
1999	6	2008	$34.00

ALL SAINTS ESTATE CHENIN BLANC ★★★

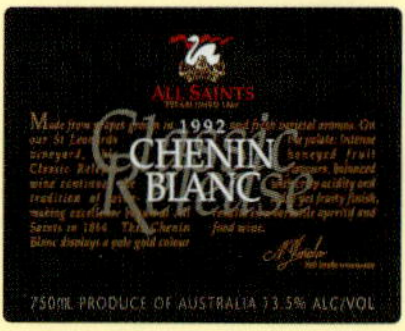

before 1995		Prior	
1995	6	Now	$15.00
1996	6	Now	$14.50
1996	6	Now	$14.00
1997	6	Now	$13.50
1998	6	Now	$13.00
1999	6	Now	$13.00

No longer made.

ALL SAINTS ESTATE DURIF ★★★★★

1998	6	2006	$40.00
1999	6	2008	$39.00
2000	6	2010	$38.00

ALL SAINTS ESTATE LATE HARVEST SEMILLON (375ml) ★★★★

1993	7	Prior	
1994	6	Now	$23.00
1995	5	Now	$18.50
1996	7	2004	$25.00
1997	6	2004	$21.00
1998	5	2004	$17.00
1999	Not made		
2000	Not made		
2001	5	2006	$15.50

ALL SAINTS MARSANNE ★★★

1992	5	Prior	
1993	Not made		
1994	5	Prior	
1995	4	Prior	
1996	6	Now	$21.00
1997	6	2004	$21.00

1998	7	2010	$24.00
1999	Not made		
2000	5	2005	$16.00
2001	5	2006	$15.50

ALL SAINTS MERLOT ★★★★

1994	4	Prior	
1995	5	Now	$21.00
1996	5	Now	$20.00
1997	6	Now	$24.00
1998	6	Now	$23.00
1999	6	2005	$22.00
2000	6	2005	$22.00

ALL SAINTS ESTATE RIESLING ★★★

1996	7	Now	$17.50
1997	7	2004	$17.00
1998	Not made		
1999	Not made		
2000	7	2010	$15.50
2001	7	2012	$15.00
2002	7	2006	$15.00

ALL SAINTS ESTATE SHIRAZ ★★★★

before 1992		Prior	
1992	7	Now	$28.00
1993	5	Now	$20.00
1994	5	Now	$19.00
1995	Not made		
1996	7	2004	$25.00
1997	6	Now	$21.00
1998	7	2004	$24.00
1999	6	Now	$20.00
2000	6	2007	$19.50

***Amberley Estate** is an impressive Margaret River producer whose surprisingly large range includes some wines unusual for the area. Winemakers: Eddie Price and David Watson.*

AMBERLEY ESTATE CABERNET SAUVIGNON RESERVE ★★★★★

1992	4	Prior	
1993	5	Now	$76.00
1994	Not made		
1995	5	2005	$70.00
1996	6	2006	$82.00
1997	4	2007	$54.00
1998	Not made		
1999	6	2010	$76.00
2000	5	2010	$62.00

AMBERLEY ESTATE CABERNET/MERLOT ★★★★

before 1993		Prior	
1993	6	Now	$30.00
1994	5	Prior	
1995	6	Now	$29.00
1996	6	Now	$28.00
1997	5	Now	$22.00
1998	4	2004	$17.50
1999	6	2006	$25.00
2000	6	2006	$25.00

AMBERLEY ESTATE CHARDONNAY ★★★★

before 1996		Prior	
1996	4	Now	$33.00
1997	4	Now	$32.00
1998	Not made		
1999	5	Now	$38.00
2000	5	2004	$36.00
2001	5	2005	$35.00

AMBERLEY ESTATE CHENIN BLANC ★★★

before 1999		Prior	
1999	6	Now	$16.00
2000	6	Now	$15.50
2001	5	Now	$12.50

AMBERLEY ESTATE SAUVIGNON BLANC ★★★

before 2000		Prior	
2000	6	Now	$19.00
2001	6	Now	$18.50

AMBERLEY ESTATE SEMILLON ★★★★

1990	4	Now	$23.00
1991	3	Prior	
1992	6	Now	$33.00
1993	5	Prior	
1994	4	Prior	
1995	5	Now	$25.00
1996	6	Now	$29.00
1997	7	Now	$33.00
1998	5	Now	$23.00
1999	6	2005	$27.00
2000	5	2006	$21.00
2001	6	2007	$25.00

AMBERLEY ESTATE SEMILLON/ SAUVIGNON BLANC ★★★

before 1999		Prior	
1999	5	Now	$18.00
2000	6	Now	$21.00
2001	5	Now	$17.00

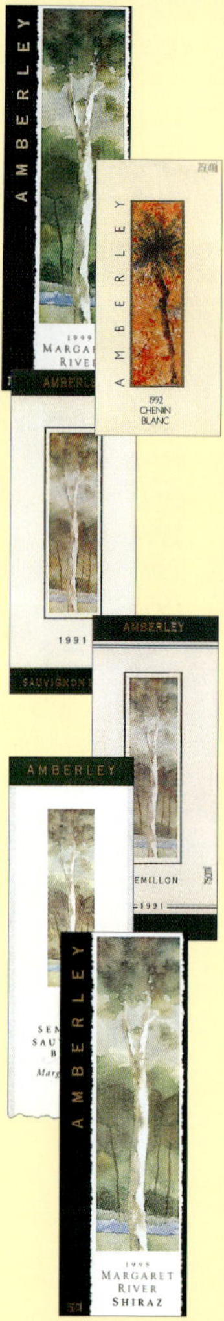

AMBERLEY ESTATE SHIRAZ ★★★★

1994	4	Prior	
1995	6	Now	$39.00
1996	7	Now	$44.00
1997	6	Now	$36.00
1998	5	Now	$29.00
1999	7	2005	$40.00
2000	6	2006	$33.00

***Amherst Winery** in Victoria's Pyrenees region is a small hobbyist operation with the admirable aspiration of producing a Shiraz of both substance and elegance. Winemaker: Norman Jones.*

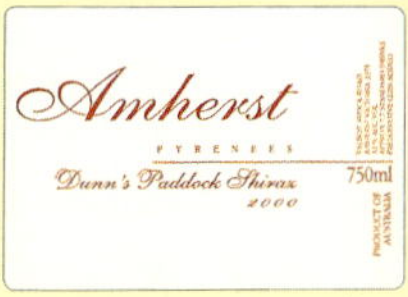

AMHERST SHIRAZ ★★★★

1998	6	2004	$28.00
1999	5	2006	$22.00
2000	6	2006	$26.00

***Andrew Garrett Wines** are McLaren Vale makers now owned by Beringer Blass. Winemaker: Charles Hargrave.*

ANDREW GARRETT CABERNET/MERLOT ★★★★

before 1992		Prior	
1992	5	Now	$15.50
1993	6	Now	$18.00
1994	5	Now	$14.50
1995	5	Now	$14.00
1996	6	Now	$16.50
1997	6	Now	$16.00
1998	7	Now	$18.00
1999	5	Now	$12.50

ANDREW GARRETT CHARDONNAY ★★★

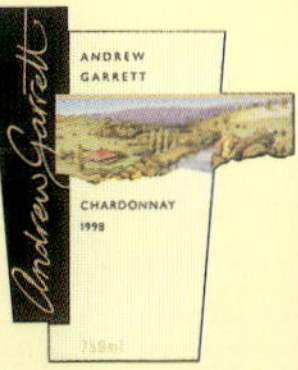

before 1995		Prior	
1995	6	Now	$15.50
1996	6	Now	$15.00
1997	6	Now	$14.50
1998	6	Now	$14.00
1999	7	Now	$16.00
2000	5	Now	$11.00
2001	6	Now	$13.00

ANDREW GARRETT SHIRAZ ★★★★

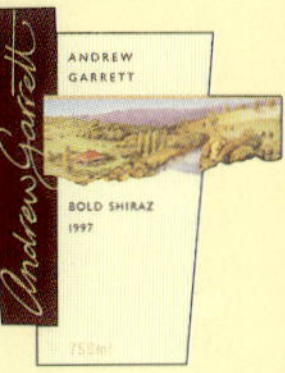

1991	7	Prior	
1992	5	Now	$14.00
1993	7	Now	$19.00
1994	6	Now	$16.00
1995	5	Now	$13.00
1996	7	Now	$17.50
1997	6	Now	$14.50
1998	7	Now	$16.50
1999	6	2005	$13.50
2000	6	2005	$13.50

***Angoves** is a large, family owned Riverland company which produces some of our finest brandies as well as a range of graceful and reliable table wines. Winemaker: Warrick Billings.*

ANGOVES BEAR CROSSING CABERNET/MERLOT ★★

2000	6	Now	$8.00
2001	6	2004	$7.75
2002	7	2006	$8.75

ANGOVES BEAR CROSSING CHARDONNAY ★★

2000	5	Prior	
2001	6	Now	$8.00
2002	7	2004	$9.25

ANGOVES BUTTERFLY RIDGE SHIRAZ /CABERNET ★★

before 1999		Prior	
1999	5	Now	$6.50
2000	5	Now	$6.25
2001	6	Now	$7.50
2002	7	Now	$8.50

ANGOVES CLASSIC RESERVE CABERNET SAUVIGNON ★★

before 2000		Prior	
2000	6	2004	$10.00
2001	6	2005	$9.75
2002	7	2007	$11.00

ANGOVES CLASSIC RESERVE CHARDONNAY ★★★

before 2001		Prior	
2001	6	Now	$9.50
2002	7	2004	$10.50

ANGOVES CLASSIC RESERVE SHIRAZ ★★

before 2000		Prior	
2000	6	Now	$10.00
2001	6	Now	$9.75
2002	7	2006	$11.00

ANGOVES SARNIA FARM CABERNET SAUVIGNON ★★★

before 1997		Prior	
1997	7	Now	$15.50
1998	7	Now	$15.00
1999	6	Now	$12.50
2000	7	2005	$14.00
2001	6	2006	$12.00
2002	7	2008	$13.50

ANGOVES SARNIA FARM CHARDONNAY ★★★★

beforee 1997		Prior	
1997	6	Now	$15.00
1998	6	Now	$14.50
1999	6	Prior	
2000	5	Prior	
2001	6	Now	$13.00
2002	7	2006	$15.00

ANGOVES SARNIA FARM SHIRAZ ★★★

2000	5	2004	$11.00
2001	6	2006	$13.00
2002	7	2008	$15.00

Annie's Lane *is a Clare Valley vineyard owned by Beringer Blass. The fruit is vinified at the old Quelltaler winery, producing most agreeable and reasonably priced wines. Winemaker: Caroline Dunn.*

ANNIE'S LANE CABERNET/MERLOT ★★★★

1995	5	Now	$15.50
1996	7	Now	$21.00
1997	6	Now	$18.00
1998	7	Now	$20.00
1999	5	2005	$14.00
2000	7	2006	$19.00

ANNIE'S LANE CHARDONNAY ★★★★

1996	5	Now	$13.50
1997	6	Now	$16.00
1998	6	Now	$15.50
1999	6	Now	$15.00
2000	6	2004	$14.50
2001	6	2004	$14.00

ANNIE'S LANE RIESLING ★★★★

1996	6	Now	$14.00
1997	7	Now	$16.00
1998	7	Now	$15.50
1999	7	Now	$15.00
2000	7	2005	$14.50
2001	7	2005	$14.00

ANNIE'S LANE SEMILLON ★★★★★

1996	5	Now	$12.50
1997	6	Now	$14.50
1998	7	Now	$16.50
1999	7	Now	$16.00
2000	7	2010	$15.50
2001	6	2008	$13.00

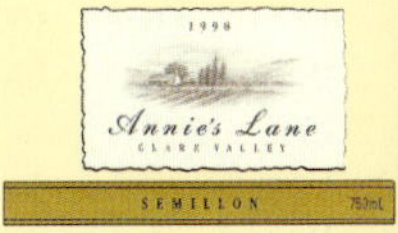

ANNIE'S LANE SHIRAZ ★★★★

1995	5	Now	$14.00
1996	7	Now	$19.00
1997	6	Now	$15.50
1998	7	2004	$18.00
1999	6	2005	$15.00
2000	6	2006	$14.50

***Antcliff's Chase** is a family owned 4 hectare vineyard in the Strathbogie Ranges in Central Victoria. Winemaker: Chris Bennett.*

ANTCLIFF'S CHASE CABERNET ENSEMBLE ★★★★

1991	6	Prior	
1992	7	Now	$25.00
1993	Not made		
1994	7	Now	$23.00
1995	Not made		
1996	6	Now	$19.00
1997	6	Now	$18.50

No data since 1997

ANTCLIFF'S CHASE CHARDONNAY ★★★★

before 1994		Prior	
1994	7	Now	$27.00
1995	6	Now	$22.00
1996	6	Now	$22.00
1997	7	Now	$25.00
1998	6	Now	$20.00
1999	7	Now	$23.00

ANTCLIFF'S CHASE PINOT NOIR ★★★★

before 1992		Prior	
1992	7	Now	$29.00
1993	Not made		
1994	7	Now	$27.00
1995	6	Now	$22.00
1996	6	Now	$22.00
1997	7	Now	$25.00
1998	Not made		
1999	6	Now	$20.00

ANTCLIFF'S CHASE RIESLING ★★★★

before 1994		Prior	
1994	7	Now	$22.00
1995	6	Prior	
1996	7	Now	$21.00
1997	7	Now	$20.00
1998	7	Now	$19.50
1999	6	2004	$16.50
2000	7	2005	$18.50

__Arrowfield's__ 100 hectare vineyard is a substantial supplier to the Sydney wine market. Much of the fruit is from Cowra as well as from the home vineyards in the Upper Hunter. Winemaker: Blair Duncan.

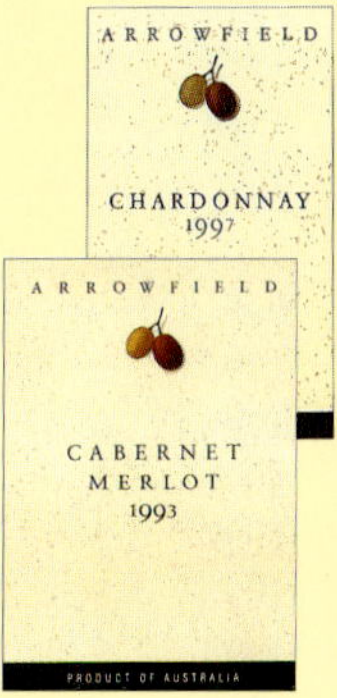

ARROWFIELD CHARDONNAY ★★

before 1999		Prior	
1999	5	Now	$13.00
2000	5	Now	$13.00

ARROWFIELD CABERNET/MERLOT ★★

before 1995		Prior	
1995	6	Now	$15.00
1996	6	Now	$14.50
1997	6	Now	$14.00
1998	6	Now	$13.50
1999	5	Now	$11.00

ARROWFIELD COWRA CHARDONNAY ★★★

1996	5	Now	$14.50
1997	7	Now	$19.50
1998	6	Now	$16.00
1999	6	Now	$15.50
2000	5	Now	$12.50

ARROWFIELD COWRA MERLOT ★★★

1996	5	Now	$14.50
1997	6	Now	$16.50
1998	6	Now	$16.00
1999	6	Now	$15.50
2000	6	Now	$15.50

ARROWFIELD HUNTER VALLEY CHARDONNAY ★★★

1994	6	Now	$18.00
1995	6	Now	$17.00
1996	7	Now	$19.50
1997	5	Now	$13.50
1998	6	Now	$16.00

ARROWFIELD HUNTER VALLEY SEMILLON ★★★

1994	5	Now	$15.00
1995	7	Now	$20.00
1996	6	Now	$17.00
1997	6	Now	$16.50
1998	7	Prior	
1999	6	Now	$15.50

ARROWFIELD SHOW RESERVE CABERNET SAUVIGNON ★★★

before 1991		Prior	
1991	5	Now	$25.00
1992	4	Prior	

1993	4	Now	$19.00
1994	4	Prior	
1995	6	Now	$26.00
1996	5	Now	$21.00
1997	6	Now	$25.00
1998	5	Now	$20.00

ARROWFIELD SHOW RESERVE CHARDONNAY ★★★

before 1994		Prior	
1994	5	Now	$18.50
1995	6	Now	$21.00
1996	7	Now	$24.00
1997	7	Now	$24.00
1998	7	Prior	
1999	5	Now	$16.00

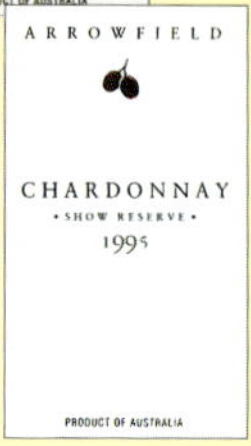

ARROWFIELD SHOW RESERVE SHIRAZ ★★★

before 1993		Prior	
1993	6	Now	$24.00
1994	5	Prior	
1995	Not made		
1996	6	Now	$22.00
1997	6	Now	$21.00

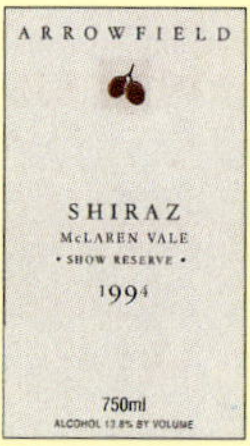

***Arthurs Creek Estate** is a small Yarra Valley vineyard established in the 1970s, and has since then irregularly released small parcels of wine, some of which have been exemplary. Winemaker: Gary Baldwin.*

ARTHURS CREEK CABERNET SAUVIGNON ★★★★★

before 1992		Prior	
1992	6	Now	$52.00
1993	7	Now	$60.00
1994	7	Now	$58.00
1995	7	Now	$56.00
1996	6	2004	$47.00
1997	6	2005	$46.00
1998	7	2006	$52.00
1999	6	2007	$43.00
2000	7	2008	$49.00

ARTHURS CREEK CHARDONNAY ★★★★

before 1998		Prior	
1998	7	Now	$37.00
1999	7	Now	$36.00
2000	6	Now	$30.00
2001	6	Now	$29.00

Ashton Hills *is a 3.5 hectare vineyard in the Piccadilly region of the Adelaide Hills. The wines are very fine indeed. Winemaker: Stephen George.*

ASHTON HILLS OBLIQUA (CABERNET/MERLOT) ★★★★

1988	5	Now	$28.00
1989	5	Now	$27.00
1990	6	Now	$32.00
1991	6	Now	$31.00
1992	6	Now	$30.00
1993	Not made		
1994	7	Now	$33.00
1995	Not made		
1996	6	Now	$26.00
1997	7	2005	$30.00
1998	6	Now	$25.00
1999	7	2005	$28.00

ASHTON HILLS CHARDONNAY ★★★★

1988	5	Now	$29.00
1989	6	Now	$34.00
1990	6	Now	$33.00
1991	7	Now	$37.00
1992	5	Now	$26.00
1993	6	Prior	
1994	Not made		
1995	6	Now	$28.00
1996	6	Now	$27.00
1997	7	Now	$31.00
1998	6	Now	$26.00
1999	7	2005	$29.00
2000	6	Now	$24.00

ASHTON HILLS PINOT NOIR ★★★★★

before 1994		Prior	
1994	6	Now	$34.00
1995	6	Now	$33.00
1996	6	Now	$32.00
1997	7	Now	$37.00
1998	6	Now	$30.00
1999	7	Now	$34.00
2000	7	2005	$33.00
2001	6	Now	$28.00

ASHTON HILLS RIESLING ★★★★

1987	5	Now	$24.00
1988	6	Now	$28.00
1989	6	Now	$27.00
1990	7	Now	$30.00
1991	7	Now	$30.00
1992	5	Now	$20.00

1993	6	Prior	
1994	6	Now	$23.00
1995	6	Now	$22.00
1996	7	Now	$25.00
1997	7	Now	$25.00
1998	6	Now	$20.00
1999	6	2005	$20.00
2000	7	2005	$23.00
2001	7	2009	$22.00
2002	Not made		

ASHTON HILLS SALMON BRUT ★★★★★

1992	6	Now	$32.00
1993	6	Now	$31.00
1994	6	Now	$30.00
1995	6	Now	$29.00
1996	6	Now	$28.00
1997	Not made		
1998	Not made		
1999	6	Now	$26.00
2000	Not made		
2001	6	Now	$25.00

Baileys*, now part of Beringer Blass, is the ultimate traditionalist Australian vineyard, situated at Taminick near Glenrowan, Victoria. It is renowned both for its long-living dry reds and its luscious fortified wines. Winemaker: Nick Walker.*

BAILEYS 1920s BLOCK SHIRAZ ★★★★★

1991	6	Now	$28.00
1992	6	2007	$27.00
1993	6	2008	$26.00
1994	6	2008	$26.00
1995	7	2009	$29.00
1996	6	2008	$24.00
1997	7	2010	$27.00
1998	7	2010	$27.00
1999	6	2010	$22.00
2000	6	2010	$21.00

BAILEYS CLASSIC SHIRAZ ★★★★

before 1973		Prior	
1973	6	Now	$43.00
1974	6	Now	$42.00
1975	7	Now	$48.00
1976	5	Prior	
1977	7	Prior	
1978	5	Prior	
1979	7	Prior	

1980	7	Now	$41.00
1981	5	Prior	
1982	6	Prior	
1983	5	Prior	
1984	5	Prior	
1985	7	Prior	
1986	6	Prior	
1987	6	Now	$29.00
1988	6	Now	$28.00
1989	5	Now	$22.00
1990	6	Now	$26.00
1991	5	Now	$21.00
1992	7	Now	$29.00
1993	6	Now	$24.00
1994	6	Now	$23.00
1995	7	2004	$26.00
1996	6	2004	$22.00
1997	7	2004	$25.00
1998	7	2005	$24.00
1999	6	2006	$20.00
2000	6	2010	$19.50

Balgownie Estate *is a once remarkable model vineyard near Bendigo, now on the resurgence. Winemaker: Tobias Ansted.*

BALGOWNIE ESTATE CABERNET SAUVIGNON ★★★★

before 1976		Prior	
1976	7	Now	$82.00
1977	4	Prior	
1978	5	Now	$54.00
1979	3	Prior	
1980	7	Now	$72.00
1981	4	Prior	
1982	5	Prior	
1983	3	Prior	
1984	4	Prior	
1985	6	Prior	
1986	7	Now	$60.00
1987	6	Now	$50.00
1988	7	Now	$58.00
1989	6	Now	$48.00
1990	7	2005	$54.00
1991	Not made		
1992	7	2007	$50.00
1993	6	Now	$42.00
1994	5	Now	$34.00
1995	5	Now	$33.00
1996	5	2005	$32.00
1997	6	2008	$38.00

1998	6	2008	$37.00
1999	5	2007	$29.00
2000	6	2009	$34.00

BALGOWNIE ESTATE SHIRAZ ★★★★

before 1986		Prior	
1986	6	Now	$49.00
1987	6	Now	$47.00
1988	6	Now	$46.00
1989	7	Now	$52.00
1990	6	Now	$43.00
1991	Not made		
1992	Not made		
1993	5	Now	$33.00
1994	6	Now	$38.00
1995	5	Now	$31.00
1996	6	2006	$36.00
1997	7	2007	$41.00
1998	6	2008	$34.00
1999	5	2007	$27.00
2000	6	2008	$32.00

***Ballandean Estate** (formerly Sundown Valley Vineyards) is a well-established maker in Queensland's Granite Belt. Winemakers: Angelo Puglisi and Phyllis Rhymer.*

BALLANDEAN ESTATE SEMILLON/ SAUVIGNON BLANC ★★

before 2001		Prior	
2000	6	Now	$14.00
2001	6	Now	$14.00

BALLANDEAN ESTATE SHIRAZ ★★★★

1989	7	Now	$32.00
1990	6	Prior	
1991	Not made		
1992	6	Now	$25.00
1993	5	Prior	
1994	6	Prior	
1995	7	Now	$27.00
1996	6	Now	$22.00
1997	7	Now	$25.00
1998	6	2006	$21.00
1999	6	2008	$20.00
2000	6	2009	$20.00
2001	6	2009	$19.00

BALLANDEAN ESTATE SYLVANER LATE HARVEST (375ml) ★★★

1989	7	Now	$26.00
1990	6	Prior	
1991	7	Now	$24.00

1992	4	Prior	
1993	7	Now	$23.00
1994	6	Now	$19.00
1995	Not made		
1996	Not made		
1997	Not made		
1998	Not made		
1999	6	2005	$16.50
2000	6	2007	$16.00
2001	6	2008	$15.50

***Balnaves of Coonawarra** became makers rather than grapegrowers in 1990 although the vineyard was established in 1975. They now have one of the modern wineries in the area. Winemaker: Peter Bissell.*

BALNAVES CABERNET/MERLOT ★★★★

1990	7	Now	$42.00
1991	6	Now	$35.00
1992	Not made		
1993	4	Prior	
1994	5	Now	$27.00
1995	Not made		
1996	6	Now	$30.00
1997	5	Now	$24.00
1998	7	2004	$33.00
1999	6	2004	$28.00
2000	6	2005	$27.00
2001	7	2005	$30.00

BALNAVES CABERNET SAUVIGNON ★★★★★

1990	7	Now	$52.00
1991	7	Now	$50.00
1992	Not made		
1993	4	Now	$27.00
1994	5	Now	$33.00
1995	5	Now	$32.00
1996	6	Now	$37.00
1997	5	Now	$30.00
1998	7	2006	$41.00
1999	6	2005	$34.00
2000	7	2008	$39.00
2001	6	2008	$32.00

BALNAVES CHARDONNAY ★★★

before 1997		Prior	
1997	6	Now	$29.00
1998	6	Prior	
1999	7	Now	$32.00
2000	6	Now	$27.00
2001	7	2004	$30.00

Bannockburn *is a purist Geelong area producer with a low-yielding vineyard whose fine fruit is annually crafted into admirable wines. Winemaker: Gary Farr.*

BANNOCKBURN CABERNET SAUVIGNON/MERLOT ★★★★

before 1985		Prior	
1985	5	Now	$49.00
1986	6	Now	$56.00
1987	6	Now	$54.00
1988	6	Now	$54.00
1989	4	Prior	
1990	5	Now	$42.00
1991	5	Now	$41.00
1992	5	Now	$40.00
1993	5	2005	$39.00
1994	5	2005	$37.00
1995	5	2005	$36.00
1996	6	2005	$42.00
1997	6	2005	$41.00
1998	Not made		
1999	6	2004	$39.00

BANNOCKBURN CHARDONNAY ★★★★★

before 1988		Prior	
1988	6	Now	$72.00
1989	4	Now	$46.00
1990	5	Now	$56.00
1991	4	Now	$44.00
1992	6	Now	$64.00
1993	7	Now	$72.00
1994	7	Now	$70.00
1995	5	Now	$48.00
1996	6	2004	$56.00
1997	7	2005	$64.00
1998	6	Now	$52.00
1999	7	2005	$60.00
2000	7	Now	$58.00

BANNOCKBURN PINOT NOIR ★★★★★

before 1988		Prior	
1988	6	Now	$70.00
1989	6	Now	$68.00
1990	5	Now	$54.00
1991	4	Now	$42.00
1992	6	Now	$62.00
1993	7	Now	$70.00
1994	7	Now	$68.00
1995	5	Now	$47.00
1996	6	2004	$54.00

1997	7	2005	$62.00
1998	6	Now	$52.00
1999	7	2005	$58.00
2000	7	2003	$56.00

BANNOCKBURN SAUVIGNON BLANC ★★★★

before 1995		Prior	
1995	6	Now	$24.00
1996	6	Now	$23.00
1997	7	Now	$27.00
1998	Not made		
1999	6	Now	$21.00
2000	7	Now	$24.00
2001	7	Now	$24.00
2002	7	Now	$23.00

BANNOCKBURN SHIRAZ ★★★★

before 1988		Prior	
1988	7	Now	$78.00
1989	6	Prior	
1990	5	Prior	
1991	5	Now	$50.00
1992	7	Now	$70.00
1993	7	Now	$68.00
1994	6	Now	$56.00
1995	5	2005	$45.00
1996	6	2005	$52.00
1997	7	2005	$60.00
1998	7	2005	$58.00
1999	7	2006	$56.00
2000	7	2005	$54.00

***Barossa Valley Estate** is an independent co-operative of Barossa Valley grapegrowers, with some distribution links with BRL Hardy. Winemaker: Natasha Mooney.*

BAROSSA VALLEY ESTATE E&E BLACK PEPPER SHIRAZ ★★★★★

1988	7	Now	$96.00
1989	5	Now	$66.00
1990	6	2007	$78.00
1991	6	2007	$76.00
1992	6	2007	$72.00
1993	5	Now	$58.00
1994	6	2007	$68.00
1995	5	Now	$56.00
1996	7	2007	$76.00
1997	5	2004	$52.00
1998	7	2010	$72.00
1999	7	2010	$70.00

BAROSSA VALLEY ESTATE E&E SPARKLING SHIRAZ ★★★★

1990	6	Now	$48.00
1991	7	Now	$54.00
1992	7	Now	$52.00
1993	5	Now	$36.00
1994	7	Now	$50.00
1995	6	Now	$41.00
1996	6	Now	$40.00
1997	6	Now	$39.00

BAROSSA VALLEY ESTATE EBENEZER CABERNET/MALBEC/MERLOT ★★★

1989	7	Now	$45.00
1990	Not made		
1991	6	Now	$36.00
1992	7	Now	$41.00
1993	5	Now	$28.00
1994	6	Now	$33.00
1995	6	Now	$32.00
1996	6	Now	$31.00
1997	6	Now	$30.00
1998	7	2005	$34.00
1999	6	2005	$28.00
2000	6	2006	$28.00

BAROSSA VALLEY ESTATE EBENEZER CHARDONNAY ★★★

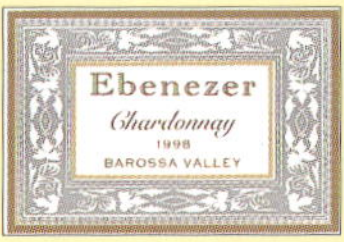

1992	7	Now	$30.00
1993	6	Now	$25.00
1994	7	Now	$28.00
1995	7	Now	$27.00
1996	7	Now	$26.00
1997	6	Now	$22.00
1998	6	Now	$21.00
1999	6	Now	$21.00
2000	6	Now	$20.00

BAROSSA VALLEY ESTATE EBENEZER SHIRAZ ★★★★

1991	7	Now	$40.00
1992	7	Now	$38.00
1993	6	Now	$32.00
1994	6	Now	$31.00
1995	7	Now	$35.00
1996	6	2004	$29.00
1997	7	2005	$33.00
1998	7	2007	$32.00
1999	7	2007	$31.00
2000	6	2006	$26.00

BAROSSA VALLEY ESTATE MOCULTA CABERNET/MERLOT ★★★

before 1989		Prior	
1989	7	Now	$25.00
1990	6	Now	$21.00
1991	7	Now	$24.00
1992	6	Prior	
1993	6	Prior	
1994	5	Prior	
1995	6	Now	$18.00
1996	7	Now	$20.00
1997	6	Now	$17.00
1998	7	Now	$19.50
1999	6	Now	$16.00
2000	6	Now	$15.50
2001	6	Now	$15.00

BAROSSA VALLEY ESTATE MOCULTA CHARDONNAY ★★★

before 1993		Prior	
1993	6	Now	$18.00
1994	7	Now	$20.00
1995	7	Now	$20.00
1996	5	Now	$13.50
1997	5	Now	$13.50
1998	6	Now	$15.50
1999	Not made		
2000	6	Now	$14.50
2001	6	Now	$14.00
2002	6	Now	$14.00

BAROSSA VALLEY ESTATE MOCULTA SHIRAZ ★★

1985	7	Now	$29.00
1986	5	Now	$20.00
1987	6	Now	$23.00
1988	5	Now	$19.00
1989	6	Now	$22.00
1990	7	Now	$25.00
1991	7	Now	$24.00
1992	6	Now	$20.00
1993	6	Now	$19.50
1994	5	Now	$16.00
1995	6	Now	$18.50
1996	7	Now	$21.00
1997	6	Now	$17.50
1998	7	Now	$20.00
1999	6	Now	$16.50
2000	6	2004	$16.00
2001	6	Now	$15.50

Barry, Brian *- see Jud's Hill*

Barry, Jim *- see Jim Barry Wines.*

Barwang *is the name of McWilliam's newest vineyard, in the Hilltops area of the Great Dividing Range near Young in NSW. Winemakers: Scott Zrna and Russell Cody.*

BARWANG CABERNET SAUVIGNON ★★★★

1990	6	Now	$31.00
1991	6	Now	$31.00
1992	6	Now	$30.00
1993	6	Now	$29.00
1994	6	Now	$28.00
1995	5	Now	$22.00
1996	6	2006	$26.00
1997	6	2006	$25.00
1998	7	2010	$29.00
1999	6	2006	$24.00
2000	6	2007	$23.00
2001	7	2011	$26.00
2002	7	2014	$26.00

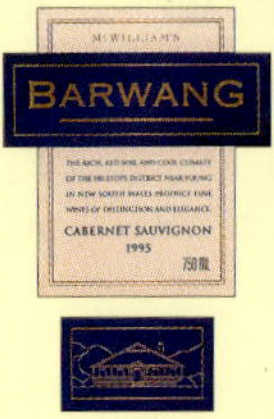

BARWANG CHARDONNAY ★★★

before 1998		Prior	
1998	6	Now	$20.00
1999	6	2004	$19.50
2000	7	2004	$22.00
2001	5	2005	$15.00
2002	7	2006	$20.00
2003	Not made		

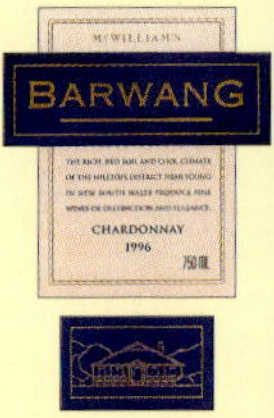

BARWANG SHIRAZ ★★★★

1990	6	Now	$31.00
1991	6	Now	$31.00
1992	6	Now	$30.00
1993	6	Now	$29.00
1994	6	Now	$28.00
1995	5	Now	$22.00
1996	6	2004	$26.00
1997	6	2004	$25.00
1998	7	2010	$29.00
1999	6	2006	$24.00
2000	6	2007	$23.00
2001	7	2011	$26.00
2002	7	2015	$26.00

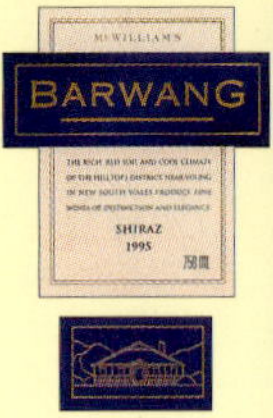

***Basedows** are long established Barossa makers whose wines over recent years have been among the valley's best, in particular the Chardonnay and the heavily oaked Semillon. Winemaker: Craig Starsborough.*

BASEDOW BAROSSA SHIRAZ ★★★★

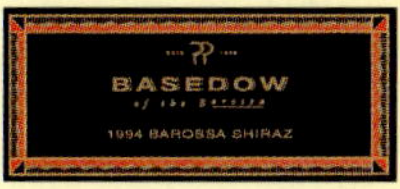

1970	7	Now	$38.00
1971	7	Now	$37.00
1972	6	Now	$31.00
1973		Prior	
1979	Not made		
1980	5	Now	$23.00
1981	6	Now	$27.00
1982	7	Prior	
1983	4	Prior	
1984	6	Now	$25.00
1985	5	Prior	
1986	6	Now	$23.00
1987	6	Now	$23.00
1988	6	Now	$22.00
1989	7	Now	$25.00
1990	7	Now	$24.00
1991	7	Now	$23.00
1992	5	Now	$16.50
1993	7	Now	$22.00
1994	7	2010	$21.00
1995	7	2010	$21.00
1996	7	2010	$20.00
1997	7	2010	$20.00

BASEDOW CHARDONNAY ★★★★

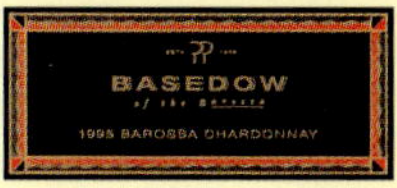

1984	5	Prior	
1985	7	Now	$25.00
1986	5	Now	$17.50
1987	7	Now	$24.00
1988	6	Prior	
1989	7	Now	$22.00
1990	6	Now	$19.00
1991	6	Now	$18.00
1992	6	Prior	
1993	7	2005	$20.00
1994	7	2010	$19.50
1995	7	2010	$19.00
1996	7	2010	$18.50
1997	6	2010	$15.00
1998	7	2012	$17.50

BASEDOW SEMILLON ★★★★

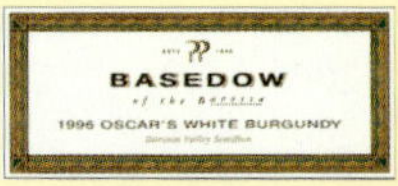

1985	7	Now	$19.00
1986	5	Now	$13.00
1987	7	Prior	

1988	7	Now	$17.50
1989	6	Now	$14.50
1990	6	Now	$14.00
1991	7	2005	$16.00
1992	6	Now	$13.50
1993	5	Now	$10.50
1994	5	Now	$10.50
1995	7	2010	$14.00
1996	7	2005	$14.00
1997	7	2008	$13.50
1998	7	2010	$13.00

***Bass Phillip** in Gippsland's Leongatha region produces a magnificent Pinot Noir. Winemaker: Phillip Jones.*

BASS PHILLIP PINOT NOIR (PREMIUM) ★★★★★

1984	6	Now	$120.00
1985	5	Now	$96.00
1986	6	Now	$110.00
1987	6	Now	$105.00
1988	6	Now	$105.00
1989	7	Now	$120.00
1990	5	Now	$82.00
1991	7	Now	$110.00
1992	7	Now	$110.00
1993	6	Now	$92.00
1994	7	Now	$100.00
1995	7	Now	$100.00
1996	7	Now	$98.00
1997	7	2004	$94.00
1998	7	2006	$92.00
1999	7	2008	$88.00
2000	6	2007	$74.00

***Beckett's Flat** is a recently established 14 hectare vineyard in Margaret River. Winemaker: Belizar Ilic.*

BECKETT'S FLAT CABERNET(/MERLOT) ★★★

1997	7	2004	$31.00
1998	5	2004	$21.00
1999	6	2005	$25.00
2000	6	2006	$24.00
2001	6	2007	$24.00

BECKETT'S FLAT SHIRAZ ★★★★

1998	5	2004	$23.00
1999	5	2004	$23.00
2000	7	2005	$31.00
2001	6	2007	$26.00

BECKETT'S FLAT MERLOT ★★★★

1999	7	2004	$27.00
2000	6	2004	$23.00
2001	Not made		

***Beckingham Wines** is a small Melbourne based winery specialising in an admirable sparkling wine using Pinot Noir and Chardonnay grapes sourced from the Mornington Peninsula, the Strathbogie Ranges and the Yarra Valley. Winemaker: Peter Beckingham.*

BECKINGHAM PAS DE DEUX ★★★★

1997	5	Now	$17.50
1998	6	Now	$20.00
1999	6	Now	$19.50
2000	5	2004	$16.00
2001	6	2006	N/R

***Belgenny Vineyard** is an enterprise based in the Hunter Valley's Pokolbin area, with a 17 hectare vineyard planted with a limited range of the noble varieties. Winemakers: Greg Silkman and Douglas Hamilton.*

BELGENNY CHARDONNAY ★★★

1995	4	Now	$21.00
1996	4	Now	$20.00
1997	Not made		
1998	5	Now	$24.00
1999	6	Now	$28.00
2000	5	Now	$22.00

BELGENNY CHARDONNAY (UNOAKED) ★★★

1996	4	Now	$15.00
1997	Not made		
1998	4	Now	$14.00
1999	5	Now	$17.00
2000	6	2004	$20.00

BELGENNY MERLOT ★★★★

1995	4	Now	$26.00
1996	4	Now	$25.00
1997	Not made		
1998	5	2004	$30.00
1999	4	2004	$23.00
2000	5	2006	$28.00

BELGENNY SEMILLON ★★★

1998	Not made		
1999	6	2009	$18.50
2000	6	2009	$18.00

BELGENNY SHIRAZ ★★★★

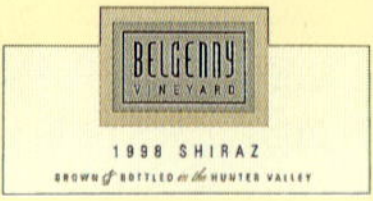

1994	5	Now	$29.00
1995	5	Now	$28.00
1996	4	Now	$21.00
1997	4	Now	$21.00
1998	7	2005	$36.00
1999	5	2005	$25.00
2000	6	2008	$29.00

Best's at Great Western *(Victoria) have produced consistently beguiling wines for many decades. Winemakers: Viv Thomson & Michael Unwin.*

BEST'S GREAT WESTERN CABERNET SAUVIGNON ★★★★

1987	4	Prior	
1988	7	Now	$46.00
1989	5	Prior	
1990	6	Now	$37.00
1991	7	Now	$42.00
1992	6	Now	$35.00
1993	6	Now	$34.00
1994	7	Now	$38.00
1995	6	Now	$32.00
1996	6	Now	$31.00
1997	6	Now	$30.00
1998	6	2008	$29.00
1999	7	2010	$33.00

BEST'S GREAT WESTERN CHARDONNAY ★★★★

before 1984		Prior	
1984	7	Now	$52.00
1985	6	Now	$44.00
1986	6	Now	$42.00
1987	6	Now	$41.00
1988	6	Now	$40.00
1989	7	Now	$45.00
1990	6	Now	$38.00
1991	5	Now	$30.00
1992	5	Now	$29.00
1993	5	Now	$28.00
1994	5	Now	$28.00
1995	6	Now	$32.00
1996	7	2004	$37.00
1997	6	2004	$30.00
1998	6	2004	$29.00
1999	5	2004	$24.00
2000	7	2005	$32.00

BEST'S GREAT WESTERN PINOT MEUNIER ★★★★

before 1987		Prior	
1987	6	Now	$50.00
1988	6	Now	$49.00
1989	5	Prior	
1990	6	Now	$46.00
1991	6	Now	$45.00
1992	6	Now	$44.00
1993	5	Prior	
1994	6	Now	$41.00
1995	5	Now	$33.00
1996	6	Now	$39.00
1997	6	Now	$38.00
1998	5	Now	$30.00

BESTS GREAT WESTERN PINOT NOIR ★★★★

1991	5	Now	$32.00
1992	7	Now	$44.00
1993	5	Now	$30.00
1994	5	Now	$29.00
1995	6	Now	$34.00
1996	5	Now	$28.00
1997	5	Now	$27.00
1998	6	Now	$31.00
1999	5	Now	$25.00
2000	7	2006	$35.00

BEST'S GREAT WESTERN RIESLING ★★★

before 1982		Prior	
1982	6	Now	$30.00
1983	5	Prior	
1984	5	Now	$24.00
1985	7	Now	$33.00
1986	5	Prior	
1987	6	Now	$26.00
1988	7	Now	$30.00
1989	4	Prior	
1990	7	Now	$28.00
1991	6	Now	$23.00
1992	6	Now	$23.00
1993	5	Prior	
1994	6	Now	$21.00
1995	7	Now	$24.00
1996	6	Now	$20.00
1997	6	Now	$19.50
1998	7	2006	$22.00
1998	5	Now	$15.50
1999	6	Now	$18.00
2000	6	Now	$17.50
2001	7	2005	$19.50

BEST'S GREAT WESTERN SHIRAZ ★★★★★

1976	7	Now	$72.00
1977	6	Now	$60.00
1978	6	Now	$58.00
1979	5	Prior	
1980	6	Now	$56.00
1981	5	Now	$45.00
1982	5	Prior	
1983	5	Now	$42.00
1984	7	Now	$58.00
1985	6	Now	$48.00
1986	5	Now	$39.00
1987	7	2004	$52.00
1988	7	2008	$50.00
1989	5	Now	$35.00
1990	6	2004	$41.00
1991	6	Now	$40.00
1992	7	2006	$45.00
1993	6	2006	$38.00
1994	6	2008	$37.00
1995	6	2006	$36.00
1996	6	2006	$35.00
1997	6	2006	$33.00
1998	7	2008	$38.00

No data since 1998

***Bethany Wines** is a small family-run winery at Bethany in the Barossa Valley, where the owners' family have been grapegrowers for a century. Winemakers: Geoff and Robert Schrapel.*

BETHANY CABERNET/MERLOT ★★★

before 1990		Prior	
1990	6	Now	$32.00
1991	7	Prior	
1992	7	Now	$36.00
1993	6	Prior	
1994	7	Now	$33.00
1995	6	Now	$28.00
1996	7	2006	$32.00
1997	5	Now	$22.00
1998	6	2006	$25.00
1999	6	2004	$25.00
2000	7	2006	$28.00
2001	6	2006	$23.00

BETHANY CHARDONNAY ★★★

before 1996		Prior	
1996	7	Now	$24.00
1997	7	Now	$23.00
1998	6	Now	$19.50

1999	5	Now	$15.50
2000	6	2004	$18.50
2001	7	2004	$21.00

BETHANY "GR" (SHIRAZ) ★★★★★

1992	7	Now	$84.00
1993	Not made		
1994	7	2006	$80.00
1995	7	Now	$78.00
1996	7	2006	$76.00
1997	7	2008	$74.00
1998	7	2010	$72.00

BETHANY GRENACHE PRESSINGS ★★★

before 1994		Prior	
1994	7	Now	$25.00
1995	6	Now	$21.00
1996	7	Now	$24.00
1997	6	Now	$20.00
1998	6	2004	$19.50
1999	6	2004	$18.50
2000	7	2006	$21.00
2001	6	2006	$17.50

BETHANY RESERVE RIESLING ★★★

before 1996		Prior	
1996	7	Now	$21.00
1997	6	Now	$17.50
1998	7	2004	$20.00
1999	6	2004	$16.50
2000	6	Now	$16.00
2001	7	2004	$18.50
2002	7	2006	$18.00

BETHANY SELECT LATE HARVEST RIESLING (CORDON PRUNED) ★★★★

before 1992		Prior	
1992	6	Now	$25.00
1993	6	Now	$24.00
1994	6	Now	$24.00
1995	7	Now	$27.00
1996	7	Now	$26.00
1997	7	Now	$25.00
1998	6	Now	$21.00
1999	6	2006	$20.00
2000	Not made		
2001	Not made		
2002	6	2007	$18.50

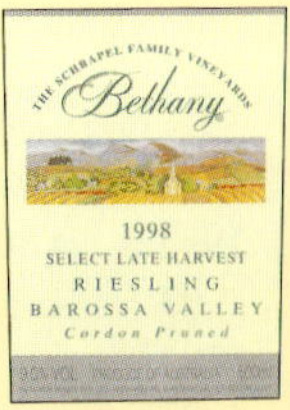

BETHANY SEMILLON ★★★★

before 1996		Prior	
1996	5	Now	$16.00
1997	7	Now	$22.00

1998	7	Now	$21.00
1999	6	Now	$18.00
2000	6	Now	$17.50
2001	7	2004	$19.50

BETHANY SHIRAZ ★★★★

before 1988		Prior	
1988	7	Now	$44.00
1989	6	Now	$36.00
1990	6	Now	$35.00
1991	5	Now	$28.00
1992	7	2004	$39.00
1993	6	Now	$32.00
1994	7	Now	$37.00
1995	6	Now	$30.00
1996	6	2006	$29.00
1997	6	Now	$29.00
1998	7	2008	$32.00
1999	6	2006	$27.00
2000	7	2008	$31.00

BETHANY "THE MANSE"
(SEMILLON/RIESLING/CHARDONNAY) ★★★

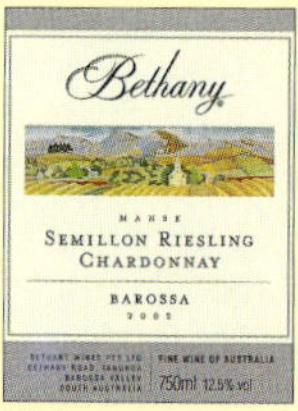

before 1998		Prior	
1998	5	Now	$13.50
1999	7	Now	$18.50
2000	6	Now	$15.00
2001	6	Now	$14.50
2002	7	2004	$16.50

***Bindi Winegrowers** are new makers in the Gisborne area of the Macedon Ranges, specialising in impressive examples of the Burgundian varieties. Winemakers: Michael Dhillon and Stuart Anderson.*

BINDI CHARDONNAY ★★★★

1991	6	Now	$64.00
1992	4	Now	$41.00
1993	4	Prior	
1994	6	Now	$58.00
1995	5	Now	$47.00
1996	4	Now	$36.00
1997	6	Now	$52.00
1998	5	Now	$43.00
1999	5	Now	$42.00
2000	6	2004	$49.00
2001	6	2005	$47.00
2002	5	2005	$38.00

BINDI CHARDONNAY "QUARTZ" ★★★★★

1995	5	Now	$58.00
1996	Not made		
1997	Not made		
1998	6	Now	$64.00
1999	5	Now	$52.00
2000	6	2004	$60.00
2001	6	2005	$60.00
2002	5	2005	N/R

BINDI PINOT NOIR ★★★★★

1992	4	Now	$54.00
1993	5	Now	$64.00
1994	6	Now	$76.00
1995	6	Now	$74.00
1996	5	Now	$60.00
1997	6	2004	$70.00
1998	6	2005	$68.00
1999	5	2006	$54.00
2000	6	2007	$64.00
2001	6	2007	$62.00
2002	5	2006	$50.00

BINDI PINOT NOIR "BLOCK FIVE" ★★★★★

1997	6	2004	$86.00
1998	6	2005	$84.00
1999	Not made		
2000	6	2006	$78.00
2001	6	2006	$76.00
2002	5	2004	N/R

***Blackjack Wines** in Central Victoria's Harcourt area are red wine specialists. Winemakers: Ian McKenzie and Ken Pollock.*

BLACKJACK CABERNET/MERLOT ★★★★★

1993	6	Now	$28.00
1994	7	Now	$32.00
1995	4	Now	$18.00
1996	6	Now	$26.00
1997	6	Now	$25.00
1998	5	Now	$20.00
1999	5	2004	$20.00
2000	6	2005	$23.00

BLACKJACK SHIRAZ ★★★★

1993	5	Now	$22.00
1994	6	Now	$25.00
1995	6	Now	$24.00
1996	6	Now	$24.00
1997	6	Now	$23.00

1998	7	2005	$26.00
1999	6	2005	$22.00
2000	7	2006	$25.00

Blass *- see Wolf Blass.*

Bleasdale's *vineyard at Langhorne Creek in South Australia produces a large range of honest, dependable and inexpensive wines. Winemaker: Michael Potts.*

BLEASDALE "MULBERRY TREE" CABERNET SAUVIGNON ★★★

before 1997		Prior	
1996	6	Now	$20.00
1997	6	Now	$19.50
1998	6	Now	$19.00
1999	5	Now	$15.00
2000	5	2004	$14.50
2001	5	2005	$14.50

BLEASDALE "FRANK POTTS" (CABERNETS/MALBEC/MERLOT/ PETIT VERDOT) ★★★★

before 1996		Prior	
1996	7	Now	$36.00
1997	5	Now	$25.00
1998	7	Now	$34.00
1999	6	Now	$28.00
2000	5	2004	$23.00

BLEASDALE MALBEC ★★

1990	6	Now	$20.00
1991	4	Prior	
1992	6	Now	$19.00
1993	Not made		
1994	6	Now	$18.00
1995	6	Now	$17.50
1996	5	Now	$14.00
1997	6	Now	$16.50
1998	7	Now	$18.50
1999	6	2004	$15.50
2000	7	2005	$17.50

BLEASDALE "BREMERVIEW" SHIRAZ ★★★

before 1997		Prior	
1997	7	Now	$20.00
1998	6	Now	$16.50
1999	6	Now	$16.00
2000	6	2004	$15.50
2001	6	2005	$15.00

Blue Pyrenees *(formerly Chateau Remy) is a French owned producer in the Avoca region of Victoria. The Estate wines are the premium ones. Well marketed and promoted, the wines have a loyal and dedicated following. Winemakers: Greg Dedman and Chris Smales.*

BLUE PYRENEES CHARDONNAY ★★★

2000	5	Now	$16.50
2001	6	Now	$19.50
2002	6	Now	$19.00

BLUE PYRENEES CABERNET SAUVIGNON ★★★

1999	5	Now	$15.50
2000	6	2004	$18.50
2001	7	2005	$21.00

BLUE PYRENEES ESTATE CHARDONNAY ★★★★

before 1996		Prior	
1996	6	Now	$25.00
1997	7	Now	$28.00
1998	6	Now	$23.00
1999	7	Now	$27.00
2000	6	2004	$22.00

BLUE PYRENEES ESTATE MIDNIGHT CUVEE ★★★★

1993	7	Now	$30.00
1994	Not made		
1995	6	Now	$24.00
1996	7	Now	$27.00
1997	7	Now	$26.00

BLUE PYRENEES ESTATE RED (CAB.SAUV/MERLOT/CAB.FRANC/SHIRAZ) ★★★★

before 1988		Prior	
1988	7	Now	$46.00
1989	5	Prior	
1990	7	Now	$43.00
1991	5	Prior	
1992	6	Prior	
1993	6	Now	$34.00
1994	7	Now	$38.00
1995	7	Now	$37.00
1996	6	2005	$31.00
1997	6	2006	$30.00
1998	6	2006	$29.00
1999	7	2010	$33.00

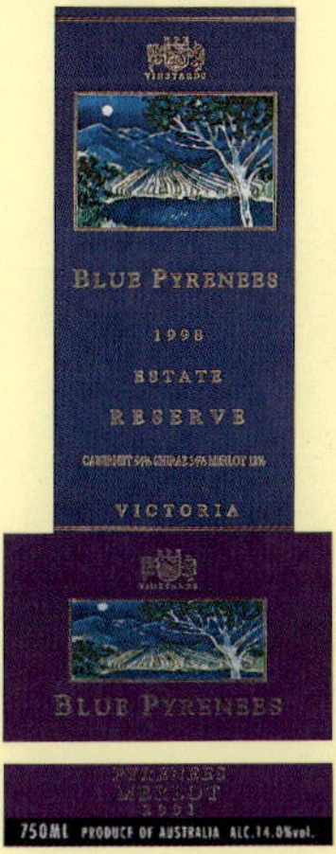

BLUE PYRENEES MERLOT ★★★

1999	6	Now	$20.00
2000	5	2004	$16.00
2001	6	2005	$19.00

BLUE PYRENEES SHIRAZ ★★★

1999	5	Now	$15.00
2000	7	2004	$20.00
2001	7	2004	$19.50

Botobolar *is a Mudgee vineyard whose organically grown wines are powerful and individual. Winemaker: Kevin Karstrom.*

BOTOBOLAR CABERNET SAUVIGNON ★★★

before 1982	Not made		
1982	7	Now	$36.00
1983	Not made		
1984	7	Now	$34.00
1985	7	Now	$33.00
1986	6	Now	$27.00
1987	7	Now	$31.00
1988	7	Now	$30.00
1989	Not made		
1990	5	Now	$20.00
1991	7	Now	$27.00
1992	6	Now	$23.00
1993	Not made		
1994	7	Now	$25.00
1995	Not made		
1996	Not made		
1997	7	Now	$23.00
1998	Not made		

BOTOBOLAR CHARDONNAY ★★

before 1988	Prior		
1988	7	Now	$29.00
1989	7	Now	$28.00
1990	7	Now	$27.00
1991	7	Now	$26.00
1992	6	Now	$22.00
1993	7	Now	$25.00
1994	5	Now	$17.00
1995	4	Now	$13.50
1996	5	Now	$16.00
1997	7	Now	$22.00
1998	7	Now	$21.00
1999	6	Now	$18.00
2000	5	Now	$14.50

BOTOBOLAR MARSANNE ★★★

1995	5	Now	$20.00
1996	5	Now	$20.00
1997	6	Now	$23.00
1998	Not made		
1999	6	Now	$22.00
2000	6	2004	$21.00

BOTOBOLAR SHIRAZ ★★★

before 1985		Prior	
1985	6	Now	$29.00
1986	5	Now	$23.00
1987	5	Now	$23.00
1988	5	Prior	
1989	7	Prior	
1990	6	Prior	
1991	6	Now	$24.00
1992	7	Now	$27.00
1993	Not made		
1994	6	Now	$22.00
1995	5	Now	$18.00
1996	6	Now	$21.00
1997	6	Now	$20.00
1998	7	2004	$23.00
1999	5	2004	$16.00

Bowen Estate *is one of Coonawarra's smaller vineyards but is making some of the area's best wines. Winemaker: Doug Bowen.*

BOWEN ESTATE CABERNET SAUVIGNON ★★★★

before 1991		Prior	
1991	7	Now	$34.00
1992	7	Now	$33.00
1993	7	Now	$32.00
1994	7	Now	$31.00
1995	6	Now	$26.00
1996	7	2004	$30.00
1997	7	Now	$29.00
1998	7	2005	$28.00
1999	6	2004	$23.00
2000	7	2006	$26.00
2001	6	2007	$22.00

BOWEN ESTATE CABERNET SAUVIGNON/MERLOT/CABERNET FRANC ★★★★★

1990	7	Prior	
1991	6	Now	$26.00
1992	6	Now	$26.00
1993	7	Now	$29.00
1994	7	Now	$28.00
1995	6	Now	$23.00
1996	7	2004	$27.00
1997	7	2005	$26.00
1998	7	2006	$25.00
1999	6	2006	$21.00
2000	7	2007	$24.00
2001	6	2008	$20.00

BOWEN ESTATE CHARDONNAY ★★★★

before 1998		Prior	
1998	7	Now	$25.00
1999	6	Now	$21.00
2000	6	Prior	
2001	6	Now	$19.50
2002	6	Now	$19.00

BOWEN ESTATE SHIRAZ ★★★★

1990	7	Now	$40.00
1991	7	Now	$39.00
1992	6	Now	$32.00
1993	6	Now	$31.00
1994	7	Now	$36.00
1995	6	Now	$29.00
1996	7	2005	$33.00
1997	7	2006	$32.00
1998	7	2007	$32.00
1999	7	2008	$31.00
2000	7	2009	$30.00

***Brands Laira** vineyard has been producing respected and sought-after wines at Coonawarra since 1965. They are part of the organisation. Winemaker: Jim Brand.*

BRANDS LAIRA CABERNET SAUVIGNON ★★★

1981	7	Now	$48.00
1982	7	Now	$46.00
1983	5	Now	$32.00
1984	7	Now	$44.00
1985	6	Now	$36.00
1986	6	Now	$35.00
1987	7	Now	$40.00
1988	5	Now	$28.00
1989	Not made		
1990	6	Now	$31.00
1991	5	Now	$25.00
1992	6	Now	$29.00
1993	5	Now	$24.00
1994	6	Now	$28.00
1995	6	2004	$27.00
1996	6	2006	$26.00
1997	6	2006	$25.00
1998	7	2008	$29.00
1999	6	2009	$24.00
2000	7	2010	$27.00
2001	7	2010	$26.00
2002	7	2012	$26.00

BRANDS LAIRA CABERNET/MERLOT ★★★★

1984	6	Now	$36.00
1985	6	Now	$35.00
1986	6	Now	$34.00
1987	7	Now	$39.00
1988	5	Now	$27.00
1989	Not made		
1990	6	Now	$30.00
1991	5	Now	$24.00
1992	6	Now	$28.00
1993	5	Now	$23.00
1994	6	2004	$27.00
1995	5	2005	$22.00
1996	6	2006	$25.00
1997	6	2006	$24.00
1998	7	2007	$28.00
1999	6	2007	$23.00
2000	Not made		
2001	Not made		
2002	Not made		

BRANDS LAIRA CHARDONNAY ★★★

1986	6	Now	$30.00
1987	5	Now	$24.00
1988	5	Now	$23.00
1989	5	Now	$22.00
1990	6	Now	$26.00
1991	5	Now	$21.00
1992	6	Now	$25.00
1993	5	Now	$20.00
1994	6	Now	$23.00
1995	5	Now	$19.00
1996	6	Now	$22.00
1997	6	Now	$21.00
1998	6	Now	$21.00
1999	6	Now	$20.00
2000	6	Now	$19.50
2001	7	2004	$22.00
2002	7	2006	$21.00

BRANDS LAIRA MERLOT ★★★★

1997	7	2006	$39.00
1998	6	2007	$33.00
1999	6	2007	$32.00
2000	7	2009	$36.00
2001	6	2008	$30.00
2002	6	2009	$29.00

BRANDS LAIRA RIESLING ★★★

1996	6	Now	$22.00
1997	7	Now	$25.00
1998	6	Now	$21.00
1999	6	Now	$20.00
2000	6	Now	$19.50
2001	6	2004	$19.00
2002	6	2006	$18.50
2003	6	2007	$18.00

BRANDS LAIRA SHIRAZ ★★★★

1980	5	Now	$37.00
1981	6	Now	$43.00
1982	7	Now	$48.00
1983	5	Now	$33.00
1984	7	Now	$46.00
1985	5	Now	$31.00
1986	6	Now	$37.00
1987	5	Now	$30.00
1988	5	Now	$29.00
1989	Not made		
1990	6	Now	$33.00
1991	6	Now	$32.00
1992	6	Now	$31.00
1993	5	Now	$25.00
1994	6	Now	$29.00
1995	6	2005	$28.00
1996	7	2006	$32.00
1997	6	2007	$26.00
1998	6	2007	$26.00
1999	7	2008	$29.00
2000	7	2004	$28.00
2001	6	2006	$23.00
2002	6	2007	$23.00

BRANDS PATRON'S RESERVE SHIRAZ/CABERNET/MERLOT ★★★★★

1996	7	2006	$74.00
1997	6	2006	$62.00
1998	7	2008	$70.00
1999	7	2010	$68.00
2000	7	2012	$66.00
2001	6	2010	N/R
2002	7	2012	N/R

BRANDS STENTIFORDS RESERVE SHIRAZ ★★★★★

1984	6	Now	$96.00
1985	Not made		
1986	7	Now	$105.00
1987	Not made		

1988	6	Now	$86.00
1989	Not made		
1990	6	Now	$80.00
1991	6	2000	$78.00
1992	Not made		
1993	Not made		
1994	Not made		
1995	6	2006	$70.00
1996	7	2008	$78.00
1997	6	2008	$66.00
1998	6	2010	$64.00
1999	7	2010	$72.00
2000	7	2012	$70.00
2001	6	2012	N/R
2002	6	2010	N/R

***Briar Ridge** are Mount View (Hunter Valley) makers whose vineyard was once known as the Robson Vineyard. Their Semillon is particularly worthy of respectful attention. Winemaker: Adrian Lockhart.*

BRIAR RIDGE CHARDONNAY ★★★

before 1996		Prior	
1996	6	Now	$24.00
1997	5	Now	$19.50
1998	7	Now	$26.00
1999	6	Now	$22.00
2000	6	Now	$21.00
2001	5	Now	$17.50
2002	5	Now	$17.00

BRIAR RIDGE STOCKHAUSEN HERMITAGE ★★★★

1991	5	Prior	
1992	5	Now	$29.00
1993	6	Prior	
1994	6	Now	$32.00
1995	7	Now	$37.00
1996	7	Now	$36.00
1997	7	Now	$35.00
1998	7	Now	$34.00
1999	6	Now	$28.00
2000	7	Now	$32.00
2001	6	Now	$26.00

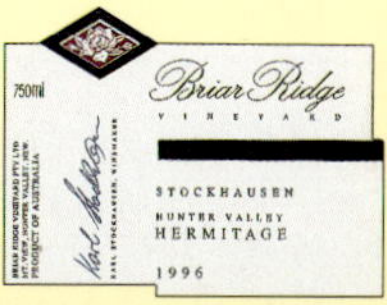

BRIAR RIDGE STOCKHAUSEN SEMILLON ★★★★

before 1994		Prior	
1994	6	Now	$29.00
1995	6	Now	$28.00
1996	7	Now	$32.00

1997	6	Now	$26.00
1998	7	2004	$30.00
1999	6	2004	$25.00
2000	7	2005	$28.00
2001	6	2005	$23.00
2002	7	2005	$27.00

***Bridgewater Mill** is the second label of Petaluma, using fruit from Clare, Coonawarra and McLaren Vale. Winemaker: Brian Croser.*

BRIDGEWATER MILL CHARDONNAY ★★★★

before 1990		Prior	
1990	5	Now	$22.00
1991	4	Now	$17.50
1992	6	Now	$25.00
1993	5	Now	$20.00
1994	4	Now	$16.00
1995	5	Now	$19.50
1996	5	Now	$18.50
1997	6	Now	$22.00
1998	4	Now	$14.00
1999	5	Now	$17.00

BRIDGEWATER MILL MILLSTONE SHIRAZ ★★★★

1989	4	Now	$21.00
1990	6	Now	$31.00
1991	5	Now	$25.00
1992	6	Now	$29.00
1993	4	Now	$19.00
1994	5	Now	$23.00
1995	5	Now	$22.00
1996	5	Now	$22.00
1997	5	2005	$21.00
1998	Not made		
1999	Not made		
2000	6	2005	$23.00

BRIDGEWATER MILL SAUVIGNON BLANC ★★★★

before 1998		Prior	
1998	6	Now	$24.00
1999	5	Now	$19.50
2000	5	Now	$19.00
2001	5	Now	$18.50
2002	5	Now	$18.00

***Brokenwood** is a small Pokolbin vineyard producing wines of very fine quality and exemplary style. Winemakers: Iain Riggs and Peter James Charteris.*

BROKENWOOD CABERNET SAUVIGNON ★★★★

before 1991		Prior	
1991	6	Now	$40.00
1992	4	Now	$25.00
1993	6	Now	$37.00
1994	5	Now	$30.00
1995	4	Now	$23.00
1996	6	Now	$34.00
1997	6	2005	$33.00
1998	6	2006	$32.00
1999	6	2007	$31.00
2000	7	2007	$35.00
2001	6	2008	$29.00

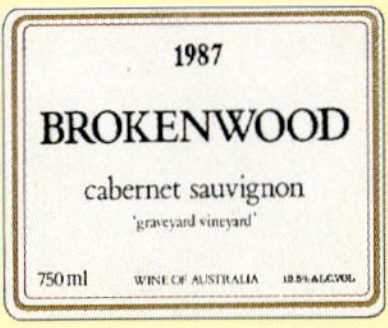

BROKENWOOD CHARDONNAY ★★★★

before 1994		Prior	
1994	5	Now	$24.00
1995	6	Now	$28.00
1996	6	Now	$27.00
1997	6	Now	$27.00
1998	7	Now	$30.00
1999	5	Now	$21.00
2000	6	Now	$24.00
2001	5	2004	$19.50
2002	5	2005	$19.00

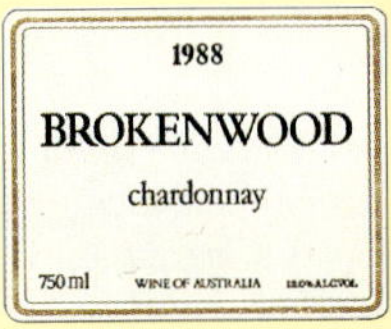

BROKENWOOD HERMITAGE (GRAVEYARD VINEYARD) ★★★★★

before 1985		Prior	
1985	5	Now	$125.00
1986	7	Now	$175.00
1987	4	Now	$96.00
1988	5	Now	$115.00
1989	6	Now	$135.00
1990	5	Now	$110.00
1991	7	Now	$150.00
1992	Not made		
1993	6	Now	$120.00
1994	6	Now	$115.00
1995	5	Now	$96.00
1996	6	2004	$110.00
1997	4	2004	$72.00
1998	6	2006	$105.00
1999	5	2007	$84.00
2000	7	2010	$115.00
2001	5	2009	$80.00

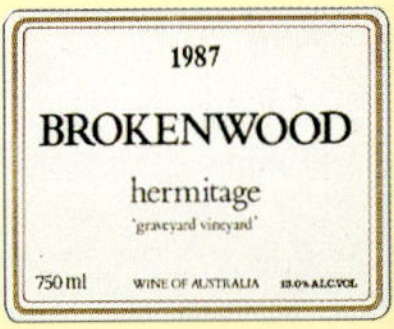

BROKENWOOD SEMILLON ★★★★

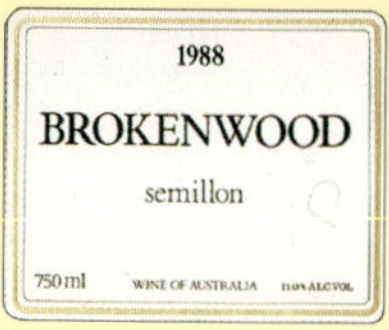

before 1986		Prior	
1986	6	Now	$32.00
1987	5	Prior	
1988	4	Prior	
1989	4	Prior	
1990	3	Prior	
1991	6	Prior	
1992	6	Now	$27.00
1993	5	Prior	
1994	6	Now	$25.00
1995	5	Now	$20.00
1996	7	Now	$28.00
1997	4	Now	$15.50
1998	5	Now	$18.50
1999	6	Now	$22.00
2000	7	2005	$24.00
2001	7	Now	$24.00
2002	5	Now	$16.50

***Brookland Valley** is a Margaret River maker in an idyllic setting (and a very fine winery restaurant). Winemaker: Garry Cherubino.*

BROOKLAND VALLEY CHARDONNAY ★★★★★

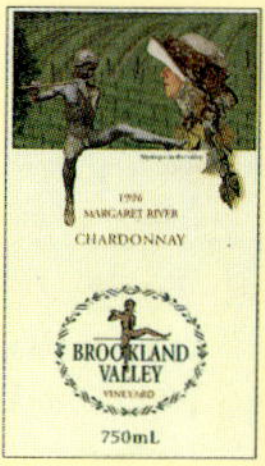

1990	7	Now	$50.00
1991	6	Now	$41.00
1992	7	Now	$47.00
1993	6	Now	$39.00
1994	7	Now	$44.00
1995	7	Now	$43.00
1996	7	Now	$42.00
1997	7	Now	$40.00
1998	6	Now	$33.00
1999	7	Now	$38.00
2000	7	2006	$37.00
2001	7	2008	$36.00

BROOKLAND VALLEY CABERNET/MERLOT ★★★★

1990	6	Now	$46.00
1991	7	Now	$52.00
1992	7	Now	$50.00
1993	7	Now	$49.00
1994	7	Now	$48.00
1995	7	Now	$47.00
1996	7	Now	$45.00
1997	6	2004	$38.00
1998	6	2005	$36.00
1999	7	2010	$41.00

BROOKLAND VALLEY MERLOT ★★★★

1995	7	Now	$50.00
1996	7	Now	$49.00
1997	7	Now	$48.00
1998	6	2004	$40.00
1999	7	2005	$45.00
2000	7	2006	$44.00

***Brown Brothers** is a medium size family owned and operated company with substantial holdings in North East Victoria and a substantial reputation, both here and overseas. Winemaker: John Brown.*

BROWN BROS BARBERA ★★★

before 1998		Prior	
1998	6	Now	$17.00
1999	6	Now	$16.50
2000	5	Now	$13.50
2001	5	2005	$13.00
2002	7	2010	$18.00

BROWN BROS CABERNET SAUVIGNON ★★★

before 1994		Prior	
1994	5	Now	$19.00
1995	4	Prior	
1996	6	2004	$22.00
1997	7	2007	$24.00
1998	6	2007	$20.00
1999	5	2006	$16.50
2000	7	2008	$22.00
2001	6	2008	N/R
2002	7	2012	N/R

BROWN BROS CHARDONNAY ★★★

before 1999		Prior	
1999	6	Now	$19.50
2000	6	2005	$19.00
2001	6	2005	$18.50
2003	7	2007	$21.00

BROWN BROS DOLCETTO/ SYRAH ★★★

before 2001		Prior	
2001	6	Now	$12.50
2002	7	Now	$14.00

BROWN BROS MERLOT ★★★

before 1997		Prior	
1997	7	Now	$21.00
1998	7	Now	$21.00
1999	5	Prior	

2000	6	2005	$17.00
2001	6	2006	N/R
2002	7	2007	N/R

BROWN BROS MOSCATO ★★

before 2001		Prior	
2001	7	Now	$13.50
2002	7	Now	$13.00

BROWN BROS NOBLE RIESLING ★★★★★

before 1996		Prior	
1996	7	2005	$58.00
1997	5	Now	$41.00
1998	5	2004	$40.00
1999	7	2007	$54.00
2000	7	2010	$52.00

BROWN BROS ORANGE MUSCAT & FLORA ★★

before 2001		Prior	
2001	5	Now	$13.50
2002	7	Now	$18.50

BROWN BROS RIESLING ★★★

before 1999		Prior	
1999	5	Now	$12.50
2000	6	2004	$14.50
2001	6	2006	$14.00
2002	7	2007	$16.00

BROWN BROS SAUVIGNON BLANC ★★★

before 2001		Prior	
2001	7	Now	$17.50
2002	7	Now	$17.00

BROWN BROS SHIRAZ ★★★

before 1996		Prior	
1996	6	Now	$23.00
1997	6	2004	$22.00
1998	6	2005	$21.00
1999	5	2005	$17.50
2000	5	2006	$17.00
2001	5	2007	$16.50
2002	7	2009	N/R

BROWN BROS TARRANGO ★★

before 2001		Prior	
2001	6	Now	$10.50
2002	7	Now	$12.00

***Bullers Calliope Wines** are long established Rutherglen producers whose range of wines includes some magnificent fortifieds. Winemaker: Richard Buller.*

BULLERS BEVERFORD CHARDONNAY ★★

before 1998		Prior	
1998	6	Now	$15.00
1999	6	Now	$14.50
2000	6	2004	$14.00
2001	Not made		
2002	5	2004	$11.00

BULLERS BEVERFORD WOODED SEMILLON ★★

before 1996		Prior	
1996	6	Now	$14.00
1997	Not made		
1998	Not made		
1999	Not made		
2000	6	Now	$12.50
2001	7	2004	$14.00

BULLERS CALLIOPE SHIRAZ ★★★★

1990	5	Prior	
1991	7	Now	$49.00
1992	5	Prior	
1993	Not made		
1994	6	Now	$39.00
1995	6	2004	$38.00
1996	6	2005	$36.00
1997	6	2005	$35.00

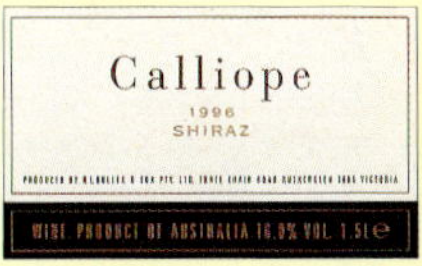

BULLERS SHIRAZ/MONDEUSE ★★★

1991	7	Now	$34.00
1992	5	Prior	
1993	4	Prior	
1994	5	Now	$22.00
1995	5	Now	$21.00
1996	7	2005	$29.00
1997	7	2005	$28.00
1998	7	2006	$27.00
1999	Not made		
2000	6	2008	$22.00

***Buring** - see Leo Buring.*

***Burra Burra** is the label applied by Ashton Hills (qv) to wine made from Spencer George's vineyard at Burra Burra in South Australia's mid North. Winemaker: Stephen George.*

BURRA BURRA LONE STAR SHIRAZ ★★★★★

1996	7	2004	$31.00
1997	6	2004	$25.00
1998	6	2006	$25.00

1999	6	2007	$24.00
2000	6	2010	$23.00
2001	7	2008	N/R

***Burton** Premium Wines is a label applied to wines made from a range of areas and, as far as I can ascertain, different winemakers. The following wine, however, is from one area and one maker. Winemaker: Pat Tocaciu.*

BURTON COONAWARRA RESERVE CABERNET ★★

1998	7	2008	$38.00
1999	6	Now	$31.00
2000	7	2005	$36.00
2001	7	2006	$34.00
2002	7	2010	$33.00

***By Farr** is the label used by purist Bannockburn winemaker Gary Farr for his small quantity hand crafted Geelong individual vineyard wines.*

CHARDONNAY BY FARR ★★★★★

1999	6	Now	$45.00
2000	7	2004	$50.00
2001	7	2005	$49.00
2002	6	2006	$41.00

PINOT NOIR BY FARR ★★★★★

1999	6	Now	$45.00
2000	7	2004	$50.00
2001	7	2005	$49.00
2002	6	2006	$41.00

SHIRAZ BY FARR ★★★★

1999	6	Now	$47.00
2000	6	2005	$45.00
2001	7	2005	$50.00
2002	6	2006	$43.00

VIOGNIER BY FARR ★★★★

1999	5	Now	$40.00
2000	6	Now	$47.00
2001	7	Now	$54.00
2002	6	2004	$45.00

***Campbells** are Rutherglen producers who have moved with the times and make some fine white wines as well as the traditionally expected North East Victorian fortifieds. Winemaker: Colin Campbell.*

CAMPBELLS BOBBIE BURNS SHIRAZ ★★★★

before 1985		Prior	
1985	5	Now	$29.00
1986	6	Now	$33.00
1987	5	Now	$27.00

1988	5	Now	$26.00
1989	4	Now	$20.00
1990	4	Now	$20.00
1991	5	2004	$24.00
1992	7	2008	$33.00
1993	6	2005	$27.00
1994	5	2004	$22.00
1995	5	2006	$21.00
1996	7	2010	$29.00
1997	6	2008	$24.00
1998	7	2010	$27.00
1999	6	2006	$23.00
2000	5	2006	$18.50
2001	6	2012	N/R
2002	7	2012	N/R

CAMPBELLS CHARDONNAY ★★★

before 1996		Prior	
1996	5	2004	$18.50
1997	4	Prior	
1998	4	Prior	
1999	5	2005	$17.00
2000	4	Now	$13.50
2001	5	2004	$16.00
2002	6	2006	$19.00

CAMPBELLS PEDRO XIMENEZ ★★★★

before 1987		Prior	
1987	6	2004	$40.00
1988	5	Prior	
1989	4	Now	$25.00
1990	5	2004	$30.00
1991	5	2004	$30.00
1992	7	Prior	
1993	5	2004	$28.00
1994	5	2004	$27.00
1995	Not made		
1996	4	Now	$20.00
1997	5	2006	$25.00
1998	5	2004	$24.00
1999	6	2010	$28.00
2000	6	2010	N/R
2001	6	2012	N/R
2002	5	2008	N/R

CAMPBELLS RIESLING ★★★

before 1986		Prior	
1986	6	2004	$29.00
1987	5	Prior	
1988	5	Now	$23.00
1989	4	Now	$18.00

1990	6	2004	$26.00
1991	4	Now	$17.00
1992	5	2004	$20.00
1993	6	2004	$24.00
1994	5	Now	$19.50
1995	6	2005	$22.00
1996	6	2005	$22.00
1997	6	2007	$21.00
1998	5	Now	$17.00
1999	5	2005	$16.50
2000	5	2006	$16.00
2001	6	2008	$19.00
2002	6	2006	$18.00

CAMPBELLS RUTHERGLEN SHIRAZ ★★★★

1986	5	2004	$28.00
1987	4	Now	$21.00
1988	4	Prior	
1989	Not made		
1990	4	Now	$20.00
1991	5	2004	$24.00
1992	6	2005	$28.00

No longer made.

CAMPBELLS "THE BARKLY" DURIF ★★★★★

1992	6	2004	$56.00
1993	6	2005	$54.00
1994	5	2008	$45.00
1995	5	2004	$43.00
1996	7	2010	$58.00
1997	6	2008	$49.00
1998	7	2010	$56.00
1999	Not made		
2000	Not made		
2001	6	2010	$44.00

Capel Vale *is an extremely fine maker near Bunbury in Western Australia. Their wines are of considerable beauty. Winemaker: Nicole Esdaile.*

CAPEL VALE CABERNET SAUVIGNON ★★★★

before 1985		Prior	
1985	5	Now	$28.00
1986	6	Now	$33.00
1987	6	Now	$32.00
1988	7	Now	$36.00
1989	7	Now	$35.00
1990	5	Now	$24.00
1991	6	Now	$28.00
1992	6	Now	$27.00
1993	7	Now	$31.00

1994	6	Now	$26.00
1995	6	Now	$25.00
1996	5	Now	$20.00
1997	5	Now	$19.50
1998	6	Now	$23.00
1999	6	2005	$22.00
2000	5	2006	$18.00
2001	7	2010	$24.00
2002	6	2010	N/R

CAPEL VALE CHARDONNAY ★★★★★

before 1985		Prior	
1985	6	Now	$34.00
1986	6	Now	$33.00
1987	7	Now	$38.00
1988	5	Now	$26.00
1989	6	Now	$30.00
1990	5	Now	$24.00
1991	5	Now	$24.00
1992	7	Now	$32.00
1993	6	Now	$27.00
1994	7	Now	$31.00
1995	7	Now	$30.00
1996	6	Now	$25.00
1997	4	Now	$16.00
1998	6	Prior	
1999	6	2005	$22.00
2000	6	2007	$22.00
2001	6	2008	$21.00
2002	7	2009	$24.00

CAPEL VALE KINNAIRD SHIRAZ ★★★★★

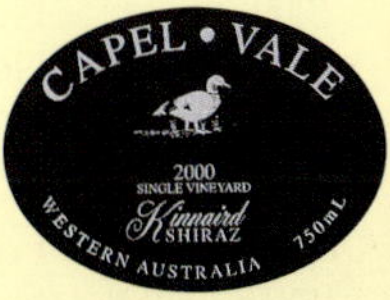

1996	7	2004	$60.00
1997	5	Now	$42.00
1998	7	2005	$56.00
1999	Not made		
2000	7	2008	$54.00
2001	7	2011	$52.00

CAPEL VALE MERLOT HOWECROFT RESERVE ★★★★

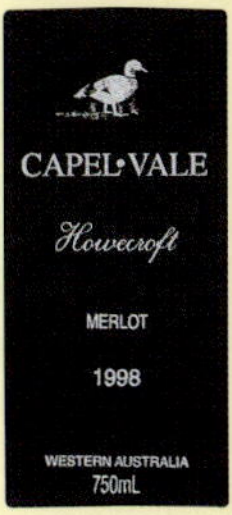

1992	5	Now	$50.00
1993	6	Now	$60.00
1994	6	Now	$58.00
1995	7	Now	$66.00
1996	6	Now	$54.00
1997	7	2004	$62.00
1998	6	2005	$52.00
1999	7	2008	$58.00
2000	7	2010	$56.00
2001	6	2011	$47.00

CAPEL VALE RIESLING WHISPERING HILL ★★★★

before 1985		Prior	
1985	5	Now	$31.00
1986	7	Now	$43.00
1987	5	Now	$29.00
1988	7	Now	$40.00
1989	7	Now	$39.00
1990	5	Now	$27.00
1991	6	Now	$31.00
1992	7	Now	$36.00
1993	6	Now	$30.00
1994	5	Now	$24.00
1995	6	Now	$28.00
1996	7	Now	$32.00
1997	5	Now	$22.00
1998	7	Now	$30.00
1999	Not made		
2000	7	2006	$28.00
2001	7	2007	$27.00
2002	7	2008	$26.00

CAPEL VALE SAUVIGNON BLANC/SEMILLON ★★★★

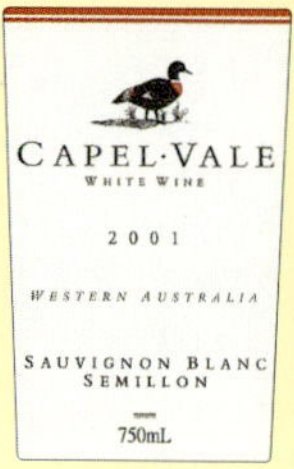

before 1993		Prior	
1993	7	Now	$25.00
1994	6	Now	$21.00
1995	7	Now	$24.00
1996	6	Now	$20.00
1997	5	Now	$16.00
1998	5	Now	$15.50
1999	6	Now	$18.50
2000	5	Now	$15.00
2001	7	Now	$20.00
2002	6	2005	$17.00

CAPEL VALE SHIRAZ ★★★★

before 1986		Prior	
1986	6	Now	$32.00
1987	6	Now	$31.00
1988	7	Now	$35.00
1989	6	Now	$29.00
1990	5	Now	$24.00
1991	6	Now	$28.00
1992	6	Now	$27.00
1993	7	2005	$31.00
1994	6	Now	$25.00
1995	6	Now	$25.00
1996	6	Now	$24.00
1997	5	Now	$19.50
1998	6	Now	$22.00

1999	7	2005	$25.00
2000	6	2007	$21.00
2001	7	2010	$24.00

***Cape Mentelle** is a very fine Margaret River producer of deep, powerful and well-balanced wines. Winemaker: John Durham.*

CAPE MENTELLE CABERNET SAUVIGNON ★★★★★

1977	4	Prior	
1978	6	Now	$110.00
1979	5	Now	$92.00
1980	4	Now	$72.00
1981	5	Now	$88.00
1982	6	Now	$100.00
1983	6	Now	$98.00
1984	4	Now	$64.00
1985	5	Now	$78.00
1986	6	Now	$90.00
1987	4	Now	$58.00
1988	6	Now	$86.00
1989	4	Now	$54.00
1990	6	Now	$80.00
1991	6	Now	$78.00
1992	5	Now	$62.00
1993	5	Now	$60.00
1994	7	Now	$84.00
1995	6	Now	$70.00
1996	6	Now	$68.00
1997	6	2005	$66.00
1998	6	2005	$64.00
1999	7	2006	$72.00
2000	6	2007	$60.00

CAPE MENTELLE CABERNET/MERLOT ★★★★

1990	3	Prior	
1991	4	Now	$25.00
1992	5	Now	$30.00
1993	4	Prior	
1994	5	Now	$28.00
1995	5	Now	$27.00
1996	5	Now	$27.00
1997	7	Now	$36.00
1998	6	Now	$30.00

CAPE MENTELLE CHARDONNAY ★★★★★

before 1992		Prior	
1992	5	Now	$34.00
1993	7	Now	$46.00
1994	6	Now	$38.00
1995	6	Now	$37.00
1996	5	Now	$30.00

1997	7	Now	$41.00
1998	6	Now	$34.00
1999	6	Now	$33.00
2000	7	2004	$37.00

CAPE MENTELLE SEMILLON/SAUVIGNON BLANC

★★★★

before 1991		Prior	
1991	6	Now	$29.00
1992	5	Now	$23.00
1993	7	Now	$32.00
1994	6	Now	$26.00
1995	6	Now	$26.00
1996	6	Now	$25.00
1997	7	Now	$28.00
1998	7	Now	$27.00
1999	6	Now	$23.00
2000	No data		
2001	7	2004	$25.00

CAPE MENTELLE SHIRAZ

★★★★★

before 1985		Prior	
1985	5	Now	$42.00
1986	5	Now	$40.00
1987	4	Prior	
1988	5	Now	$38.00
1989	5	Now	$37.00
1990	5	Now	$36.00
1991	6	Now	$42.00
1992	4	Now	$27.00
1993	6	Now	$39.00
1994	5	Now	$32.00
1995	7	Now	$43.00
1996	6	Now	$36.00
1997	7	Now	$41.00
1998	6	Now	$34.00
1999	6	2005	$33.00
2000	7	2007	$37.00

CAPE MENTELLE ZINFANDEL

★★★★

before 1990		Prior	
1990	6	Now	$47.00
1991	5	Now	$38.00
1992	4	Now	$30.00
1993	5	Now	$36.00
1994	4	Now	$28.00
1995	7	Now	$48.00
1996	6	Now	$40.00
1997	6	Now	$39.00
1998	5	Now	$31.00
1999	7	2005	$42.00
2000	6	2005	$35.00

***Capercaillie** (formerly the Dawson Estate) is a Hunter Valley producer of a range of agreeable and reasonably priced wines. Winemaker: Alasdair Sutherland.*

CAPERCAILLIE CHARDONNAY ★★★

1996	5	Now	$20.00
1997	5	Now	$19.00
1998	Not made		
1999	6	Now	$21.00
2000	6	2005	$21.00
2001	6	2005	$20.00
2002	6	2006	$20.00

CAPERCAILLIE SEMILLON ★★★★

1996	6	Now	$22.00
1997	4	Now	$14.50
1998	5	2004	$17.50
1999	6	2005	$20.00
2000	5	2006	$16.50
2001	6	2007	$19.00
2002	6	2008	$18.50

CAPERCAILLIE SHIRAZ ★★★★

1997	5	2005	$18.50
1998	6	2007	$21.00
1999	6	2008	$21.00

CAPERCAILLIE "THE CLAN" CABERNETS ★★★★

1994	5	Now	$28.00
1995	Not made		
1996	6	2005	$32.00
1997	5	2005	$25.00
1998	6	2008	$30.00
1999	5	2006	$24.00
2000	6	2008	$28.00
2001	5	2008	$23.00

***Carlyle Wines** in Wahgunyah in Victoria's North East is a venture owned and operated by Chris Pfeiffer. The white wines are made for longevity. Winemaker: Chris Pfeiffer.*

CARLYLE CABERNET SAUVIGNON ★★★

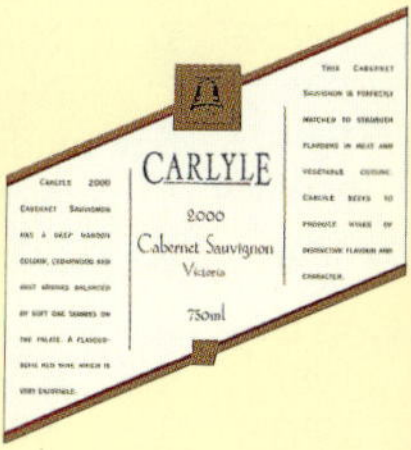

1996	5	Now	$17.00
1997	6	Now	$20.00
1998	5	Now	$16.00
1999	7	2005	$22.00
2000	6	2007	$18.50
2001	6	2007	$18.00
2002	7	2010	N/R

CARLYLE LATE HARVEST RIESLING ★★★

1997	6	2005	$19.00
1998	6	2006	$18.50
1999	Not made		
2000	7	2008	$20.00

CARLYLE MARSANNE ★★★

1997	6	2005	$16.00
1998	6	2006	$15.50
1999	7	2009	$18.00
2000	Not made		
2001	7	2010	N/R
2002	6	2010	N/R

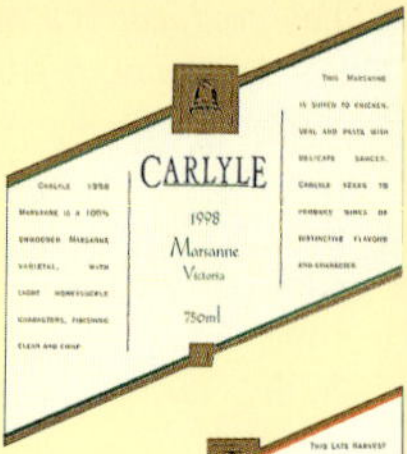

CARLYLE RIESLING ★★★

1995	7	2008	$23.00
1996	Not made		
1997	Not made		
1998	6	2008	$18.00
1999	5	2004	$14.50
2000	5	2006	$14.00
2001	7	2011	$19.00
2002	7	2015	$18.50

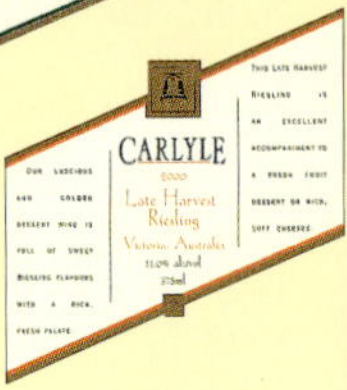

CARLYLE SHIRAZ ★★★

1996	5	Now	$16.50
1997	6	Now	$19.50
1998	5	Now	$15.50
1999	6	2006	$18.50
2000	7	2007	$21.00
2001	6	2007	N/R
2002	7	2010	N/R

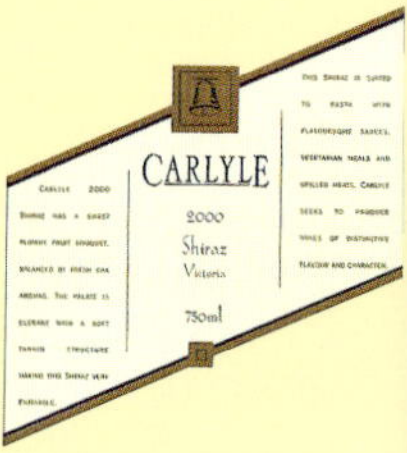

***Cassegrain Vineyards** are innovative and painstaking makers in the Hastings Valley area near Port Macquarie in northern New South Wales. Winemaker: John Cassegrain.*

CASSEGRAIN CHARDONNAY ★★★★

before 1991		Prior	
1991	7	Now	$29.00
1992	6	Now	$24.00
1993	7	Now	$28.00
1994	6	Now	$23.00
1995	7	Now	$26.00
1996	5	Now	$18.00
1997	7	Now	$25.00
1998	7	Now	$24.00
1999	Not made		
2000	6	Now	$19.50
2001	5	2004	$15.50

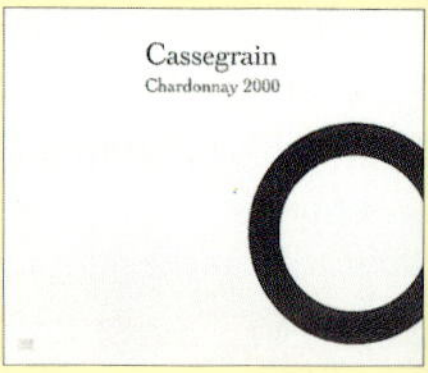

CASSEGRAIN CHAMBOURCIN ★★★

1987	6	Now	$31.00
1988	5	Now	$25.00
1989	5	Now	$24.00
1990	6	Now	$28.00
1991	6	Now	$27.00
1992	6	Now	$26.00

1993	6	Now	$26.00
1994	6	Now	$25.00
1995	6	Now	$24.00
1996	6	Now	$23.00
1997	7	Now	$27.00
1998	5	Now	$18.50
1999	5	Now	$18.00
2000	5	Now	$17.50
2001	5	Now	$17.00
2002	6	2004	$20.00

CASSEGRAIN FROMENTEAU CHARDONNAY

★★★★★

before 1987		Prior	
1987	5	Now	$37.00
1988	Not made		
1989	7	Now	$49.00
1990	5	Prior	
1991	7	Now	$47.00
1992	5	Now	$32.00
1993	6	Now	$38.00
1994	Not made		
1995	6	Now	$35.00
1996	6	Now	$34.00
1997	6	Now	$33.00
1998	7	Now	$38.00
1999	Not made		
2000	6	Now	$30.00
2001	6	2004	$30.00

CASSEGRAIN PINOT NOIR

★★★★

1991	6	Now	$27.00
1992	5	Now	$22.00
1993	6	Now	$25.00
1994	6	Now	$25.00
1995	Not made		
1996	Not made		
1997	6	Now	$22.00
1998	4	Now	$14.50
1999	Not made		
2000	6	Now	$21.00

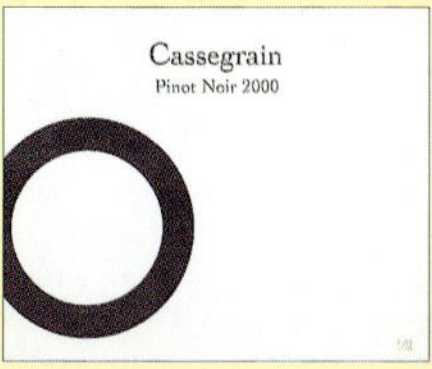

CASSEGRAIN SEMILLON

★★★

1985	7	Now	$37.00
1986	6	Now	$31.00
1987	Not made		
1988	5	Now	$24.00
1989	7	Now	$33.00
1990	Not made		
1991	6	Now	$27.00
1992	6	Now	$26.00
1993	5	Now	$21.00

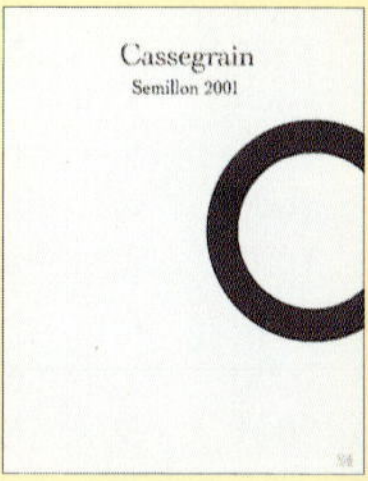

1994	5	Now	$20.00
1995	6	Now	$24.00
1996	5	2004	$19.50
1997	6	2005	$22.00
1998	6	2006	$22.00
1999	4	Now	$14.00
2000	7	Now	$24.00
2001	6	Now	$20.00
2002	6	2004	$19.50

***Castle Rock Estate** is a Mount Barker region vineyard. Their Riesling is a wine of considerable beauty. Winemakers: Michael Staniford and Rob Diletti.*

CASTLE ROCK CABERNET SAUVIGNON ★★★

before 1994		Prior	
1994	5	Now	$21.00
1995	Not made		
1996	7	Now	$29.00
1997	6	2004	$24.00
1998	6	2004	$23.00
1999	5	2004	$18.50

CASTLE ROCK CHARDONNAY ★★★

before 1995		Prior	
1995	Not made		
1996	5	Now	$19.00
1997	7	Now	$26.00
1998	6	Now	$21.00
1999	5	Now	$17.50
2000	6	Now	$20.00

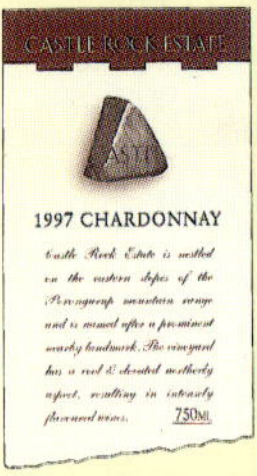

CASTLE ROCK PINOT NOIR ★★★

before 1996		Prior	
1996	7	Now	$27.00
1997	Not made		
1998	7	Now	$26.00
1999	6	Now	$21.00

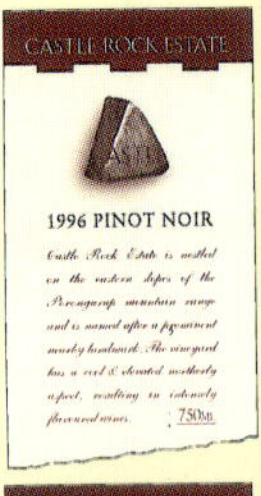

CASTLE ROCK RIESLING ★★★★★

before 1993		Prior	
1993	5	Now	$19.00
1994	6	Now	$22.00
1995	Not made		
1996	7	Prior	
1997	6	Now	$20.00
1998	6	Now	$19.50
1999	6	Now	$19.00
2000	7	Now	$21.00
2001	5	Now	$15.00

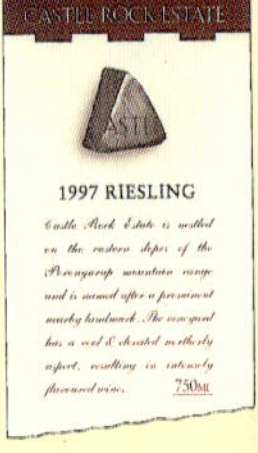

***Cathcart Ridge Estate** is a small Grampians (Great Western district) vineyard producing a blockbuster of a Cabernet and a very fine Merlot. Winemaker: David Farnhill.*

CATHCART RIDGE CABERNET SAUVIGNON ★★★★

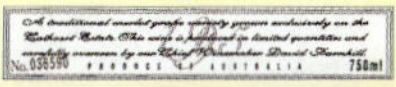

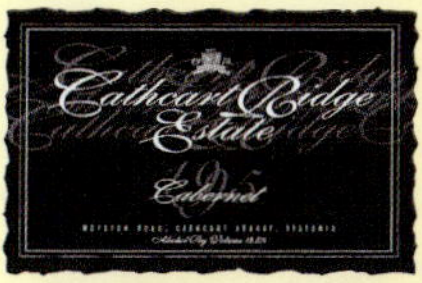

1994	7	2004	$39.00
1995	6	Now	$32.00
1996	5	Now	$26.00
1997	Not made		
1998	7	2012	$35.00
1999	6	2010	$29.00
2000	7	2010	$33.00

CATHCART RIDGE CABERNET/MERLOT ★★★★

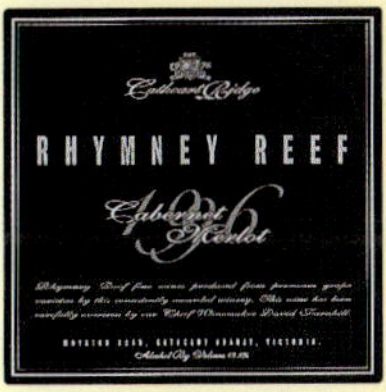

before 1996		Prior	
1996	5	Now	$16.50
1997	Not made		
1998	7	2012	$22.00
1999	6	2008	$18.50
2000	6	2009	$18.00

CATHCART RIDGE CHARDONNAY ★★★

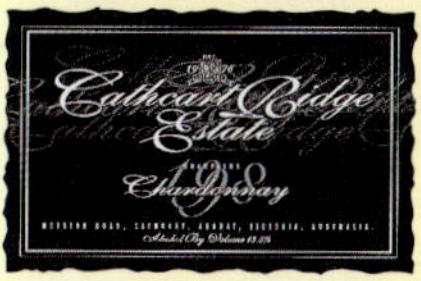

before 1997		Prior	
1997	6	2004	$18.00
1998	7	2006	$20.00
1999	Not made		
2000	7	2006	$19.00
2001	7	2007	$18.50

CATHCART RIDGE MERLOT ★★★★★

1989	6	Now	$43.00
1990	Not made		
1991	Not made		
1992	5	Prior	
1993	7	2005	$45.00
1994	5	Prior	
1995	7	2008	$42.00
1996	6	2006	$35.00
1997	Not made		
1998	Not made		
1999	6	2010	$32.00
2000	7	2012	$37.00
2001	7	2012	$36.00

CATHCART RIDGE SHIRAZ ★★★★

before 1996		Prior	
1996	7	2006	$38.00
1997	6	2008	$32.00
1998	7	2010	$36.00
1999	7	2014	$35.00
2000	6	2012	$29.00
2001	7	2013	$33.00

***Chain of Ponds** is the label under which a growing range of wines is released made from fruit from the Gumeracha Vineyard in the Adelaide Hills. Winemaker: Neville Falkenberg.*

CHAIN OF PONDS CABERNET SAUVIGNON "AMADEUS" ★★★★

1993	7	Now	$45.00
1994	6	Now	$37.00
1995	Not made		
1996	7	Now	$41.00
1997	6	Now	$34.00
1998	7	Now	$38.00
1999	6	2004	$32.00

CHAIN OF PONDS CHARDONNAY "CORKSCREW ROAD" ★★★★

1993	6	Now	$39.00
1994	7	Now	$45.00
1995	6	Now	$37.00
1996	6	Now	$36.00
1997	7	Now	$41.00
1998	7	Now	$39.00
1999	6	Now	$33.00
2000	7	2005	$37.00

CHAIN OF PONDS RIESLING "PURPLE PATCH" ★★★

1994	7	Now	$26.00
1995	Not made		
1996	6	Now	$21.00
1997	7	2004	$23.00
1998	7	Now	$23.00
1999	6	Now	$19.00
2000	6	Now	$18.50
2001	7	2006	$21.00

CHAIN OF PONDS SEMILLON "SQUARE CUT" ★★★★★

1993	6	Now	$23.00
1994	7	Now	$26.00
1995	6	Now	$22.00
1996	6	Now	$21.00
1997	6	Now	$20.00
1998	7	Now	$23.00
1999	6	2004	$19.50
2000	7	2006	$22.00
2001	7	2007	$21.00

CHAIN OF PONDS SEMILLON/ SAUVIGNON BLANC "BLACK THURSDAY" ★★★★

1996	7	Now	$25.00
1997	6	Prior	
1998	6	Prior	

1999	7	Now	$23.00
2000	6	Now	$19.50
2001	6	Now	$18.50

***Chalice Bridge Estate** is a large (120 ha) vineyard 16km South East of the Margaret River township. Winemaker: Margaret River Wines.*

CHALICE BRIDGE CABERNET SAUVIGNON ★★★★

1999	7	2006	$24.00
2000	7	2005	$23.00
2001	6	2006	$19.50
2002	5	2006	$16.00

CHALICE BRIDGE SHIRAZ

★★★★

1999	7	2006	$27.00
2000	7	2006	$26.00
2001	Not made		
2002	6	2007	$21.00

***Chapel Hill** is a very fine part Swiss owned winery in McLaren Vale producing a range of highly regarded wines. Winemakers: Pam Dunsford and Angela Meaney.*

CHAPEL HILL CABERNET SAUVIGNON ★★★★★

1990	7	Now	$42.00
1991	5	Now	$29.00
1992	7	2005	$39.00
1993	5	Now	$27.00
1994	6	Now	$32.00
1995	5	Now	$25.00
1996	7	2008	$35.00
1997	5	Now	$24.00
1998	6	2008	$28.00
1999	6	2005	$27.00
2000	6	2006	$26.00

CHAPEL HILL SHIRAZ ★★★★★

1990	6	Now	$35.00
1991	7	Now	$40.00
1992	5	Now	$27.00
1993	5	Now	$27.00
1994	7	2005	$36.00
1995	5	Now	$25.00
1996	7	2008	$34.00
1997	5	Now	$24.00
1998	6	2008	$28.00
1999	6	2004	$27.00
2000	6	2007	$26.00

CHAPEL HILL VERDELHO ★★★★

1997	6	2005	$22.00
1998	5	Now	$17.50
1999	5	Now	$17.00

2000	6	Now	$20.00
2001	6	2007	$19.50
2002	6	2007	$19.00

Charles Melton Wines *is a very small Barossa Valley producer with a range of wines which have excited an intensely loyal following. No ratings have been received from the maker. Winemakers: Charles Melton and Jo Ahearne.*

CHARLES MELTON CABERNET SAUVIGNON ★★★★

CHARLES MELTON NINE POPES (SHIRAZ/GRENACHE/MOURVERDRE) ★★★★★

Chateau Francois *is a small Pokolbin maker of hobbyist size but perfectionist aspirations. Winemaker: Don Francois.*

CHATEAU FRANCOIS SHIRAZ/PINOT NOIR ★★★

1986	6	Now	$22.00
1987	6	Now	$21.00
1988	4	Prior	
1989	6	Now	$20.00
1990	7	Now	$22.00
1991	6	Now	$19.00
1992	5	Now	$15.00
1993	6	Now	$17.50
1994	6	Now	$17.00
1995	6	Now	$16.50
1996	6	Now	$16.00
1997	7	Now	$18.50
1998	6	Now	$15.00
1999	7	2005	$17.50
2000	6	2004	N/R

CHATEAU FRANCOIS SEMILLON ★★★★

before 1988		Prior	
1988	6	Now	$17.00
1989	6	Now	$16.50
1990	6	Now	$16.00
1991	6	Now	$15.50
1992	7	Now	$18.00
1993	7	Now	$17.50
1994	7	Now	$17.00
1995	7	Now	$16.50
1996	7	Now	$16.00
1997	6	Now	$13.00
1998	6	Now	$13.00
1999	6	Now	N/R
2000	7	2004	N/R

***Chateau Reynella** is an historic McLaren Vale maker now owned and operated by BRL Hardy. The label has now been deleted except for Vintage Port. Winemaker: Eric Semler.*

CHATEAU REYNELLA VINTAGE PORT ★★★★

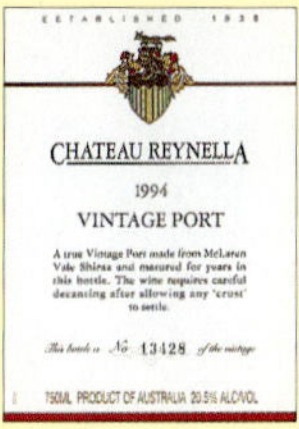

1966	4	Now	$38.00
1967	7	Now	$64.00
1968	3	Now	$27.00
1969	Not made		
1970	6	Now	$50.00
1971	6	Now	$50.00
1972	6	Now	$48.00
1973	Not made		
1974	4	Now	$30.00
1975	7	Now	$52.00
1976	6	Now	$43.00
1977	7	Now	$49.00
1978	6	Now	$40.00
1979	7	2005	$46.00
1980	6	Now	$38.00
1981	7	Now	$43.00
1982	7	Now	$42.00
1983	6	Now	$35.00
1984	Not made		
1985	Not made		
1986	Not made		
1987	7	2012	$36.00
1988	6	2005	$30.00
1989	Not made		
1990	6	2010	$28.00
1991	Not made		
1992	Not made		
1993	Not made		
1994	6	2014	$25.00
1995	Not made		
1996	6	2016	$24.00

***Chateau Tahbilk** - see Tahbilk*

***Chateau Xanadu** - see Xanadu.*

***Chatsfield Wines' Mount Barker** fruit produces three greatly respected white wines and, unusually for the area, a fine Shiraz. Winemaker: Bob Lee.*

CHATSFIELD CHARDONNAY ★★★★

before 1995		Prior	
1995	5	Now	$17.00
1996	6	Now	$20.00
1997	7	Now	$22.00
1998	6	2005	$19.00

1999	Not made		
2000	6	2005	$18.00
2001	7	2005	$20.00

CHATSFIELD GEWURZTRAMINER ★★★

before 1990		Prior	
1990	6	Now	$23.00
1991	Not made		
1992	5	Prior	
1993	5	Now	$17.50
1994	6	Now	$20.00
1995	6	Now	$20.00
1996	6	Now	$19.50
1997	6	2005	$19.00
1998	7	2005	$21.00
1999	5	Now	$15.00
2000	5	Now	$14.50
2001	5	2004	$14.00

CHATSFIELD MERIDIAN (CABERNET FRANC) ★★★

before 1995		Prior	
1995	6	Now	$25.00
1996	7	Now	$28.00
1997	5	Now	$19.50
1998	5	2005	$19.00
1999	5	2007	$18.50
2000	6	2009	$21.00
2001	6	2005	$21.00

CHATSFIELD RIESLING ★★★

before 1990		Prior	
1990	6	Now	$22.00
1991	Not made		
1992	5	Prior	
1993	5	Now	$17.00
1994	6	Now	$20.00
1995	6	Now	$19.50
1996	6	2005	$19.00
1997	6	2005	$18.50
1998	7	2005	$21.00
1999	5	Now	$14.50
2000	5	Now	$14.00
2001	7	2006	$19.00

CHATSFIELD SHIRAZ ★★★★

before 1990		Prior	
1990	7	Now	$35.00
1991	7	Now	$34.00
1992	7	Now	$33.00
1993	6	Now	$27.00
1994	7	2005	$31.00
1995	6	2005	$26.00

1996	6	2005	$25.00
1997	5	Now	$20.00
1998	5	2005	$20.00
1999	5	2007	$19.00
2000	6	2006	$22.00

Chestnut Grove Wines *is a Manjimup (WA) producer with 18 hectares of vines together with olive trees and, of course, a chestnut grove. Winemaker: Kim Horton.*

CHESTNUT GROVE CABERNET/MERLOT ★★★★

before 1998		Prior	
1998	5	Now	$19.50
1999	6	2005	$23.00
2000	6	2006	$22.00
2001	6	2008	$21.00

CHESTNUT GROVE MERLOT ★★★★

1997	5	Prior	
1998	6	Now	$35.00
1999	7	2005	$40.00
2000	6	2006	$33.00
2001	7	2007	$38.00

CHESTNUT GROVE PINOT NOIR ★★★★

before 1997		Prior	
1997	6	Now	$41.00
1998	Not made		
1999	6	Now	$38.00
2000	Not made		
2001	6	2005	$36.00
2002	7	2006	$41.00

CHESTNUT GROVE SAUVIGNON BLANC ★★★★

before 2000		Prior	
2000	6	Now	$19.00
2001	6	2004	$18.50

CHESTNUT GROVE VERDELHO ★★★★

before 2000		Prior	
2000	7	2004	$20.00
2001	6	2005	$16.50
2002	7	2006	$18.50

Clairault *is yet another maker whose product attests to the extreme quality of Margaret River as a wine area. Winemaker: Peter Stark.*

CLAIRAULT CABERNET/MERLOT ★★★★

1998	5	Now	$25.00
1999	7	Now	$34.00
2000	6	2004	$28.00
2001	6	2005	$28.00

CLAIRAULT RESERVE (CABERNET SAUVIGNON/FRANC/MERLOT) ★★★★★

before 1994		Prior	
1994	6	Now	$64.00
1995	7	Now	$74.00
1996	7	Now	$70.00
1997	6	Now	$58.00
1998	7	2006	$66.00
1999	7	2007	$64.00
2000	6	2008	$54.00

CLAIRAULT SAUVIGNON BLANC ★★★★

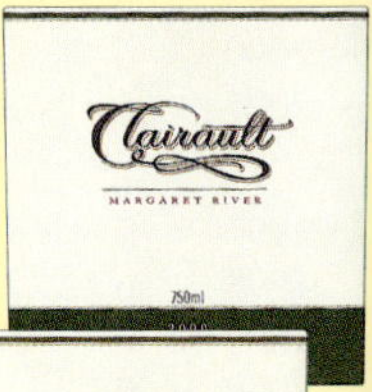

before 2000		Prior	
2000	6	Now	$21.00
2001	6	Now	$21.00

CLAIRAULT SEMILLON/ SAUVIGNON BLANC ★★★★

before 1996		Prior	
1996	5	Now	$22.00
1997	5	Prior	
1998	6	Prior	
1999	6	Now	$24.00
2000	6	Now	$23.00
2001	5	Now	$19.00

***Clarendon Hills** is a McLaren Vale maker with a range of blockbusting wines, including some very fine but massive Shiraz. The dollar values printed below are not misprints, but are based on the current prices given to me by the owner/winemaker. Winemaker: Roman Bratasiuk.*

CLARENDON HILLS ASTRALIS SHIRAZ ★★★★★

1994	7	2016	$195.00
1995	7	2020	$190.00
1996	7	2018	$180.00
1997	7	2020	$180.00
1998	7	2018	$170.00

CLARENDON HILLS BLEWITT SPRINGS OLD VINE GRENACHE ★★★★

1991	7	Now	$100.00
1992	7	Now	$100.00
1993	6	Now	$84.00
1994	7	Now	$94.00
1995	7	2005	$92.00
1996	7	Now	$90.00
1997	7	Now	$86.00
1998	7	2005	$84.00
1999	6	2008	$70.00

CLARENDON HILLS CABERNET SAUVIGNON ★★★★

1991	7	Now	$86.00
1992	7	Now	$84.00
1993	7	2005	$80.00
1994	Not made		
1995	7	2010	$76.00
1995	Not made		
1996	Not made		
1997	7	2010	$70.00
1998	7	2015	$68.00
1999	6	2008	$56.00

CLARENDON HILLS KANGARILLA CHARDONNAY ★★★★

1996	6	Now	$52.00
1997	7	Now	$58.00
1998	7	2005	$56.00

CLARENDON HILLS MERLOT ★★★★

1990	5	Now	$96.00
1991	6	Now	$110.00
1992	7	2005	$125.00
1993	6	Now	$105.00
1994	7	2005	$120.00
1995	7	Now	$115.00
1996	7	Now	$110.00
1997	7	2005	$105.00
1998	7	2006	$105.00

***Cleveland Estate** is a small maker in Victoria's Macedon region. The wines are reliable and sometimes very good indeed. Winemaker: Keith Brien.*

CLEVELAND ESTATE BRUT MACEDON ★★★★

before 1994		Prior	
1994	6	Now	$41.00
1995	6	Now	$40.00
1996	6	Now	$39.00
1997	6	Now	$38.00
1998	6	Now	$37.00

CLEVELAND ESTATE CABERNET SAUVIGNON "MINUS FIVE" ★★★★

1988	5	Prior	
1989	6	Now	$49.00
1990	5	Prior	
1991	7	Now	$54.00
1992	6	Now	$45.00
1993	6	Now	$43.00
1994	Not made		
1995	6	Now	$41.00

1996	Not made		
1997	5	2005	$32.00
1998	7	2006	$43.00

No longer made

CLEVELAND ESTATE CHARDONNAY ★★★★

1988	5	Now	$36.00
1989	5	Prior	
1990	5	Prior	
1991	6	Prior	
1992	6	Now	$38.00
1993	6	Now	$37.00
1994	7	Now	$42.00
1995	6	Now	$35.00
1996	6	Now	$34.00
1997	7	2004	$38.00
1998	6	2004	$32.00
1999	6	2004	$31.00
2000	6	2004	$30.00

CLEVELAND ESTATE PINOT NOIR ★★★★

before 1992		Prior	
1992	6	Now	$40.00
1993	5	Prior	
1994	7	Now	$44.00
1995	5	Prior	
1996	6	2004	$36.00
1997	7	Now	$40.00
1998	7	2005	$39.00
1999	7	2005	$38.00

CLEVELAND ESTATE SHIRAZ ★★★★

1998	5	Now	$28.00
1999	6	2010	$32.00
2000	6	2008	$31.00

***Clonakilla** is a Canberra district maker who predates the Doonkuna Estate as Murrumbateman's longest established producer. Winemaker: Tim Kirk.*

CLONAKILLA CABERNET/MERLOT ★★★★

before 1988		Prior	
1988	6	Now	$52.00
1989	Not made		
1990	3	Prior	
1991	4	Now	$31.00
1992	6	Now	$46.00
1993	5	Now	$37.00
1994	6	2004	$43.00
1995	5	Now	$35.00
1996	5	2004	$34.00
1997	7	2006	$46.00

1998	6	2008	$38.00
1999	6	2006	$37.00
2000	6	2006	$36.00
2001	7	2008	$41.00
2002	6	2004	$34.00

CLONAKILLA RIESLING ★★★★

1986	6	Now	$43.00
1987	5	Now	$34.00
1988	6	Now	$40.00
1989	2	Prior	
1990	4	Prior	
1991	5	Now	$30.00
1992	5	Now	$30.00
1993	7	2004	$40.00
1994	6	2004	$34.00
1995	6	2005	$33.00
1996	6	2004	$32.00
1997	7	2007	$36.00
1998	6	2006	$30.00
1999	6	2009	$29.00
2000	5	2008	$23.00
2001	7	2009	$32.00
2002	6	2012	$26.00

CLONAKILLA SEMILLON/ SAUVIGNON BLANC ★★★

before 1995		Prior	
1995	6	Now	$23.00
1996	5	Now	$18.50
1997	5	Now	$18.00
1998	6	Now	$21.00
1999	7	Now	$24.00
2000	6	Now	$20.00
2001	No data		
2002	5	Now	$15.50

CLONAKILLA SHIRAZ/VIOGNIER ★★★★★

1990	3	Now	$48.00
1991	4	Now	$62.00
1992	5	Now	$76.00
1993	5	Now	$74.00
1994	7	2006	$100.00
1995	6	Now	$84.00
1996	5	Now	$68.00
1997	7	2007	$92.00
1998	7	2009	$88.00
1999	5	2010	$62.00
2000	6	2008	$72.00
2001	7	2010	$82.00
2002	7	2012	$78.00

Clover Hill *is a very fine sparkling wine crafted by Taltarni (qv) from premium Tasmanian grapes. Winemaker: Peter Steer.*

CLOVER HILL METHODE CHAMPENOISE ★★★★★

1991	6	Now	$46.00
1992	6	Now	$45.00
1993	6	Now	$44.00
1994	6	Now	$42.00
1995	6	Now	$41.00
1996	5	Now	$33.00
1997	5	Now	$32.00
1998	6	Now	$38.00

Cockfighter's Ghost *is a 12 hectare vineyard at Broke in the Hunter Valley owned and operated by Harbridge Fine Wines. Wines from other regions are produced under the same label. Winemaker: John Wade.*

COCKFIGHTER'S GHOST CHARDONNAY ★★★★

1996	5	Now	$17.00
1997	6	Now	$20.00
1998	6	Now	$19.50
1999	7	Now	$22.00

COCKFIGHTER'S GHOST CHARDONNAY (UNWOODED) ★★★

1996	5	Now	$17.00
1997	5	Now	$16.50
1998	5	Now	$16.00
1999	6	Now	$18.50
2000	7	Now	$21.00

COCKFIGHTER'S GHOST PINOT NOIR ★★★★

1995	5	Now	$24.00
1996	6	Now	$28.00
1997	5	Now	$23.00
1998	7	Now	$31.00
1999	5	Now	$22.00
2000	7	Now	$30.00

COCKFIGHTER'S GHOST SEMILLON ★★★

1995	5	Now	$17.00
1996	6	Now	$20.00
1997	5	Now	$16.00
1998	7	Now	$22.00
1999	6	2004	$18.00
2000	6	2005	$17.50
2001	6	2005	$17.00

COCKFIGHTER'S GHOST PINOT NOIR (PEMBERTON) ★★★★

1997	6	Now	$22.00
1998	7	Now	$25.00
1999	7	Now	$24.00

COCKFIGHTER'S GHOST SHIRAZ ★★★★

1995	5	Now	$21.00
1996	5	Now	$20.00
1997	6	Now	$24.00
1998	6	2004	$23.00
1999	7	2005	$26.00

COCKFIGHTER'S GHOST VERDELHO ★★★

1999	7	Now	$18.50
2000	6	Now	$15.50
2001	7	Now	$17.50

***Coldstream Hills**, now owned by Southcorp, is a leading Yarra Valley vineyard and winery founded by Australia's leading wine writer, James Halliday. Winemaker: Paul Lapsley.*

COLDSTREAM BRIARSTON HILLS CABERNET/MERLOT ★★★★★

before 1991		Prior	
1991	7	Now	$40.00
1992	6	Now	$33.00
1993	5	Now	$27.00
1994	5	Prior	
1995	5	Now	$25.00
1996	4	Prior	
1997	6	Now	$29.00
1998	7	2004	$33.00
1999	4	Now	$18.00
2000	7	2010	$31.00

COLDSTREAM HILLS RESERVE CABERNET SAUVIGNON ★★★★★

1985	5	Now	$50.00
1986	6	Now	$58.00
1987	5	Now	$47.00
1988	7	Now	$64.00
1989	4	Now	$36.00
1990	6	Now	$52.00
1991	7	2005	$58.00
1992	7	2010	$56.00
1993	6	Now	$48.00
1994	6	2004	$46.00
1995	6	2005	$45.00
1996	Not made		
1997	7	2006	$49.00

1998	7	2008	$48.00
1999	Not made		
2000	7	2010	$45.00

COLDSTREAM HILLS RESERVE CHARDONNAY

★★★★★

1986	6	Now	$62.00
1987	5	Now	$50.00
1988	7	Now	$68.00
1989	3	Prior	
1990	5	Now	$46.00
1991	7	Now	$62.00
1992	7	Now	$60.00
1993	7	Now	$58.00
1994	7	Now	$56.00
1995	5	Prior	
1996	6	2005	$46.00
1997	6	Now	$45.00
1998	5	Now	$36.00
1999	5	Now	$35.00
2000	6	2004	$41.00

COLDSTREAM HILLS RESERVE PINOT NOIR

★★★★★

before 1987		Prior	
1987	6	Now	$62.00
1988	7	Now	$70.00
1989	4	Prior	
1990	3	Prior	
1991	7	Now	$64.00
1992	7	Now	$62.00
1993	4	Now	$34.00
1994	7	Now	$58.00
1995	5	Now	$40.00
1996	7	2006	$54.00
1997	7	2008	$52.00
1998	6	2004	$44.00
1999	Not made		
2000	7	2010	$49.00

COLDSTREAM HILLS SAUVIGNON BLANC (SEMILLON/ until 1997)

★★★★

1985	3	Now	$20.00
1986	5	Now	$32.00
1987	6	Now	$38.00
1988	5	Now	$31.00
1989	4	Now	$24.00
1990	6	Now	$35.00
1991	6	Now	$34.00
1992	7	Now	$38.00
1993	Not made		
1994	7	Now	$36.00

1995	5	Now	$25.00
1996	6	Now	$29.00
1997	6	Now	$28.00
1998	7	Now	$32.00
1999	7	Now	$31.00
2000	6	Now	$26.00

***Coolangatta Estate** is an admirable resort/golfcourse/tourist operation in the Shoalhaven area of NSW. Their viticultural practices are of an exemplary standard, resulting in some impressive wines (made by Tyrrells). Winemaker: Andrew Spinaze.*

COOLANGATTA ESTATE ALEXANDER BERRY CHARDONNAY ★★★★

1991	6	Now	$30.00
1992	Not made		
1993	5	Now	$24.00
1994	6	Now	$28.00
1995	6	Now	$27.00
1996	6	Now	$26.00
1997	6	Now	$25.00
1998	6	Now	$25.00
1999	Not made		
2000	6	2004	$23.00
2001	6	2005	$23.00
2002	6	2006	$22.00

COOLANGATTA ESTATE CHAMBOURCIN ★★★

1996	5	Now	$19.00
1997	6	Now	$22.00
1998	6	Now	$21.00
1999	6	Now	$21.00
2000	6	Now	$20.00
2001	6	2003	$20.00
2002	6	2004	$19.00

COOLANGATTA ESTATE VERDELHO ★★★

1997	5	Now	$17.50
1998	6	Now	$20.00
1999	6	Now	$20.00
2000	6	Now	$19.50
2001	6	2002	$19.00
2002	6	2003	$18.50

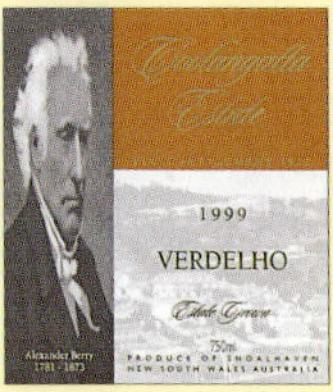

***Cope-Williams** is a small, cool climate Romsey (Victoria) maker, particularly well-regarded for some skilfully crafted sparkling wines. Winemaker: Michael Cope-Williams.*

COPE-WILLIAMS CABERNET/MERLOT ★★★★

1988	6	Now	$37.00
1989	5	Prior	
1990	6	Now	$35.00

1991	5	Now	$28.00
1992	6	Now	$33.00
1993	6	Now	$32.00
1994	4	Now	$20.00
1995	5	Now	$25.00
1996	4	Now	$19.50
1997	6	2006	$28.00
1998	6	2005	$27.00

COPE-WILLIAMS CHARDONNAY ★★★

before 1988		Prior	
1988	6	Now	$24.00
1989	7	Now	$27.00
1990	6	Now	$22.00
1991	7	Now	$25.00
1992	6	Now	$21.00
1993	Not made		
1994	6	Now	$20.00
1995	7	Now	$22.00
1996	Not made		
1997	6	Now	$18.50
1998	6	Now	$18.00

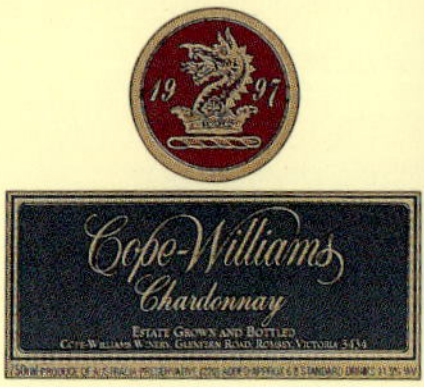

COPE-WILLIAMS "ROMSEY BRUT" (METHODE CHAMPENOISE) ★★★★

before 1988		Prior	
1988	5	Now	$34.00
1989	4	Prior	
1990	7	Now	$45.00
1991	7	Now	$44.00
1992	5	Prior	
1993	6	Now	$35.00
1994	4	Now	$23.00
1995	6	Now	$33.00
1996	6	Now	$32.00
1997	7	Now	$37.00
1998	7	Now	$36.00

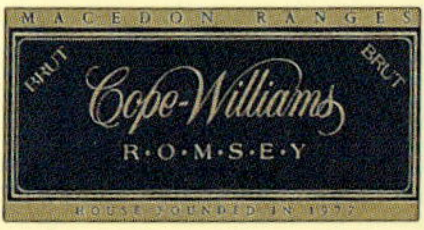

COPE-WILLIAMS PINOT NOIR ★★★

before 1988		Prior	
1988	7	Now	$34.00
1989	2	Prior	
1990	6	Now	$28.00
1991	5	Prior	
1992	7	Now	$30.00
1993	Not made		
1994	5	Now	$20.00
1995	4	Now	$16.00
1996	5	Now	$19.50
1997	7	Now	$26.00
1998	6	Now	$22.00

Coriole, in McLaren Vale, has been long known for unusually elegant reds. Of recent years the whites have improved greatly to bolster this fine maker's reputation still further. Winemaker: Grant Harrison.

CORIOLE CHARDONNAY ★★★★

before 1993		Prior	
1993	6	Now	$21.00
1994	7	Now	$24.00
1995	6	Now	$20.00
1996	6	Now	$19.50
1997	6	Now	$19.00

No data since 1997

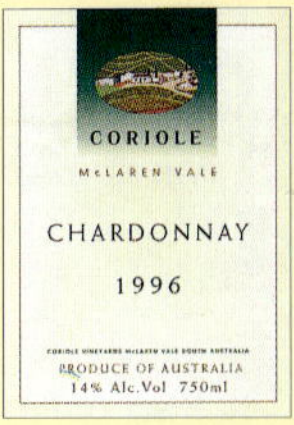

CORIOLE CHENIN BLANC ★★★

before 1993		Prior	
1993	5	Now	$15.00
1994	5	Now	$14.50
1995	5	Now	$14.00
1996	7	Now	$19.00
1997	6	Now	$16.00
1998	7	Now	$18.00
1999	6	Now	$15.00
2000	7	Now	$17.00
2001	7	2004	$16.50

CORIOLE MARY KATHLEEN CABERNET/MERLOT ★★★★

1992	5	Now	$40.00
1993	6	Now	$47.00
1994	7	Now	$54.00
1995	5	Now	$37.00
1996	6	Now	$43.00
1997	6	Now	$42.00
1998	7	2006	$48.00
1999	6	2007	$40.00

CORIOLE LLOYD RESERVE SHIRAZ ★★★★★

1989	7	Now	$120.00
1990	5	Now	$86.00
1991	7	Now	$115.00
1992	6	Now	$98.00
1993	6	Now	$94.00
1994	6	Now	$92.00
1995	7	Now	$100.00
1996	7	Now	$100.00
1997	5	Now	$70.00
1998	7	2005	$96.00
1999	7	2006	$92.00

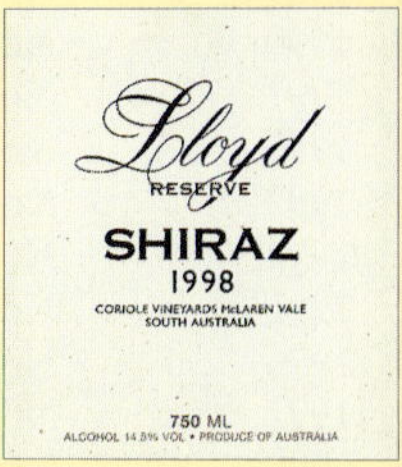

CORIOLE REDSTONE (SHIRAZ/CABERNET/GRENACHE) ★★★

1992	7	Now	$27.00
1993	7	Now	$26.00
1994	7	Now	$25.00
1995	6	Now	$21.00
1996	6	Now	$20.00
1997	5	2004	$16.50
1998	6	2004	$19.00
1999	5	2004	$15.50
2000	7	2006	$21.00

CORIOLE SANGIOVESE ★★★

before 1994		Prior	
1994	5	Now	$20.00
1995	6	Now	$24.00
1996	6	Now	$23.00
1997	5	Now	$19.00
1998	5	Now	$18.50
1999	6	2006	$21.00
2000	5	2005	$17.50

CORIOLE SEMILLON ★★★★

1989	7	Prior	
1990	7	Now	$34.00
1991	4	Prior	
1992	7	Now	$32.00
1993	6	Now	$26.00
1994	7	Now	$30.00
1995	5	Now	$21.00
1996	6	Now	$24.00
1997	6	Now	$23.00
1998	7	Now	$27.00
1999	5	Now	$18.50
2000	7	2004	$25.00
2001	7	2005	$24.00

CORIOLE SHIRAZ ★★★★

before 1989		Prior	
1989	6	Now	$37.00
1990	6	Now	$36.00
1991	5	Now	$29.00
1992	5	Now	$28.00
1993	7	Now	$38.00
1994	6	Now	$32.00
1995	6	Now	$31.00
1996	7	Now	$35.00
1997	6	Now	$29.00
1998	7	2005	$33.00
1999	7	Now	$32.00
2000	7	2007	$31.00

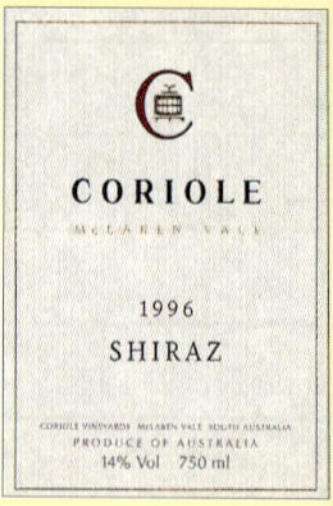

***Cowra Estate** is a substantial producer taking advantage of the reputation for generous fruit earned by earlier Cowra wines from Petaluma and Rothbury. The wines are remarkably inexpensive. Winemaker: Simon Gilbert.*

COWRA ESTATE CABERNET FRANC ROSE ★★★

before 1999		Prior	
1999	5	Now	$12.00
2000	6	Now	$14.00

COWRA ESTATE CABERNETS ★★★

1988	4	Prior	
1989	4	Now	$12.50
1990	Not made		
1994	5	Now	$15.00
1995	4	Now	$11.50
1996	7	Prior	
1997	6	Now	$16.50
1998	7	Now	$18.50
1999	6	2005	$15.50

COWRA ESTATE CHARDONNAY ★★★

1992	4	Prior	
1993	4	Now	$12.50
1994	Not made		
1995	6	Now	$17.50
1996	6	2005	$17.00
1997	7	Now	$19.00
1998	4	Now	$10.50
1999	6	Prior	
2000	7	2010	$17.50

***Crabtree of Watervale** is a Clare Valley producer previously known as Watervale Cellars. Their particularly fine wood-aged Semillon should be sought out. Winemaker: Robert Crabtree.*

CRABTREE RIESLING ★★★★

before 1994		Prior	
1994	6	Now	$18.00
1995	5	Now	$14.50
1996	6	Now	$17.00
1997	6	Now	$16.50
1998	6	Now	$16.00
1999	6	Now	$15.50
2000	6	2006	$15.00
2001	7	2010	$17.50

CRABTREE SEMILLON ★★★★

1988	5	Now	$20.00
1989	7	Now	$27.00
1990	6	Now	$23.00

1991	6	Now	$22.00
1992	5	Now	$18.00
1993	5	Now	$17.50
1994	6	Now	$20.00
1995	5	Now	$16.50
1996	6	Now	$19.00
1997	6	Now	$18.50
1998	6	Now	$18.00
1999	6	Now	$17.50

CRABTREE SHIRAZ/CABERNET ★★★

1982	5	Prior	
1983	Not made		
1984	7	Prior	
1985	5	Prior	
1986	7	Now	$33.00
1987	6	Now	$27.00
1988	6	Now	$27.00
1989	6	Now	$26.00
1990	7	Now	$29.00
1991	5	Now	$20.00
1992	6	Now	$24.00
1993	6	Now	$23.00
1994	6	Now	$22.00
1995	6	Now	$22.00
1996	7	Now	$25.00
1997	6	2004	$20.00
1998	6	2005	$20.00
1999	7	2006	$22.00

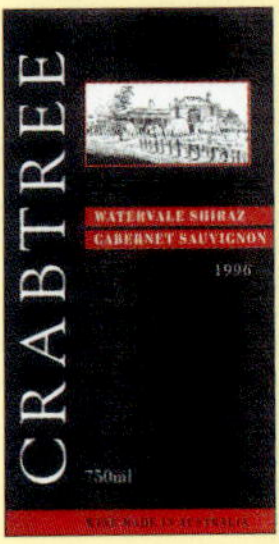

Craigie Knowe *is a very small vineyard on the rocky soil at Cranbrook on Tasmania's east coast, and annually produce a powerful but complex Cabernet. Winemaker: John Austwick.*

CRAIGIE KNOWE CABERNET SAUVIGNON ★★★★

1984	5	Now	$43.00
1985	5	Now	$42.00
1986	Not made		
1987	Not made		
1988	4	Now	$30.00
1989	5	Now	$37.00
1990	5	Now	$36.00
1991	5	Now	$35.00
1992	5	Now	$34.00
1993	5	Now	$33.00
1994	6	Now	$38.00
1995	5	Now	$31.00
1996	4	Now	$24.00
1997	4	Now	$23.00
1998	4	Now	$23.00

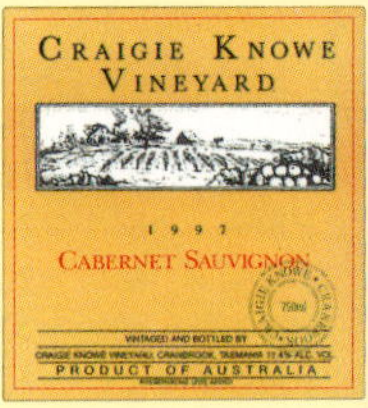

1999	5	2002	$27.00
2000	4	2004	$21.00
2001	5	2005	$26.00

***Craiglee** is a re-establishment of a 19th century vineyard at Sunbury near Melbourne. Winemaker: Pat Carmody.*

CRAIGLEE CHARDONNAY ★★★★

before 1992		Prior	
1992	5	Now	$34.00
1993	6	Now	$40.00
1994	6	Now	$38.00
1995	6	Now	$37.00
1996	6	Now	$36.00
1997	6	Now	$35.00
1998	5	Now	$28.00
1999	6	Now	$33.00
2000	6	Now	$32.00
2001	5	2004	$26.00

CRAIGLEE SHIRAZ ★★★★★

before 1981		Prior	
1981	3	Now	$35.00
1982	3	Now	$34.00
1983	5	Now	$56.00
1984	6	Now	$64.00
1985	6	Now	$62.00
1986	6	Now	$62.00
1987	5	Now	$50.00
1988	6	Now	$58.00
1989	5	Now	$47.00
1990	7	Now	$64.00
1991	6	Now	$52.00
1992	5	Now	$43.00
1993	6	Now	$50.00
1994	6	2004	$49.00
1995	5	Now	$39.00
1996	6	Now	$46.00
1997	6	2008	$44.00
1998	6	2008	$43.00
1999	5	2007	$35.00
2000	6	2008	$41.00

***Craigmoor** is an historic Mudgee winery which is now part of the Orlando Wyndham group. Wines are no longer released under this label. Winemaker: James Manners.*

CRAIGMOOR CABERNET SAUVIGNON ★★★

before 1990		Prior	
1991	7	Now	$20.00
1992	5	Now	$14.50
1993	6	Now	$16.50

1994	6	Now	$16.00
1995	5	Now	$13.00
1996	7	Now	$18.00
1997	5	Now	$12.50
1998	5	Now	$12.00

CRAIGMOOR CHARDONNAY ★★★

before 1994		Prior	
1994	7	Now	$17.00
1995	6	Now	$14.50
1996	6	Now	$14.00
1997	7	Now	$15.50
1998	6	Now	$13.00
1999	7	Now	$15.00

CRAIGMOOR SEMILLON ★★★

1993	6	Now	$17.50
1994	5	Now	$14.00
1995	5	Now	$13.50
1996	6	Now	$16.00
1997	6	Now	$15.50
1998	5	Now	$12.50

CRAIGMOOR SHIRAZ ★★★

1988	4	Now	$13.00
1989	Not made		
1990	6	Now	$18.50
1991	6	Now	$18.00
1992	Not made		
1993	6	Now	$17.00
1994	6	Now	$16.50
1995	7	Now	$18.50
1996	6	Now	$15.50
1997	4	Now	$10.00
1998	6	Now	$14.50

***Craneford** is a Springton (Adelaide Hills) maker who produce an admirable Chardonnay. Winemaker: John Zilm.*

CRANEFORD CHARDONNAY ★★★★

1986	5	Now	$20.00
1987	6	Now	$24.00
1988	6	Now	$23.00
1989	5	Now	$18.50
1990	Not made		
1991	Not made		
1992	5	Now	$17.00
1993	Not made		
1994	6	Now	$19.50
1995	4	Now	$12.50
1996	6	Now	$18.00
1997	6	Now	$17.50

1998	6	2004	$17.00
1999	6	2005	$16.50
2000	No data		
2001	7	2005	$18.50

CRANEFORD RIESLING ★★★★

1993	5	Now	$20.00
1994	6	Now	$23.00
1995	4	Now	$15.00
1996	6	Now	$22.00
1997	7	Now	$25.00
1998	6	2008	$21.00
1999	6	2009	$20.00
2000	No data		
2001	7	2005	$22.00

CRANEFORD SHIRAZ ★★★★

1988	7	Now	$36.00
1989	6	Now	$30.00
1990	7	Now	$34.00
1991	6	Now	$28.00
1992	6	Now	$27.00
1993	Not made		
1994	Not made		
1995	Not made		
1996	6	Now	$24.00
1997	7	2006	$27.00
1998	7	2008	$26.00

***Croser** is a methode champenoise wine of a quality unprecedented (for an Australian sparkling wine) when it was first released. The wine is made at Petaluma. Winemaker: Brian Croser.*

CROSER ★★★★★

1985	4	Now	$39.00
1986	4	Now	$38.00
1987	5	Now	$46.00
1988	5	Now	$45.00
1989	Not made		
1990	7	Now	$58.00
1991	4	Now	$32.00
1992	7	Now	$56.00
1993	5	Now	$38.00
1994	6	Now	$45.00
1995	4	Now	$29.00
1996	5	2010	$35.00
1997	5	Now	$34.00
1998	5	2005	$33.00
1999	5	2005	$32.00
2000	5	2004	$31.00

Cullen Wines are low key but high quality producers in an area where the fruit is so often outstanding - Margaret River. Cullen wines are powerful, individual and long-living. Winemaker: Vanya Cullen.

CULLEN CABERNET SAUVIGNON/MERLOT ★★★★★

1975	4	Now	$120.00
1976	5	Now	$145.00
1977	4	Now	$115.00
1978	4	Now	$110.00
1979	3	2005	$82.00
1980	5	Now	$130.00
1981	5	Now	$125.00
1982	6	Now	$150.00
1983	5	Now	$120.00
1984	6	Now	$140.00
1985	6	Now	$135.00
1986	6	Now	$130.00
1987	4	Now	$86.00
1988	6	2005	$125.00
1989	4	Now	$80.00
1990	6	2005	$115.00
1991	7	2010	$130.00
1992	6	2005	$110.00
1993	5	Now	$90.00
1994	6	2010	$100.00
1995	7	2020	$115.00
1996	6	2010	$98.00
1997	6	2020	$96.00
1998	6	2020	$92.00
1999	7	2020	$105.00
2000	6	2020	$88.00

CULLEN CHARDONNAY ★★★★

1980	3	Now	$37.00
1981	5	Now	$60.00
1982	6	Now	$70.00
1983	5	Now	$56.00
1984	6	Now	$66.00
1985	5	Now	$54.00
1986	4	Now	$41.00
1987	5	Now	$50.00
1988	5	Now	$49.00
1989	3	Now	$28.00
1990	4	Now	$37.00
1991	3	Now	$27.00
1992	5	Now	$43.00
1993	5	Now	$42.00
1994	6	Now	$49.00
1995	5	Now	$40.00

1996	6	2005	$46.00
1997	6	2009	$45.00
1998	6	2010	$44.00
1999	6	2010	$42.00
2000	7	2010	$48.00

CULLEN PINOT NOIR ★★★★

1984	5	Now	$52.00
1985	5	Now	$52.00
1986	5	Now	$50.00
1987	4	Now	$39.00
1988	4	Now	$38.00
1989	3	Now	$27.00
1990	5	Now	$45.00
1991	4	Now	$35.00
1992	6	Now	$50.00
1993	6	Now	$49.00
1994	5	Now	$40.00
1995	6	Now	$46.00
1996	6	Now	$45.00
1997	6	Now	$44.00
1998	6	Now	$42.00
1999	5	Now	$34.00

CULLEN SAUVIGNON BLANC/SEMILLON ★★★★

1991	4	Now	$24.00
1992	5	Now	$29.00
1993	7	Now	$40.00
1994	5	Now	$28.00
1995	6	Now	$32.00
1996	6	2005	$31.00
1997	6	Now	$31.00
1998	6	2005	$30.00
1999	6	Now	$29.00
2000	6	2005	$28.00
2001	6	2004	$27.00
2002	7	2005	$31.00

***The Curlewis Winery** in the Geelong region specialises in Pinot Noir, with most notable success. Winemaker: Rainer Breit.*

CURLEWIS PINOT NOIR ★★★★

1998	5	Now	$36.00
1999	Not made		
2000	7	2005	$48.00
2001	6	2005	$40.00

CURLEWIS PINOT NOIR RESERVE ★★★★★

1998	5	2005	$58.00
1999	Not made		
2000	7	2008	$78.00
2001	6	2007	$64.00

Dalwhinnie Winery *is a high country Moonambel (Victoria) maker with eighteen hectares of vines. The Shiraz is magnificent, and the other wines not far behind. Winemaker: David Jones.*

DALWHINNIE CABERNET SAUVIGNON

★★★★★

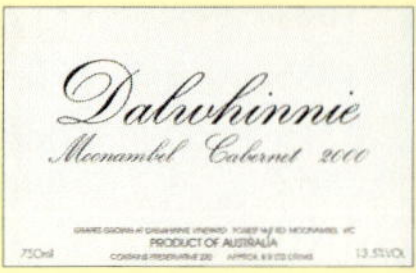

1980	7	Now	$100.00
1981	5	Prior	
1982	6	Prior	
1983	6	Prior	
1984	7	Now	$90.00
1985	5	Now	$62.00
1986	7	Now	$84.00
1987	5	Now	$58.00
1988	7	Now	$80.00
1989	5	Prior	
1990	7	Now	$76.00
1991	6	Now	$62.00
1992	6	2004	$60.00
1993	7	2005	$68.00
1994	7	2006	$66.00
1995	7	2008	$64.00
1996	6	2010	$54.00
1997	7	2012	$60.00
1998	7	2013	$60.00
1999	7	2014	$58.00
2000	7	2015	$56.00
2001	6	2015	$47.00

DALWHINNIE CHARDONNAY

★★★★★

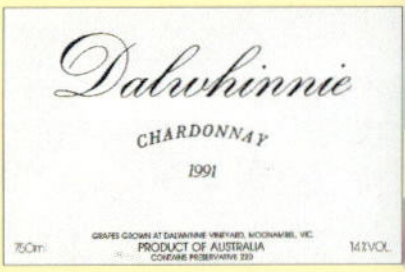

before 1988		Prior	
1988	7	Now	$64.00
1989	4	Prior	
1990	7	Now	$60.00
1991	6	Now	$50.00
1992	7	Now	$56.00
1993	6	Now	$47.00
1994	6	Now	$46.00
1995	5	Now	$37.00
1996	7	2004	$50.00
1997	6	2005	$42.00
1998	7	2006	$47.00
1999	7	2007	$46.00
2000	7	2007	$45.00
2001	6	2007	$37.00

DALWHINNIE PINOT NOIR

★★★★★

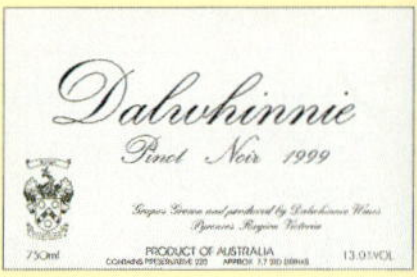

1995	4	Now	$41.00
1996	5	Now	$50.00
1997	4	Now	$39.00

1998	5	2004	$47.00
1999	6	2004	$54.00
2000	6	2005	$54.00
2001	6	2005	$52.00

DALWHINNIE SHIRAZ

★★★★★

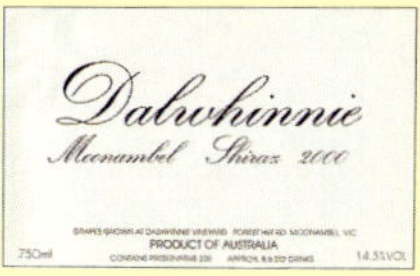

1980	7	Now	$110.00
1981	5	Prior	
1982	6	Prior	
1983	Not made		
1984	6	Now	$86.00
1985	7	Now	$98.00
1986	6	Now	$82.00
1987	5	Now	$66.00
1988	7	Now	$90.00
1989	5	Now	$62.00
1990	7	Now	$84.00
1991	7	2004	$82.00
1992	7	2006	$80.00
1993	5	2004	$54.00
1994	7	2006	$74.00
1995	6	2008	$62.00
1996	6	2008	$60.00
1997	7	2010	$68.00
1998	7	2010	$66.00
1999	7	2011	$64.00
2000	7	2011	$62.00
2001	7	2012	$60.00

***d'Arenberg** are reliable, well-distributed McLaren Vale makers with a large range of respected wines. Winemakers: Chester Osborn and Phillip Dean.*

d'ARENBERG THE VINTAGE FORTIFIED SHIRAZ

★★★★

1971	6	Now	$54.00
1972	Not made		
1973	7	Now	$60.00
1974	Not made		
1975	7	2006	$56.00
1976	7	2004	$54.00
1977	Not made		
1978	6	Now	$44.00
1979	Not made		
1987	7	2010	$49.00
1988	Not made		
1993	5	2010	$33.00
1994	Not made		
1995	7	2017	$43.00
1996	Not made		
1997	6	2020	$35.00

1998	7	2025	$39.00
1999	7	2030	$38.00
2000	6	2027	$32.00

d'ARENBERG HIGH TRELLIS CABERNET SAUVIGNON ★★★★

before 1976		Prior	
1976	7	2005	$58.00
1977	6	Prior	
1978	6	2008	$46.00
1979	6	Prior	
1980	Not made		
1981	5	Prior	
1982	6	Now	$41.00
1983	5	Prior	
1984	6	Prior	
1985	6	2010	$38.00
1986	6	2005	$37.00
1987	5	Now	$29.00
1988	5	Now	$29.00
1989	6	Now	$33.00
1990	6	Now	$32.00
1991	7	2010	$37.00
1992	5	2006	$25.00
1993	4	2005	$20.00
1994	5	2008	$24.00
1995	7	2012	$33.00
1996	6	2012	$27.00
1997	5	2014	$22.00
1998	7	2015	$30.00
1999	6	2015	$25.00
2000	6	2015	$24.00
2001	6	2015	$23.00

d'ARENBERG IRONSTONE PRESSINGS (GRENACHE/SHIRAZ) ★★★★★

1988	5	Now	$74.00
1989	6	Now	$86.00
1990	6	2004	$84.00
1991	6	2006	$82.00
1992	6	2005	$80.00
1993	5	2005	$64.00
1994	6	2010	$74.00
1995	7	2015	$84.00
1996	6	2013	$70.00
1997	7	2025	$80.00
1998	7	2022	$78.00
1999	7	2023	$76.00
2000	6	2020	$62.00

d'ARENBERG NOBLE RIESLING (375ml) ★★★★

1985	7	Now	$52.00
1986	Not made		
1987	6	Prior	
1988	Not made		
1989	6	Prior	
1990	Not made		
1991	6	Now	$38.00
1992	7	Now	$43.00
1993	4	Now	$23.00
1994	5	Now	$28.00
1995	6	2005	$33.00
1996	5	2007	$27.00
1997	7	2010	$37.00
1998	6	2011	$30.00
1999	7	2011	$35.00

d'ARENBERG OLIVE GROVE CHARDONNAY ★★★★

before 1990		Prior	
1990	6	Now	$24.00
1991	6	Now	$24.00
1992	6	Now	$23.00
1993	7	2004	$26.00
1994	7	2005	$25.00
1995	7	2005	$24.00
1996	6	2007	$20.00
1997	6	2010	$20.00
1998	5	2011	$16.00
1999	6	2011	$18.50
2000	7	2012	$21.00
2001	7	2013	$20.00
2002	7	2013	$20.00

d'ARENBERG THE FOOTBOLT SHIRAZ ★★★★

1970	4	Now	$39.00
1971	6	Now	$56.00
1972	6	Prior	
1973	7	Prior	
1974	Not made		
1975	4	Prior	
1976	6	2005	$49.00
1977	Not made		
1978	5	Prior	
1979	Not made		
1980	5	Prior	
1981	Not made		
1982	5	2010	$34.00
1983	Not made		
1984	Not made		
1985	6	2005	$37.00
1986	Not made		

1987	6	Now	$35.00
1988	6	Now	$34.00
1989	6	Now	$33.00
1990	7	2005	$37.00
1991	7	2010	$36.00
1992	6	2015	$30.00
1993	4	2006	$19.50
1994	6	2008	$28.00
1995	7	2015	$32.00
1996	6	2010	$27.00
1997	5	2011	$22.00
1998	7	2015	$29.00
1999	6	2015	$24.00
2000	7	2017	$28.00
2000	7	2028	$27.00

d'ARENBERG d'ARRY'S ORIGINAL SHIRAZ/GRENACHE ★★★★

1961	6	Now	$72.00
1962	Not made		
1963	7	2005	$80.00
1964	6	Now	$66.00
1965	5	Now	$54.00
1966	4	Now	$42.00
1967	7	2008	$70.00
1968	5	Now	$49.00
1969	5	Now	$48.00
1970	6	2010	$56.00
1971	6	Now	$54.00
1972	5	Now	$44.00
1973	4	Now	$34.00
1974	Not made		
1975	5	Now	$40.00
1976	7	2005	$54.00
1977	Not made		
1978	Not made		
1979	5	Now	$35.00
1980	Not made		
1981	Not made		
1982	6	2010	$39.00
1983	Not made		
1984	Not made		
1985	Not made		
1986	6	2016	$34.00
1987	7	2020	$39.00
1988	6	2015	$32.00
1989	5	2014	$26.00
1990	6	2018	$31.00
1991	7	2019	$35.00
1992	7	2020	$34.00

1993	5	2015	$23.00
1994	5	2015	$23.00
1995	7	2030	$31.00
1996	6	2025	$26.00
1997	7	2030	$29.00
1998	6	2025	$24.00
1999	6	2025	$23.00
2000	6	2025	$23.00

d'ARENBERG THE FISHPLATE SAUVIGNON BLANC ★★★

2000	7	Now	$23.00
2001	5	Now	$16.00
2002	7	2004	$22.00

d'ARENBERG THE COPPERMINE ROAD CABERNET SAUVIGNON ★★★★★

1995	6	2022	$70.00
1996	6	2020	$68.00
1997	6	2022	$66.00
1998	7	2028	$74.00
1999	7	2028	$72.00
2000	7	2028	$70.00
2001	7	2028	$68.00

d'ARENBERG THE DEAD ARM SHIRAZ ★★★★★

1993	4	Now	$52.00
1994	6	2010	$76.00
1995	7	2023	$86.00
1996	6	2016	$70.00
1997	6	2018	$68.00
1998	7	2025	$78.00
1999	6	2020	$64.00
2000	7	2027	$74.00

d'ARENBERG THE CUSTODIAN GRENACHE ★★★★

1994	6	2005	$25.00
1995	7	2007	$29.00
1996	7	2008	$28.00
1997	7	2009	$27.00
1998	6	2008	$22.00
1999	6	2010	$22.00
2000	6	2011	$21.00

d'ARENBERG THE DRY DAM RIESLING ★★★★

before 1982		Prior	
1982	6	Now	$34.00
1983	4	Prior	
1984	4	Prior	

1985	6	Now	$31.00
1986	Not made		
1987	6	Now	$29.00
1988	Not made		
1989	7	Now	$32.00
1990	6	Now	$26.00
1991	Not made		
1992	7	2005	$29.00
1993	7	2007	$28.00
1994	2	Now	$7.75
1995	6	2008	$23.00
1996	6	2010	$22.00
1997	6	2011	$21.00
1998	Not made		
1999	7	2012	$23.00
2000	7	2013	$23.00
2001	6	2012	$19.00
2002	7	2020	$21.00

d'ARENBERG THE PEPPERMINT PADDOCK CHAMBOURCIN ★★★

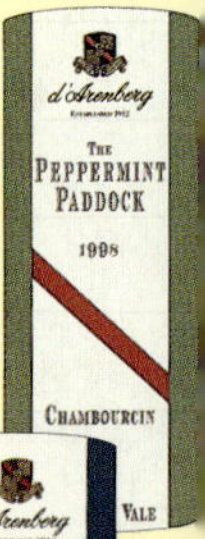

1993	4	Prior	
1994	5	Now	$24.00
1995	6	Now	$28.00
1996	5	Now	$22.00
1997	5	Now	$22.00
1998	6	2005	$25.00
1999	5	2005	$20.00

d'ARENBERG THE TWENTY EIGHT ROAD MOURVEDRE ★★★★

1995	5	Now	$34.00
1996	6	2010	$39.00
1997	7	2015	$44.00
1998	6	2015	$37.00
1999	6	2015	$36.00
2000	7	2018	$41.00
2001	6	2016	$34.00

David Wynn Wines *are made at the Mountadam winery from fruit sourced from the Eden Valley. Winemaker: Adam Wynn.*

DAVID WYNN PATRIARCH SHIRAZ ★★★★

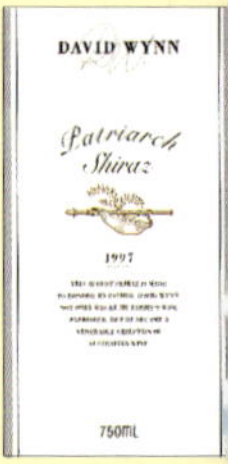

before 1993		Prior	
1993	7	Now	$50.00
1994	7	Now	$49.00
1995	6	Now	$41.00
1996	7	Now	$46.00
1997	5	Now	$32.00
1998	6	Now	$37.00

***De Bortoli** are Griffith and Yarra Valley producers whose wide range of wines includes an astonishingly good botrytis-affected Sauternes style. Winemakers: Darren De Bortoli (chief), Ralph Graham, Julie Mortlock, Helen Foggo-Paschkow (Bilbul), Stephen Webber , David Bickall and David Slingsby-Smith (Yarra Valley).*

DE BORTOLI "NOBLE ONE" (375 ml) ★★★★★

– 1990 –

1982	7	Now	$56.00
1983	6	Now	$46.00
1984	5	Now	$38.00
1985	5	Now	$36.00
1986	5	Now	$35.00
1987	7	Now	$48.00
1988	6	Now	$40.00
1989	Not made		
1990	7	Now	$44.00
1991	6	Now	$37.00
1992	6	Now	$36.00
1993	7	Now	$40.00
1994	7	Now	$39.00
1995	7	Now	$38.00
1996	7	2007	$37.00
1997	5	2005	$25.00
1998	7	2009	$35.00
1999	7	2010	$34.00
2000	7	2008	$33.00

DE BORTOLI YARRA VALLEY CABERNET SAUVIGNON ★★★★

1988	6	Now	$40.00
1989	5	Now	$33.00
1990	5	Now	$32.00
1991	6	Now	$37.00
1992	7	Now	$42.00
1993	7	2006	$41.00
1994	6	2004	$34.00
1995	7	2010	$38.00
1996	5	2004	$26.00
1997	6	2005	$31.00
1998	6	2005	$30.00
1999	7	2008	$34.00

DE BORTOLI YARRA VALLEY CHARDONNAY ★★★★

1989	5	Now	$26.00
1990	5	Now	$25.00
1991	6	Now	$29.00
1992	6	Now	$28.00
1993	6	Now	$28.00
1994	6	Now	$27.00
1995	7	Now	$30.00
1996	7	Now	$29.00

1997	7	2004	$29.00
1998	7	Now	$28.00
1999	7	2004	$27.00
2000	5	2004	$19.00
2001	7	2006	$25.00

DE BORTOLI YARRA VALLEY PINOT NOIR ★★★★

1994	5	Now	$28.00
1995	6	Now	$33.00
1996	7	Now	$37.00
1997	6	2005	$31.00
1998	7	Now	$35.00
1999	6	Now	$29.00
2000	7	2008	$33.00

DE BORTOLI YARRA VALLEY SHIRAZ ★★★★

1988	5	Now	$35.00
1989	5	Now	$34.00
1990	5	Now	$33.00
1991	Not made		
1992	6	Now	$38.00
1993	7	Now	$43.00
1994	6	Now	$35.00
1995	6	Now	$34.00
1996	5	Now	$28.00
1997	6	2004	$32.00
1998	7	2006	$37.00
1999	6	2007	$30.00

***Delamere Vineyard** is a Pipers Brook (Tasmania) producer specialising in the Burgundian varieties. Winemaker: Richard Richardson.*

DELAMERE CHARDONNAY ★★★

before 1992		Prior	
1992	6	Now	$33.00
1993	4	Prior	
1994	5	Now	$26.00
1995	6	Now	$30.00
1996	Not made		
1997	4	Prior	
1998	7	Now	$32.00
1999	6	Now	$26.00
2000	6	Now	$26.00

DELAMERE PINOT NOIR ★★★

1995	6	Now	$24.00
1996	Not made		
1997	5	1999	$19.00
1998	5	Now	$18.50
1999	6	2003	$21.00

DELAMERE PINOT NOIR RESERVE ★★★★

before 1988		Prior	
1988	6	Now	$37.00
1989	5	Prior	
1990	6	Now	$35.00
1991	6	Now	$34.00
1992	6	Now	$33.00
1993	5	Prior	
1994	7	Now	$36.00
1995	6	Now	$30.00
1996	6	Now	$29.00
1997	6	Now	$28.00
1998	6	Now	$27.00
1999	6	2004	$26.00

***Delatite** is a small, extremely good vineyard in Victoria's Mansfield region. Winemaker: Ros Ritchie.*

DELATITE DEVIL'S RIVER (CABERNET SAUVIGNON/MERLOT to 1986) ★★★★

1984	6	Now	$40.00
1985	5	Now	$32.00
1986	6	Now	$38.00
1987	6	Now	$37.00
1988	7	Now	$42.00
1989	4	Now	$23.00
1990	6	Now	$34.00
1991	7	Now	$38.00
1992	6	Now	$32.00
1993	5	Now	$25.00
1994	6	Now	$30.00
1995	5	Now	$24.00
1996	6	Now	$28.00
1997	6	Now	$27.00
1998	6	2005	$26.00
1999	5	2005	$21.00

DELATITE CHARDONNAY ★★★

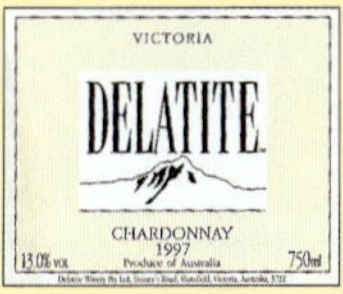

1987	5	Now	$29.00
1988	5	Now	$28.00
1989	6	Now	$33.00
1990	6	Now	$32.00
1991	7	Now	$36.00
1992	6	Now	$30.00
1993	5	Now	$24.00
1994	6	Now	$28.00
1995	6	Now	$28.00
1996	6	Now	$27.00

1997	6	Now	$26.00
1998	7	2004	$29.00
1999	6	Now	$24.00
2000	6	Now	$24.00
2001	5	2004	$19.50

DELATITE GEWURZTRAMINER ★★★★

before 1987		Prior	
1987	7	Now	$35.00
1988	6	Now	$29.00
1989	5	Now	$23.00
1990	6	Now	$27.00
1991	6	Now	$26.00
1992	6	Now	$26.00
1993	6	Now	$25.00
1994	5	Now	$20.00
1995	6	Now	$23.00
1996	7	Now	$27.00
1997	6	Now	$22.00
1998	6	Now	$21.00
1999	5	Now	$17.50
2000	6	2004	$20.00
2001	7	2004	$23.00

DELATITE PINOT NOIR ★★★

before 1986		Prior	
1986	6	Now	$34.00
1987	5	Now	$27.00
1988	6	Now	$32.00
1989	7	Now	$36.00
1990	6	Now	$30.00
1991	Not made		
1992	7	Now	$33.00
1993	6	Now	$27.00
1994	6	Now	$27.00
1995	5	Now	$21.00
1996	6	Now	$25.00
1997	7	Now	$28.00
1998	6	2004	$24.00
1999	6	2005	$23.00
2000	6	2005	$22.00

DELATITE RIESLING ★★★★

1982	7	Now	$36.00
1983	6	Now	$30.00
1984	5	Now	$24.00
1985	5	Now	$24.00
1986	6	Now	$28.00
1987	7	Now	$31.00

1988	5	Now	$22.00
1989	5	Now	$21.00
1990	6	Now	$24.00
1991	7	Now	$28.00
1992	6	Now	$23.00
1993	6	Now	$22.00
1994	7	Now	$25.00
1995	5	Now	$17.50
1996	6	2006	$20.00
1997	6	Now	$20.00
1998	7	2005	$22.00
1999	6	2004	$19.00
2000	6	2004	$18.50
2001	6	2005	$18.00

***Devil's Lair** is a substantial Margaret River vineyard owned by Southcorp and planted with the noble Bordelaise and Burgundian varieties. Winemaker: Stuart Pym.*

DEVIL'S LAIR CHARDONNAY ★★★★

before 1996		Prior	
1996	5	Now	$34.00
1997	7	2005	$46.00
1998	6	2005	$39.00
1999	7	2008	$44.00
2000	6	2007	$36.00

DEVIL'S LAIR "MARGARET RIVER" (CABERNET SAUVIGNON) ★★★★

1990	6	Now	$76.00
1991	5	Prior	
1992	5	Prior	
1993	6	2005	$70.00
1994	6	2007	$68.00
1995	6	2006	$66.00
1996	5	2006	$54.00
1997	5	2007	$52.00
1998	6	2008	$60.00
1999	7	2009	$68.00
2000	6	2008	$56.00

DEVIL'S LAIR PINOT NOIR ★★★★

1992	5	Prior	
1993	6	Now	$37.00
1994	5	Now	$30.00
1995	5	Now	$29.00
1996	5	Now	$28.00
1997	6	Now	$33.00

No longer made.

Diamond Valley Vineyards *are high quality Yarra Valley makers who are also developing a vineyard at Phillip Island. Only the "Estate" wines are made wholly from their own fruit. Winemaker: David Lance.*

DIAMOND VALLEY VINEYARDS BLUE LABEL CHARDONNAY ★★★★

before 1995		Prior	
1995	6	Now	$25.00
1996	7	Now	$29.00
1997	6	Now	$24.00
1998	7	Now	$27.00
1999	6	Now	$22.00
2000	7	2004	$25.00
2001	7	2005	$25.00
2002	7	2006	$24.00

DIAMOND VALLEY VINEYARDS BLUE LABEL CABERNET/MERLOT ★★★★

before 1994		Prior	
1994	6	Now	$28.00
1995	Not made		
1996	5	Now	$22.00
1997	6	Now	$25.00
1998	6	2004	$25.00
1999	6	2004	$24.00
2000	6	2005	$23.00
2001	7	2006	$26.00

DIAMOND VALLEY VINEYARDS BLUE LABEL PINOT NOIR ★★★★

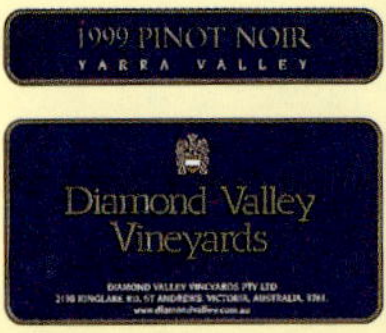

before 1992		Prior	
1992	6	Now	$32.00
1993	6	Now	$31.00
1994	7	Now	$35.00
1995	6	Now	$29.00
1996	7	Now	$33.00
1997	6	Now	$28.00
1998	7	Now	$31.00
1999	7	Now	$30.00
2000	6	2004	$25.00
2001	6	2005	$24.00
2002	7	2006	$28.00

DIAMOND VALLEY VINEYARDS BLUE LABEL SAUVIGNON BLANC ★★★

1999	6	Now	$18.00
2000	7	Now	$20.00
2001	6	Now	$17.00
2002	7	Now	$19.00

DIAMOND VALLEY VINEYARDS CLOSE PLANTED PINOT NOIR ★★★★★

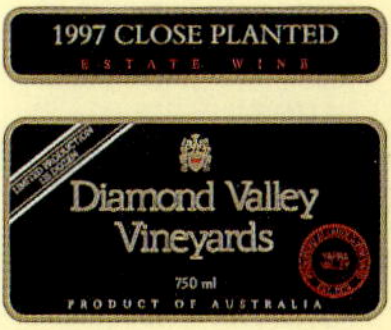

1992	7	Now	$90.00
1993	6	Prior	
1994	5	Prior	
1995	7	Now	$82.00
1996	7	Now	$80.00
1997	7	2004	$76.00
1998	Not made		
1999	7	2006	$72.00
2000	7	2007	$70.00
2001	7	2007	$68.00

DIAMOND VALLEY VINEYARDS ESTATE CABERNET ★★★★

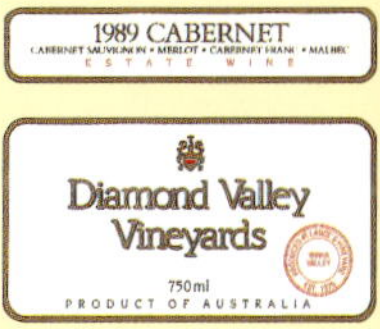

before 1988		Prior	
1988	6	Now	$41.00
1989	6	Prior	
1990	7	Now	$45.00
1991	6	Now	$37.00
1992	7	Now	$42.00
1993	Not made		
1994	6	Now	$34.00
1995	Not made		
1996	5	2004	$27.00
1997	7	2006	$36.00
1998	7	2006	$35.00
1999	7	2006	$34.00
2000	7	2007	$33.00

DIAMOND VALLEY VINEYARDS ESTATE CHARDONNAY ★★★★★

before 1990		Prior	
1990	7	Now	$45.00
1991	6	Prior	
1992	7	Now	$42.00
1993	6	Now	$35.00
1994	6	Now	$34.00
1995	7	Now	$38.00
1996	7	Now	$37.00
1997	7	Now	$36.00
1998	7	2004	$35.00
1999	6	2004	$29.00
2000	7	2005	$33.00
2001	7	2006	$32.00

DIAMOND VALLEY VINEYARDS ESTATE PINOT NOIR ★★★★★

before 1991		Prior	
1991	7	Now	$96.00
1992	5	Now	$66.00

1993	7	Now	$92.00
1994	6	Now	$76.00
1995	5	Now	$62.00
1996	7	Now	$84.00
1997	7	2004	$80.00
1998	7	2005	$78.00
1999	7	2006	$76.00
2000	Not made		
2001	7	2007	$72.00
2002	7	2008	$70.00

***Domaine A** is the label under which the elite best of Stoney Vineyard's wines are released. The Pinot is superb. Winemaker: Peter Althaus.*

DOMAINE A CABERNET SAUVIGNON ★★★★★

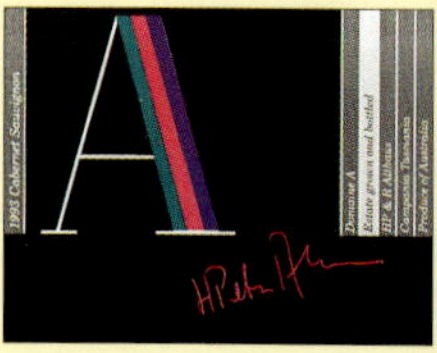

1990	6	Now	$86.00
1991	6	Now	$82.00
1992	7	2005	$94.00
1993	5	2005	$64.00
1994	7	2010	$88.00
1995	6	2005	$74.00
1996	Not made		
1997	6	2008	$70.00
1998	7	2010	$78.00
1999	6	2010	$66.00
2000	7	208	N/R
2001	7	2010	N/R

DOMAINE A "LADY A" FUME BLANC ★★★★

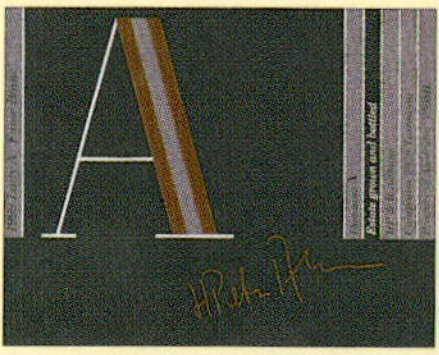

1996	5	2004	$43.00
1997	7	2010	$58.00
1998	Not made		
1999	7	2008	$54.00
2000	Not made		
2001	6	2008	$45.00
2002	7	2010	N/R

DOMAINE A PINOT NOIR ★★★★★

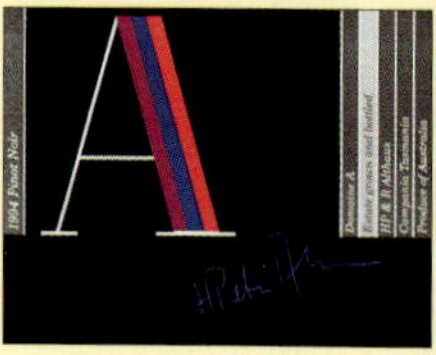

1990	5	Prior	
1991	6	Now	$86.00
1992	7	Now	$96.00
1993	5	Now	$66.00
1994	7	2005	$90.00
1995	6	Now	$76.00
1996	Not made		
1997	7	2006	$84.00
1998	7	2010	$80.00
1999	7	2008	$78.00
2000	7	2008	$76.00
2001	6	2009	N/R
2002	Not made		

Domaine Chandon *was established in the Yarra Valley in 1985 as part of Moet et Chandon's expansion into New World sparkling wine production. Small quantities of still wine have been produced since 1990, but production is now expanding, and it is expected that by 2010 still wine will account for 50% of the output. Winemakers: Dr Tony Jordan, Neville Rowe, James Gosper and John Harris.*

DOMAINE CHANDON GREEN POINT CHARDONNAY

★★★★★

1989	5	Now	$39.00
1990	4	Now	$30.00
1991	5	Now	$36.00
1992	4	Now	$28.00
1993	5	Now	$34.00
1994	6	Now	$40.00
1995	6	Now	$39.00
1996	7	Now	$44.00
1997	No data		
1998	4	Now	$24.00
1999	Not made		
2000	5	Now	$28.00
2001	6	Now	$32.00
2002	6	2004	$32.00

DOMAINE CHANDON GREEN POINT MCLAREN VALE SHIRAZ

★★★★

1998	5	Now	$28.00
1999	6	2004	$33.00
2000	Not made		
2001	6	2004	$31.00

DOMAINE CHANDON GREEN POINT PINOT NOIR

★★★★

1998	4	Now	$28.00
1999	Not made		
2000	5	2004	$33.00
2001	5	Now	$32.00

DOMAINE CHANDON VINTAGE BRUT

★★★★★

1987	4	Now	$30.00
1988	5	Now	$37.00
1989	6	Now	$43.00
1990	7	Now	$49.00
1991	6	Now	$41.00
1992	7	Now	$46.00
1993	6	Now	$38.00
1994	7	Now	$43.00

1995	6	Now	$36.00
1996	4	Now	$23.00
1997	6	Now	$34.00
1998	6	Now	$33.00
1999	7	Now	$37.00

DOMAINE CHANDON VINTAGE BLANC DE BLANCS

★★★★

1986	6	Now	$47.00
1987	Not made		
1988	Not made		
1989	6	Now	$43.00
1990	6	Now	$41.00
1991	7	Now	$47.00
1992	6	Now	$39.00
1993	7	Now	$44.00
1994	Not made		
1995	6	Now	$36.00
1996	5	Now	$29.00
1997	6	Now	$34.00
1998	6	Now	$33.00
1999	7	Now	$37.00
2000	6	Now	$31.00

DOMAINE CHANDON VINTAGE BLANC DE NOIRS

★★★★

1988	6	Prior	
1989	Not made		
1990	7	Now	$47.00
1991	6	Now	$39.00
1992	7	Now	$44.00
1993	6	Now	$37.00
1994	5	Now	$30.00
1995	5	Now	$29.00
1996	4	Now	$22.00
1997	6	Now	$33.00
1998	Not made		

DOMAINE CHANDON VINTAGE BRUT ROSE

★★★★

1990	7	Now	$48.00
1991	5	Now	$33.00
1992	6	Now	$39.00
1993	6	Now	$38.00
1994	7	Now	$43.00
1995	6	Now	$36.00
1996	4	Now	$23.00
1997	6	Now	$33.00
1998	6	Now	$32.00
1999	7	Now	$37.00

Doonkuna Estate *is one of the longest established of the Canberra area producers. The quality of their wines, particularly in recent vintages, is admirable. Winemaker: Malcolm Burdett.*

DOONKUNA ESTATE CABERNET SAUVIGNON/MERLOT ★★★

before 1995		Prior	
1995	7	Now	$33.00
1996	6	Now	$27.00
1997	7	Now	$31.00
1998	7	Now	$30.00
1999	Not made		
2000	6	Now	$24.00
2001	7	2004	$27.00
2002	7	2005	$27.00

DOONKUNA ESTATE CHARDONNAY ★★★★

before 1998		Prior	
1998	6	Now	$23.00
1999	Not made		
2000	7	Now	$25.00
2001	7	Now	$24.00
2002	7	2004	$23.00

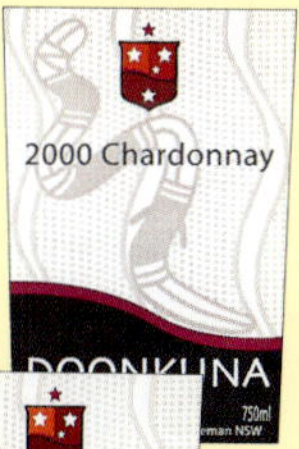

DOONKUNA ESTATE PINOT NOIR ★★★

before 1998		Prior	
1998	5	Now	$22.00
1999	Not made		
2000	6	Now	$25.00
2001	6	Now	$24.00
2002	6	2004	$24.00

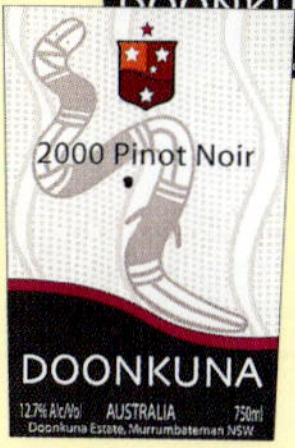

DOONKUNA ESTATE RIESLING ★★★★

before 1997		Prior	
1997	6	Now	$21.00
1998	6	Now	$21.00
1999	Not made		
2000	7	Now	$23.00
2001	7	Now	$22.00
2002	6	Now	$18.50

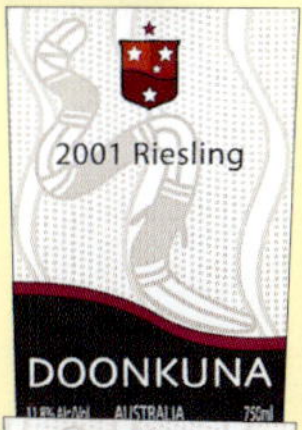

DOONKUNA ESTATE SAUVIGNON BLANC/SEMILLON ★★★★

before 1999		Prior	
1999	7	Now	$21.00
2000	7	Now	$20.00
2001	7	Now	$20.00
2002	6	Now	$16.50

DOONKUNA ESTATE SHIRAZ ★★★★

before 1992		Prior	
1992	6	Now	$37.00
1993	6	Prior	

1994	7	Prior	
1995	6	Now	$34.00
1996	6	Now	$33.00
1997	7	Now	$37.00
1998	7	Now	$36.00
1999	7	Now	$35.00
2000	7	Now	$34.00
2001	7	2004	$33.00
2002	7	2005	$32.00

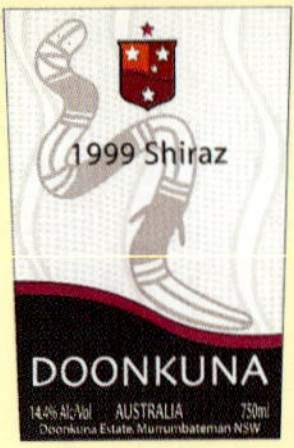

***Draytons** are long established and much respected Pokolbin makers with a small range of reliably good wines. Winemaker: Trevor Drayton.*

DRAYTONS CABERNET SAUVIGNON ★★★

1988	5	Now	$17.50
1989	Not made		
1990	Not made		
1991	7	Now	$23.00
1992	6	Now	$19.00
1993	6	Now	$18.50
1994	Not made		
1995	5	Now	$14.50
1996	6	Now	$17.00
1997	5	Now	$13.50
1998	5	Now	$13.00
1999	7	2005	$18.00

DRAYTONS CHARDONNAY ★★★

before 1989		Prior	
1989	7	Now	$22.00
1990	5	Now	$15.50
1991	7	Now	$21.00
1992	7	Now	$20.00
1993	4	Prior	
1994	5	Now	$14.00
1995	6	Now	$16.00
1996	5	Now	$13.00
1997	5	Now	$12.50
1998	6	Now	$15.00
1999	7	2005	$17.00
2000	7	2006	$16.50

DRAYTONS CHARDONNAY/SEMILLON ★★★

before 1987		Prior	
1987	7	Now	$20.00
1988	6	Now	$17.00
1989	6	Now	$16.50
1990	5	Now	$13.50
1991	7	Now	$18.00
1992	5	Now	$12.50
1993	6	Now	$14.50

1994	4	Now	$9.50
1995	6	Now	$14.00

No longer made.

DRAYTONS BIN 5555 SHIRAZ
(formerly IVANHOE HERMITAGE) ★★★

before 1988		Prior	
1988	7	Now	$24.00
1989	5	Now	$17.00
1990	5	Now	$16.50
1991	7	Now	$22.00
1992	5	Now	$15.50
1993	6	Now	$18.00
1994	4	Now	$11.50
1995	7	Now	$19.50
1996	6	Now	$16.50
1997	6	Now	$16.00
1998	6	2004	$15.50
1999	7	2006	$17.50

DRAYTON VERDELHO ★★★

before 1991		Prior	
1991	6	Now	$18.50
1992	5	Prior	
1993	7	Now	$20.00
1994	5	Now	$14.00
1995	6	Now	$16.50
1996	5	Now	$13.50
1997	5	Now	$13.00
1998	5	Now	$12.50
1999	7	2005	$17.00
2000	7	2005	$16.50

DRAYTON VINEYARD RESERVE CHARDONNAY ★★★★

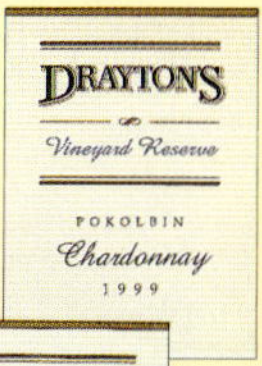

1997	6	2008	$25.00
1998	6	2009	$24.00
1999	7	2010	$27.00

DRAYTON VINEYARD RESERVE MERLOT ★★★★

1997	6	2005	$25.00
1998	6	2006	$24.00
1999	7	2008	$27.00

DRAYTON VINEYARD RESERVE SEMILLON ★★★

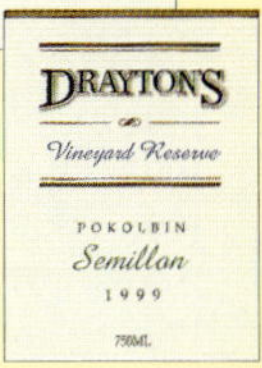

1997	7	2007	$29.00
1998	6	2005	$24.00
1999	6	2007	$23.00
2000	7	2010	$26.00

DRAYTON VINEYARD RESERVE SHIRAZ ★★★★

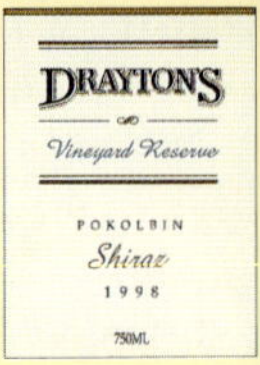

1997	6	2008	$25.00
1998	6	2009	$24.00
1999	7	2010	$27.00

DRAYTON WILLIAM SHIRAZ ★★★★★

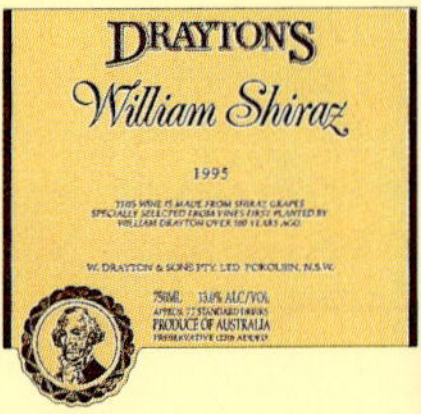

1988	7	Now	$60.00
1989	6	Now	$50.00
1990	7	2005	$56.00
1991	7	2005	$54.00
1992	Not made		
1993	6	2004	$44.00
1994	Not made		
1995	6	2008	$42.00
1996	7	2008	$47.00

***Dromana Estate** is a Mornington Peninsula producer of some of the Australia's finest wines (see also Yarra Valley Hills). Winemaker: Garry Crittenden.*

DROMANA ESTATE CABERNET/MERLOT ★★★★

1986	6	Now	$42.00
1987	5	Now	$34.00
1988	6	Now	$40.00
1989	5	Now	$32.00
1990	6	Now	$37.00
1991	5	Now	$30.00
1992	6	Now	$35.00
1993	6	Now	$34.00
1994	6	Now	$33.00
1995	5	Now	$27.00
1996	6	Now	$31.00
1997	6	Now	$30.00
1998	6	Now	$29.00
1999	7	2005	$33.00

DROMANA ESTATE CHARDONNAY ★★★★★

1986	6	Now	$46.00
1987	5	Now	$37.00
1988	6	Now	$44.00
1989	6	Now	$42.00
1990	6	Now	$41.00
1991	7	Now	$47.00
1992	6	Now	$39.00
1993	6	Now	$38.00
1994	7	Now	$43.00
1995	6	Now	$35.00
1996	5	Now	$28.00
1997	5	Now	$28.00
1998	6	Now	$32.00

1999	7	2005	$37.00
2000	7	2005	$36.00
2001	5	2005	$25.00

DROMANA ESTATE PINOT NOIR ★★★★★

1986	5	Prior	
1987	5	Now	$37.00
1988	6	Now	$44.00
1989	6	Now	$42.00
1990	5	Now	$34.00
1991	7	Now	$47.00
1992	6	Now	$39.00
1993	6	Now	$38.00
1994	6	Now	$36.00
1995	6	Now	$35.00
1996	7	Now	$40.00
1997	6	Now	$33.00
1998	6	Now	$32.00
1999	6	2004	$31.00
2000	7	2005	$36.00
2001	6	2005	$30.00

Dulcinea Vineyard *is a small producer at Sulky, near Ballarat in Victoria. Winemaker: Rod Stott.*

DULCINEA CABERNET SAUVIGNON ★★★

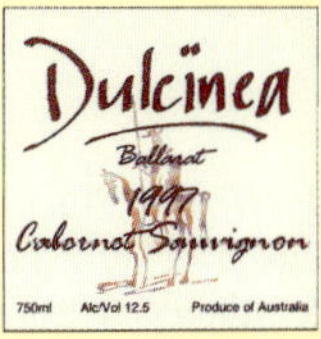

1995	4	Now	$13.50
1996	6	Now	$20.00
1997	5	Now	$16.00
1998	6	Now	$19.00
1999	5	Now	$15.00

DULCINEA CHARDONNAY ★★★

1994	4	Now	$13.00
1995	5	Now	$16.00
1996	7	Now	$22.00
1997	6	Now	$18.50
1998	5	Now	$14.50
1999	6	Now	$17.00

DULCINEA PINOT NOIR ★★★

1995	4	Now	$12.00
1996	6	Now	$18.00
1997	6	Now	$17.50
1998	7	Now	$19.50
1999	6	Now	$16.50

Eaglehawk *by Wolf Blass is the name under which moderately priced wines from the Wolf Blass empire are released. Winemakers: Wendy Stuckey and John Glaetzer.*

EAGLEHAWK CHARDONNAY ★★★

before 1998		Prior	
1998	6	Now	$11.00
1999	7	Now	$12.50

2000	5	Now	$8.75
2001	6	Now	$10.00
2002	6	Now	$10.00

EAGLEHAWK RIESLING ★★★

before 1998		Prior	
1998	5	Now	$9.00
1999	6	Now	$10.50
2000	7	2005	$11.50
2001	6	2005	$9.75
2002	7	2005	$11.00

EAGLEHAWK SEMILLON/
SAUVIGNON BLANC ★★

before 1998		Prior	
1998	7	Now	$11.00
1999	6	Now	$9.00
2000	6	Now	$8.75
2001	6	Now	$8.50

No longer made.

EAGLEHAWK ESTATE
SHIRAZ/MERLOT/CABERNET ★★★

before 1999		Prior	
1999	6	Now	$11.00
2000	5	2004	$9.00
2001	6	2004	$10.50

***East Arm Vineyard** in Tasmania's Tamar Valley is currently only 2 hectares, but the property has the potential for another 10 or so. The wines are delicate - almost fragile, but of considerable beauty. Winemakers: Bert Sundstrop and Nick Butler.*

EAST ARM CHARDONNAY ★★★

1998	5	Now	$20.00
1999	5	Now	$19.50
2000	5	2004	$18.50
2001	4	Now	$14.50

EAST ARM PINOT NÒIR ★★★

1998	6	2004	$25.00
1999	6	2005	$24.00
2000	5	2005	$19.50
2001	6	2006	$22.00

EAST ARM RIESLING ★★★★

1997	4	Prior	
1998	7	Now	$25.00
1999	6	Now	$21.00
2000	7	2004	$24.00
2001	5	2004	$16.50
2002	7	2005	$22.00

***Eastern Peake** is a 4.5 hectare vineyard near Creswick in Central Victoria, planted with the Burgundian varieties. Winemaker: Norman Latta.*

EASTERN PEAKE CHARDONNAY ★★★★

1996	6	2006	$32.00
1997	5	2005	$26.00
1998	6	2006	$30.00
1999	7	2008	$35.00

EASTERN PEAKE "PERSUASION" (PINOT NOIR ROSE) ★★★

before 1997		Prior	
1997	6	Now	$19.00
1998	5	Now	$15.00
1999	7	2004	$21.00
2000	6	Now	$17.00

EASTERN PEAKE PINOT NOIR ★★★★

1993	6	Now	$36.00
1994	6	2004	$35.00
1995	6	Now	$34.00
1996	5	2004	$27.00
1997	6	2007	$32.00
1998	5	2006	$26.00
1999	7	2008	$35.00

***Edwards and Chaffey** was split from the Seaview label, and was the dedicated McLaren Vale label of the Southcorp group. The label has now been discontinued. Winemaker: Fiona Donald.*

EDWARDS AND CHAFFEY CABERNET ★★★★

1992	7	Now	$50.00
1993	Not made		
1994	6	Now	$41.00
1995	Not made		
1996	6	Now	$39.00
1997	6	Now	$38.00
1998	7	2005	$43.00
1999	6	2005	$36.00

EDWARDS AND CHAFFEY CHARDONNAY ★★★★

before 1996		Prior	
1996	7	Now	$30.00
1997	6	Now	$25.00
1998	6	Now	$24.00
1999	6	Now	$24.00
2000	5	Now	$19.50

EDWARDS AND CHAFFEY SHIRAZ ★★★★

1992	7	Now	$52.00
1993	Not made		
1994	6	Now	$43.00

1995	5	Now	$34.00
1996	6	2004	$40.00
1997	6	2004	$39.00
1998	7	2006	$44.00
2000	6	2005	$37.00

***Elderton Wines** are successful Barossa Valley makers who are enjoying the rewards of quality production and vigourous marketing. Winemakers: Richard Sheedy, Allister Ashmead and James Irvine.*

ELDERTON CABERNET SAUVIGNON ★★★★

before 1990		Prior	
1990	6	Now	$29.00
1991	7	Now	$33.00
1992	7	Now	$32.00
1993	6	Now	$27.00
1994	6	Now	$26.00
1995	6	Now	$25.00
1996	7	2006	$28.00
1997	6	2005	$24.00
1998	7	2006	$27.00
1999	6	2005	$22.00
2000	6	2005	$21.00
2001	7	2010	$24.00
2002	7	2010	N/R

ELDERTON CABERNET/SHIRAZ/MERLOT ★★★★

1992	7	Now	$54.00
1993	Not made		
1994	7	Now	$50.00
1995	7	Now	$49.00
1996	7	Now	$48.00
1997	6	2005	$40.00
1998	7	2006	$45.00
1999	6	2008	$38.00
2000	5	2006	$30.00

ELDERTON COMMAND SHIRAZ ★★★★★

1984	5	Now	$105.00
1985	6	Now	$120.00
1986	6	Now	$120.00
1987	6	Now	$115.00
1988	6	Now	$110.00
1989	Not made		
1990	7	Now	$125.00
1991	Not made		
1992	7	Now	$115.00
1993	6	Now	$98.00
1994	7	2005	$110.00

1995	6	2005	$92.00
1996	7	2007	$100.00
1997	7	2008	$100.00
1998	7	2010	$98.00
1999	6	2010	$82.00
2000	6	2009	$80.00

ELDERTON RIESLING ★★★

before 1990		Prior	
1990	6	Now	$23.00
1991	Not made		
1992	6	Now	$22.00
1993	6	Now	$21.00
1994	6	Now	$20.00
1995	Not made		
1996	Not made		
1997	6	Now	$19.00
1998	7	2005	$21.00
1999	6	2005	$17.50
2000	6	2005	$17.00
2001	6	2007	$16.50
2002	7	2007	$19.00

ELDERTON SHIRAZ ★★★★

before 1988		Prior	
1988	7	Now	$42.00
1989	6	Now	$35.00
1990	7	Now	$40.00
1991	7	Now	$38.00
1992	7	Now	$37.00
1993	6	Now	$31.00
1994	7	Now	$35.00
1995	6	Now	$29.00
1996	7	2005	$33.00
1997	6	2005	$27.00
1998	7	2006	$31.00
1999	6	2006	$26.00
2000	5	2004	$21.00
2001	7	2008	$28.00
2002	7	2009	N/R

***Eldridge Estate** of Red Hill is a small Red Hill (Mornington Peninsula) vineyard specialising in the Burgundian varieties. Their range includes a frivolous but quite delightful Gamay. Winemaker: David Lloyd.*

ELDRIDGE ESTATE CABERNET /MERLOT ★★★

1995	5	2005	$28.00
1996	3	Now	$16.50
1997	6	2006	$32.00
1998	5	2006	$26.00

ELDRIDGE ESTATE CHARDONNAY ★★★★

1996	4	Prior	
1997	5	2005	$31.00
1998	7	2008	$42.00
1999	7	2008	$40.00
2000	7	2006	$39.00
2001	7	2008	$38.00

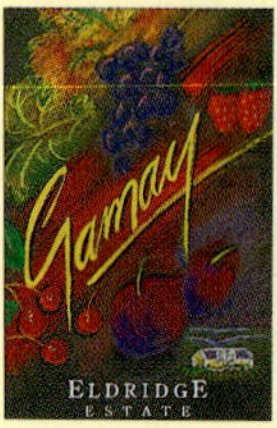

ELDRIDGE ESTATE GAMAY ★★★

2000	6	2005	$21.00
2001	5	2004	$17.00
2002	7	2010	$23.00

ELDRIDGE ESTATE PINOT NOIR ★★★★

1996	3	Prior	
1997	6	2004	$41.00
1998	5	2005	$33.00
1999	6	2006	$39.00
2000	6	2009	$38.00
2001	7	2009	$43.00

ELDRIDGE ESTATE SEMILLON/ SAUVIGNON BLANC ★★★

before 2000		Prior	
2000	6	2005	$20.00
2001	7	2005	$22.00
2002	6	2005	$18.50

Elgee Park *is one of the first Mornington Peninsula vineyards (established in 1972) whose graceful wines are of very good quality. Winemaker: Tod Dexter.*

ELGEE PARK FAMILY RESERVE CABERNET/MERLOT ★★★★

before 1997		Prior	
1997	6	Now	$29.00
1998	5	2004	$24.00
1999	5	2005	$23.00

ELGEE PARK FAMILY RESERVE CHARDONNAY ★★★★

before 1997		Prior	
1997	6	Now	$35.00
1998	5	Now	$28.00
1999	6	2004	$33.00
2000	5	2004	$27.00

ELGEE PARK FAMILY RESERVE RIESLING ★★★

before 1999		Prior	
1999	5	Now	$15.50
2000	5	Now	$15.00
2001	6	Now	$18.00

Elsewhere Vineyard *is a Southern Tasmanian maker who produces a very highly regarded Pinot Noir. The maker is apparently reluctant to supply ratings, so these are my own. Winemaker: Andrew Hood.*

ELSEWHERE VINEYARD PINOT NOIR ★★★★

1993	6	Now	$37.00
1994	5	Now	$30.00
1995	6	Now	$35.00
1996	4	Now	$22.00
1997	5	Now	$27.00
1998	7	Now	$37.00
1999	7	Now	$36.00
2000	7	2005	$35.00

Eppalock Ridge *(formerly Romany Rye Vineyards) are Redesdale (Bendigo district) makers with a small crush of individual wines. Winemaker: Rod Hourigan.*

EPPALOCK RIDGE CABERNET/MERLOT ★★★★

before 1996		Prior	
1996	4	Now	$32.00
1997	4	Now	$31.00
1998	5	Prior	
1999	Not made		
2000	6	2005	$43.00
2001	6	2007	$41.00
2002	6	2010	$40.00

EPPALOCK RIDGE SHIRAZ ★★★

before 1998		Prior	
1998	5	2004	$36.00
1999	5	2004	$35.00
2000	5	2005	$34.00
2001	6	2008	$40.00
2002	6	2010	$38.00

Evans and Tate *are West Australian makers whose focus is now on their Redbrook vineyard at Margaret River. Winemaker: Richard Rowe.*

EVANS AND TATE MARGARET RIVER CABERNET/MERLOT ★★★

1999	7	Now	$22.00
2000	7	2004	$22.00
2001	7	2005	$21.00
2002	6	2005	$17.50

EVANS AND TATE MARGARET RIVER CABERNET SAUVIGNON ★★★★

1988	6	Now	$64.00
1989	5	Prior	
1990	6	Now	$60.00

1991	6	Now	$58.00
1992	6	Now	$56.00
1993	7	Now	$64.00
1994	6	Now	$54.00
1995	7	Now	$60.00
1996	7	Now	$58.00
1997	7	Now	$56.00
1998	7	2005	$56.00
1999	7	2006	$54.00

EVANS AND TATE MARGARET RIVER CHARDONNAY ★★★★★

before 1999		Prior	
1999	7	Now	$23.00
2000	6	2004	$19.50
2001	7	2004	$22.00
2002	6	2004	$18.00

EVANS AND TATE MARGARET RIVER MERLOT ★★★★

before 1994		Prior	
1994	6	Now	$41.00
1995	7	Now	$47.00
1996	7	Now	$46.00
1997	Not made		
1998	7	2008	$43.00
1999	7	2009	$42.00
2000	7	2009	$40.00

EVANS AND TATE MARGARET RIVER SAUVIGNON BLANC(/SEMILLON) ★★★

before 2001		Prior	
2001	7	Now	$19.50
2002	7	Now	$19.00

EVANS AND TATE MARGARET RIVER SEMILLON ★★★★

before 2000		Prior	
2000	7	Now	$20.00
2001	7	2004	$19.50
2002	7	2004	$19.00

EVANS AND TATE MARGARET RIVER SHIRAZ ★★★★

before 1995		Prior	
1995	7	Now	$24.00
1996	6	Now	$20.00
1997	7	Now	$23.00
1998	6	2005	$19.50
1999	7	2007	$22.00
2000	7	2009	$21.00
2001	7	2009	$20.00

EVANS AND TATE TWO VINEYARDS CHARDONNAY ★★★

before 1997		Prior	
1997	6	Now	$19.00
1998	7	Now	$22.00
1999	7	Now	$21.00
2000	7	2005	$20.00

***Eyton on Yarra** is a new and well-funded Yarra Valley winery and restaurant enterprise of considerable promise. Winemaker: Matt Aldridge.*

EYTON ON YARRA CABERNET/MERLOT ★★★★

1995	4	2004	$25.00
1996	3	Prior	
1997	5	2004	$30.00
1998	6	2005	$35.00
1999	4	2005	$22.00
2000	5	2006	$27.00

EYTON ON YARRA CHARDONNAY ★★★★

before 1997		Prior	
1997	6	Now	$34.00
1998	5	Now	$27.00
1999	4	Now	$21.00
2000	5	2005	$26.00
2001	5	2006	$25.00

EYTON ON YARRA PINOT/CHARDONNAY BRUT ★★★★

before 1995		Prior	
1995	5	Now	$29.00
1996	5	Now	$28.00
1997	6	Now	$33.00
1998	6	2004	$32.00

EYTON ON YARRA PINOT NOIR ★★★★★

before 1997		Prior	
1997	5	Now	$31.00
1998	4	Now	$24.00
1999	4	Now	$23.00
2000	5	2005	$29.00
2001	6	2006	$33.00

***Fergussons** are Yarra Valley makers whose estate grown wines are densely flavoured and emphatic. Winemaker: Chris Keyes.*

FERGUSSONS CABERNET SAUVIGNON ★★★★

before 1982		Prior	
1982	7	Now	$58.00
1983	7	Now	$56.00
1984	3	Now	$24.00

1985	Not made		
1986	7	Now	$52.00
1987	6	Now	$44.00
1988	Destroyed by fire		
1989	Destroyed by fire		
1990	7	2010	$47.00
1991	6	Now	$39.00
1992	6	Now	$38.00
1993	6	Now	$36.00
1994	6	2005	$35.00
1995	6	2010	$34.00
1996	6	2015	$33.00
1997	6	2015	$32.00
1998	7	2020	$37.00
1999	6	2015	$30.00
2000	7	2015	$35.00
2001	6	2020	$29.00
2002	6	2020	N/R

FERGUSSONS CHARDONNAY ★★★★

before 1992		Prior	
1992	6	Now	$43.00
1993	3	Now	$21.00
1994	5	Now	$34.00
1995	5	Now	$33.00
1996	5	Now	$32.00
1997	6	2005	$37.00
1998	7	2010	$42.00
1999	6	2005	$35.00
2000	6	2010	$34.00
2001	6	2010	$33.00
2002	6	2010	$32.00

FERGUSSONS SHIRAZ ★★★★★

before 1982		Prior	
1982	6	Now	$52.00
1983	7	Now	$58.00
1984	4	Prior	
1985	Not made		
1986	7	Now	$54.00
1987	5	Now	$37.00
1988	Destroyed by fire		
1989	Destroyed by fire		
1990	Not made		
1991	6	Now	$40.00
1992	6	Now	$39.00
1993	6	Now	$38.00
1994	6	Now	$36.00

1995	5	2005	$29.00
1996	7	2005	$40.00
1997	6	2005	$33.00
1998	7	2015	$38.00
1999	6	2010	$31.00
2000	6	2010	$30.00
2001	6	2010	$30.00
2002	6	2010	N/R

***Fermoy Estate** is a Margaret River maker whose exceedingly elegant Cabernet Sauvignon is complemented by a graceful Semillon and a most intriguing Merlot. Winemaker: Michael Kelly.*

FERMOY ESTATE CABERNET SAUVIGNON ★★★★★

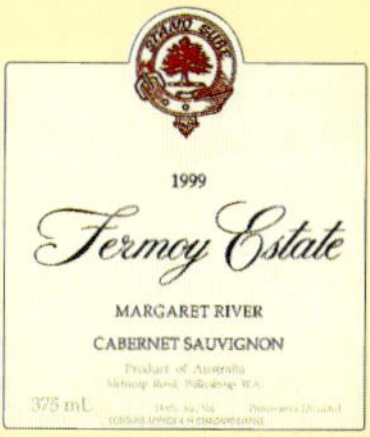

1988	6	Now	$50.00
1989	6	Now	$49.00
1990	5	Now	$39.00
1991	6	Now	$46.00
1992	7	Now	$52.00
1993	6	Now	$43.00
1994	6	2004	$42.00
1995	6	2004	$41.00
1996	4	Now	$26.00
1997	4	Now	$25.00
1998	4	Now	$25.00
1999	6	2006	$36.00
2000	6	2006	$35.00
2001	6	2008	$34.00

FERMOY ESTATE MERLOT ★★★★★

1991	6	Now	$47.00
1992	7	Now	$52.00
1993	Not made		
1994	6	Now	$43.00
1995	5	Now	$34.00
1996	5	Now	$33.00
1997	5	Now	$32.00
1998	6	2004	$38.00
1999	6	2006	$37.00
2000	7	2006	$42.00
2001	7	2007	$40.00

FERMOY ESTATE SEMILLON ★★★★

1990	4	Now	$22.00
1991	5	Now	$27.00
1992	5	Now	$26.00
1993	6	Now	$31.00
1994	6	Now	$30.00

1995	5	Now	$24.00
1996	7	Now	$33.00
1997	5	Now	$23.00
1998	5	Now	$22.00
1999	5	Now	$21.00
2000	6	2004	$25.00
2001	7	2005	$28.00
2002	6	2005	$23.00

***Fox Creek Wines** is a recently established McLaren maker with high quality aspirations. Winemakers: Dan Hills and Tony Walker.*

FOX CREEK RESERVE CABERNET ★★★★

1995	6	Now	$41.00
1996	7	Now	$46.00
1997	6	Now	$38.00
1998	7	2005	$43.00
1999	6	2005	$36.00
2000	6	2006	$35.00
2001	6	2007	$34.00

FOX CREEK RESERVE MERLOT ★★★★

1997	7	Now	$45.00
1998	7	2004	$44.00
1999	5	Now	$30.00
2000	6	2005	$35.00
2001	6	2006	$34.00

FOX CREEK RESERVE SHIRAZ ★★★★

1994	5	Now	$68.00
1995	4	Now	$52.00
1996	7	2005	$88.00
1997	6	2005	$74.00
1998	7	2008	$84.00
1999	6	2007	$70.00
2000	5	2007	$56.00
2010	7	2010	$76.00

FOX CREEK SEMILLON/ SAUVIGNON BLANC ★★★

2000	7	Now	$17.50
2001	6	2004	$14.50
2002	7	2005	$16.50

FOX CREEK SHIRAZ/CABERNET FRANC ★★★

1996	5	Now	$24.00
1997	7	Now	$32.00
1998	7	2004	$31.00
1999	7	2005	$30.00
2000	6	2005	$25.00
2001	7	2007	$29.00

FOX CREEK SHORT ROW SHIRAZ ★★★

1999	7	2006	$28.00
2000	6	2005	$24.00
2001	7	2008	$27.00

FOX CREEK VERDELHO ★★★

before 1999		Prior	
1999	6	Now	$16.50
2000	7	Now	$19.00
2001	5	Now	$13.00
2002	7	2004	$17.50

***Fox River** is the second label of Mount Barker's respected maker Goundrey Wines. Winemaker: David Martin.*

FOX RIVER CHENIN/SEMILLON ★★

before 1998		Prior	
1998	7	Now	$17.50
1999	6	Now	$14.50
2000	6	Now	$14.50
2001	7	2004	$16.00
2002	7	2005	$15.50

FOX RIVER SHIRAZ ★★

1995	6	Now	$22.00
1996	5	Now	$18.00
1997	6	Now	$21.00
1998	7	2005	$23.00
1999	6	2005	$19.50
2000	6	2005	$19.00
2001	7	2010	$21.00
2002	7	2010	$21.00

FOX RIVER SHIRAZ/CABERNET ★★★

1995	5	Prior	
1996	5	Now	$14.50
1997	6	Now	$17.00
1998	7	2005	$19.50
1999	7	2005	$19.00
2000	5	Now	$13.00
2001	6	2008	$15.00

***Frankland Estate** in Western Australia's Frankland River region is a grower turned winemaker whose product is well worth seeking out (particularly the beautifully elegant Chardonnay). Winemakers: Judi Cullam and Barrie Smith.*

FRANKLAND ESTATE CABERNET SAUVIGNON ★★★★

1991	5	Prior	
1992	5	Now	$27.00
1993	6	Now	$31.00
1994	6	Now	$30.00

1995	6	Now	$29.00
1996	5	Now	$24.00
1997	6	Now	$28.00
1998	6	Now	$27.00
1999	6	Now	$26.00

FRANKLAND ESTATE CHARDONNAY ★★★★★

before 1998		Prior	
1998	5	Now	$21.00
1999	6	Now	$25.00
2000	6	2004	$24.00
2001	6	2005	$24.00

FRANKLAND ESTATE ISOLATION RIDGE RIESLING ★★★★★

1991	6	Now	$33.00
1992	5	Now	$26.00
1993	6	Now	$31.00
1994	6	Now	$30.00
1995	5	Now	$24.00
1996	6	2004	$28.00
1997	6	2008	$27.00
1998	6	2009	$27.00
1999	6	2010	$26.00
2000	6	2010	$25.00
2001	6	2012	$24.00

FRANKLAND ESTATE ISOLATION RIDGE SHIRAZ ★★★★

1991	5	Prior	
1992	5	Now	$29.00
1993	6	Now	$34.00
1994	6	Prior	
1995	6	Now	$32.00
1996	6	2004	$31.00
1997	6	2005	$30.00
1998	6	2006	$29.00
1999	6	2009	$28.00
2000	6	2010	$27.00

FRANKLAND ESTATE OLMO'S REWARD (CAB.FRANC/MERLOT/MALBEC/CAB.SAUVIGNON) ★★★★

1992	5	Now	$35.00
1993	6	Now	$41.00
1994	6	2004	$40.00
1995	6	2005	$39.00
1996	6	2006	$37.00
1997	6	2007	$36.00
1998	6	2009	$35.00
1999	6	2010	$34.00

Galah Wine*, in spite of the name, is neither a joke nor made from or by Galahs. In essence this operation is an underpriced mail-order negociant label controlled and administered by Stephen George of Ashton Hills fame (q.v). Wines can be purchased only by writing to Box 231 Ashton 5137. Winemaker/Wine Selector: Stephen George.*

GALAH CLARE VALLEY CABERNET/MALBEC ★★★★

1986	7	Now	$40.00
1987	6	Now	$34.00
1988	6	Now	$33.00
1989	7	Now	$37.00
1990	Not made		
1991	5	Now	$25.00
1992	7	Now	$34.00
1993	6	Now	$28.00
1994	7	Now	$32.00
1995	Not made		
1996	7	Now	$30.00
1997	6	2004	$25.00
1998	7	2006	$28.00
1999	6	2009	$23.00
2000	7	2007	$27.00

GALAH WINE CLARE VALLEY SHIRAZ ★★★★

1986	6	Now	$35.00
1987	6	Now	$34.00
1988	7	Now	$38.00
1989	7	Now	$37.00
1990	7	Now	$36.00
1991	5	Now	$25.00
1992	7	Now	$34.00
1993	6	Now	$28.00
1994	7	Now	$32.00
1995	6	Now	$27.00
1996	6	Now	$26.00
1997	6	Now	$25.00
1998	7	2004	$29.00
1999	6	2007	$24.00
2000	7	2005	$27.00

Gapsted Wines *in Victoria's King Valley have about 10 hectares of vines, but also call on fruit from a great many small growers in the area. Winemakers: Michael Cope-Williams and Shayne Cunningham.*

GAPSTED CABERNET FRANC ★★★★

1997	7	Now	$27.00
1998	Not made		
1999	6	2004	$22.00
2000	6	2005	$21.00
2001	7	2007	$24.00

GAPSTED CABERNET SAUVIGNON ★★★★

1998	7	Now	$25.00
1999	6	2004	$21.00
2000	7	2007	$24.00

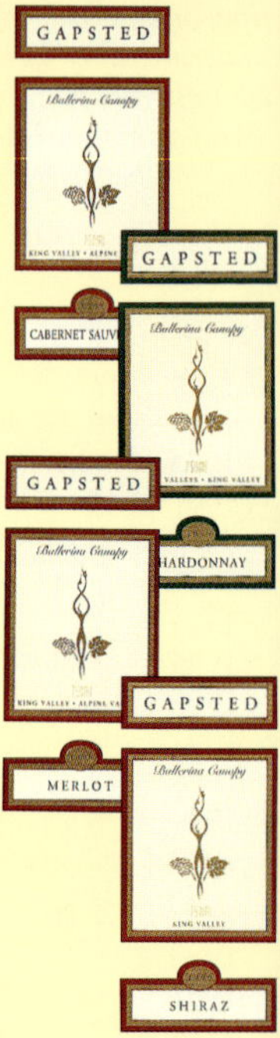

GAPSTED CHARDONNAY ★★★★

1998	6	Now	$22.00
1999	7	Now	$25.00
2000	5	2004	$17.50
2001	6	2005	$20.00
2002	6	2005	$20.00

GAPSTED DURIF ★★★★

1998	6	2004	$34.00
1999	5	2005	$28.00
2000	Not made		
2001	6	2007	$31.00

GAPSTED MERLOT ★★★★

1998	7	Now	$29.00
1999	6	2004	$24.00
2000	6	2005	$23.00

GAPSTED SHIRAZ ★★★★

1997	7	Now	$30.00
1998	Not made		
1999	6	2004	$24.00
2000	6	2005	$23.00

Garden Gully Vineyards *in Victoria's Great Western district is a syndicate-owned operation producing very agreeable wines, sometimes from sourced grapes, but the following wines are usually estate grown. Winemakers: Brian Fletcher and Warren Randall.*

GARDEN GULLY SHIRAZ ★★★

before 1991		Prior	
1991	6	Now	$27.00
1992	Not made		
1993	5	Now	$21.00
1994	6	Now	$24.00
1995	7	2005	$27.00
1996	7	Now	$27.00
1997	6	2004	$22.00
1998	7	2005	$25.00

GARDEN GULLY SPARKLING SHIRAZ ★★★★

1991	6	Now	$36.00
1992	5	Now	$29.00
1993	5	Now	$28.00
1994	7	2004	$39.00
1995	Not made		

1996	6	2004	$31.00
1997	7	2008	$36.00
1998	6	2008	$30.00

GARDEN GULLY RIESLING ★★★

1992	6	Now	$18.50
1993	Not made		
1994	6	Now	$17.50
1995	Not made		
1996	Not made		
1997	5	Now	$13.50
1998	7	2004	$18.00
1999	5	2004	$12.50
2000	No data		
2001	6	Now	$14.00

Garrett, Andrew *- see Andrew Garrett.*

Gartelmann Hunter Valley Estate *(formerly the George Hunter Estate) is a vineyard with 16 hectares of well established vines at Lovedale. Winemakers: Monach Winemaking Services and David Lowe.*

GARTELMANNN CHARDONNAY ★★★

before 2000		Prior	
2000	7	Now	$21.00
2001	6	Now	$17.50
2002	7	2004	$19.50

GARTELMANN SEMILLON ★★★★

1998	6	Now	$20.00
1999	7	2004	$22.00
2000	6	Now	$19.00
2001	5	Now	$15.00
2002	6	2005	$18.00

GARTELMANN SHIRAZ ★★★

1997	5	Prior	
1998	7	Now	$32.00
1999	5	Now	$22.00
2000	7	Now	$30.00
2001	6	2004	$25.00
2002	7	2005	N/R

Geoff Hardy Kuitpo Wines *are all from a 26 hectare vineyard in the Adelaide Hills. The same two winemakers produce the Pertaringa wines (q.v.) Winemakers: Geoff Hardy and Ben Riggs.*

GEOFF HARDY KUITPO CABERNET ★★★★

1993	6	Now	$37.00
1994	6	Now	$36.00
1995	Not made		

1996	7	2004	$39.00
1997	5	Now	$27.00
1998	7	2004	$37.00
1999	6	2005	$31.00

GEOFF HARDY KUITPO SHIRAZ ★★★★★

1993	7	Now	$41.00
1994	6	Now	$34.00
1995	Not made		
1996	Not made		
1997	6	Now	$31.00
1998	7	2007	$36.00
1999	6	2007	$30.00

***Geoff Merrill Wines** are McLaren Vale makers whose range spans a gamut between inexpensive and very much not. Winemaker: Geoff Merrill.*

GEOFF MERRILL CABERNET SAUVIGNON ★★★

1990	6	Now	$28.00
1991	6	Now	$27.00
1992	5	Now	$22.00
1993	6	Now	$26.00
1994	6	Now	$25.00
1995	6	Now	$24.00
1996	7	Now	$28.00
1997	6	Now	$23.00
1998	7	2004	$26.00
1999	5	2004	$18.00

GEOFF MERRILL HENLEY SHIRAZ ★★★★★

1996	7	2008	$155.00
1997	7	2007	$150.00
1998	7	2010	$145.00

GEOFF MERRILL RESERVE CABERNET SAUVIGNON ★★★★

1988	6	Now	$60.00
1989	6	Now	$58.00
1990	7	Now	$64.00
1991	6	Now	$54.00
1992	5	Now	$44.00
1993	5	Now	$43.00
1994	6	Now	$50.00
1995	7	2005	$56.00
1996	7	2006	$54.00
1997	6	2006	$45.00
1998	7	2010	$52.00

GEOFF MERRILL RESERVE CHARDONNAY ★★★★

1993	6	Now	$39.00
1994	6	Now	$38.00
1995	6	Now	$37.00
1996	7	2004	$42.00
1997	5	2004	$29.00
1998	7	2005	$39.00

GEOFF MERRILL RESERVE SHIRAZ ★★★★

1994	7	2004	$54.00
1995	6	2005	$45.00
1996	7	2006	$50.00
1997	6	2006	$43.00
1998	7	2010	$48.00

GEOFF MERRILL SAUVIGNON BLANC ★★★

before 1999		Prior	
1999	7	Now	$26.00
2000	6	Now	$22.00
2001	5	Now	$18.00
2002	7	Now	$24.00

GEOFF MERRILL SHIRAZ ★★★

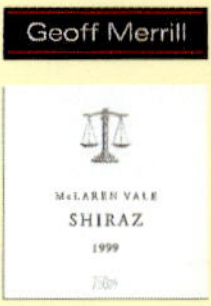

1990	6	Now	$28.00
1991	5	Now	$22.00
1992	5	Now	$22.00
1993	6	Now	$25.00
1994	7	Now	$29.00
1995	6	Now	$24.00
1996	7	Now	$27.00
1997	6	Now	$22.00
1998	7	2004	$26.00
1999	6	2005	$21.00

***Geoff Weaver** (formerly Stafford Ridge) is the label under which wines are released from the Lenswood (high Adelaide Hills) vineyard of the gifted winemaker. Winemaker: Geoff Weaver.*

GEOFF WEAVER CHARDONNAY ★★★★★

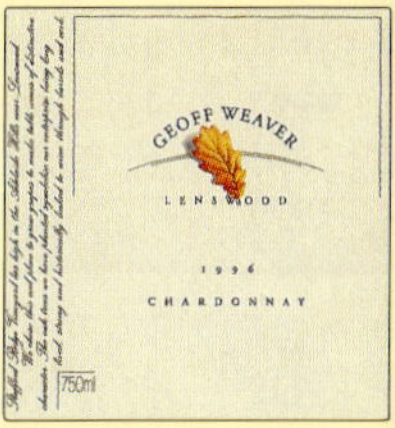

before 1992		Prior	
1992	4	Now	$36.00
1993	5	Now	$44.00
1994	5	Now	$43.00
1995	6	Now	$50.00
1996	5	Now	$41.00
1997	5	Now	$39.00
1998	6	2004	$46.00
1999	5	2004	$37.00
2000	6	2005	$43.00
2001	6	2007	$42.00

GEOFF WEAVER RIESLING ★★★★

before 1998		Prior	
1998	6	Now	$27.00
1999	5	Prior	
2000	5	2004	$21.00
2001	5	2004	$20.00
2002	Not made		

GEOFF WEAVER SAUVIGNON BLANC ★★★★

before 1999		Prior	
1999	6	Now	$24.00
2000	6	Now	$23.00
2001	6	Now	$22.00
2002	6	Now	$22.00

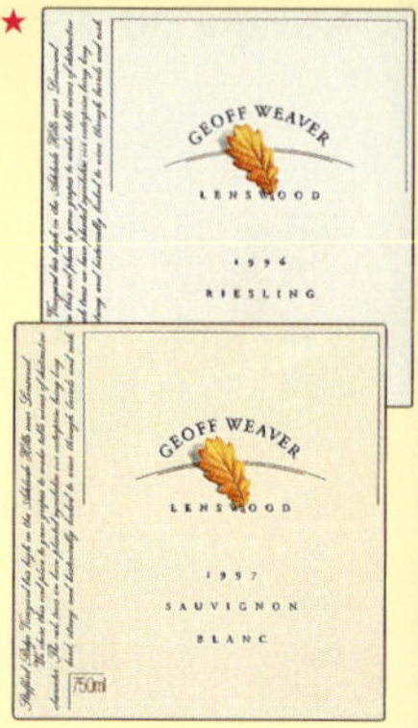

***Glenara Wines** are Adelaide Hills makers whose vineyard is 400 metres above sea level. The wines are stylish and elegant. Winemaker: Trevor Jones.*

GLENARA CABERNET ROSE ★★★

before 1998		Prior	
1998	7	Now	$15.00
1999	7	Now	$15.00
2000	Not made		

GLENARA RIESLING ★★★★

before 1993		Prior	
1993	7	Now	$21.00
1994	6	Now	$17.50
1995	7	Now	$19.50
1996	6	Now	$16.50
1997	6	Now	$16.00
1998	7	Now	$18.00
1999	6	2004	$15.00
2000	7	2005	$17.00

***Glenguin** are Hunter Valley winemakers who present individual vineyard wines (the particular vineyards being identified on the labels). Winemaker: Robin Tedder.*

GLENGUIN CHARDONNAY ★★★

1996	4	Now	$19.00
1997	4	Now	$18.50
1998	6	Now	$27.00
1999	5	Now	$22.00

GLENGUIN SEMILLON ★★★★

1996	4	Now	$17.50
1997	5	Now	$21.00
1998	4	Now	$16.50
1999	5	Now	$20.00
2000	5	Now	$19.50

Gloucester Ridge Vineyards*, on the outskirts of the Pemberton township, produce a range of wines of impressive weight and finesse. Winemaker: Brendan Smith.*

GLOUCESTER RIDGE CABERNET SAUVIGNON ★★★★

1996	7	2004	$35.00
1997	5	203	$24.00
1998	7	2004	$33.00
1999	7	2008	$32.00
2000	7	2010	$31.00

GLOUCESTER RIDGE CHARDONNAY ★★★★

1996	5	Now	$29.00
1997	5	Now	$28.00
1998	5	Now	$28.00
1999	6	Now	$32.00
2000	7	Now	$37.00
2001	7	2006	$36.00
2002	7	2007	$35.00

GLOUCESTER RIDGE SAUVIGNON BLANC ★★★

before 1998		Prior	
1998	5	Now	$17.00
1999	5	Now	$16.50
2000	6	Now	$19.50
2001	6	2005	$19.00
2002	7	2006	$21.00

Gnangara *- see Evans and Tate.*

Goona Warra Vineyard *is a re-establishment of a then elaborate 19th century vineyard at Sunbury in Victoria. Winemaker: Nick Bickford.*

GOONA WARRA CABERNET FRANC ★★★★

before 1994		Prior	
1994	5	Now	$26.00
1995	6	Now	$31.00
1996	5	Now	$25.00
1997	6	2005	$29.00
1998	5	2006	$23.00
1999	Not made		
2000	6	2008	$27.00
2001	7	2009	$30.00

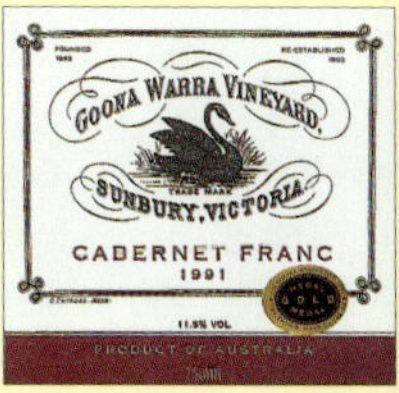

GOONA WARRA CHARDONNAY ★★★★

before 1997		Prior	
1997	7	2005	$29.00
1998	5	Now	$20.00
1999	5	Now	$20.00

2000	6	2004	$23.00
2001	6	2006	$22.00
2002	7	2007	$25.00

GOONA WARRA PINOT NOIR ★★★

before 1997		Prior	
1997	6	Now	$32.00
1998	6	Now	$31.00
1999	Not made		
2000	5	Now	$24.00
2001	7	2006	$33.00
2002	6	2007	$28.00

GOONA WARRA SEMILLON (/SAUVIGNON BLANC) ★★★

before 1991		Prior	
1991	7	Now	$32.00
1992	7	Now	$31.00
1993	5	Now	$21.00
1994	5	Now	$21.00
1995	5	Now	$20.00
1996	5	Now	$20.00
1997	6	2006	$23.00
1998	6	2007	$22.00
1999	Not made		
2000	5	Now	$17.50
2001	5	Now	$17.00
2002	6	2008	$20.00

***Goundrey Wines** were the pioneers of the Mount Barker area on the South Coast of Western Australia. Their 100 hectares of prime vineyards give them a formidable basis for an increasing impact on the quality market. Winemaker: David Martin.*

GOUNDREY CHARDONNAY (UNWOODED) ★★★

before 1998		Prior	
1998	7	Now	$22.00
1999	7	Now	$22.00
2000	6	Now	$18.50
2001	7	Now	$21.00
2002	7	2004	$20.00

GOUNDREY CHENIN BLANC ★★★

before 1999		Prior	
1999	5	Now	$13.50
2000	6	Now	$16.00
2001	7	Now	$18.00
2002	7	Now	$17.50

GOUNDREY CLASSIC WHITE ★★★

1997	5	Prior	
1998	7	Now	$18.00
1999	7	Now	$17.50

GOUNDREY RESERVE CABERNET SAUVIGNON ★★★★

before 1990		Prior	
1990	4	Now	$19.00
1991	5	Now	$23.00
1992	6	Now	$27.00
1993	5	Now	$22.00
1994	6	Now	$25.00
1995	6	Now	$24.00
1996	7	Now	$28.00
1997	6	2004	$23.00
1998	7	2005	$26.00

GOUNDREY CABERNET/MERLOT ★★★

1996	7	Now	$21.00
1997	6	Now	$17.50
1998	7	Now	$20.00
1999	6	2004	$16.50
2000	7	2006	$18.50
2001	7	2006	$18.00

GOUNDREY RESERVE CHARDONNAY ★★★★

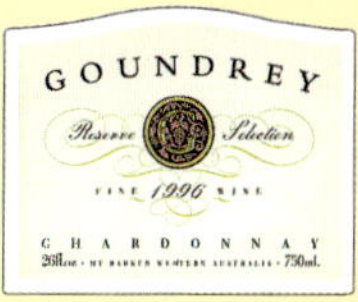

before 1995		Prior	
1995	7	Now	$40.00
1996	5	Now	$28.00
1997	6	Now	$32.00
1998	7	Now	$37.00
1999	7	Now	$36.00

GOUNDREY RESERVE RIESLING ★★★★

before 1992		Prior	
1992	6	Now	$17.00
1993	5	Now	$14.00
1994	6	Now	$16.00
1995	6	Now	$15.50
1996	5	Now	$12.50
1997	7	Now	$17.50
1998	6	2005	$14.50
1999	6	2006	$14.00
2000	7	2010	$16.00
2001	Not made		
2002	6	2012	$13.00

GOUNDREY RESERVE SHIRAZ ★★★★

before 1991		Prior	
1991	5	Now	$23.00
1992	7	Now	$32.00
1993	6	Now	$26.00
1994	6	Now	$26.00
1995	7	2005	$29.00
1996	6	2010	$24.00
1997	6	2011	$23.00

1998	6	2005	$23.00
1999	7	2012	$26.00
2000	6	2011	$21.00

***Grace Devlin Wines** is a new vineyard in Victoria's Redesdale region, an area notable for its distinctive red wines. The Cabernet is an impressively profound, complex wine. Winemakers: Brian and Lee Paterson.*

GRACE DEVLIN CABERNET SAUVIGNON ★★★★

1999	5	2006	$26.00
2000	4	2005	$20.00
2001	6	2006	$30.00

***Grand Cru** - see Karl Seppelt Estate.*

***Granite Hills** in Victoria's Baynton area are cool climate makers of intensely flavoured wines. Winemaker: Llew Knight.*

GRANITE HILLS CABERNET SAUVIGNON ★★★★

before 1982		Prior	
1982	5	Now	$36.00
1983	4	Prior	
1984	4	Prior	
1985	4	Prior	
1986	5	Now	$32.00
1987	4	Now	$25.00
1988	4	Now	$24.00
1989	4	Now	$23.00
1990	Not made		
1991	5	Now	$27.00
1992	5	Now	$26.00
1993	Not made		
1994	4	Now	$20.00
1995	6	2005	$29.00
1996	6	2006	$28.00
1997	6	2010	$27.00
1998	7	2010	$31.00

GRANITE HILLS CHARDONNAY ★★★★

1986	5	Now	$28.00
1987	4	Prior	
1988	4	Now	$21.00
1989	4	Now	$20.00
1990	5	Now	$24.00
1991	4	Now	$19.00
1992	4	Now	$18.50
1993	5	Now	$22.00
1994	5	Now	$22.00
1995	6	Now	$25.00

1996	7	2006	$29.00
1997	6	2006	$24.00
1998	7	2006	$27.00

GRANITE HILLS RIESLING ★★★★

1986	7	Now	$32.00
1987	4	Now	$18.00
1988	6	Now	$26.00
1989	4	Now	$17.00
1990	7	Now	$29.00
1991	5	Now	$20.00
1992	5	Now	$19.50
1993	6	Now	$22.00
1994	5	Now	$18.50
1995	6	2004	$21.00
1996	6	2006	$20.00
1997	6	2008	$20.00
1998	7	2006	$23.00
1999	7	2007	$22.00
2000	6	2006	$18.50

GRANITE HILLS SHIRAZ ★★★★

before 1986		Prior	
1986	6	Now	$38.00
1987	4	Now	$24.00
1988	7	Now	$41.00
1989	4	Now	$23.00
1990	Not made		
1991	5	Now	$27.00
1992	5	Now	$26.00
1993	Not made		
1994	Not made		
1995	6	2007	$29.00
1996	5	2008	$23.00
1997	7	2010	$32.00
1998	7	2010	$31.00

***Grant Burge** is a family owned and operated Barossa Valley based producer whose substantial range of wines includes a very fine Shiraz - "Meshach". Winemaker: Grant Burge.*

GRANT BURGE CAMERON VALE CABERNET SAUVIGNON ★★★

1988	6	Now	$33.00
1989	5	Now	$27.00
1990	6	Now	$31.00
1991	7	Now	$35.00
1992	6	Now	$29.00
1993	7	Now	$33.00
1994	6	Now	$28.00
1995	6	Now	$27.00

1996	6	2004	$26.00
1997	6	2005	$25.00
1998	7	2008	$29.00
1999	6	2006	$24.00
2000	7	2008	$27.00
2001	7	2013	$26.00

GRANT BURGE CHARDONNAY ★★★★

before 1993		Prior	
1993	7	Now	$26.00
1994	6	Now	$22.00
1995	5	Now	$17.50
1996	6	Now	$20.00
1997	6	Now	$20.00
1998	6	Now	$19.50
1999	7	2004	$22.00
2000	6	2004	$18.00
2001	7	2008	$20.00
2002	6	2009	$17.00

GRANT BURGE EDEN VALLEY RIESLING ★★★

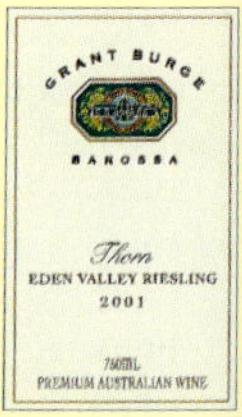

before 1994		Prior	
1994	5	Now	$16.00
1995	5	Now	$15.50
1996	6	Now	$18.00
1997	7	Now	$20.00
1998	7	2004	$19.50
1999	6	2005	$16.50
2000	7	2005	$18.50
2001	7	2006	$18.00
2002	7	2010	$17.50

GRANT BURGE GRENACHE/SHIRAZ/MOURVEDRE ★★★★

1995	6	2008	$24.00
1996	7	2010	$27.00
1997	6	2010	$23.00
1998	7	2013	$26.00
1999	7	2016	$25.00

GRANT BURGE MERLOT ★★★★

1988	6	Now	$27.00
1989	6	Now	$26.00
1990	7	Now	$29.00
1991	7	Now	$29.00
1992	6	Now	$24.00
1993	5	Now	$19.50
1994	6	Now	$22.00
1995	6	Now	$22.00
1996	6	Now	$21.00
1997	5	Now	$17.00
1998	6	2004	$20.00

1999	6	2006	$19.50
2000	6	2009	$19.00
2001	7	2010	$21.00
2002	6	2012	$18.00

GRANT BURGE MESHACH SHIRAZ ★★★★★

1988	6	Now	$120.00
1989	Not made		
1990	7	2010	$135.00
1991	7	2009	$130.00
1992	6	2007	$110.00
1993	6	2007	$105.00
1994	7	2010	$120.00
1995	6	2015	$100.00
1996	7	2017	$110.00
1997	Not made		
1998	7	2020	$105.00
1999	7	2022	$105.00

GRANT BURGE SAUVIGNON BLANC ★★★

before 1998		Prior	
1998	6	Now	$15.50
1999	6	Now	$15.00
2000	6	Now	$14.50
2001	7	Now	$16.50
2002	7	Now	$16.00

GRANT BURGE SEMILLON ★★★

before 1994		Prior	
1992	5	Now	$19.00
1993	6	Now	$22.00
1994	5	Now	$17.50
1995	5	Now	$17.00
1996	6	Now	$20.00
1997	7	Now	$22.00
1998	7	Now	$22.00
1999	6	Now	$18.50
2000	7	2005	$21.00
2001	6	2006	$17.50
2002	6	2007	$17.00

GRANT BURGE SHADRACH CABERNET ★★★★★

1993	6	Now	$48.00
1994	6	2004	$46.00
1995	Not made		
1996	7	2006	$50.00
1997	Not made		
1998	7	2013	$48.00

GRANT BURGE SHIRAZ ★★★★

1988	6	Now	$40.00
1989	6	Now	$39.00
1990	7	Now	$44.00

1991	7	Now	$43.00
1992	6	Now	$36.00
1993	6	Now	$35.00
1994	5	Now	$28.00
1995	7	2004	$38.00
1996	7	2005	$37.00
1997	7	2007	$36.00
1998	7	2010	$35.00
1999	6	2008	$29.00
2000	7	2010	$33.00
2001	7	2012	$32.00

***Grosset Wines** is a Clare Valley maker whose wines are of remarkable finesse and elegance. Winemaker: Jeffrey Grosset.*

GROSSET GAIA (BORDEAUX BLEND) ★★★★★

1989	4	Prior	
1990	7	Now	$94.00
1991	6	Now	$78.00
1992	6	2005	$76.00
1993	5	2004	$62.00
1994	7	2008	$84.00
1995	6	2006	$70.00
1996	6	2008	$68.00
1997	6	2007	$66.00
1998	7	2012	$74.00
1999	6	2011	$62.00
2000	6	2014	$60.00
2001	6	2015	$58.00

GROSSET PICCADILLY (CHARDONNAY) ★★★★

1993	5	Now	$52.00
1994	5	Now	$52.00
1995	6	2004	$60.00
1996	7	2008	$68.00
1997	5	2005	$47.00
1998	5	2005	$46.00
1999	7	2010	$62.00
2000	6	2010	$52.00
2001	6	2011	$50.00
2002	6	2012	$49.00

GROSSET POLISH HILL RIESLING ★★★★★

before 1990		Prior	
1990	6	Now	$54.00
1991	5	Now	$43.00
1992	6	Now	$50.00
1993	6	Now	$49.00
1994	7	2007	$56.00
1995	7	2008	$54.00
1996	6	2009	$45.00

1997	6	2004	$44.00
1998	6	2008	$42.00
1999	6	2008	$41.00
2000	6	2010	$40.00
2001	6	2015	$39.00
2002	7	2018	$44.00

GROSSET SEMILLON/SAUVIGNON BLANC ★★★

1993	6	Prior	
1994	6	Now	$36.00
1995	6	Now	$35.00
1996	6	Now	$34.00
1997	7	Now	$39.00
1998	6	Now	$32.00
1999	7	2004	$37.00
2000	6	2005	$30.00
2001	6	2006	$29.00
2002	6	2007	$29.00

GROSSET WATERVALE RIESLING ★★★★

before 1990		Prior	
1990	6	Now	$41.00
1991	5	Now	$33.00
1992	6	Now	$39.00
1993	6	Now	$38.00
1994	7	2004	$43.00
1995	7	2005	$41.00
1996	6	2007	$34.00
1997	6	2005	$33.00
1998	6	2006	$32.00
1999	6	2005	$31.00
2000	6	2007	$31.00
2001	6	2012	$30.00
2002	7	2015	$34.00

***Hamilton** is one of the oldest names in Australian wine - established in 1837. Their fine McLaren Vale vineyards are undergoing a renaissance. Winemaker: Paul Gordon.*

HAMILTON BURTONS VINEYARD SHIRAZ/GRENACHE ★★★★

1995	6	2005	$36.00
1996	4	Now	$23.00
1997	4	Now	$22.00
1998	7	2008	$38.00
1999	7	2010	$37.00

HAMILTON CABERNET SAUVIGNON "HUT BLOCK" ★★★

1992	5	Now	$21.00
1993	5	Now	$20.00
1994	6	Now	$23.00

1995	5	Now	$19.00
1996	7	Now	$26.00
1997	6	Now	$21.00
1998	7	2008	$24.00
1999	6	2006	$20.00
2000	7	Now	$23.00

HAMILTON CENTURION SHIRAZ ★★★★

1993	6	Now	$56.00
1994	6	Now	$54.00
1995	5	Now	$44.00
1996	7	2008	$60.00
1997	6	2010	$50.00
1998	7	2010	$56.00
1999	7	2010	$54.00

HAMILTON CHARDONNAY ★★★

1993	5	Now	$18.50
1994	6	Now	$21.00
1995	6	Now	$21.00
1996	7	Now	$23.00
1997	7	2004	$23.00
1998	5	Now	$16.00
1999	6	2004	$18.50
200	7	2005	$21.00
2001	6	Now	$17.50

HAMILTON GUMPR'S BLOCK SHIRAZ ★★★

1995	5	Now	$19.00
1996	6	2006	$22.00
1997	5	2005	$18.00
1998	7	2008	$24.00
1999	6	2005	$20.00
2000	7	2006	$23.00

***Hanging Rock Winery** is the Macedon area vineyard and winery of the redoubtable John Ellis. The wines are made both from his own fruit and from selected cool-climate fruit. Winemaker: John Ellis.*

HANGING ROCK HEATHCOTE SHIRAZ ★★★★

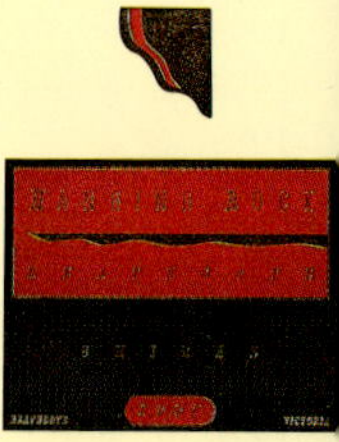

1987	7	Now	$82.00
1988	5	Now	$56.00
1989	4	Prior	
1990	6	Now	$64.00
1991	7	Now	$74.00
1992	7	Now	$70.00
1993	Not made		
1997	7	2007	$66.00
1998	6	2007	$56.00
1999	6	2009	$54.00
2000	7	2010	$62.00

HANGING ROCK JIM JIM ESTATE-GROWN SAUVIGNON BLANC ★★★★

1987	4	Prior	
1988	6	Now	$38.00
1989	4	Prior	
1990	6	Now	$36.00
1991	Not made		
1992	6	Now	$34.00
1993	7	Now	$38.00
1994	6	Now	$32.00
1995	6	Now	$31.00
1996	6	Now	$30.00
1997	5	Now	$24.00
1998	6	Now	$28.00
1999	6	Now	$27.00
2000	6	Now	$27.00
2001	6	Now	$26.00

HANGING ROCK VICTORIA CHARDONNAY ★★★

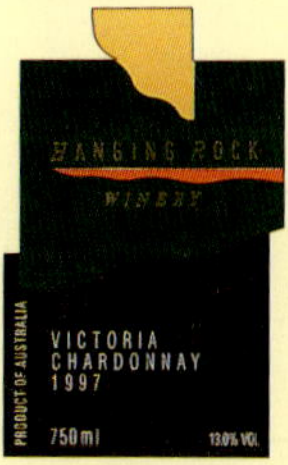

before 1990		Prior	
1990	6	Now	$26.00
1991	6	Now	$25.00
1992	6	Now	$24.00
1993	6	Now	$24.00
1994	5	Now	$19.50
1995	5	Now	$18.50
1996	5	Now	$18.00
1997	5	Now	$17.50
1998	6	Now	$20.00
1999	6	Now	$20.00
2000	6	Now	$19.50
2001	6	Now	$19.00

***Hardy's** (now BRL Hardy) is one of the vinous corporate giants with vineyards in McLaren Vale, Barossa Valley, Keppoch and the Riverland. Winemakers: Peter Dawson, Glen James, Stephen Pannell. Ed Carr, Eric Semler.*

HARDY EILEEN HARDY CHARDONNAY ★★★★

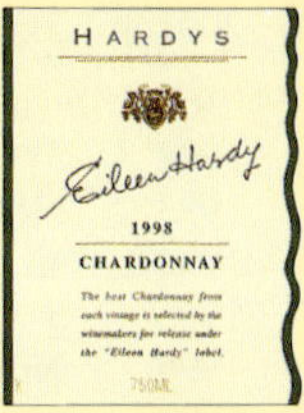

1986	7	Now	$68.00
1987	6	Now	$56.00
1988	6	Now	$54.00
1989	7	Now	$62.00
1990	7	Now	$60.00
1991	6	Now	$50.00
1992	7	Now	$56.00
1993	5	Now	$39.00
1994	7	Now	$54.00
1995	6	Now	$45.00
1996	7	Now	$50.00

1997	7	Now	$49.00
1998	7	Now	$48.00
1999	7	2004	$46.00
2000	7	2005	$45.00
2001	6	2006	$37.00
2002	6	2008	$36.00

HARDY EILEEN HARDY SHIRAZ ★★★★★

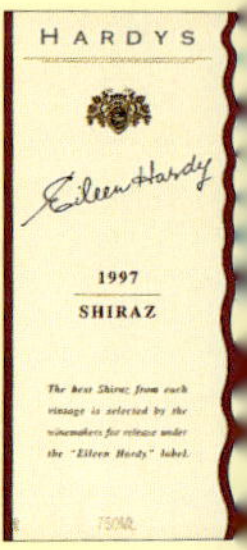

1970	7	Now	$260.00
1971	6	Now	$215.00
1972	4	Prior	
1973	6	Now	$200.00
1974	4	Prior	
1975	6	Now	$190.00
1976	6	Now	$185.00
1977	4	Prior	
1978	Not made		
1979	7	Now	$200.00
1980	6	Now	$165.00
1981	7	Now	$185.00
1982	6	Now	$155.00
1983	Not made		
1984	4	Now	$98.00
1985	5	Now	$115.00
1986	6	Now	$135.00
1987	7	Now	$155.00
1988	7	Now	$150.00
1989	6	Now	$125.00
1990	7	Now	$140.00
1991	7	2005	$140.00
1992	6	2005	$115.00
1993	7	2007	$130.00
1994	6	2006	$110.00
1995	7	2008	$120.00
1996	7	2009	$120.00
1997	6	2009	$100.00
1998	7	2010	$110.00
1999	6	2011	$94.00
2000	6	2012	$92.00
2001	5	2011	$74.00

HARDY SIR JAMES VINTAGE ★★★★

1992	3	Prior	
1993	Not made		
1994	4	Prior	
1995	5	Prior	
1996	Not made		
1997	6	Now	$30.00
1998	7	Now	$34.00
1999	7	Now	$33.00
2000	7	Now	$32.00

HARDY VINTAGE PORT ★★★★

1965	6	Now	$64.00
1966	6	Now	$62.00
1967	5	Now	$50.00
1968	6	Now	$58.00
1969	7	Now	$66.00
1970	6	Now	$54.00
1971	7	Now	$62.00
1972	6	Now	$52.00
1973	5	Now	$42.00
1974	4	Now	$33.00
1975	7	Now	$56.00
1976	7	Now	$54.00
1977	5	Now	$37.00
1978	6	Now	$44.00
1979	5	Now	$35.00
1980	5	Now	$34.00
1981	7	2005	$47.00
1982	5	Now	$32.00
1983	5	2005	$31.00
1984	Not made		
1985	Not made		
1986	Not made		
1987	6	2010	$33.00
1988	6	2010	$32.00
1989	No data		
1993	6	2013	$30.00
1994	6	2014	$30.00
1995	Not made		
1996	6	2016	$28.00
1997	6	2017	$27.00
1998	6	2018	$26.00

***Harewood Estate** is a very fine vineyard at Denmark, in Western Australia's Great Southern region. Grape suppliers to other makers, they produce a little of their own wine. Winemaker: Michael Kerrigan.*

HAREWOOD ESTATE CHARDONNAY ★★★★

1997	5	Now	$28.00
1998	6	Now	$32.00
1999	6	Now	$31.00
2000	Not made		
2001	7	2004	$35.00

HAREWOOD ESTATE PINOT NOIR ★★★

1997	6	Now	$36.00
1998	5	Now	$29.00
1999	5	Now	$28.00
2000	5	Now	$27.00
2001	6	2004	$32.00

Heggies *is a very good vineyard at 550 metres up in the Eden Valley, owned by S. Smith and Sons who also own the labels Yalumba and Pewsey Vale. Winemaker: Peter Gambetta.*

HEGGIES VINEYARD BOTRYTIS RIESLING (375ml) ★★★★

before 1994		Prior	
1994	5	Now	$16.50
1995	5	Now	$16.00
1996	6	Now	$19.00
1997	5	Now	$15.00
1998	7	Now	$21.00
1999	7	Now	$20.00
2000	Not made		

HEGGIES VINEYARD CHARDONNAY ★★★★

before 1993		Prior	
1993	6	Now	$31.00
1994	6	Now	$30.00
1995	5	Prior	
1996	6	Now	$28.00
1997	7	Now	$32.00
1998	5	Prior	
1999	5	Now	$21.00
2000	7	Now	$29.00
2001	7	2004	$28.00
2002	6	2004	$24.00

HEGGIES VINEYARD MERLOT ★★★★

1990	6	Now	$31.00
1991	5	Now	$25.00
1992	6	Now	$30.00
1993	7	Now	$34.00
1994	7	Now	$33.00
1995	5	Now	$22.00
1996	6	Now	$26.00
1997	6	Now	$25.00
1998	5	Now	$20.00
1999	5	2004	$20.00
2000	6	2004	$23.00

HEGGIES VINEYARD PINOT NOIR ★★★★

1993	6	Now	$29.00
1994	5	Now	$24.00
1995	5	Now	$23.00
1996	4	Prior	
1997	5	Now	$22.00
1998	6	Now	$25.00
1999	6	Now	$24.00

HEGGIES VINEYARD RIESLING ★★★★

before 1995		Prior	
1995	6	Now	$24.00
1996	5	Now	$20.00
1997	5	Now	$19.50
1998	6	Now	$22.00
1999	6	Now	$22.00
2000	6	Now	$21.00
2001	6	2005	$20.00
2002	5	Now	$16.50

HEGGIES VINEYARD VIOGNIER ★★★★

before 1999		Prior	
1999	6	Now	$28.00
2000	7	Now	$31.00
2001	7	Now	$30.00
2002	7	Now	$30.00

***Helm Wines** are well-established Murrumbateman (A.C.T.) producers whose wines have helped create considerable interest in the region. Winemaker: Ken Helm.*

HELM CABERNET SAUVIGNON (/MERLOT from 1989) ★★★★

before 1983		Prior	
1983	7	Now	$38.00
1984	5	Now	$26.00
1985	5	Now	$26.00
1986	7	Now	$35.00
1987	7	Now	$34.00
1988	6	Now	$28.00
1989	7	Now	$32.00
1990	7	Now	$31.00
1991	7	Now	$30.00
1992	6	Now	$25.00
1993	5	Now	$20.00
1994	5	Now	$20.00
1995	7	Now	$27.00
1996	6	Now	$22.00
1997	7	2004	$25.00
1998	6	Now	$21.00
1999	7	Now	$24.00
2000	7	2004	$23.00
2001	6	2004	$19.50

HELM CHARDONNAY (NON-OAKED) ★★★

1990	7	Now	$31.00
1991	6	Now	$26.00
1992	6	Now	$25.00
1993	6	Now	$24.00
1994	6	Now	$23.00

1995	7	Now	$26.00
1996	6	Now	$22.00
1997	6	Now	$21.00
1998	7	Now	$24.00
1999	6	Now	$20.00
2000	7	Now	$23.00
2001	6	Now	$19.00
2002	7	2004	$21.00

HELM (CABERNET BLEND) ★★★★

1994	7	Now	$24.00
1995	Not made		
1996	7	Now	$23.00
1997	7	Now	$22.00
1998	Not made		
1999	Not made		
2000	7	Now	$20.00
2001	7	2004	$20.00

HELM RIESLING ★★★★

before 1990		Prior	
1990	7	Now	$30.00
1991	6	Now	$25.00
1992	6	Now	$24.00
1993	7	Now	$27.00
1994	6	Now	$23.00
1995	6	Now	$22.00
1996	6	Now	$21.00
1997	7	Now	$24.00
1998	7	Now	$24.00
1999	7	Now	$23.00
2000	7	Now	$22.00
2001	7	Now	$22.00
2002	7	2004	$21.00

***Henschke**, a family-owned winery established for five generations in the Keyneton and Eden Valley area of the Barossa ranges, produce some of Australia's finest wines. Winemaker: Stephen Henschke.*

HENSCHKE CABERNET SAUVIGNON
CYRIL HENSCHKE ★★★★★

before 1988		Prior	
1988	5	Now	$120.00
1989	7	Now	$160.00
1990	6	Now	$135.00
1991	6	Now	$130.00
1992	4	Now	$86.00
1993	7	Now	$145.00
1994	7	2004	$140.00
1995	5	2005	$98.00

1996	6	2007	$110.00
1997	5	2007	$92.00
1998	7	2008	$125.00
1999	5	2009	$86.00
2000	5	2010	$84.00

HENSCHKE HILL OF GRACE

★★★★★

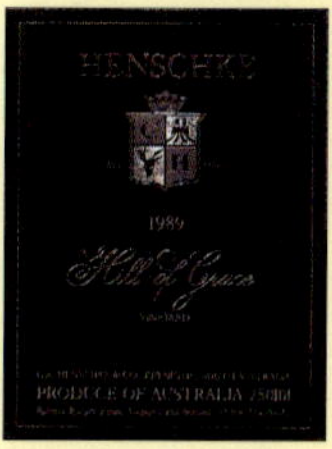

1958	4	Prior	
1959	7	Now	$1260.00
1960	5	Prior	
1961	3	Prior	
1962	6	Now	$980.00
1963	2	Prior	
1964	5	Now	$780.00
1965	6	Prior	
1966	6	Now	$880.00
1967	7	Now	$1000.00
1968	4	Prior	
1969	1	Prior	
1970	3	Prior	
1971	4	Prior	
1972	7	Now	$860.00
1973	6	Now	$700.00
1974	Not made		
1975	3	Prior	
1976	4	Prior	
1977	5	Prior	
1978	7	Now	$720.00
1979	5	Now	$500.00
1980	5	Prior	
1981	4	Prior	
1982	6	2007	$540.00
1983	4	Prior	
1984	7	2009	$600.00
1985	5	2010	$410.00
1986	7	2011	$560.00
1987	6	2012	$470.00
1988	7	2013	$520.00
1989	5	2009	$370.00
1990	7	2010	$500.00
1991	6	2011	$420.00
1992	6	2012	$400.00
1993	5	2008	$330.00
1994	7	2009	$450.00
1995	4	2009	$245.00
1996	7	2011	$420.00
1997	5	2007	$290.00
1998	7	2018	$400.00

HENSCHKE EDEN VALLEY "JULIUS" RIESLING ★★★★

before 1994		Prior	
1994	5	Now	$27.00
1995	6	Now	$32.00
1996	5	Now	$26.00
1997	6	Now	$30.00
1998	5	Now	$24.00
1999	5	Now	$24.00
2000	4	2004	$18.50
2001	6	2005	$27.00
2002	7	2007	$30.00

HENSCHKE KEYNETON ESTATE (SHIRAZ/CABERNET/MALBEC) ★★★★★

1989	7	Now	$60.00
1990	7	2005	$58.00
1991	5	2006	$40.00
1992	4	Now	$31.00
1993	5	Now	$38.00
1994	7	2004	$52.00
1995	4	2005	$29.00
1996	6	2006	$42.00
1997	4	2007	$27.00
1998	6	2007	$39.00
1999	6	2009	$38.00
2000	4	2010	$25.00

HENSCHKE LENSWOOD ABBOTT'S PRAYER ★★★★★

1989	5	Now	$78.00
1990	6	Now	$90.00
1991	6	Now	$88.00
1992	4	Now	$56.00
1993	7	Now	$96.00
1994	7	Now	$94.00
1995	4	Now	$52.00
1996	7	2006	$88.00
1997	5	2007	$60.00
1998	6	2008	$70.00
1999	6	2009	$68.00
2000	5	2010	$56.00

HENSCHKE LOUIS EDEN VALLEY SEMILLON ★★★★

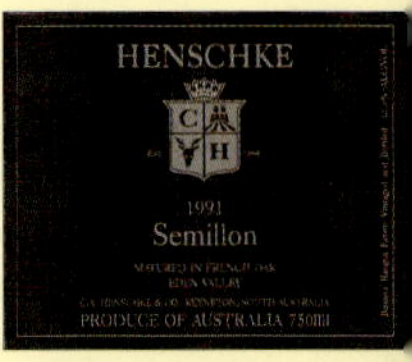

before 1989		Prior	
1989	6	Now	$31.00
1990	5	Now	$25.00
1991	4	Prior	
1992	6	Now	$29.00
1993	5	Now	$23.00

1994	4	Now	$18.00
1995	6	Now	$26.00
1996	6	2004	$25.00
1997	5	Now	$20.00
1998	6	2004	$24.00
1999	6	2005	$23.00
2000	7	2008	$26.00

HENSCHKE MOUNT EDELSTONE ★★★★★

before 1978		Prior	
1978	6	Now	$140.00
1979	3	Prior	
1980	5	Now	$110.00
1981	4	Now	$86.00
1982	7	2007	$145.00
1983	5	Now	$100.00
1984	6	2009	$115.00
1985	4	Now	$76.00
1986	7	2006	$130.00
1987	5	2012	$90.00
1988	7	2008	$120.00
1989	5	2004	$84.00
1990	7	2010	$110.00
1991	5	2006	$80.00
1992	6	2006	$92.00
1993	5	2008	$74.00
1994	7	2009	$100.00
1995	4	2005	$56.00
1996	6	2006	$82.00
1997	4	2007	$52.00
1998	6	2008	$78.00
1999	6	2009	$76.00
2000	5	2010	$60.00

***Hickinbotham** of Dromana is a 10 hectare vineyard and winery in the Mornington Peninsula, using its own and local contract grown grapes. Winemaker: Andrew Hickinbotham.*

HICKINBOTHAM CHARDONNAY ★★★★

1992	7	Now	$38.00
1993	6	Prior	
1994	6	Now	$31.00
1995	5	2005	$25.00
1996	6	Now	$29.00
1997	7	2005	$33.00
1998	7	2005	$32.00
1999	Not made		
2000	7	Now	$30.00

HICKINBOTHAM MERLOT ★★★★

1991	6	Now	$28.00
1992	7	Now	$32.00
1993	7	2010	$31.00
1994	6	Now	$26.00
1995	6	2005	$25.00
1996	Not made		
1997	7	2005	$28.00

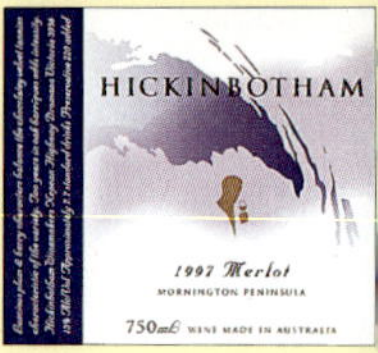

HICKINBOTHAM PINOT NOIR ★★★★

before 1994		Prior	
1994	6	Now	$28.00
1995	Not made		
1996	7	Prior	
1997	7	Now	$30.00
1998	7	Now	$29.00

***Hidden Valley** is the second label of St Peters Winery and Distillery, the premium label being Wilton Estate (q.v.) Winemaker: Not stated.*

HIDDEN VALLEY CHARDONNAY ★★

before 1999		Prior	
1999	6	Now	$10.50
2000	Not made		
2001	6	Now	$10.00

HIDDEN VALLEY SEMILLON/ CHARDONNAY ★★

before 1998		Prior	
1998	6	Now	$8.50
1999	6	Now	$8.25
2000	5	Now	$6.75
2001	6	Now	$7.75
2002	6	Now	$7.75

HIDDEN VALLEY SHIRAZ/ CABERNET/MERLOT ★★

before 1999		Prior	
1999	6	Now	$10.50
2000	Not made		
2001	6	Now	$10.00

***Hill-Smith Estate** is a high Barossa ranges vineyard owned and operated by the Hill Smith family. Winemaker: Louisa Rose.*

HILL-SMITH ESTATE CHARDONNAY ★★★★

before 1997		Prior	
1997	5	Now	$17.00
1998	6	Now	$20.00
1999	7	Now	$22.00

No longer made.

HILL-SMITH ESTATE SAUVIGNON BLANC ★★★

before 2001		Prior	
2001	6	Now	$16.50
2002	7	Now	$18.50

Hillstowe Wines *are Adelaide Hills based makers with exemplary vineyards in McLaren Vale and the high Adelaide Hills. Winemaker: Justin McNamee.*

HILLSTOWE ADELAIDE HILLS/ MCLAREN VALE SAUVIGNON BLANC ★★★

before 1997		Prior	
1997	7	Now	$23.00
1998	6	Now	$19.50
1999	7	Now	$22.00
2000	6	Now	$18.50
2001	5	Now	$15.00
2002	6	Now	$17.50

HILLSTOWE BUXTON MCLAREN VALE CHARDONNAY ★★★

1991	6	Now	$20.00
1992	6	Now	$19.50
1993	6	Now	$19.00
1994	6	Now	$18.50
1995	5	Now	$15.00
1996	6	Now	$17.50
1997	6	Now	$17.00
1998	6	Now	$16.50
1999	No data		
2000	No data		
2001	6	Now	$15.00

HILLSTOWE BUXTON MCLAREN VALE CABERNET/MERLOT ★★★

1991	6	Now	$27.00
1992	5	Now	$21.00
1993	6	2004	$25.00
1994	6	2005	$24.00
1995	Not made		
1996	6	2006	$23.00
1997	6	2006	$22.00
1998	7	2008	$25.00

HILLSTOWE "MARY'S HUNDRED" MCLAREN VALE SHIRAZ ★★★★

1994	6	Now	$46.00
1995	Not made		
1996	7	2008	$50.00
1997	7	2010	$49.00
1998	7	2012	$47.00
1999	7	2010	$46.00

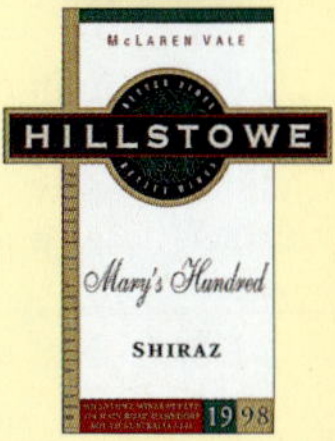

HILLSTOWE UDY'S MILL LENSWOOD CHARDONNAY

★★★★

1992	6	Now	$29.00
1993	6	Now	$28.00
1994	6	Now	$27.00
1995	7	Now	$31.00
1996	7	Now	$30.00
1997	7	Now	$29.00
1998	7	2004	$28.00
1999	7	2006	$27.00
2000	5	2005	$19.00
2001	6	2005	$22.00
2002	6	2007	$21.00

HILLSTOWE UDY'S MILL LENSWOOD PINOT NOIR

★★★★

1991	6	Now	$39.00
1992	4	Now	$25.00
1993	6	Now	$37.00
1994	6	Now	$36.00
1995	5	Now	$29.00
1996	6	Now	$34.00
1997	7	Now	$38.00
1998	7	2005	$37.00
1999	7	2005	$36.00
2000	5	2005	$25.00

***Hollick Wines** are Coonawarra small makers whose large range of wines includes one of the best Cabernets that this premium area has seen. Winemakers: Ian Hollick and Matt Pellew.*

HOLLICK "THE NECTAR" BOTRYTIS RIESLING (375ml)

★★★★

1985	6	Now	$31.00
1986	Not made		
1987	Not made		
1988	Not made		
1989	6	Now	$28.00
1990	7	Now	$32.00
1991	Not made		
1992	6	Now	$25.00
1993	Not made		
1994	6	2004	$24.00
1995	Not made		
1996	7	2006	$26.00
1997	6	2007	$22.00
1998	Not made		
1999	7	2010	$24.00
2000	Not made		
2001	7	2011	$23.00

HOLLICK "COONAWARRA" (CABERNET/MERLOT/CAB. FRANC) ★★★★

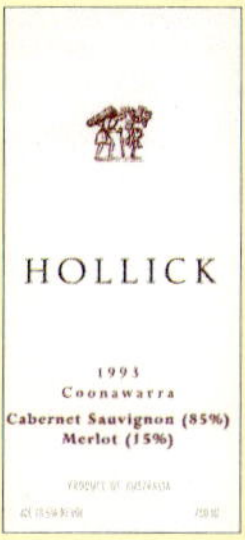

before 1986		Prior	
1986	5	Now	$29.00
1987	5	Prior	
1988	7	Now	$38.00
1989	6	Now	$32.00
1990	7	Now	$36.00
1991	7	Now	$35.00
1992	6	Now	$29.00
1993	6	Now	$28.00
1994	7	2004	$32.00
1995	5	Now	$22.00
1996	6	2004	$26.00
1997	6	2005	$25.00
1998	7	2008	$28.00
1999	6	2006	$23.00
2000	7	2009	$27.00

HOLLICK CHARDONNAY (RESERVE) ★★★★

before 1993		Prior	
1993	6	Now	$26.00
1994	6	Now	$26.00
1995	6	Now	$25.00
1996	5	Now	$20.00
1997	6	Now	$23.00
1998	7	Now	$27.00
1999	6	2004	$22.00
2000	7	2005	$25.00

HOLLICK PINOT NOIR ★★★★

before 1990		Prior	
1990	6	Now	$26.00
1991	Not made		
1992	6	Now	$24.00
1993	6	Now	$24.00
1994	Not made		
1995	6	Now	$22.00
1996	6	Now	$22.00
1997	6	Now	$21.00
1998	7	Now	$24.00
1999	6	Now	$20.00
2000	7	Now	$22.00
2001	7	2005	$22.00

HOLLICK RIESLING ★★★★

before 1991		Prior	
1991	6	Now	$21.00
1992	7	Now	$23.00
1993	Not made		
1994	5	Now	$16.00

1995	6	Now	$18.50
1996	Not made		
1997	6	Now	$17.50
1998	6	Now	$17.00
1999	6	Now	$16.50
2000	7	2006	$18.50
2001	6	2007	$15.50

HOLLICK RAVENSWOOD (CABERNET SAUVIGNON)

★★★★★

1988	6	Now	$72.00
1989	6	2004	$70.00
1990	7	2005	$80.00
1991	7	2006	$78.00
1992	7	2007	$74.00
1993	7	2009	$72.00
1994	7	2009	$70.00
1995	Not made		
1996	7	2011	$66.00
1997	Not made		
1998	7	2013	$62.00
1999	7	2012	$60.00

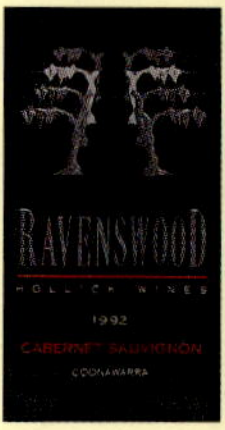

HOLLICK SAUVIGNON BLANC/SEMILLON

★★★★

1997	6	Now	$18.50
1998	6	Now	$17.50
1999	6	Now	$17.00
2000	7	Now	$19.50
2001	6	Now	$16.00

HOLLICK SHIRAZ/CABERNET SAUVIGNON

★★★

1991	6	Prior	
1992	6	Now	$23.00
1993	6	Now	$23.00
1994	7	Now	$26.00
1995	6	Now	$21.00
1996	6	Now	$21.00
1997	6	Now	$20.00
1998	7	Now	$23.00
1999	6	2004	$19.00
2000	7	2007	$21.00
2001	6	2006	$18.00

HOLLICK WILGHA SHIRAZ

★★★★★

1988	6	Now	$58.00
1989	5	Now	$47.00
1990	6	Now	$54.00

1991	6	Now	$52.00
1992	6	Now	$50.00
1993	6	Now	$50.00
1994	6	Now	$48.00
1995	Not made		
1996	7	2006	$52.00
1997	6	2007	$44.00
1998	7	2010	$50.00
1999	6	2010	$42.00
2000	7	2012	$47.00

Hope Estate *was created when Michael Hope purchased a 15 hectare vineyard near Broke in the Hunter Valley in 1994. Since then, he has added an 80 hectare property at Fordwich, together with the old Saxonvale winery. Winemaker: Josti Steele.*

HOPE ESTATE CHARDONNAY ★★★★

1998	4	Prior	
1999	7	Now	$23.00
2000	6	2006	$19.00
2001	6	2007	$18.50

HOPE ESTATE SEMILLON ★★★

1998	5	2004	$16.00
1999	4	2004	$12.50
2000	5	2005	$15.00
2001	5	2006	$14.50
2002	7	2007	$20.00

HOPE ESTATE MERLOT ★★★

1999	4	Prior	
2000	5	2004	$22.00
2001	5	2006	$21.00
2002	5	2006	$21.00

HOPE ESTATE SHIRAZ ★★★

1997	4	Now	$19.00
1998	5	Now	$23.00
1999	4	2004	$18.00
2000	6	2005	$26.00
2001	5	2005	$21.00
2002	5	2006	$20.00

HOPE ESTATE VERDELHO ★★★★

1997	6	Now	$17.00
1998	5	Now	$14.00
1999	5	Now	$13.50
2000	7	Now	$18.50
2001	No data		
2002	7	2004	$17.50

***Houghtons** are the largest producers in Western Australia with vineyards in the Swan Valley, Moondah Brook (q.v.), Frankland River, Mount Barker and Pemberton. The wines have earned a consistent reputation for reliability over the years. Winemaker: Larry Cherubino.*

HOUGHTON WHITE BURGUNDY ★★

before 1991		Prior	
1991	7	Now	$18.50
1992	4	Now	$10.00
1993	6	Now	$15.00
1994	5	Now	$12.00
1995	5	Now	$11.50
1996	5	Now	$11.50
1997	5	Now	$11.00
1998	5	2004	$10.50
1999	7	2010	$14.50
2000	6	2008	$12.00
2001	6	2008	$11.50
2002	7	2008	$13.50

***Howard Park** is a tiny Denmark (Western Australia) producer who now has another new winery in Margaret River. The wines are meticulously made Winemaker: Michael Kerrigan.*

HOWARD PARK CABERNET SAUVIGNON/MERLOT ★★★★★

1986	7	Now	$130.00
1987	5	Prior	
1988	6	Now	$105.00
1989	4	Prior	
1990	6	Now	$100.00
1991	6	2005	$98.00
1992	7	2006	$110.00
1993	6	2006	$92.00
1994	7	2008	$100.00
1995	5	2005	$72.00
1996	6	2007	$84.00
1997	5	2005	$68.00
1998	6	2009	$80.00
1999	7	2010	$90.00
2000	6	2010	$74.00

HOWARD PARK CHARDONNAY ★★★★

1993	7	Now	$50.00
1994	4	Prior	
1995	6	Prior	
1996	6	Now	$39.00
1997	6	Now	$38.00
1998	6	Now	$37.00

1999	7	Now	$42.00
2000	6	2004	$35.00
2001	7	2006	$40.00

HOWARD PARK RIESLING ★★★★

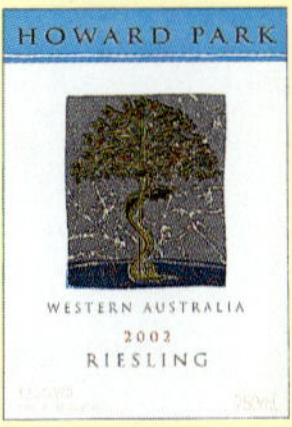

1986	7	Now	$48.00
1987	5	Prior	
1988	5	Prior	
1989	5	Prior	
1990	6	Prior	
1991	7	Now	$41.00
1992	7	Now	$40.00
1993	5	Now	$28.00
1994	5	Now	$27.00
1995	6	Now	$31.00
1996	6	Now	$30.00
1997	6	2005	$29.00
1998	5	Now	$24.00
1999	5	2005	$23.00
2000	6	2007	$27.00
2001	7	2012	$30.00
2002	6	2010	$25.00

***Hugh Hamilton Wines** has a 15 hectare vineyard in McLaren Vale. The wines can sometimes include fruit from the Adelaide Hills. Winemaker: Hugh Hamilton.*

HUGH HAMILTON CHARDONNAY ★★★

before 1999		Prior	
1999	6	Now	$18.50
2000	5	Now	$14.50
2001	6	Now	$17.00

HUGH HAMILTON SHIRAZ ★★★★

1994	7	Now	$30.00
1995	5	Now	$21.00
1996	5	Now	$20.00
1997	5	Now	$20.00
1998	6	Now	$23.00

HUGH HAMILTON SPARKLING SHIRAZ ★★★

before 1996		Prior	
1996	5	Now	$19.00
1997	5	Now	$18.50
1998	6	Now	$21.00

***The Hugo Winery** is yet another McLaren Flat maker to stun the winelover with a quality most would have thought unachievable for the area until a few years ago. Winemaker: John Hugo.*

HUGO CABERNET SAUVIGNON ★★★★

before 1990		Prior	
1990	7	Now	$29.00
1991	6	Now	$24.00

1992	7	Now	$28.00
1993	6	Now	$23.00
1994	7	Now	$26.00
1995	6	Now	$22.00
1996	7	2004	$24.00
1997	6	2004	$20.00
1998	7	2006	$23.00
1999	6	2007	$19.50
2000	6	2008	$19.00
2001	7	2009	$21.00

HUGO CHARDONNAY ★★★★

before 1994		Prior	
1994	7	Now	$21.00
1995	6	Now	$17.50
1996	6	Now	$17.00
1997	7	Now	$19.00
1998	6	Now	$16.00
1999	7	2004	$18.00
2000	Not made		
2001	Not made		

HUGO RIESLING ★★★

before 1989		Prior	
1989	7	Now	$18.00
1990	5	Now	$12.50
1991	6	Now	$14.50
1992	Not made		
1993	6	Now	$13.50
1994	Not made		
1995	7	Now	$15.00
1996	6	Now	$12.50

No longer made.

HUGO SAUVIGNON BLANC ★★★

1998	6	Now	$17.50
1999	6	Now	$17.00
2000	7	Now	$19.50
2001	6	Now	$16.00

HUGO SHIRAZ ★★★★

before 1988		Prior	
1988	6	Now	$28.00
1989	6	Now	$27.00
1990	7	Now	$31.00
1991	7	Now	$30.00
1992	7	Now	$29.00
1993	6	Now	$24.00
1994	6	Now	$23.00
1995	6	Now	$23.00
1996	7	2004	$26.00
1997	6	2004	$21.00

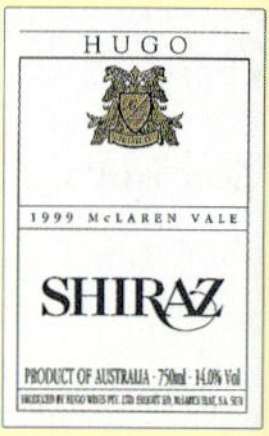

1998	7	2006	$24.00
1999	6	2006	$20.00
2000	7	2008	$23.00
2001	7	2009	$22.00

HUGO UNWOODED CHARDONNAY ★★★

1998	6	Prior	
1999	6	Now	$16.00
2000	7	Now	$18.00
2001	6	Now	$15.00

***Hungerford Hill**, now owned by Cassegrain, are middle sized Hunter Valley based producers of a range of table wines from the NSW fruit. The vintages below are all from the time when the operation was owned by Southcorp. Winemaker: Geoff Jarratt.*

HUNGERFORD HILL HILLTOPS CABERNET SAUVIGNON ★★★

1994	5	Now	$19.50
1995	6	Now	$23.00
1996	6	Now	$22.00
1997	7	Now	$25.00
1998	6	Now	$21.00
1999	5	Now	$17.00
2000	Not made		

HUNGERFORD HILL COWRA CHARDONNAY ★★★

before 1996		Prior	
1996	5	Now	$14.50
1997	6	Now	$17.00
1998	5	Now	$14.00
1999	6	Now	$16.00
2000	Not made		

HUNGERFORD HILL SEMILLON ★★★

1995	5	Now	$15.00
1996	6	Now	$17.50
1997	Not made		
1998	5	Now	$14.00

HUNGERFORD HILL TUMBARUMBA SAUVIGNON BLANC ★★★

before 1995		Prior	
1995	6	Now	$20.00
1996	5	Now	$16.50
1997	6	Now	$19.00
1998	6	Now	$18.50
1999	7	Now	$21.00
2000	5	Now	$14.50

***Huntington Estate** is one of the more impressive of the Mudgee producers, well established and distinctively styled. Winemaker: Susie Roberts.*

HUNTINGTON ESTATE CABERNET SAUVIGNON/MERLOT ★★★★

before 1984		Prior	
1984	7	Now	$24.00
1985	6	Now	$20.00
1986	7	Now	$23.00
1987	5	Now	$16.00
1988	6	Now	$18.50
1989	6	Now	$18.00
1990	7	Now	$20.00
1991	7	Now	$20.00
1992	6	Now	$16.50
1993	6	Now	$16.00
1994	6	Now	$15.50
1995	Not made		
1996	5	Now	$12.00
1997	7	Now	$16.50

Not made since 1997

HUNTINGTON ESTATE CABERNET SAUVIGNON ★★★★

before 1981		Prior	
1981	7	Now	$38.00
1982	6	Now	$31.00
1983	6	Now	$30.00
1984	7	Now	$34.00
1985	6	Now	$29.00
1986	7	Now	$32.00
1987	5	Now	$22.00
1988	6	Now	$26.00
1989	6	Now	$25.00
1990	7	Now	$29.00
1991	6	Now	$24.00
1992	6	Now	$23.00
1993	6	Now	$22.00
1994	6	Now	$22.00
1995	6	Now	$21.00
1996	5	Now	$17.50
1997	7	Now	$23.00
1998	6	2004	$19.50
1999	7	2004	$22.00
2000	5	2004	$15.50
2001	6	2005	$18.00
2002	6	2006	$17.50

HUNTINGTON ESTATE SHIRAZ ★★★

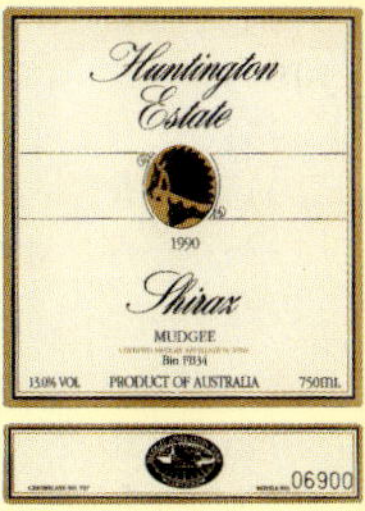

before 1981		Prior	
1981	7	Now	$38.00
1982	6	Now	$31.00
1983	6	Now	$30.00
1984	7	Now	$34.00
1985	6	Now	$29.00
1986	7	Now	$32.00
1987	5	Now	$22.00
1988	6	Now	$26.00
1989	7	Now	$30.00
1990	6	Now	$25.00
1991	6	Now	$24.00
1992	6	Now	$23.00
1993	7	Now	$26.00
1994	6	Now	$22.00
1995	6	Now	$21.00
1996	3	Now	$10.50
1997	7	Now	$23.00
1998	5	Now	$16.50
1999	7	Now	$22.00
2000	7	2004	$21.00
2001	6	2005	$18.00
2002	6	2006	$17.50

***Idyll Vineyard** was the first planted in the re-establishment of the Geelong vignoble. The wines have been supple and attractive. The vineyard is now under new ownership. Winemaker: Daryl Sefton (for the vintages below).*

BONE IDYLL (SHIRAZ) ★★

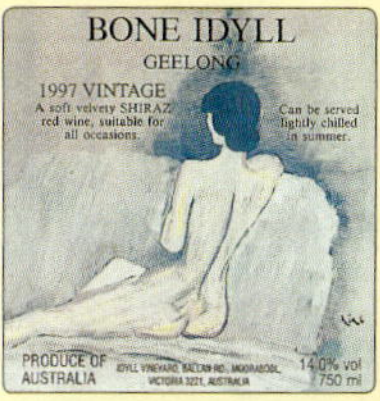

before 1996		Prior	
1996	5	Now	$13.00
1997	7	Now	$18.00
1998	6	Now	$15.00

IDYLL CABERNET SAUVIGNON (CABERNET SAUVIGNON/ SHIRAZ until 1987) ★★★★

before 1980		Prior	
1980	6	Now	$32.00
1981	7	Now	$36.00
1982	6	Now	$30.00
1983	5	Now	$24.00
1984	4	Now	$18.50
1985	5	Now	$23.00
1986	6	Now	$26.00
1987	5	Now	$21.00
1988	5	Now	$21.00
1989	5	Now	$20.00
1990	6	Now	$23.00

1991	6	Now	$23.00
1992	6	Now	$22.00
1993	5	Now	$18.00
1994	6	Now	$21.00
1995	6	Now	$20.00
1996	6	Now	$19.50
1997	7	2005	$22.00

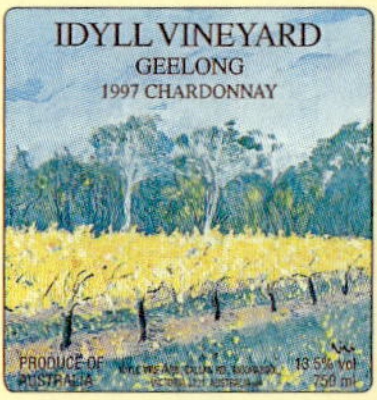

IDYLL CHARDONNAY ★★★

1995	6	Now	$17.50
1996	5	Now	$14.00
1997	5	Now	$14.00
1998	6	Now	$16.00

IDYLL GEWURZTRAMINER ★★★★

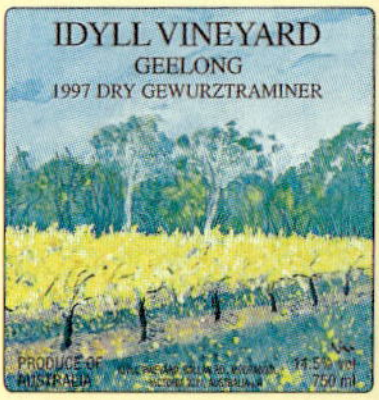

before 1990		Prior	
1990	5	Now	$16.50
1991	6	Now	$19.50
1992	5	Now	$15.50
1993	6	Now	$18.00
1994	5	Now	$14.50
1995	6	Now	$17.00
1996	6	Now	$16.50
1997	6	Now	$16.00
1998	6	Now	$15.50

IDYLL SHIRAZ ★★★★

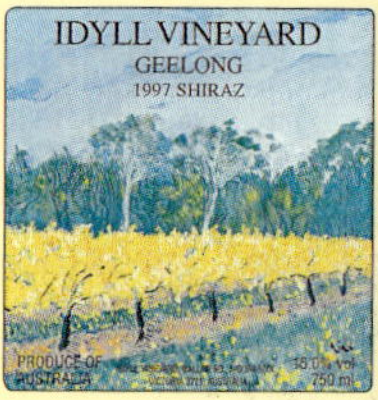

1990	7	Now	$26.00
1991	5	Now	$18.50
1992	5	Now	$18.00
1993	5	Now	$17.50
1994	6	Now	$20.00
1995	6	Now	$19.50
1996	6	Now	$19.00
1997	7	2005	$21.00

***Ingoldby Wines** are McLaren Flat makers whose flagship wine is a fine Cabernet Sauvignon. The operation is now owned by Beringer Blass. Winemaker: Charles Hargrave.*

INGOLDBY CABERNET SAUVIGNON ★★★★

before 1990		Prior	
1990	7	Now	$24.00
1991	7	Now	$23.00
1992	6	Now	$19.00
1993	7	Now	$22.00
1994	7	2005	$21.00
1995	6	Now	$17.50
1996	6	2004	$17.00

1997	6	2004	$16.50
1998	7	2006	$19.00
1999	7	2010	$18.00
2000	7	2011	$17.50

INGOLDBY CHARDONNAY ★★★★

before 1998		Prior	
1998	7	Now	$19.00
1999	6	Now	$15.50
2000	6	Now	$15.00
2001	7	2005	$17.00
2002	7	2007	$16.50

INGOLDBY SHIRAZ ★★★★

before 1990		Prior	
1990	7	Now	$25.00
1991	5	Now	$17.50
1992	6	2005	$20.00
1993	7	2005	$23.00
1994	7	Now	$22.00
1995	6	Now	$18.50
1996	6	Now	$18.00
1997	6	Now	$17.50
1998	7	2005	$20.00
1999	7	2008	$19.00
2000	7	2009	$18.50
2001	7	2010	$18.00

***Jamiesons Run** is a Coonawarra based label owned by Beringer Blass and representing quality for value wines. Winemaker: Andrew Hales.*

JAMIESONS RUN CHARDONNAY ★★★

before 1999		Prior	
1999	6	Now	$16.00
2000	6	2004	$15.50
2001	6	2005	$15.00
2002	6	2006	$15.00

JAMIESONS RUN COONAWARRA (DRY RED) ★★★

before 1992		Prior	
1992	6	Now	$19.00
1993	7	Now	$21.00
1993	6	Now	$17.50
1994	6	2004	$17.00
1995	5	Now	$14.00
1996	7	2005	$19.00
1997	6	Now	$15.50
1998	7	2006	$18.00
1999	6	2008	$15.00
2000	6	2009	$14.50

Jane Brook Estate *is a Swan Valley producer not in the traditional Swan Valley mould, producing stylish and appealingly crisp wines, made even more impressive from their Pemberton fruit. Winemakers: Julie White and David Atkinson.*

JANE BROOK ESTATE CABERNET/MERLOT ★★★★

before 1995		Prior	
1995	6	Now	$28.00
1996	5	Now	$23.00
1997	6	Now	$27.00
1998	7	2006	$30.00
1999	6	2007	$25.00
2000	3	Now	$12.00
2001	6	2008	$24.00

JANE BROOK ESTATE CHARDONNAY ★★★

before 1995		Prior	
1995	4	Now	$18.00
1996	5	Now	$22.00
1997	5	Now	$21.00
1998	5	Now	$20.00
1999	5	Now	$20.00
2000	6	2004	$23.00
2001	5	2006	$19.00

JANE BROOK ESTATE CHENIN BLANC WOOD-AGED ★★★★

before 1995		Prior	
1995	5	Now	$16.00
1996	4	Now	$12.50
1997	6	Now	$18.50
1998	7	2005	$21.00

No longer made.

JANE BROOK ESTATE METHODE CHAMPENOISE PINOT CHARDONNAY ★★★

1992	4	Prior	
1993	Not made		
1994	6	Prior	
1995	Not made		
1996	Not made		
1997	Not made		
1998	Not made		
1999	6	2007	$29.00
2000	6	2007	$28.00

JANE BROOK ESTATE METHODE CHAMPENOISE SHIRAZ ★★★

1992	5	Prior	
1993	Not made		
1994	Not made		
1995	Not made		
1996	6	2006	$31.00

1997	6	2007	$30.00
1998	Not made		
1999	5	2005	$24.00

JANE BROOK ESTATE SAUVIGNON BLANC ★★★

before 1998		Prior	
1998	6	Now	$22.00
1999	6	Now	$21.00
2000	6	2004	$20.00
2001	5	2004	$16.50
2002	6	2006	$19.50

JANE BROOK ESTATE SHIRAZ ★★★★

before 1995		Prior	
1995	7	2007	$31.00
1996	6	Now	$26.00
1997	5	Now	$21.00
1998	5	Now	$20.00
1999	6	2004	$23.00
2000	4	2004	$15.50
2001	6	2009	$22.00

JANE BROOK ESTATE VERDELHO ★★★

1998	4	Now	$15.50
1999	5	Now	$19.00
2000	6	Now	$22.00
2001	6	2004	$21.00
2002	6	2006	$21.00

***Jasper Hill** is a cool climate producer in Victoria's Heathcote area. The wines are both convincing and impressive. Winemaker: Ron Laughton.*

JASPER HILL EMILY'S PADDOCK SHIRAZ/CABERNET FRANC ★★★★★

1982	5	Prior	
1983	7	Now	$150.00
1984	5	Prior	
1985	6	Now	$120.00
1986	7	Now	$135.00
1987	5	Now	$96.00
1988	6	Now	$110.00
1989	5	Prior	
1990	6	Now	$100.00
1991	7	Now	$115.00
1992	7	Now	$110.00
1993	7	Now	$110.00
1994	6	2004	$92.00
1995	7	2005	$105.00
1996	7	2006	$100.00
1997	7	2007	$100.00
1998	7	2008	$96.00

1999	6	2006	$80.00
2000	7	2009	$90.00
2001	6	2009	$76.00

JASPER HILL GEORGIA'S PADDOCK SHIRAZ ★★★★

1982	6	Prior	
1983	7	Now	$125.00
1984	5	Prior	
1985	6	Now	$100.00
1986	7	Now	$115.00
1987	Not made		
1988	6	Now	$96.00
1989	4	Prior	
1990	6	Now	$90.00
1991	7	Now	$100.00
1992	7	Now	$98.00
1993	7	Now	$96.00
1994	6	Now	$80.00
1995	7	2005	$90.00
1996	7	2006	$88.00
1997	7	2007	$84.00
1998	7	2008	$82.00
1999	7	2007	$80.00
2000	7	2009	$78.00
2001	6	2009	$64.00

JASPER HILL GEORGIA'S PADDOCK RIESLING ★★★

before 1989		Prior	
1989	5	Now	$33.00
1990	6	Now	$39.00
1991	6	Now	$38.00
1992	6	Now	$37.00
1993	6	Now	$36.00
1994	5	Now	$29.00
1995	Not made		
1996	6	Now	$33.00
1997	6	Now	$32.00
1998	7	Now	$36.00
1999	7	2004	$35.00
2000	6	2004	$29.00
2001	6	2006	$28.00
2002	7	2008	$32.00

***Jim Barry Wines** are Clare Valley makers with a sizeable range of reliable wines including one of the world's best Shiraz. Winemaker: Mark Barry.*

JIM BARRY ARMAGH SHIRAZ ★★★★★

1985	6	2005	$210.00
1986	Not made		
1987	7	2008	$235.00

1988	7	2005	$230.00
1989	7	2010	$220.00
1990	7	2010	$215.00
1991	7	Now	$210.00
1992	7	2010	$200.00
1993	7	2015	$195.00
1994	7	2006	$190.00
1995	7	2010	$185.00
1996	7	2010	$180.00
1997	7	2010	$175.00
1998	7	2010	$170.00
1999	7	2015	$165.00
2000	7	2015	$160.00

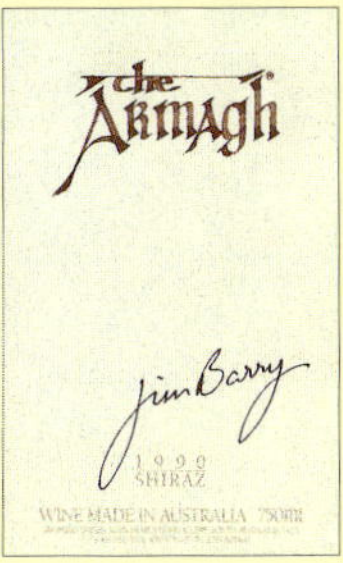

JIM BARRY CABERNET/MERLOT ★★★

before 1989		Prior	
1989	6	Now	$14.00
1990	6	Now	$13.50
1991	6	Now	$13.00
1992	6	Now	$12.50
1993	6	Now	$12.50
1994	7	Now	$14.00
1995	6	Now	$11.50
1996	7	Now	$13.00

Not made after 1996

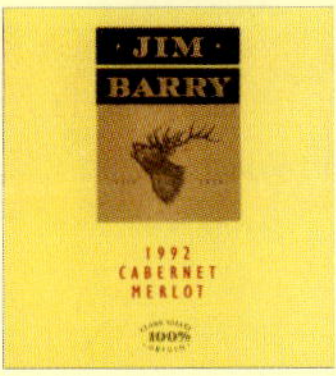

JIM BARRY CABERNET SAUVIGNON ★★★★

before 1985		Prior	
1985	5	Now	$34.00
1986	6	Now	$40.00
1987	6	Now	$38.00
1988	5	Now	$31.00
1989	7	Now	$42.00
1990	6	Now	$35.00
1991	Not made		
1992	7	Now	$39.00
1993	6	Now	$32.00
1994	7	2005	$36.00
1995	6	2006	$30.00
1996	6	2007	$29.00
1997	6	2008	$29.00
1998	6	2005	$28.00
1999	7	2007	$31.00

JIM BARRY CHARDONNAY ★★★

before 1990		Prior	
1990	6	Now	$20.00
1991	6	Now	$19.50
1992	6	Now	$18.50
1993	7	Now	$21.00
1994	No data		

1995	6	Now	$17.00
1996	6	Now	$16.50
1997	7	Now	$19.00
1998	7	Now	$18.50
1999	6	Now	$15.00
2000	5	Now	$12.00
2001	6	2004	$14.50

Discontinued.

JIM BARRY LODGE HILL RIESLING ★★★★

1997	6	Now	$20.00
1998	7	Now	$23.00
1999	7	2004	$22.00
2000	7	2005	$21.00
2001	7	2005	$21.00
2002	7	2006	$20.00

JIM BARRY McCRAE WOOD CABERNET/MALBEC ★★★★

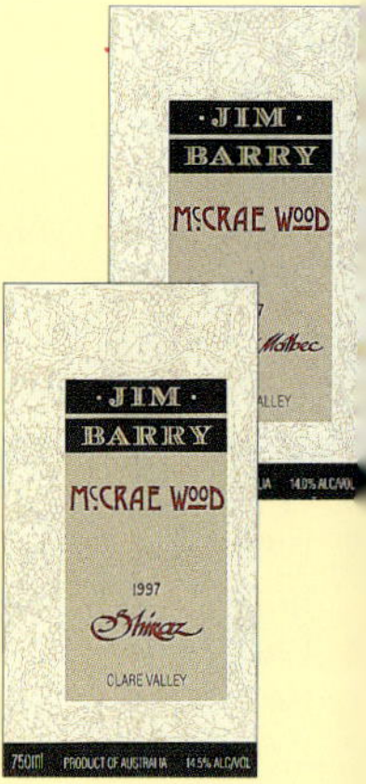

1995	6	Now	$33.00
1996	7	Now	$37.00
1997	7	2004	$36.00
1998	Not made		

Discontinued.

JIM BARRY McCRAE WOOD SHIRAZ ★★★★

1992	6	Now	$50.00
1993	7	Now	$58.00
1994	6	2005	$48.00
1995	7	2005	$54.00
1996	7	2005	$52.00
1997	7	2008	$50.00
1998	6	2008	$42.00
1999	7	2010	$48.00
2000	7	2010	$47.00

JIM BARRY WATERVALE RIESLING ★★★

before 1990		Prior	
1990	4	Now	$14.00
1991	4	Now	$13.50
1992	7	2005	$23.00
1993	6	Now	$19.00
1994	6	Now	$18.50
1995	6	Now	$18.00
1996	6	Now	$17.50
1997	6	Now	$17.00
1998	7	Prior	
1999	7	2010	$18.50
2000	6	2005	$15.50
2001	7	2010	$17.50
2002	7	2010	$17.00

Jud's Hill *is one of the Clare Valley's respected makers. Winemaker: Brian Barry.*

JUD'S HILL CABERNET SAUVIGNON ★★★★

before 1992		Prior	
1992	7	Now	$31.00
1993	7	Now	$30.00
1994	7	Now	$29.00
1995	7	Prior	
1996	7	Now	$27.00
1997	7	Now	$27.00
1998	7	Now	$26.00
1999	7	2004	$25.00
2000	7	2004	$24.00
2001	7	2004	$24.00
2002	7	2008	N/R

JUD'S HILL MERLOT ★★★★★

1992	7	Now	$48.00
1993	Not made		
1994	7	Now	$46.00
1995	7	Prior	
1996	7	Now	$43.00
1997	7	Prior	
1998	7	2007	$40.00
1999	7	2007	$39.00
2000	7	2007	$38.00
2001	6	2004	N/R
2002	7	2008	N/R

JUD'S HILL RIESLING ★★★

before 2000		Prior	
2000	7	Now	$19.00
2001	7	2004	$18.50
2002	7	2007	$18.00

Kangaroo Island Trading Company *is an operation where the grapes are grown by Genny and Michael Florance, but the production is by Caj and Jenny who also own the Chain of Ponds label. The grapes are grown on Kangaroo Island's first producing vineyard - the Florance vineyard. Winemaker: Neville Falkenberg.*

KANGAROO ISLAND CABERNET/MERLOT ★★★★

1991	5	Prior	
1992	5	Now	$36.00
1993	6	Now	$42.00
1994	7	Now	$47.00
1995	6	Now	$39.00
1996	7	Now	$45.00
1997	6	Now	$37.00

1998	6	Now	$36.00
1999	7	2005	$41.00
2000	6	2005	$34.00

***The Karina Vineyard** is a beautifully tended small vineyard in the Dromana area of the Mornington Peninsula. Winemaker: Gerard Terpstra.*

KARINA VINEYARD CABERNET/MERLOT ★★★★

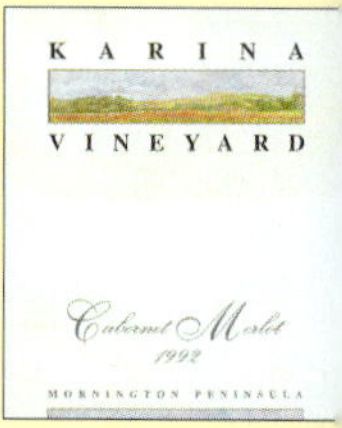

before 1994		Prior	
1994	7	Now	$28.00
1995	6	Now	$23.00
1996	4	Prior	
1997	6	Now	$22.00
1998	6	Now	$21.00
1999	6	2004	$20.00
2000	7	2005	$23.00
2001	7	2006	$22.00
2002	Not made		

KARINA VINEYARD CHARDONNAY ★★★★★

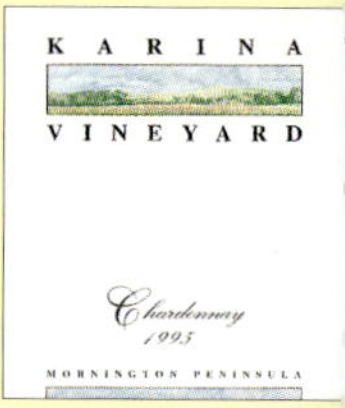

before 1996		Prior	
1996	5	Now	$18.50
1997	7	Now	$25.00
1998	7	Now	$24.00
1999	7	2004	$23.00
2000	7	2005	$23.00
2001	7	2006	$22.00
2002	7	2007	$21.00

KARINA VINEYARD RIESLING ★★★★

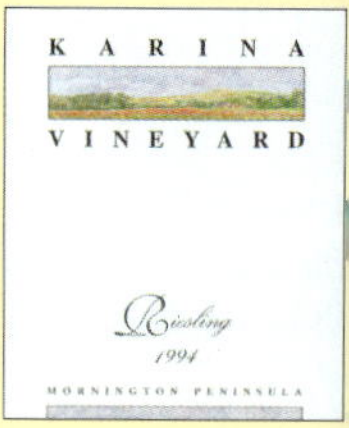

before 1995		Prior	
1995	7	Now	$22.00
1996	6	Now	$18.50
1997	7	Now	$21.00
1998	6	Now	$17.50
1999	7	Now	$20.00
2000	6	Now	$16.50
2001	6	Now	$16.00
2002	7	2004	$18.00

KARINA VINEYARD SAUVIGNON BLANC ★★★★

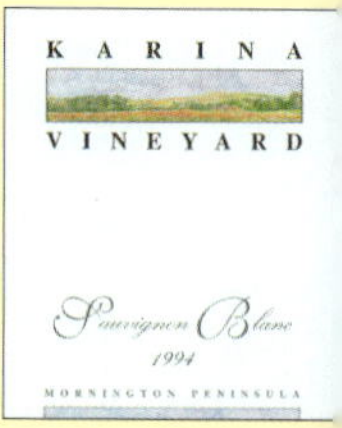

before 1997		Prior	
1997	6	Now	$20.00
1998	6	Now	$19.50
1999	7	Now	$22.00
2000	6	Now	$18.50
2001	7	Now	$21.00
2002	7	2004	$20.00

Karl Seppelt Estate *(formerly Grand Cru) is a small Springton (Eden Valley) producer whose wines are worthy of considerable respect. Winemaker: Karl Seppelt.*

KARL SEPPELT BRUT SAUVAGE ★★★★

1989	6	Prior	
1990	Not made		
1991	Not made		
1992	7	Now	$24.00
1993	Not made		
1997	6	2004	$19.50
1998	6	2005	$19.00

KARL SEPPELT ESTATE CABERNET SAUVIGNON ★★★★

before 1991		Prior	
1991	No data		
1992	No data		
1993	6	Now	$22.00
1994	7	Now	$24.00
1996	7	2005	$24.00
1997	6	2005	$20.00
1998	6	2006	$19.50

KARL SEPPELT ESTATE CHARDONNAY ★★★

before 1994		Prior	
1994	5	Now	$21.00
1995	6	Now	$25.00
1996	7	Now	$28.00
1997	Not made		
1998	Not made		
1999	Not made		
2000	5	Now	$17.50
2001	Not made		
2002	5	2004	$16.50

KARL SEPPELT ESTATE CHARDONNAY BRUT ★★★★

1990	6	Now	$23.00
1991	7	Now	$26.00
1992	7	Now	$25.00
1993	Not made		
1994	Not made		
1995	7	2005	$23.00
1996	No data		
1997	6	2004	$19.00
1998	6	2005	$18.00

KARL SEPPELT ESTATE MERLOT ★★★★

1998	6	2005	$24.00
1999	Not made		
2000	6	2006	$22.00
2001	6	2007	$22.00

KARL SEPPELT ESTATE SHIRAZ ★★★

1986	5	Prior	
1987	Not made		
1988	5	Now	$21.00
1989	5	Now	$21.00
1990	Not made		
1996	5	2005	$20.00
1997	6	2005	$23.00
1998	6	2005	$22.00
1999	6	2005	$22.00

KARL SEPPELT ESTATE SPARKLING SHIRAZ ★★★★

before 1992		Prior	
1992	6	Now	$25.00
1993	Not made		
1994	6	Now	$24.00
1995	Not made		
1996	6	2005	$22.00
1997	6	2005	$22.00

***Karriview**, in Western Australia's Denmark region, pioneered the area's production of Pinot Noir and Chardonnay with their 1989 vintage. Their quality is such that others will surely follow. Winemaker: John Wade.*

KARRIVIEW CHARDONNAY ★★★★

before 1993		Prior	
1993	6	Now	$32.00
1994	5	Prior	
1995	7	Now	$35.00
1996	6	Now	$29.00
1997	7	Now	$33.00
1998	6	Now	$28.00
1999	7	Now	$31.00

KARRIVIEW PINOT NOIR ★★★★

before 1994		Prior	
1994	7	Now	$38.00
1995	5	Now	$26.00
1996	6	Now	$31.00
1997	No data		
1998	5	Now	$24.00

***Katnook** are Coonawarra makers of wines of extremely impressive quality. Winemaker: Wayne Stehbens.*

KATNOOK CABERNET SAUVIGNON ★★★★★

1980	6	Now	$94.00
1981	5	Now	$76.00
1982	5	Now	$74.00
1983	4	Now	$58.00

1984	5	Now	$70.00
1985	5	Now	$68.00
1986	6	Now	$80.00
1987	5	Now	$64.00
1988	5	Now	$62.00
1989	Not made		
1990	6	Now	$70.00
1991	6	Now	$68.00
1992	6	Now	$66.00
1993	5	Now	$54.00
1994	6	Now	$62.00
1995	5	Now	$50.00
1996	6	Now	$58.00
1997	7	2008	$66.00
1998	7	2009	$64.00
1999	7	2010	$62.00
2000	6	2009	$52.00

KATNOOK CHARDONNAY ★★★★

1980	5	Now	$48.00
1981	4	Now	$37.00
1982	5	Now	$45.00
1983	4	Now	$35.00
1984	5	Now	$42.00
1985	5	Now	$41.00
1986	6	Now	$48.00
1987	5	Now	$39.00
1988	5	Now	$38.00
1989	6	Now	$44.00
1990	7	Now	$50.00
1991	5	Now	$34.00
1992	6	Now	$40.00
1993	5	Now	$32.00
1994	7	Now	$44.00
1995	7	Now	$43.00
1996	6	Now	$36.00
1997	6	2004	$35.00
1998	7	2005	$39.00
1999	6	2005	$32.00
2000	6	2006	$32.00

KATNOOK ESTATE CHARDONNAY BRUT ★★★★

1984	5	Now	$38.00
1985	5	Now	$37.00
1986	5	Now	$36.00
1987	5	Now	$35.00
1988	Not made		
1989	Not made		
1990	6	Now	$38.00
1991	Not made		
1992	Not made		

1993	6	Now	$35.00
1994	5	Now	$28.00
1995	6	Now	$33.00
1996	7	Now	$37.00

KATNOOK MERLOT ★★★★

1987	4	Now	$39.00
1988	5	Now	$47.00
1989	Not made		
1990	5	Now	$45.00
1991	Not made		
1992	6	Now	$50.00
1993	5	Now	$41.00
1994	6	Now	$48.00
1995	5	Now	$38.00
1996	7	Now	$52.00
1997	6	2004	$43.00
1998	7	2006	$49.00
1999	6	2005	$41.00
2000	6	2005	$40.00

KATNOOK ODYSSEY (CABERNET) ★★★★★

1991	7	2006	$100.00
1992	7	2007	$100.00
1993	Not made		
1994	7	2010	$94.00
1995	Not made		
1996	7	2012	$88.00
1997	6	2010	$74.00
1998	6	2011	$72.00

KATNOOK RIESLING ★★★

1980	6	Now	$32.00
1981	5	Now	$26.00
1982	5	Now	$25.00
1983	Not made		
1984	5	Now	$23.00
1985	5	Now	$23.00
1986	6	Now	$26.00
1987	5	Now	$21.00
1988	6	Now	$25.00
1989	6	Now	$24.00
1990	Not made		
1994	6	Now	$23.00
1995	5	Now	$18.50
1996	6	Now	$21.00
1997	7	Now	$24.00
1998	5	Now	$17.00
1999	7	Now	$23.00
2000	6	2004	$19.00
2001	6	2005	$18.50

KATNOOK SAUVIGNON BLANC ★★★

before 1991		Prior	
1991	6	Now	$33.00
1992	6	Now	$32.00
1993	5	Now	$25.00
1994	6	Now	$30.00
1995	7	Now	$34.00
1996	7	Now	$33.00
1997	6	Now	$27.00
1998	6	Now	$26.00
1999	6	Now	$26.00
2000	6	Now	$25.00
2001	6	2004	$24.00

***Kays** are long established and respected McLaren Vale producers with a large range of traditionally styled wines. Winemaker: Colin Kay.*

KAYS AMERY BLOCK 6 SHIRAZ ★★★★

before 1989		Prior	
1989	6	Now	$60.00
1990	7	Now	$68.00
1991	6	Now	$56.00
1992	7	Now	$64.00
1993	6	Now	$54.00
1994	6	Now	$52.00
1995	6	Now	$50.00
1996	7	2006	$56.00
1997	6	2004	$48.00
1998	7	2008	$54.00
1999	6	2007	$45.00
2000	7	2010	$50.00
2001	7	2011	$49.00
2002	7	2012	$48.00

KAYS AMERY CABERNET SAUVIGNON ★★★

before 1992		Prior	
1992	7	Now	$36.00
1993	5	Now	$25.00
1994	6	Now	$29.00
1995	5	Now	$24.00
1996	7	2004	$32.00
1997	6	Now	$27.00
1998	7	2006	$30.00
1999	6	2007	$25.00
2000	7	2008	$29.00
2001	7	2010	$28.00
2002	7	2012	$27.00

KAYS AMERY GRENACHE ★★★

1994	5	Now	$19.00
1995	6	Now	$22.00
1996	7	Now	$25.00

1997	Not made		
1998	7	Now	$23.00
1999	Not made		
2000	Not made		
2001	7	2005	$21.00

KAYS AMERY HILLSIDE SHIRAZ ★★★★

1997	7	2005	$40.00
1998	7	2010	$39.00
1999	7	2008	$38.00
2000	7	2010	$37.00
2001	7	2011	$36.00
2002	7	2012	$35.00

KAYS AMERY MERLOT ★★★★

1998	7	2005	$29.00
1999	6	2006	$24.00
2000	6	2006	$24.00
2001	7	2007	$27.00
2002	7	2008	$26.00

KAYS AMERY SHIRAZ ★★★★

1992	6	Now	$31.00
1993	5	Now	$25.00
1994	6	Now	$29.00
1995	6	Now	$28.00
1996	7	2004	$32.00
1997	6	Now	$26.00
1998	7	2006	$30.00
1999	7	2008	$29.00
2000	7	2008	$28.00
2001	7	2010	$27.00
2002	7	2010	$27.00

***Kellybrook Winery** is a Yarra Valley producer whose peerless cider-making mastery unfairly limits the respect accorded the very fine wines. The sparkling wine is particularly recommendable. Winemakers: Darren Kelly and Philip Kelly.*

KELLYBROOK CABERNET SAUVIGNON (/MERLOT) ★★★★

before 1988		Prior	
1988	6	Now	$37.00
1989	Not made		
1990	Not made		
1991	5	Now	$28.00
1992	6	Now	$33.00
1993	6	Now	$32.00
1994	6	Now	$31.00
1995	Not made		
1996	6	Now	$29.00

1997	7	2007	$33.00
1998	6	2008	$27.00
1999	7	2010	$31.00
2000	7	2010	$30.00
2001	7	2011	$29.00
2002	7	2012	$28.00

KELLYBROOK CHARDONNAY ★★★

before 1996		Prior	
1996	6	Now	$26.00
1997	6	Now	$26.00
1998	5	Now	$21.00
1999	6	Now	$24.00
2000	6	2004	$23.00
2001	7	2005	$26.00
2002	7	2006	$26.00

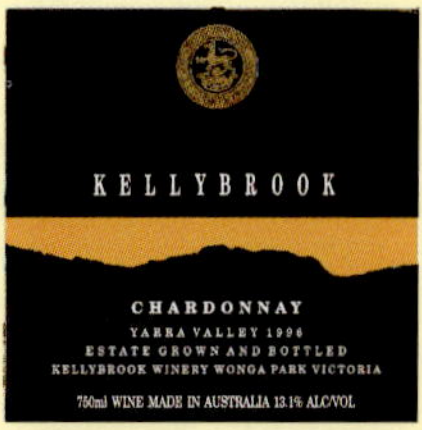

KELLYBROOK PINOT NOIR ★★★

before 1994		Prior	
1994	5	Now	$29.00
1995	5	Now	$28.00
1996	5	Now	$27.00
1997	5	Now	$26.00
1998	6	Now	$31.00
1999	6	2004	$30.00
2000	6	2005	$29.00
2001	6	2006	$28.00

KELLYBROOK PINOT NOIR/CHARDONNAY METHODE CHAMPENOISE ★★★★★

before 1990		Prior	
1990	6	Now	$36.00
1991	6	Prior	
1992	6	Prior	
1993	6	Now	$33.00
1994	6	Now	$32.00
1995	6	Now	$31.00
1996	Not made		
1997	Not made		
1998	6	Now	$29.00

KELLYBROOK SHIRAZ ★★★★

1984	6	Prior	
1985	Not made		
1986	Not made		
1987	Not made		
1988	6	Now	$39.00
1989	Not made		
1990	Not made		
1991	5	Now	$29.00
1992	Not made		
1993	5	Now	$28.00

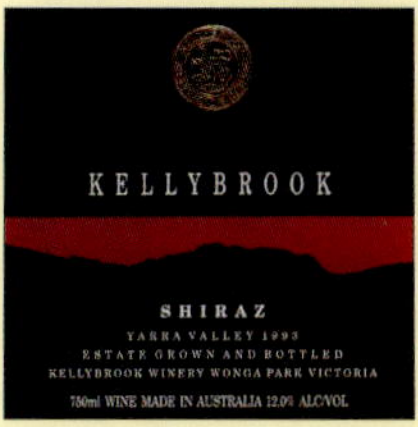

1994	7	Now	$38.00
1995	4	Now	$21.00
1996	6	Now	$31.00
1997	7	2004	$35.00
1998	6	2005	$29.00
1999	6	2006	$28.00
2000	6	2007	$27.00
2001	7	2008	$31.00
2002	7	2007	$30.00

***Killerby Vineyards** is a Capel, and now also Margaret River (Western Australia) area producer whose change of name was accompanied by a marked quality improvement. The acquisition of the new Margaret River vineyard augurs well for still greater vinous achievements. Winemaker: Paul Boulden.*

KILLERBY CABERNET SAUVIGNON ★★★★

before 1988		Prior	
1988	Not made		
1989	6	Now	$35.00
1990	Not made		
1991	5	Prior	
1992	6	Prior	
1993	6	Now	$31.00
1994	5	Now	$25.00
1995	5	Now	$24.00
1996	5	Now	$24.00
1997	5	2004	$23.00
1998	7	2008	$31.00
1999	7	2009	$30.00
2000	7	2010	$30.00

KILLERBY CHARDONNAY ★★★★★

before 1989		Prior	
1989	5	Now	$46.00
1990	4	Prior	
1991	5	Now	$43.00
1992	5	Now	$42.00
1993	4	Now	$32.00
1994	6	Now	$47.00
1995	5	Now	$38.00
1996	6	Now	$45.00
1997	7	Now	$50.00
1998	6	2004	$42.00
1999	5	2005	$34.00
2000	7	2005	$46.00
2001	5	2005	$32.00

KILLERBY SEMILLON ★★★★

before 1989		Prior	
1989	6	Now	$38.00
1990	4	Prior	

1991	5	Now	$30.00
1992	5	Now	$29.00
1993	4	Now	$23.00
1994	6	Now	$33.00
1995	5	Now	$27.00
1996	6	Now	$31.00
1997	4	Now	$20.00
1998	5	Now	$24.00
1999	5	Now	$24.00
2000	5	2004	$23.00

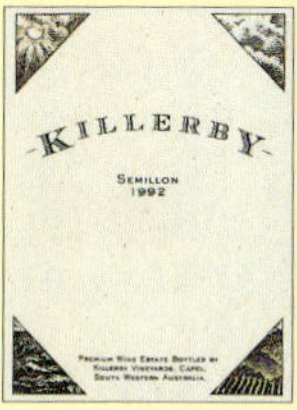

KILLERBY SHIRAZ ★★★★

1989	3	Prior	
1990	Not made		
1991	5	Now	$31.00
1992	4	Prior	
1993	5	Now	$29.00
1994	6	Now	$34.00
1995	6	Now	$33.00
1996	5	Now	$27.00
1997	5	Now	$26.00
1998	7	2008	$35.00
1999	5	2008	$24.00
2000	6	2008	$28.00

***Knappstein Wines** (formerly Tim Knappstein Wines) is a good quality producer in the Clare Valley. In 1995 a new 120 acre vineyard, Yertabulti, was developed. Winemaker: Andrew Hardy.*

KNAPPSTEIN CABERNET/MERLOT ★★★

before 1991		Prior	
1991	7	Now	$32.00
1992	6	Now	$27.00
1993	6	Now	$26.00
1994	7	Now	$30.00
1995	6	Now	$25.00
1996	6	Now	$24.00
1997	5	Now	$19.50
1998	6	Now	$22.00
1999	6	Now	$22.00
2000	6	2004	$21.00

KNAPPSTEIN CHARDONNAY ★★★★

before 1998		Prior	
1998	6	Now	$20.00
1999	6	Now	$20.00
2000	6	Now	$19.50
2001	6	Now	$18.50
2002	7	Now	$21.00

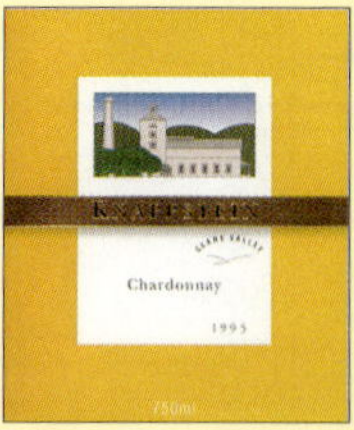

KNAPPSTEIN ENTERPRISE CABERNET SAUVIGNON ★★★★

before 1985		Prior	
1985	5	Now	$50.00
1986	7	Now	$70.00
1987	4	Now	$38.00
1988	6	Now	$56.00
1989	6	Now	$54.00
1990	7	Now	$62.00
1991	Not made		
1992	Not made		
1993	6	Now	$48.00
1994	7	2005	$54.00
1995	6	2006	$46.00
1996	7	2006	$52.00
1997	5	2005	$36.00
1998	7	2008	$49.00
1999	7	2008	$47.00

KNAPPSTEIN ENTERPRISE SHIRAZ ★★★★

1994	7	2004	$50.00
1995	6	Now	$42.00
1996	6	2004	$41.00
1997	7	2007	$46.00
1998	7	2008	$45.00
1999	7	2008	$44.00

KNAPPSTEIN GEWURZTRAMINER ★★★

before 1998		Prior	
1998	6	Now	$20.00
1999	6	Now	$20.00
2000	6	Now	$19.50
2001	7	Now	$22.00

KNAPPSTEIN RIESLING ★★★

before 1985		Prior	
1985	7	Now	$38.00
1986	6	Now	$31.00
1987	6	Now	$30.00
1988	6	Now	$30.00
1989	6	Now	$29.00
1990	7	Now	$33.00
1991	5	Now	$22.00
1992	6	Now	$26.00
1993	6	Now	$25.00
1994	6	Now	$25.00
1995	7	Now	$28.00
1996	6	Now	$23.00
1997	7	Now	$26.00
1998	6	2004	$22.00
1999	7	2006	$25.00

2000	7	2009	$24.00
2001	6	Now	$20.00
2002	7	2012	$23.00

KNAPPSTEIN SHIRAZ ★★★★

1994	6	Now	$22.00
1995	6	Now	$21.00
1996	7	Now	$24.00
1997	7	Now	$23.00
1998	7	2004	$23.00
1999	7	2005	$22.00
2000	7	2006	$21.00

KNAPPSTEIN SEMILLON/
SAUVIGNON BLANC ★★★

1997	6	Prior	
1998	7	Now	$22.00
1999	6	Now	$18.00
2000	7	Now	$20.00
2001	7	nOW	$20.00

***Knight's Granite Hille** - see Granite Hills.*

***Krondorf** was a Barossa winery processing grapes from far afield as well as from the original Tanunda area vineyard. It is owned by Beringer Blass who have now discontinued the label. Winemaker: Nick Walker.*

KRONDORF BAROSSA RIESLING ★★★

before 1991		Prior	
1991	6	Now	$12.00
1992	7	Now	$14.00
1993	6	Now	$11.50
1994	5	Now	$9.50
1995	7	Now	$12.50
1996	7	Now	$12.50
1997	7	Now	$12.00
1998	7	Now	$11.50

KRONDORF CHARDONNAY ★★★

before 1991		Prior	
1991	6	Now	$12.00
1992	5	Now	$9.75
1993	6	Now	$11.50
1994	7	Now	$13.00
1995	7	Now	$12.50
1996	7	Now	$12.00
1997	7	Now	$11.50

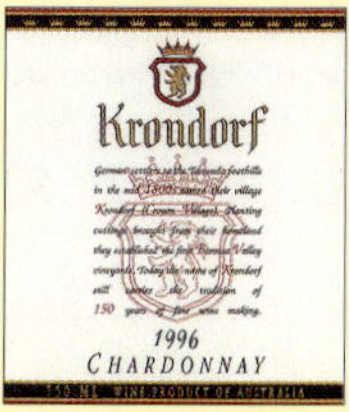

KRONDORF FAMILY RESERVE
CHARDONNAY ★★★★

1985	7	Now	$24.00
1986	7	Now	$23.00
1987	5	Prior	

1988	5	Now	$15.50
1989	6	Now	$18.00
1990	7	Now	$20.00
1991	6	Now	$17.00
1992	6	Now	$16.50
1993	6	Now	$16.00
1994	7	Now	$18.00
1995	6	Now	$15.00
1996	7	Now	$17.00
1997	6	Now	$14.00

KRONDORF FAMILY RESERVE
SHOW CABERNET ★★★★

1991	5	Now	$17.00
1992	6	Now	$20.00
1993	5	Now	$16.00
1994	7	Now	$22.00
1995	6	2004	$18.50
1996	7	2004	$21.00

KRONDORF SEMILLON ★★★

before 1991		Prior	
1991	6	Now	$13.00
1992	5	Now	$10.50
1993	6	Now	$12.00
1994	5	Now	$10.00
1995	6	Now	$11.50
1996	7	Now	$13.00
1997	7	Now	$12.50
1998	7	Now	$12.50

KRONDORF SHIRAZ ★★★

1993	5	Now	$13.50
1994	5	Now	$13.00
1995	4	Now	$10.00
1996	6	Now	$14.50
1997	5	Now	$12.00

***Lake Breeze Wines** is a Langhorne Creek vineyard which has been producing grapes since 1930, but only (comparitively) recently making wine. The quality so far has been admirable. Winemaker: Greg Follett.*

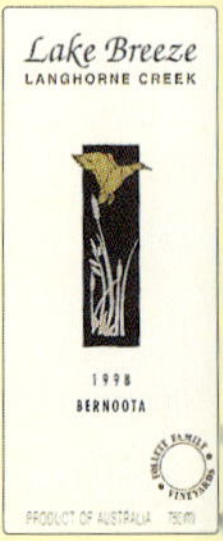

LAKE BREEZE BERNOOTA
SHIRAZ/CABERNET ★★★

1992	7	2004	$29.00
1993	6	Prior	
1994	6	Now	$24.00
1995	5	Now	$19.50
1996	7	2005	$26.00
1997	5	Now	$18.00
1998	7	2004	$25.00

1999	6	2005	$20.00
2000	6	2007	$20.00
2001	6	2007	$19.50

LAKE BREEZE CABERNET SAUVIGNON ★★★★

1991	5	Prior	
1992	7	2004	$36.00
1993	6	Now	$30.00
1994	6	2004	$29.00
1995	6	Now	$28.00
1996	6	2007	$27.00
1997	5	2005	$22.00
1998	6	2008	$25.00
1999	5	2005	$20.00
2000	6	2008	$24.00
2001	6	2007	$23.00

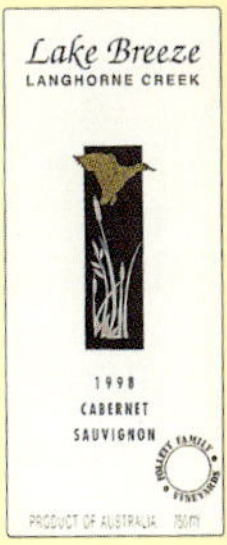

LAKE BREEZE WINEMAKER'S SELECTION SHIRAZ ★★★★★

1994	7	2004	$49.00
1995	Not made		
1996	7	2008	$46.00
1997	Not made		
1998	7	2010	$43.00
1999	6	2006	$36.00
2000	7	2010	$41.00
2001	Not made		

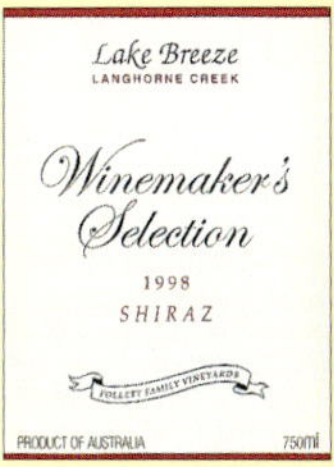

Lake George Winery *was the seminal Canberra district winemaking venture, and has remained small and markedly individual. It has now been sold, and recent vintages remain a mystery. Winemaker: Angus Campbell.*

LAKE GEORGE CHARDONNAY ★★★

before 1995		Prior	
1995	5	Now	$30.00
1996	5	Now	$30.00

LAKE GEORGE MERLOT ★★★

1991	4	Now	$27.00
1992	3	Prior	
1994	3	Prior	
1994	4	Now	$25.00
1995	5	Now	$30.00
1996	6	Now	$36.00

LAKE GEORGE PINOT NOIR ★★★

before 1991		Prior	
1991	3	Now	$25.00
1992	3	Prior	
1993	3	Now	$24.00
1994	4	Now	$31.00
1995	5	Now	$38.00
1996	5	Now	$37.00

***Lakes Folly** is a superb small vineyard at Pokolbin. The wines are among the most sought-after in Australia. Winemaker: Rodney Kempe.*

LAKES FOLLY (CABERNET SAUVIGNON/PETIT VERDOT/SHIRAZ/MERLOT)

★★★★★

before 1980		Prior	
1980	5	Now	$74.00
1981	6	Now	$88.00
1982	4	Prior	
1983	5	Prior	
1984	3	Prior	
1985	6	Now	$78.00
1986	5	Now	$62.00
1987	6	Now	$72.00
1988	5	Now	$58.00
1989	7	Now	$80.00
1990	5	Now	$56.00
1991	6	Now	$64.00
1992	5	Now	$52.00
1993	7	Now	$72.00
1994	6	2007	$60.00
1995	5	Now	$48.00
1996	7	2010	$66.00
1997	6	2008	$54.00
1998	7	2014	$62.00
1999	6	2011	$50.00
2000	7	2014	$58.00
2001	6	2014	$48.00
2002	6	2014	$47.00

LAKES FOLLY CHARDONNAY

★★★★★

before 1989		Prior	
1989	6	Now	$66.00
1990	5	Prior	
1991	6	Now	$62.00
1992	6	Now	$60.00
1993	6	Prior	
1994	7	Now	$66.00
1995	6	Now	$54.00
1996	7	Now	$62.00
1997	6	Now	$52.00
1998	5	Now	$42.00
1999	6	2004	$49.00
2000	7	2004	$54.00
2001	6	2005	$46.00
2002	5	2006	$37.00

***Lark Hill** is a Canberra district maker of the area's best wines, a fact not probably unconnected with the vineyard's altitude - over 800 metres. Winemakers: Dr David and Sue Carpenter.*

LARK HILL CABERNET/MERLOT ★★★★

1991	6	Now	$34.00
1992	5	Now	$27.00
1993	7	Now	$37.00
1994	6	Now	$31.00
1995	7	Now	$35.00
1996	7	Now	$34.00
1997	6	Now	$28.00
1998	7	2004	$32.00
1999	7	2005	$31.00
2000	6	2004	$26.00

LARK HILL CHARDONNAY ★★★★

before 1991		Prior	
1991	6	Now	$35.00
1992	5	Prior	
1993	7	Now	$39.00
1994	5	Prior	
1995	6	Now	$31.00
1996	7	Now	$36.00
1997	7	Now	$35.00
1998	6	Now	$29.00
1999	6	2004	$28.00
2000	7	2005	$32.00
2001	7	2006	$31.00

LARK HILL METHODE CHAMPENOISE ★★★★

1993	6	Now	$31.00
1994	6	Now	$30.00
1995	6	Now	$29.00
1996	7	Now	$33.00
1997	7	2004	$32.00

LARK HILL PINOT NOIR ★★★★★

1994	5	Prior	
1995	5	Now	$32.00
1996	7	Now	$44.00
1997	7	Now	$42.00
1998	6	Now	$35.00
1999	7	2004	$40.00
2000	7	2005	$39.00
2001	7	2006	$38.00
2002	7	2008	$36.00

LARK HILL RIESLING ★★★★

before 1993		Prior	
1993	6	Now	$27.00
1994	7	Now	$31.00

1995	5	Prior	
1996	6	Now	$25.00
1997	7	Now	$28.00
1998	5	Prior	
1999	7	Now	$26.00
2000	7	2004	$26.00
2001	7	2005	$25.00
2002	7	2005	$24.00
2003	7	2006	$23.00

***Leasingham** is a 100 year old Clare Valley producer now owned and operated by BRL Hardy. Winemakers: Kerri Thompson and Anna Flowerday.*

LEASINGHAM BIN 7 RIESLING ★★★

1994	4	Now	$13.00
1995	4	Now	$13.00
1996	6	Now	$18.50
1997	7	Now	$21.00
1998	6	Now	$17.50
1999	5	Now	$14.00
2000	6	2010	$16.50
2001	6	2012	$16.00
2001	7	2020	$18.50

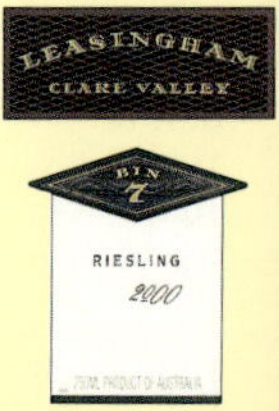

LEASINGHAM BIN 37 CHARDONNAY ★★★

before 1996		Prior	
1996	5	Now	$14.00
1997	6	Now	$16.50
1998	6	Now	$16.00
1999	No data		
2000	No data		
2001	5	2005	$12.00

LEASINGHAM BIN 56 CABERNET SAUVIGNON/MALBEC ★★★

before 1980		Prior	
1980	7	Now	$42.00
1981	7	Now	$41.00
1982	5	Now	$28.00
1983	7	Now	$39.00
1984	7	Now	$37.00
1985	5	Now	$26.00
1986	5	Now	$25.00
1987	5	Now	$24.00
1988	6	Now	$28.00
1989	7	Now	$32.00
1990	7	2005	$31.00
1991	6	Now	$26.00
1992	6	Now	$25.00

1993	5	Now	$20.00
1994	7	Now	$28.00
1995	6	Now	$23.00
1996	5	Now	$19.00
1997	5	Now	$18.00
1998	7	2010	$25.00
1999	6	2008	$20.00
2000	6	2006	$20.00
2001	7	2025	$22.00

LEASINGHAM BIN 61 SHIRAZ ★★★

1988	5	Now	$28.00
1989	4	Now	$22.00
1990	7	Now	$37.00
1991	7	Now	$36.00
1992	7	Now	$35.00
1993	5	Now	$24.00
1994	7	2005	$33.00
1995	6	2004	$27.00
1996	5	2004	$22.00
1997	5	Now	$21.00
1998	7	2005	$29.00
1999	5	2004	$20.00
2000	6	2008	$23.00
2001	7	2012	$27.00

LEASINGHAM CLASSIC CLARE CABERNET SAUVIGNON ★★★★

1991	6	Now	$54.00
1992	7	Now	$62.00
1993	6	Now	$50.00
1994	7	2005	$58.00
1995	6	2004	$48.00
1996	7	2010	$54.00
1997	5	Now	$38.00
1998	7	2010	$52.00
1999	5	2010	$36.00

LEASINGHAM CLASSIC CLARE SHIRAZ ★★★★

1991	7	Now	$64.00
1992	6	Now	$54.00
1993	5	Now	$43.00
1994	7	2010	$58.00
1995	6	2007	$49.00
1996	7	2015	$56.00
1997	5	2007	$39.00
1998	7	2010	$52.00
1999	5	2008	$36.00

LEASINGHAM CLASSIC CLARE SPARKLING SHIRAZ ★★★★

1991	5	Now	$33.00
1992	6	Now	$39.00
1993	Not made		
1994	6	2005	$37.00

***Leconfield**, a 25 hectare Coonawarra vineyard owned and operated by the Hamilton Wine Group, specialises in premium Cabernets. Winemaker: Paul Gordon.*

LECONFIELD CABERNET SAUVIGNON ★★★★

before 1982		Prior	
1982	6	Now	$54.00
1983	Not made		
1984	4	Prior	
1985	Not made		
1986	4	Prior	
1987	Not made		
1988	5	Now	$38.00
1989	4	Now	$29.00
1990	6	Now	$43.00
1991	7	Now	$49.00
1992	5	Now	$34.00
1993	6	2004	$39.00
1994	7	2005	$45.00
1995	5	Now	$31.00
1996	6	2006	$36.00
1997	7	2008	$41.00
1998	6	2010	$34.00
1999	5	2009	$27.00
2000	6	2010	$32.00

LECONFIELD CHARDONNAY ★★★

before 1991		Prior	
1991	6	Now	$29.00
1992	5	Now	$23.00
1993	6	Now	$27.00
1994	6	Now	$27.00
1995	4	Now	$17.50
1996	6	Now	$25.00
1997	5	Now	$20.00
1998	5	2004	$20.00
1999	5	2005	$19.00
2000	6	2008	$22.00
2001	6	2005	$22.00

LECONFIELD MERLOT ★★★★

1991	7	Now	$42.00
1992	6	Now	$34.00
1993	6	Now	$33.00

1994	7	Now	$38.00
1995	6	2004	$32.00
1996	6	2005	$31.00
1997	No data		
2000	5	2008	$24.00

LECONFIELD RIESLING ★★★★

1990	5	Now	$21.00
1991	5	Now	$21.00
1992	6	Now	$24.00
1993	5	Now	$20.00
1994	7	Now	$27.00
1995	5	Now	$18.50
1996	7	2006	$25.00
1997	7	2007	$24.00
1998	6	2006	$20.00
1999	4	2004	$13.00
2000	6	2010	$19.50
2001	6	2006	$19.00
2002	7	2007	$21.00

LECONFIELD SHIRAZ ★★★★

before 1990		Prior	
1990	6	Now	$42.00
1991	5	Now	$34.00
1992	5	Now	$33.00
1993	6	Now	$39.00
1994	5	Now	$31.00
1995	7	2005	$43.00
1996	6	2006	$35.00
1997	7	2007	$40.00
1998	5	Now	$28.00
1999	5	2004	$27.00
2000	5	2005	$26.00

***Leeuwin Estate** is Australia's largest extreme quality producer, the grapes being grown on their 90 hectare Margaret River vineyard. Their habit of affixing an Art Series label to the best vintages (at very substantial prices) makes the lesser labelled wines remarkably good buying. Winemaker: Bob Cartwright.*

LEEUWIN ESTATE CABERNET SAUVIGNON ★★★★

before 1985		Prior	
1985	6	Now	$82.00
1986	6	Prior	
1987	7	Now	$90.00
1988	6	Now	$74.00
1989	7	Now	$84.00
1990	5	Now	$58.00
1991	6	Now	$68.00

1992	6	Now	$66.00
1993	5	Now	$52.00
1994	5	Now	$52.00
1995	6	Now	$60.00
1996	5	Now	$49.00
1997	6	Now	$56.00
1998	5	Now	$46.00
1999	7	2005	$62.00
2000	5	2005	$43.00

LEEUWIN ESTATE CHARDONNAY

★★★★★

before 1985		Prior	
1985	7	Now	$130.00
1986	6	Now	$110.00
1987	7	Now	$125.00
1988	6	Now	$100.00
1989	6	Now	$100.00
1990	5	Now	$82.00
1991	6	Now	$96.00
1992	6	Now	$92.00
1993	6	Now	$90.00
1994	6	Now	$88.00
1995	6	Now	$84.00
1996	5	Now	$68.00
1997	6	Now	$80.00
1998	5	Now	$64.00
1999	5	2004	$62.00
2000	7	2005	$86.00

LEEUWIN ESTATE PINOT NOIR

★★★★★

before 1993		Prior	
1993	4	Now	$36.00
1994	5	Now	$44.00
1995	6	Prior	
1996	6	Now	$49.00
1997	5	Now	$40.00
1998	4	Now	$31.00
1999	4	Now	$30.00
2000	4	Now	$29.00
2001	6	2004	$42.00

LEEUWIN ESTATE RIESLING

★★★★

before 1993		Prior	
1993	5	Now	$23.00
1994	5	Now	$22.00
1995	6	Now	$26.00
1996	6	Now	$25.00
1997	5	Now	$20.00
1998	6	Now	$24.00

1999	6	Now	$23.00
2000	7	Now	$26.00
2001	6	Now	$22.00
2002	6	Now	$21.00

LEEUWIN ESTATE SAUVIGNON BLANC ★★★★

before 1996		Prior	
1995	6	Now	$37.00
1996	6	Now	$36.00
1997	5	Now	$29.00
1998	6	Now	$34.00
1999	5	Now	$27.00
2000	6	Now	$32.00
2001	6	Now	$31.00
2002	7	Now	$35.00

Lehmann *- see Peter Lehmann.*

Leland Estate *is an Adelaide Hills vineyard established by Robb Cootes (of Yalumba fame) 500 metres above sea level. Winemaker: Robb Cootes.*

LELAND ESTATE ADELE (SPARKLING) ★★★★

before 1998		Prior	
1998	6	Now	$27.00
1999	Not made		
2000	7	Now	$30.00

LELAND ESTATE PINOT NOIR ★★★★

before 1996		Prior	
1996	7	Now	$34.00
1997	6	Prior	
1998	6	Now	$28.00
1999	6	Now	$27.00
2000	5	Now	$22.00
2001	6	2004	$25.00

LELAND ESTATE SAUVIGNON BLANC ★★★

before 1998		Prior	
1998	6	Now	$21.00
1999	6	Now	$21.00
2000	7	Now	$23.00
2001	6	Now	$19.50
2002	6	Now	$19.00

Lenswood Vineyards *is the name under which Tim Knappstein is producing high quality wines from his Lenswood (Adelaide Hills) plantings. Winemaker: Tim Knappstein.*

LENSWOOD CHARDONNAY ★★★★★

before 1995		Prior	
1995	7	Now	$43.00
1996	6	Now	$36.00

1997	6	Now	$34.00
1998	7	Now	$39.00
1999	6	Now	$32.00
2000	7	2004	$37.00
2001	7	2004	$36.00

LENSWOOD PINOT NOIR ★★★★

before 1993		Prior	
1993	6	Now	$60.00
1994	6	Prior	
1995	5	Prior	
1996	7	Now	$64.00
1997	6	Now	$54.00
1998	7	Now	$60.00
1999	6	2004	$50.00
2000	7	2005	$58.00
2001	6	2005	$48.00
2002	7	2007	$54.00

LENSWOOD SAUVIGNON BLANC ★★★★

before 1996		Prior	
1996	6	Now	$24.00
1997	6	Prior	
1998	7	Now	$26.00
1999	5	Now	$18.50
2000	7	Now	$25.00
2001	7	2003	$24.00
2002	7	2004	$23.00

***Lenton Brae** is a Margaret River vineyard and winery (designed and built by the architect/owner). Wine quality has been a little patchy, but the better vintages show much promise. Winemaker: Edward Tomlinson.*

LENTON BRAE "MARGARET RIVER" (CABERNET SAUVIGNON/MERLOT/ PETIT VERDOT) ★★★★

1988	6	Now	$58.00
1989	4	Prior	
1990	5	Prior	
1991	6	Now	$52.00
1992	4	Prior	
1993	3	Prior	
1994	6	Now	$48.00
1995	5	Now	$39.00
1996	6	2005	$45.00
1997	5	2008	$37.00
1998	6	2010	$43.00
1999	6	2012	$41.00
2000	5	2015	$33.00

LENTON BRAE CABERNET/MERLOT ★★★

1991	5	Prior	
1992	Not made		
1993	3	Prior	
1994	5	Now	$27.00
1995	5	Now	$26.00
1996	4	Now	$20.00
1997	4	2004	$20.00
1998	6	2006	$29.00
1999	6	2007	$28.00
2000	6	2007	$27.00
2001	7	2008	$31.00

LENTON BRAE CHARDONNAY ★★★★

before 1992		Prior	
1992	7	2004	$50.00
1993	4	Prior	
1994	4	Prior	
1995	4	Prior	
1996	5	Now	$32.00
1997	7	2005	$43.00
1998	7	2006	$42.00
1999	5	2005	$29.00
2000	5	2005	$28.00
2001	6	2008	$33.00

LENTON BRAE SEMILLON/SAUVIGNON BLANC ★★★★

before 1995		Prior	
1995	7	2005	$30.00
1996	5	Now	$20.00
1997	6	2004	$24.00
1998	5	Now	$19.50
1999	6	2005	$22.00
2000	7	2007	$25.00
2001	5	2006	$18.00
2002	7	2012	$24.00

***Leo Buring** is a Barossa Valley based maker in the Southcorp Wines aegis. They are particularly renowned for their uniquely beautiful premium Rieslings - wines which possess remarkable longevity. Winemaker: Oliver Crawford.*

LEO BURING LEONAY EDEN VALLEY RIESLING ★★★★★

before 1972		Prior	
1972	7	Now	$52.00
1973	7	Prior	
1974	Not made		
1975	6	Now	$41.00
1976	6	Prior	

1977	5	Prior	
1978	5	Prior	
1979	7	Now	$43.00
1980	4	Now	$23.00
1981	4	Now	$23.00
1982	5	Now	$28.00
1983	Not made		
1984	5	2004	$26.00
1985	Not made		
1986	5	Now	$24.00
1987	5	Now	$24.00
1988	Not made		
1989	5	Now	$22.00
1990	7	Now	$31.00
1991	6	Now	$25.00
1992	4	Now	$16.50
1993	3	Now	$12.00
1994	7	2008	$27.00
1995	5	2004	$19.00
1996	Not made		
1997	7	2008	$25.00
1998	6	2008	$21.00
1999	No data		
2000	5	2005	$16.50
2001	Not made		
2002	5	2005	$15.50

LEO BURING RESERVE BIN BAROSSA/COONAWARRA CABERNET SAUVIGNON ★★★

1984	7	Now	$35.00
1985	5	Now	$24.00
1986	6	Now	$28.00
1987	4	Now	$18.50
1988	7	Now	$31.00
1989	4	Now	$17.50
1990	6	Now	$25.00
1991	7	Now	$28.00
1992	5	Now	$20.00
1993	6	Now	$23.00
1994	6	Now	$22.00
1995	5	Now	$18.00
1996	6	2004	$21.00
1997	7	2006	$24.00

No longer made.

LEO BURING WATERVALE RIESLING (LEONAY) ★★★★★

1975	7	Now	$72.00
1976	5	Prior	
1977	5	Prior	

1978	6	Prior	
1979	7	Now	$64.00
1980	4	Now	$35.00
1981	3	Prior	
1982	4	Now	$33.00
1983	Not made		
1984	Not made		
1985	Not made		
1986	Not made		
1987	Not made		
1988	4	Prior	
1989	Not made		
1990	6	Now	$40.00
1991	7	Now	$45.00
1992	5	Now	$31.00
1993	Not made		
1994	6	2005	$35.00
1995	Not made		
2002	6	2015	$33.00

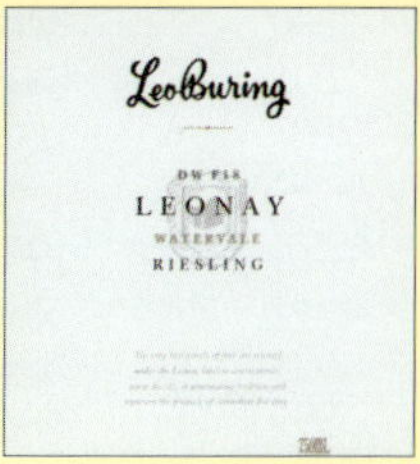

***Leydens Vale** was the label under which Blue Pyrenees Estate (qv) released a range of reasonably priced varietals from grapes grown virtually anywhere in the better areas of Australia. The label has now been discontinued. Winemakers: Greg Dedman and Kim Hart.*

LEYDENS VALE PINOT NOIR ★★★

before 1995		Prior	
1995	5	Now	$14.50
1996	6	Now	$17.00
1997	6	Now	$16.50
1998	5	Now	$13.50
No longer made			

LEYDENS VALE SHIRAZ ★★★

before 1995		Prior	
1995	4	Now	$13.50
1996	5	Now	$16.00
1997	5	Now	$15.50
1998	6	Now	$18.50
No longer made			

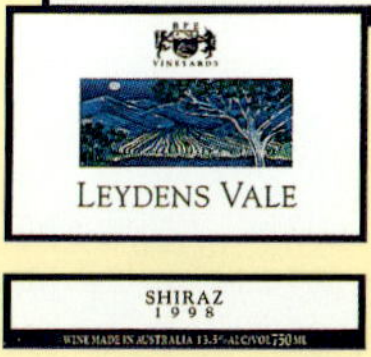

***Lillydale Vineyards** is a respected Yarra Valley operation now owned by McWilliams. Winemakers: Scott Zrna and Russell Cody.*

LILLYDALE VINEYARDS CABERNET/MERLOT ★★★★

before 1997		Prior	
1997	7	2004	$28.00
1998	6	2005	$23.00
1999	6	2007	$23.00

2000	7	2008	$26.00
2001	7	2010	$25.00
2002	6	2007	$21.00

LILLYDALE VINEYARDS CHARDONNAY ★★★★

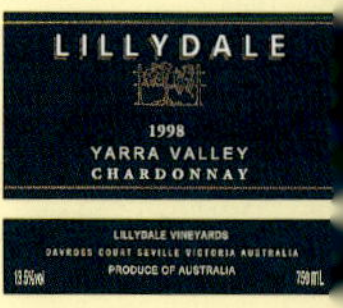

before 1997		Prior	
1997	6	Now	$20.00
1998	6	Now	$19.50
1999	6	Now	$19.00
2000	6	Now	$18.50
2001	7	2008	$21.00
2002	7	2006	$20.00

LILLYDALE VINEYARDS PINOT NOIR ★★★★

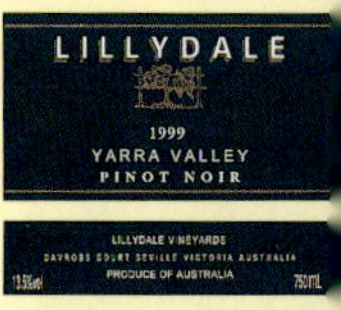

before 2000		Prior	
2000	6	Now	$23.00
2001	7	2005	$26.00
2002	6	2006	$21.00

LILLYDALE VINEYARDS SAUVIGNON BLANC ★★★

before 2000		Prior	
2000	7	Now	$20.00
2001	6	Now	$17.00
2002	7	2004	$19.50
2003	7	2005	$19.00

***Lindemans**, part of Southcorp Wines, is a very large maker with holdings in the Hunter Valley, Coonawarra, Clare, Padthaway and North West Victoria. In spite of their necessarily substantial production of high volume lines, they consistently make small quantities of very fine wines. Winemakers: Patrick Auld (Hunter Valley), Greg Clayfield (Coonawarra and Padthaway), Phillip John (Overall).*

LINDEMANS HUNTER RIVER SHIRAZ ★★★★

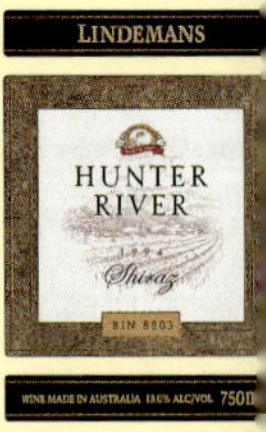

1975	5	Now	$30.00
1976	Not made		
1977	5	Now	$28.00
1978	5	Now	$28.00
1979	6	Now	$32.00
1980	7	Now	$37.00
1981	Not made		
1982	5	Now	$24.00
1983	7	Now	$33.00
1984	Not made		
1985	4	Now	$18.00
1986	7	Now	$31.00
1987	7	Now	$30.00
1988	5	Now	$20.00
1989	5	Now	$20.00
1990	6	Now	$23.00

1991	7	2005	$26.00
1992	Not made		
1993	Not made		
1994	6	2005	$20.00
1995	6	2007	$20.00
1996	5	2009	$16.00
1997	6	2010	$19.00
1998	6	2012	$18.50

No longer made.

LINDEMANS HUNTER RIVER CHABLIS (UNOAKED CHARDONNAY from 1994)

★★★★

1975	6	Now	$27.00
1976	4	Now	$17.50
1977	5	Now	$21.00
1978	6	Now	$25.00
1979	7	Now	$28.00
1980	5	Now	$19.50
1981	5	Now	$19.00
1982	4	Now	$14.50
1983	5	Now	$18.00
1984	5	Now	$17.50
1985	3	Now	$10.00
1986	6	Now	$19.50
1987	7	Now	$22.00
1988	4	Now	$12.00
1989	4	Now	$12.00
1990	5	Now	$14.50
1991	7	Now	$20.00
1992	6	Now	$16.50
1993	5	Now	$13.00
1994	5	Now	$13.00
1995	7	2004	$17.50
1996	5	2005	$12.00

No longer made.

LINDEMANS HUNTER RIVER CHARDONNAY

★★★★

1981	5	Now	$22.00
1982	4	Now	$17.50
1983	5	Now	$21.00
1984	4	Now	$16.50
1985	4	Now	$16.00
1986	5	Now	$19.50
1987	5	Now	$18.50
1988	7	Now	$25.00
1989	6	Now	$21.00
1990	5	Now	$17.00
1991	7	Now	$23.00
1992	7	Now	$22.00
1993	6	Now	$19.00

1994	5	Now	$15.00
1995	7	2004	$20.00
1996	5	2005	$14.50
1997	Not made		
1998	6	2005	$16.00

No longer made.

LINDEMANS HUNTER RIVER RESERVE PORPHYRY ★★★★

1975	6	Now	$19.00
1976	Not made		
1977	5	Now	$15.00
1978	6	Now	$17.50
1979	Not made		
1980	Not made		
1981	Not made		
1982	4	Now	$10.50
1983	6	Now	$15.00
1984	Not made		
1985	Not made		
1986	Not made		
1987	6	Now	$13.50
1988	5	Now	$11.00
1989	5	Now	$10.50
1990	6	Now	$12.00
1991	Not made		
1992	Not made		
1993	6	Now	$11.00
1994	6	Now	$11.00
1995	6	2004	$10.50

No longer made.

LINDEMANS HUNTER RIVER SEMILLON ★★★★

1975	5	Now	$34.00
1976	4	Now	$27.00
1977	5	Now	$32.00
1978	5	Now	$31.00
1979	7	Now	$43.00
1980	6	Now	$35.00
1981	4	Now	$23.00
1982	4	Now	$22.00
1983	5	Now	$27.00
1984	4	Now	$21.00
1985	5	Now	$25.00
1986	6	Now	$30.00
1987	7	Now	$34.00
1988	5	Now	$23.00
1989	5	Now	$22.00
1990	5	Now	$22.00
1991	7	Now	$30.00
1992	6	Now	$25.00

1993	5	Now	$20.00
1994	5	Now	$19.50
1995	7	2004	$26.00
1996	5	2005	$18.50
1997	Not made		
1998	7	2008	$24.00

No longer made.

LINDEMANS LIMESTONE RIDGE SHIRAZ/CABERNET

★★★★★

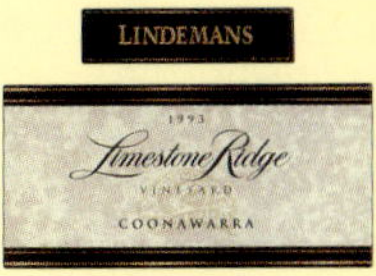

1976	7	Now	$78.00
1977	5	Now	$54.00
1978	6	Now	$64.00
1979	6	Now	$62.00
1980	7	Now	$70.00
1981	5	Now	$49.00
1982	7	Now	$66.00
1983	Not made		
1984	5	Now	$45.00
1985	6	Now	$52.00
1986	7	Now	$58.00
1987	6	Now	$49.00
1988	6	Now	$48.00
1989	5	Now	$38.00
1990	7	Now	$52.00
1991	7	2004	$50.00
1992	6	2005	$42.00
1993	7	2006	$48.00
1994	6	2007	$40.00
1995	Not made		
1996	5	2006	$31.00
1997	5	2008	$30.00
1998	6	2010	$35.00
1999	No data		
2000	No data		

LINDEMANS PADTHAWAY CHARDONNAY

★★★

1980	4	Now	$16.00
1981	Not made		
1982	4	Now	$15.50
1983	6	Now	$22.00
1984	5	Now	$18.00
1985	6	Now	$21.00
1986	6	Now	$20.00
1987	7	Now	$23.00
1988	7	Now	$22.00
1989	6	Now	$18.50
1990	7	Now	$21.00
1991	7	Now	$20.00
1992	5	Now	$14.00

1993	6	Now	$16.50
1994	7	Now	$19.00
1995	6	2005	$15.50
1996	6	2005	$15.00
1997	7	2006	$17.00
1998	6	2007	$14.50

LINDEMANS PADTHAWAY PINOT NOIR ★★★

before 1987		Prior	
1987	5	Now	$21.00
1988	5	Now	$20.00
1989	5	Now	$20.00
1990	6	Now	$23.00
1991	6	Now	$22.00
1992	5	Now	$18.00
1993	5	Now	$17.50
1994	6	Now	$20.00
1995	6	Now	$20.00
1996	5	Now	$16.00
1997	6	Now	$19.00
1998	6	2004	$18.50

LINDEMANS PYRUS COONAWARRA RED BLEND ★★★★★

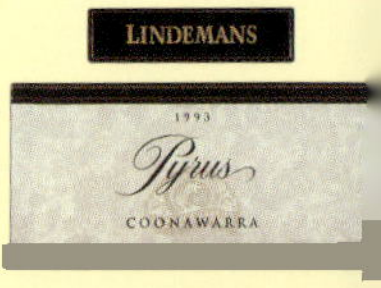

1985	7	Now	$60.00
1986	6	Now	$50.00
1987	6	Now	$49.00
1988	6	Now	$48.00
1989	Not made		
1990	6	Now	$45.00
1991	7	Now	$50.00
1992	5	Now	$35.00
1993	6	2004	$41.00
1994	6	2005	$40.00
1995	6	2007	$39.00
1996	6	2008	$38.00
1997	6	2009	$37.00
1998	6	2010	$36.00
1999	5	2009	$29.00

LINDEMANS ST GEORGE CABERNET SAUVIGNON ★★★★★

1976	6	Now	$50.00
1977	5	Now	$41.00
1978	6	Now	$47.00
1979	5	Now	$38.00
1980	7	Now	$52.00
1981	5	Now	$36.00
1982	6	Now	$42.00
1983	Not made		
1984	5	Now	$33.00

1985	7	Now	$45.00
1986	6	Now	$37.00
1987	5	Now	$30.00
1988	6	Now	$35.00
1989	5	Now	$28.00
1990	7	Now	$39.00
1991	7	2004	$38.00
1992	5	2005	$26.00
1993	6	2006	$30.00
1994	6	2007	$29.00
1995	5	2006	$24.00
1996	5	Now	$23.00
1997	6	2005	$27.00
1998	7	2006	$30.00
1999	6	2006	$25.00

***Long Gully Estate** is a Healesville (Yarra Valley) producer some of whose releases to date have been impressive. Winemaker: Peter Florance.*

LONG GULLY IRMA'S CABERNET ★★★★

before 1988		Prior	
1988	7	Now	$36.00
1989	6	Prior	
1990	7	Prior	
1991	7	Now	$33.00
1992	7	Now	$32.00
1993	7	Now	$31.00
1994	6	Prior	
1995	6	2004	$25.00
1996	6	2005	$24.00
1997	6	2004	$24.00
1998	6	2006	$23.00
1999	5	2005	$18.50

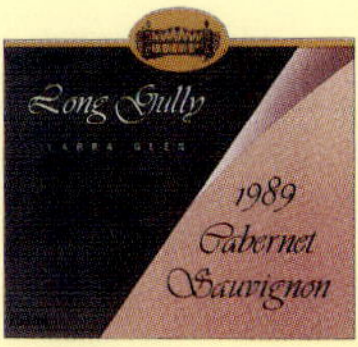

LONG GULLY CHARDONNAY ★★★★

before 1995		Prior	
1995	7	Now	$27.00
1996	7	Now	$26.00
1997	7	Now	$25.00
1998	6	Now	$21.00
1999	6	Now	$20.00
2000	6	Now	$20.00

LONG GULLY ICE RIESLING (375ml) ★★★★

1998	7	Now	$28.00
1999	6	Now	$24.00
2000	6	2004	$23.00
2001	6	2005	$22.00
2002	6	2006	$22.00
2003	6	2007	$21.00

LONG GULLY PINOT NOIR ★★★

1986	7	Now	$37.00
1987	6	Prior	
1988	6	Now	$30.00
1989	7	Now	$34.00
1990	6	Now	$28.00
1991	7	Now	$32.00
1992	7	Now	$31.00
1993	6	Now	$26.00
1994	6	Now	$25.00
1995	6	Now	$24.00
1996	7	Now	$28.00
1997	7	2005	$27.00
1998	6	2004	$22.00
1999	6	2005	$21.00
2000	6	2004	$21.00
2001	6	2005	$20.00

LONG GULLY RESERVE MERLOT ★★★★

before 1995		Prior	
1995	7	Now	$35.00
1996	7	Now	$34.00
1997	7	Now	$33.00
1998	6	2004	$28.00
1999	6	2005	$27.00

LONG GULLY RIESLING ★★★★

before 1997		Prior	
1997	7	Now	$17.50
1998	7	Now	$17.00
1999	6	Now	$14.00
2000	6	Now	$13.50

LONG GULLY SAUVIGNON BLANC ★★★

before 1997		Prior	
1997	6	Now	$21.00
1998	Not made		
1999	6	Now	$19.50
2000	6	2004	$19.00
2001	5	2005	$15.50

LONG GULLY SHIRAZ ★★★

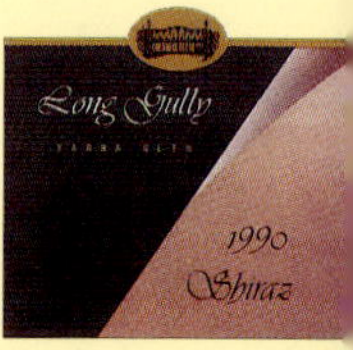

before 1994		Prior	
1994	6	Now	$24.00
1995	6	2004	$24.00
1996	6	Now	$23.00
1997	7	Now	$26.00
1998	7	Now	$25.00
1999	5	2006	$17.50

***Longleat** are long established Goulburn Valley growers with close ties to Chateau Tahbilk. Winemaker: David Traeger.*

LONGLEAT CABERNET SAUVIGNON ★★★

1989	5	Prior	
1990	7	Now	$41.00
1991	5	Now	$28.00
1992	7	Now	$39.00
1993	4	Prior	
1994	5	Prior	
1995	4	Prior	
1996	5	Now	$24.00
1997	5	Now	$24.00
1998	6	Now	$28.00
1999	6	2004	$27.00
2000	6	2005	$26.00

LONGLEAT RIESLING ★★★

1998	7	Now	$19.00
1999	5	Now	$13.00
2000	6	Now	$15.00
2001	6	2004	$15.00

LONGLEAT SEMILLON ★★★

1998	7	Now	$19.50
1999	5	Now	$13.50
2000	5	2004	$13.00
2001	6	2005	$15.50

LONGLEAT SHIRAZ ★★★

before 1996		Prior	
1996	4	Now	$19.00
1997	5	Now	$23.00
1998	6	Now	$27.00
1999	7	2004	$30.00
2000	6	2005	$25.00

***Lowe Family Wines** is a Hunter Valley operation run by contract winemakers David Lowe and Jane Wilson. Fruit can come from Mudgee, Orange and the Hunter. Winemakers: Jane Wilson and David Lowe.*

LOWE CHARDONNAY ★★★★

1997	4	Now	$21.00
1998	4	Now	$20.00
1999	6	Now	$29.00
2000	5	Now	$24.00

LOWE MERLOT ★★★★

1997	3	Prior	
1998	4	Now	$23.00
1999	6	2005	$34.00
2000	5	2005	$27.00
2001	6	2006	$32.00

LOWE SEMILLON ★★★★

1997	6	Now	$26.00
1998	4	Now	$17.00
1999	7	2006	$29.00
2000	6	2004	$24.00
2001	4	2004	$15.50
2002	6	2006	$22.00

LOWE SHIRAZ ★★★★

1997	4	Now	$20.00
1998	6	2004	$30.00
1999	6	2006	$29.00
2000	7	2006	$33.00
2001	5	2006	$23.00

***McAlister Vineyards** is a Longford (Gippsland) maker producing just the one wine, a Bordeaux styled red from four of the five noble Bordeaux varieties (no Malbec). Winemaker: Peter Edwards.*

The McALISTER ★★★★★

before 1980		Prior	
1980	6	Now	$82.00
1981	Not made		
1982	2	Prior	
1983	Not made		
1984	6	Now	$74.00
1985	5	Prior	
1986	5	Now	$58.00
1987	7	2005	$78.00
1988	6	2005	$66.00
1989	5	Now	$52.00
1990	7	2008	$72.00
1991	7	2005	$70.00
1992	6	2005	$58.00
1993	7	2007	$66.00
1994	7	2005	$64.00
1995	7	2010	$62.00
1996	5	2005	$43.00
1997	6	2010	$50.00
1998	7	2012	$56.00
1999	7	2010	$54.00
2000	7	2014	$54.00

***McWilliams Mount Pleasant** - see Mount Pleasant.*

***McGuigan Wines** is a successful publicly listed company much of whose production is exported. Only one wine has the necessary three vintages rated for inclusion in this edition. Winemaker: Brian McGuigan.*

McGUIGAN SEMILLON ★★★

1999	4	Now	$10.00
2000	5	Now	$12.00
2001	6	2004	$14.00

***McWilliams** is a large company with vineyards in the Hunter Valley, Yarra Valley, Coonawarra, Young and the Murrumbidgee Irrigation Area. Winemaker: Jim Brayne.*

McWILLIAMS HANWOOD CABERNET SAUVIGNON ★★

before 1998		Prior	
1998	6	Now	$12.50
1999	5	Now	$10.00
2000	5	Now	$10.00
2001	6	2004	$11.50
2002	7	2004	$13.00
2003	6	2005	N/R

McWILLIAMS HANWOOD CHARDONNAY ★★

before 2000		Prior	
2000	6	Now	$11.00
2001	6	Now	$10.50
2002	7	2004	$12.00
2003	7	2005	$11.50

McWILLIAMS HANWOOD MERLOT ★★

1999	5	Now	$10.50
2000	6	Now	$12.00
2001	6	2005	$12.00
2002	6	2005	$11.50
2003	6	2004	$11.00

McWILLIAMS HANWOOD SEMILLON/CHARDONNAY ★★

before 2000		Prior	
2000	6	Now	$10.50
2001	7	Now	$12.00
2002	7	2004	$11.50
2003	7	2005	$11.00

McWILLIAMS HANWOOD VERDELHO ★★

before 2001		Prior	
2001	6	Now	$10.50
2002	7	2004	$11.50
2003	7	2005	$11.50

McWILLIAMS LIMITED RELEASE RIVERINA BORTYTIS ★★★

before 1996		Prior	
1996	7	Now	$27.00
1997	7	Now	$26.00
1998	6	Now	$22.00
1999	6	2004	$21.00
2000	6	2005	$20.00
2001	7	2006	$23.00

Main Ridge Estate *was the first of the Mornington Peninsula (Victoria) makers to achieve commercial production. Since then the wines have achieved a beauty and reliability to establish an enviable reputation for this maker. Winemaker: Nat White.*

MAIN RIDGE ESTATE CHARDONNAY ★★★★★

before 1992		Prior	
1992	7	Now	$70.00
1993	6	Now	$58.00
1994	7	2006	$66.00
1995	6	Now	$54.00
1996	6	Now	$52.00
1997	7	2005	$60.00
1998	7	2008	$58.00
1999	7	2009	$56.00
2000	7	2010	$54.00
2001	7	2012	$54.00

MAIN RIDGE ESTATE HALF ACRE PINOT NOIR ★★★★★

before 1992		Prior	
1992	6	Now	$68.00
1993	6	Now	$66.00
1994	7	2004	$74.00
1995	6	Now	$62.00
1996	5	Now	$50.00
1997	7	2007	$68.00
1998	7	2007	$66.00
1999	7	2009	$64.00
2000	7	2010	$62.00
2001	7	2011	$60.00

Malcolm Creek Vineyard *is a small maker at Kersbrook in the Adelaide Hills, established as a "hobby" for winemaking identity Reg Tolley. Winemaker: Reg Tolley.*

MALCOLM CREEK CABERNET SAUVIGNON ★★★

before 1993		Prior	
1993	6	Now	$24.00
1994	6	2004	$23.00
1995	6	2005	$23.00

1996	7	2006	$26.00
1997	7	2007	$25.00
1998	6	2006	$21.00
1999	6	2007	$20.00
2000	7	2010	N/R
2001	6	2011	N/R
2002	7	2012	N/R

MALCOLM CREEK CHARDONNAY ★★★

before 1994		Prior	
1994	7	Now	$25.00
1995	6	Now	$21.00
1996	6	Now	$20.00
1997	7	Now	$23.00
1998	7	Now	$23.00
1999	6	Now	$19.00
2000	Not made		
2001	6	2005	$18.00
2002	7	2006	$20.00

***Margan Family Winegrowers** are recently established Hunter Valley makers benefiting from owner Andrew Margan's substantial experience in the Hunter and in Europe. Winemaker: Andrew Margan.*

MARGAN FAMILY BOTRYTIS SEMILLON (375ML) ★★★★

1999	7	2005	$29.00
2000	6	2005	$24.00
2001	6	2004	$23.00
2002	7	2010	$26.00

MARGAN FAMILY CABERNET SAUVIGNON ★★★★

1997	6	Now	$21.00
1998	7	2005	$24.00
1999	5	2003	$17.00
2000	7	2010	$23.00
2001	6	2007	$19.50
2002	7	2015	$22.00

MARGAN FAMILY CHARDONNAY ★★★

before 2001		Prior	
2001	6	2005	$19.00
2002	7	2007	$21.00

MARGAN FAMILY MERLOT ★★★★

1997	6	Prior	
1998	5	Now	$20.00
1999	5	2004	$19.50
2000	6	2010	$23.00
2001	5	2010	$18.50
2002	6	2012	$21.00

MARGAN FAMILY SEMILLON ★★★★

1997	5	Prior	
1998	5	2008	$15.50
1999	6	2009	$18.50
2000	7	2015	$21.00
2001	7	2015	$20.00
2002	6	2017	$17.00

MARGAN FAMILY SHIRAZ ★★★★

1997	5	2002	$20.00
1998	5	2010	$19.50
1999	5	2010	$19.00
2000	6	2020	$22.00
2001	7	2020	$25.00
2002	6	2020	$21.00

MARGAN FAMILY VERDELHO ★★★

before 2001		Prior	
2001	5	Now	$15.50
2002	6	Now	$18.50

***Marsh Estate** is an unirrigated Pokolbin vineyard originally established by Quentin Taperell, but acquired by Peter Marsh in 1978. Winemaker: Andrew Marsh.*

MARSH ESTATE CABERNET SAUVIGNON ★★★

before 1990		Prior	
1990	6	Now	$26.00
1991	7	Now	$30.00
1992	6	Now	$25.00
1993	6	Now	$24.00
1994	7	Now	$27.00
1995	6	Now	$23.00
1996	6	Now	$22.00
1997	6	Now	$21.00
1998	7	2005	$24.00
1999	6	Now	$20.00
2000	6	2004	$20.00

MARSH ESTATE CHARDONNAY ★★★

before 1991		Prior	
1991	7	Now	$29.00
1992	6	Now	$24.00
1993	6	Now	$23.00
1994	7	Now	$26.00
1995	6	Now	$22.00
1996	6	Now	$21.00
1997	6	Now	$21.00
1998	7	Now	$23.00
1999	6	Now	$19.50
2000	5	Now	$16.00

MARSH ESTATE SHIRAZ VAT R ★★★

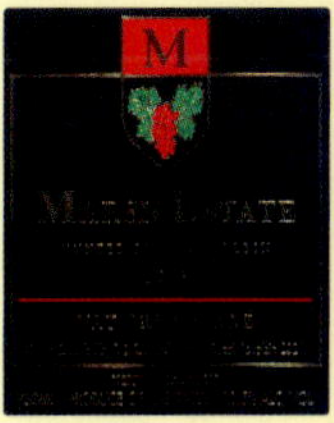

1981	6	Now	$36.00
1982	5	Now	$29.00
1983	5	Now	$28.00
1984	5	Now	$28.00
1985	6	Now	$32.00
1986	6	Now	$31.00
1987	6	Now	$30.00
1988	6	Now	$29.00
1989	6	Now	$29.00
1990	6	Now	$28.00
1991	7	Now	$31.00
1992	6	Now	$26.00
1993	6	Now	$25.00
1994	7	Now	$29.00
1995	6	Now	$24.00
1996	6	Now	$23.00
1997	6	Now	$22.00
1998	7	2005	$25.00
1999	6	Now	$21.00
2000	6	2004	$21.00

***Massoni** is a 1.5 hectare vineyard at Red Hill in the Mornington Peninsula, and is now owned by Ian Home, who created the renowned Yellowglen sparkling wines. Winemaker: Sam Tyrrell.*

MASSONI HOMES CHARDONNAY ★★★

1998	7	Prior	
1999	7	Now	$26.00
2000	7	Now	$25.00
2001	7	Now	$25.00

MASSONI HOMES PINOT NOIR ★★★

1998	6	Now	$25.00
1999	7	Now	$28.00
2000	6	Now	$23.00
2001	7	Now	$26.00

MASSONI RED HILL CHARDONNAY ★★★★

before 1997		Prior	
1997	7	Now	$38.00
1998	7	Now	$37.00
1999	7	2004	$36.00
2000	7	Now	$35.00

MASSONI RED HILL PINOT NOIR ★★★★

before 1994		Prior	
1994	7	Now	$48.00
1995	6	Now	$40.00
1996	7	Now	$45.00
1997	7	Now	$44.00

1998	7	Now	$43.00
1999	7	Now	$42.00
2000	7	2005	$40.00

Maxwell Wines and Mead *is a McLaren Vale producer of just that. Their wines are elegant, convincing and underpriced. Winemaker: Mark Maxwell.*

MAXWELL CABERNET SAUVIGNON ★★★

before 1990		Prior	
1990	5	Now	$25.00
1991	6	Now	$30.00
1992	5	Now	$24.00
1993	5	Prior	
1994	7	Now	$32.00
1995	6	Now	$26.00
1996	7	2005	$30.00
1997	6	Now	$25.00
1998	7	2005	$28.00
1999	7	2006	$27.00
2000	5	2007	$19.00

MAXWELL CABERNET/MERLOT ★★★

1988	5	Prior	
1989	Not made		
1990	5	Now	$16.00
1991	4	Prior	
1992	6	Now	$18.00
1993	5	Prior	
1994	6	Now	$17.00
1995	6	Prior	
1996	5	Now	$13.50
1997	6	Now	$15.50
1998	7	Now	$17.50

MAXWELL SHIRAZ ★★★★

before 1991		Prior	
1991	6	Now	$32.00
1992	5	Now	$26.00
1993	5	Now	$25.00
1994	7	Now	$34.00
1995	6	Now	$28.00
1996	7	Now	$32.00
1997	6	Now	$27.00
1998	6	Now	$26.00
1999	7	2004	$30.00
2000	5	2004	$20.00

***Meadowbank Wines** are well established growers in the Coal River Bay region in southern Tasmania. (It is notable that the winery restaurant has some of the best food in Tasmania.) Winemaker: Andrew Hood.*

MEADOWBANK CHARDONNAY ★★★★

before 1995		Prior	
1995	6	Now	$38.00
1996	3	Now	$18.50
1997	5	Now	$30.00
1998	6	2005	$35.00
1999	6	2006	$34.00
2000	7	2006	$38.00
2001	6	2005	$32.00
2002	7	2007	$36.00

MEADOWBANK PINOT NOIR ★★★★

before 1992		Prior	
1992	6	Now	$40.00
1993	7	2005	$46.00
1994	6	Now	$38.00
1995	6	Now	$37.00
1996	3	Now	$18.00
1997	5	2005	$29.00
1998	6	2004	$34.00
1999	6	2005	$33.00
2000	6	2008	$32.00
2001	6	2008	$31.00
2002	7	2010	$35.00

MEADOWBANK RIESLING ★★★★

before 1993		Prior	
1993	6	Now	$37.00
1994	4	Prior	
1995	4	Prior	
1996	4	Now	$22.00
1997	5	Now	$27.00
1998	6	2005	$32.00
1999	6	2007	$31.00
2000	6	2010	$30.00
2001	6	2010	$29.00
2002	5	2015	$24.00

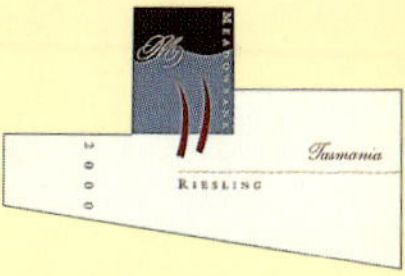

***Meerea Park** in the Hunter Valley's Singleton area is a small producer of admirable barrel-fermented Chardonnay. Winemaker: Rhys Eather.*

MEEREA PARK CABERNET/MERLOT ★★★

1996	6	Now	$24.00
1997	5	Now	$20.00
1998	7	Now	$27.00
1999	6	2005	$22.00
2000	6	2005	$22.00

MEEREA PARK CHARDONNAY (BARREL FERMENTED) ★★★★

1991	5	Prior	
1992	6	Now	$33.00
1993	5	Now	$26.00
1994	6	Now	$31.00
1995	5	Now	$25.00
1996	6	nOW	$25.00
1997	6	Now	$28.00
1998	6	Now	$27.00
1999	6	2004	$27.00
2000	6	2004	$26.00

MEEREA PARK CHARDONNAY (UNOAKED) ★★★

1996	5	Prior	
1997	5	Now	$15.00
1998	6	Now	$17.50
1999	6	Now	$17.00

MEEREA PARK "LINDSAY HILL" VERDELHO ★★★

1997	6	Now	$20.00
1998	5	Now	$16.00
1999	6	Now	$19.00

MEEREA PARK SAUVIGNON BLANC/SEMILLON ★★★

1997	5	Now	$14.50
1998	6	Now	$16.50
1999	7	Now	$19.00

***Merrebee Estate** is a small Mount Barker producer who, since the first vintage in 1995, has made some remarkably fine wines. Winemaker: Contract.*

MERREBEE ESTATE CHARDONNAY ★★★★

1995	7	Prior	
1996	Not made		
1997	Not made		
1998	6	Now	$23.00
1999	Not made		
2000	7	2004	$26.00

MERREBEE ESTATE RIESLING ★★★★

before 1997		Prior	
1997	6	Now	$19.00
1998	Not made		
1999	7	2004	$21.00
2000	7	2005	$20.00

MERREBEE ESTATE SHIRAZ ★★★★

before 1998		Prior	
1998	7	Now	$25.00
1999	7	2004	$24.00
2000	7	2005	$24.00

Merricks Estate *is a Mornington Peninsula maker with a small range of fine wines. Winemaker: Michael Zitzlaff*

MERRICKS ESTATE CABERNET SAUVIGNON ★★★★

1984	5	Now	$35.00
1985	Not made		
1986	6	Now	$39.00
1987	4	Now	$25.00
1988	6	Now	$37.00
1989	6	Now	$36.00
1990	7	Now	$41.00
1991	6	Now	$34.00
1992	6	Now	$33.00
1993	7	2005	$37.00
1994	No data		
1995	No data		
1996	Not made		
1997	7	2005	$33.00
1998	6	2006	$27.00
1999	6	2007	$27.00

MERRICKS ESTATE CHARDONNAY ★★★★

1986	5	Now	$38.00
1987	5	Now	$36.00
1988	5	Now	$35.00
1989	6	Now	$41.00
1990	6	Now	$40.00
1991	6	Now	$39.00
1992	7	Now	$44.00
1993	7	Now	$43.00
1994	7	Now	$42.00
1995	4	Now	$23.00
1996	6	Now	$33.00
1997	5	Now	$27.00
1998	6	Now	$32.00
1999	6	2004	$31.00

MERRICKS ESTATE SHIRAZ ★★★

1984	5	Now	$40.00
1985	5	Now	$38.00
1986	Not made		
1987	Not made		
1988	7	Now	$49.00
1989	6	Now	$41.00

1990	7	Now	$47.00
1991	6	Now	$39.00
1992	6	Now	$38.00
1993	7	Now	$43.00
1994	Not made		
1995	4	Now	$23.00
1996	Not made		
1997	Not made		
1998	6	2008	$31.00
1999	5	2009	$25.00

***Metala** is a long respected label now in the hands of Beringer Blass. Winemaker: Nigel Dolan.*

METALA CABERNET SAUVIGNON/SHIRAZ ★★★★

before 1988		Prior	
1988	7	Now	$30.00
1989	6	Now	$25.00
1990	6	Now	$24.00
1991	6	Now	$23.00
1992	7	Now	$26.00
1993	7	Now	$26.00
1994	6	Now	$21.00
1995	6	Now	$21.00
1996	7	2004	$23.00
1997	7	2005	$23.00
1998	7	2006	$22.00
1999	6	2008	$18.50
2000	6	2009	$18.00
2001	6	2010	$17.50

METALA ORIGINAL PLANTINGS SHIRAZ ★★★★

1994	6	2006	$44.00
1995	6	2008	$42.00
1996	7	2010	$48.00
1997	No data		
1998	7	2015	$45.00
1999	7	2017	$44.00

***Milbrovale** is a second label of Oakvale (qv). The wines are vineyard specific to the Milbrovale property at Broke in the Hunter Valley. Winemaker: Richard Owens.*

MILBROVALE OWENS FAMILY CHARDONNAY ★★★

1998	5	Now	$18.50
1999	6	Now	$21.00
2000	6	Now	$21.00

MILBROVALE OWENS FAMILY SEMILLON ★★★

1998	6	2004	$21.00
1999	6	2005	$20.00
2000	6	2006	$20.00

MILBROVALE OWENS FAMILY SHIRAZ ★★★

1998	6	Now	$21.00
1999	5	Now	$17.00
2000	7	2006	$23.00

MILBROVALE OWENS FAMILY VERDELHO ★★★

1998	5	Prior	
1999	7	Now	$22.00
2000	7	Now	$22.00

***Mildara** (now Beringer Blass) is a large and long-established producer whose wines have for decades been at the upper end of the quality spectrum. Winemaker: David O'Leary.*

MILDARA COONAWARRA CABERNET SAUVIGNON ★★★★

before 1989		Prior	
1989	5	Now	$28.00
1990	7	Now	$38.00
1991	7	Now	$37.00
1992	7	2004	$35.00
1993	5	Now	$24.00
1994	6	2004	$29.00
1995	5	Now	$23.00
1996	7	2006	$31.00
1997	6	2005	$26.00
1998	7	2010	$30.00
1999	6	2010	$25.00
2000	6	2011	$24.00

***Millfield** is a Lower Hunter Valley winery whose initial releases have been admirably neat (and sensibly priced) examples of good winemaking. Winemaker: David Lowe.*

MILLFIELD CHARDONNAY ★★★★

1998	6	Now	$29.00
1999	6	Now	$28.00
2000	5	Now	$23.00
2001	5	2005	$22.00

MILLFIELD SEMILLON ★★★★

1998	6	2008	$24.00
1999	7	2009	$27.00
2000	5	2010	$18.50
2001	5	2011	$18.00
2002	5	2012	$17.50

MILLFIELD SHIRAZ ★★★★

1998	5	Now	$24.00
1999	5	Now	$24.00
2000	6	2006	$28.00

***Miramar** is a Mudgee winery producing sensitively made wines with good balance and fruit. Winemaker: Ian MacRae.*

MIRAMAR CABERNET SAUVIGNON ★★★

before 1984		Prior	
1984	7	Now	$40.00
1985	6	Now	$33.00
1986	7	Now	$37.00
1987	5	Now	$26.00
1988	5	Now	$25.00
1989	Not made		
1990	5	Now	$24.00
1991	6	Now	$28.00
1992	Not made		
1993	Not made		
1994	6	Now	$25.00
1995	5	Now	$20.00
1996	5	Now	$20.00
1997	6	Now	$23.00
1998	5	Now	$18.50
1999	6	Now	$22.00

MIRAMAR DOUX BLANC ★★★

1989	5	Now	$18.50
1990	Not made		
1995	5	Now	$17.50
1996	Not made		
1999	6	2005	$20.00

MIRAMAR ROSE ★★

before 1994		Prior	
1994	6	Now	$15.50
1995	5	Now	$12.50
1996	6	Now	$14.50
1997	5	Now	$12.00
1998	5	Now	$11.50
1999	5	Now	$11.00
2000	6	Now	$13.00

MIRAMAR SEMILLON ★★★

before 1990		Prior	
1990	6	Now	$21.00
1991	5	Now	$17.50
1992	6	Now	$20.00
1993	4	Prior	
1994	6	Now	$19.00
1995	6	Now	$18.50

1996	5	Now	$15.00
1997	6	2004	$17.50
1998	Not made		
1999	Not made		
2000	6	2005	$16.00

MIRAMAR SHIRAZ ★★★

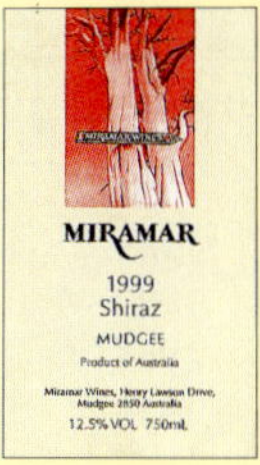

before 1980		Prior	
1980	7	Now	$38.00
1981	5	Prior	
1982	5	Prior	
1983	6	Now	$30.00
1984	6	Now	$29.00
1985	5	Now	$23.00
1986	Not made		
1987	Not made		
1988	6	Now	$26.00
1989	6	Now	$25.00
1990	6	Now	$24.00
1991	6	Now	$23.00
1992	Not made		
1993	6	Now	$22.00
1994	6	Now	$21.00
1995	5	Now	$17.50
1996	5	Now	$17.00
1997	6	2004	$20.00
1998	5	Now	$16.00
1999	6	2004	$18.50

***Mitchell Cellars** is a small Clare Valley maker with two high quality vineyards in the area. Winemaker: Andrew Mitchell.*

MITCHELL CELLARS CABERNET SAUVIGNON ★★★★

1976	6	Now	$54.00
1977	6	Now	$52.00
1978	Not made		
1979	4	Prior	
1980	7	Now	$56.00
1981	5	Now	$39.00
1982	6	Now	$46.00
1983	5	Now	$37.00
1984	6	Now	$43.00
1985	5	Now	$35.00
1986	7	Now	$47.00
1987	6	Now	$39.00
1988	5	Now	$32.00
1989	Not made		
1990	7	Now	$42.00
1991	7	Now	$41.00

1992	5	Now	$28.00
1993	5	Now	$27.00
1994	6	Now	$32.00
1995	5	Now	$26.00
1996	7	2004	$35.00
1997	6	2005	$29.00
1998	7	2008	$33.00

MITCHELL CELLARS PEPPERTREE VINEYARD SHIRAZ

★★★★

1984	6	Now	$45.00
1985	4	Now	$29.00
1986	6	Now	$42.00
1987	7	Now	$48.00
1988	5	Now	$33.00
1989	4	Now	$26.00
1990	6	Now	$38.00
1991	6	Now	$37.00
1992	5	Now	$29.00
1993	6	Now	$34.00
1994	6	Now	$33.00
1995	5	Now	$27.00
1996	6	2004	$31.00
1997	7	2006	$36.00
1998	7	2008	$35.00
1999	6	2007	$29.00

MITCHELL CELLARS WATERVALE RIESLING

★★★★

1978	7	Now	$44.00
1979	4	Prior	
1980	7	Now	$41.00
1981	4	Prior	
1982	7	Now	$39.00
1983	6	Now	$32.00
1984	7	2004	$36.00
1985	6	Now	$30.00
1986	6	Now	$29.00
1987	6	Now	$28.00
1988	5	Now	$23.00
1989	5	Now	$22.00
1990	6	Now	$26.00
1991	4	Now	$17.00
1992	6	Now	$24.00
1993	6	Now	$24.00
1994	6	Now	$23.00
1995	6	Now	$22.00
1996	6	Now	$22.00
1997	7	2004	$25.00
1998	6	2005	$20.00

1999	6	2006	$20.00
2000	7	2008	$22.00
2001	7	2008	$22.00

MITCHELL CELLARS SEMILLON ★★★★

before 1990		Prior	
1990	6	Now	$26.00
1991	4	Now	$17.00
1992	5	Now	$20.00
1993	6	Now	$24.00
1994	6	Now	$23.00
1995	5	Now	$18.50
1996	6	Now	$22.00
1997	7	Now	$24.00
1998	7	Now	$24.00
1999	6	Now	$20.00
2000	6	Now	$19.50

***Mitchelton** in Victoria's Goulburn Valley is a highly respected medium-sized producer of some of the State's better wines. Winemaker: Don Lewis.*

MITCHELTON BLACKWOOD PARK RIESLING ★★★★

before 1981		Prior	
1981	7	Now	$32.00
1982	6	Now	$26.00
1983	6	Prior	
1984	6	Now	$25.00
1985	6	Prior	
1986	6	Now	$23.00
1987	5	Now	$19.00
1988	6	Now	$22.00
1989	6	Now	$21.00
1990	6	Now	$21.00
1991	7	Now	$23.00
1992	7	2005	$23.00
1993	5	Now	$16.00
1994	6	Now	$18.50
1995	7	2005	$21.00
1996	6	2006	$17.50
1997	6	2006	$17.00
1998	7	2007	$19.00
1999	6	2008	$16.00
2000	6	2009	$15.50
2001	6	2010	$15.00
2002	5	2009	$12.00

MITCHELTON CABERNET SAUVIGNON ★★★★

before 1985		Prior	
1985	7	Now	$37.00
1986	7	Now	$36.00

1987	7	Now	$35.00
1988	6	Now	$29.00
1989	6	Now	$28.00
1990	7	Prior	
1991	7	Prior	
1992	6	Prior	
1993	7	2005	$29.00
1994	6	2008	$24.00
1995	6	2010	$24.00
1996	6	2010	$23.00
1997	6	2011	$22.00
1998	7	2010	$25.00

MITCHELTON CHARDONNAY ★★★★

before 1995		Prior	
1995	7	2005	$25.00
1996	6	2005	$21.00
1997	7	2005	$24.00
1998	6	2006	$20.00
1999	6	2005	$19.50
2000	6	2006	$18.50

MITCHELTON MARSANNE ★★★★

1979	5	Now	$36.00
1980	6	Now	$42.00
1981	5	Now	$34.00
1982	6	Now	$40.00
1983	5	Now	$32.00
1984	6	Now	$38.00
1985	5	Now	$30.00
1986	7	Now	$41.00
1987	6	Now	$34.00
1988	7	Now	$39.00
1989	6	Now	$32.00
1990	7	Now	$37.00
1991	6	Now	$31.00
1992	6	2005	$30.00
1993	6	2008	$29.00
1994	7	2010	$33.00
1995	6	2005	$27.00
1996	5	2005	$22.00
1997	6	2006	$25.00
1998	6	2006	$25.00

MITCHELTON PRINT SHIRAZ ★★★★★

1980	6	Now	$80.00
1981	6	Now	$78.00
1982	6	Now	$76.00
1983	Not made		
1984	5	Prior	
1985	6	Prior	

1986	Not made		
1987	6	Prior	
1988	Not made		
1989	Not made		
1990	7	2005	$70.00
1991	6	2008	$58.00
1992	7	2010	$66.00
1993	6	2010	$54.00
1994	7	2010	$62.00
1995	7	2010	$60.00
1996	6	2011	$50.00
1997	6	2011	$49.00
1998	7	2015	$54.00

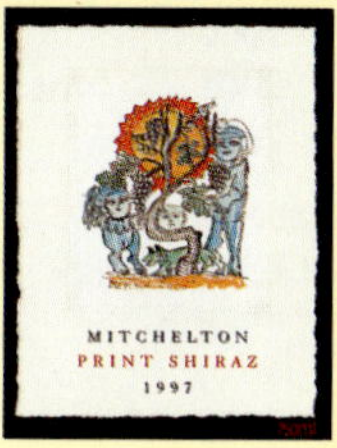

MITCHELTON SEMILLON (CLASSIC RELEASE) ★★★★

1980	5	Prior	
1981	7	Now	$41.00
1982	6	Now	$34.00
1983	6	Now	$33.00
1984	7	Now	$38.00
1985	6	Now	$31.00
1986	7	Now	$35.00
1987	Not made		
1988	6	Now	$28.00
1989	Not made		
1990	Not made		
1991	7	Now	$30.00

No longer made.

***Montrose Wines** in Mudgee have been acquired by the Orlando Wyndham group, sharing a common winemaker with Craigmoor and Poet's Corner. Winemaker: James Manners*

MONTROSE BARBERA ★★★

1996	6	Now	$26.00
1997	6	Now	$25.00
1998	Not made		
1999	6	2006	$24.00
2000	5	2004	$19.00
2001	Not made		
2002	7	2007	$25.00

MONTROSE BLACK SHIRAZ ★★★

1994	6	Now	$22.00
1995	6	Now	$21.00
1996	7	Now	$24.00
1997	6	Now	$20.00
1998	6	Now	$19.50
1999	6	2005	$19.00

2000	7	2005	$21.00
2001	Not made		
2002	5	2007	$14.50

MONTROSE CABERNET SAUVIGNON ★★★

before 1988		Prior	
1988	6	Now	$24.00
1989	6	Now	$24.00
1990	7	Now	$27.00
1991	7	Now	$26.00
1992	5	Now	$18.00
1993	6	Now	$21.00
1994	7	Now	$24.00
1995	6	Now	$20.00
1996	7	Now	$22.00
1997	6	2004	$18.50
1998	5	Now	$15.00

No longer made.

MONTROSE CHARDONNAY ★★★

before 1991		Prior	
1991	7	Now	$21.00
1992	5	Now	$14.50
1993	6	Now	$17.00
1994	6	Now	$16.50
1995	7	Now	$18.50
1996	7	Now	$18.00
1997	5	Now	$12.50
1998	6	Now	$14.50

No longer made.

MONTROSE SANGIOVESE ★★★★

1996	6	Now	$26.00
1997	7	Now	$29.00
1998	6	Now	$24.00
1999	No data		
2000	Not made		
2001	Not made		
2002	6	2005	$22.00

MONTROSE STONY CREEK CHARDONNAY ★★★

1994	7	Now	$21.00
1995	Not made		
1996	7	Now	$20.00
1997	6	Now	$16.50
1998	Not made		
1999	7	Now	$18.00
2000	Not made		
2001	6	Now	$14.50
2002	7	2005	$16.50

__Moondah Brook__ is the Gingin (80 km north of Perth) vineyard of the Houghton company. Winemaker: Larry Cherubino.

MOONDAH BROOK CABERNET SAUVIGNON

★★★

before 1990		Prior	
1990	6	Now	$22.00
1991	5	Now	$18.00
1992	5	Now	$17.50
1993	5	Now	$17.00
1994	6	Now	$20.00
1995	No data		
1996	5	Now	$15.50
1997	5	2004	$15.00
1998	7	2008	$21.00
1999	7	2008	$20.00
2000	6	2008	$16.50
2001	7	2008	$19.00

MOONDAH BROOK CHARDONNAY

★★★

1991	6	Now	$20.00
1992	5	Now	$16.50
1993	6	Now	$19.50
1994	5	Now	$15.50
1995	5	Now	$15.50
1996	No data		
1997	5	Now	$14.50
1998	5	Now	$14.00
1999	5	Now	$13.50
2000	6	2005	$16.00
2001	6	2006	$15.50
2002	7	2008	$17.50

MOONDAH BROOK CHENIN BLANC

★★★

1989	6	Now	$22.00
1990	4	Now	$14.00
1991	6	Now	$20.00
1992	6	Now	$20.00
1993	6	Now	$19.50
1994	5	Now	$16.00
1995	5	Now	$15.50
1996	5	Now	$15.00
1997	5	Now	$14.50
1998	5	2004	$14.00
1999	Not made		
2000	6	2006	$16.00
2001	6	2007	$15.50
2002	7	2008	$17.50

MOONDAH BROOK VERDELHO ★★

1989	6	Now	$22.00
1990	5	Now	$18.00
1991	6	Now	$21.00
1992	4	Now	$13.50
1993	6	Now	$19.50
1994	5	Now	$16.00
1995	4	Now	$12.50
1996	5	Now	$15.00
1997	5	Now	$14.50
1998	5	Now	$14.00
1999	7	2005	$19.00
2000	6	2004	$16.00
2001	6	2005	$15.50
2002	7	2008	$17.50

***Moorilla Estate** is a small Hobart maker who painstakingly produce some very fine, rare wines. Winemaker: Alain Rousseau.*

MOORILLA ESTATE CABERNET SAUVIGNON ★★★★

before 1993		Prior	
1993	5	Now	$27.00
1994	7	Now	$37.00
1995	5	Now	$25.00
1996	6	Now	$30.00
1997	7	Now	$34.00
1998	7	2004	$33.00
1999	7	2005	$32.00

MOORILLA ESTATE CHARDONNAY ★★★★

before 1993		Prior	
1993	7	Now	$37.00
1994	7	Now	$36.00
1995	7	Now	$34.00
1996	5	Now	$24.00
1997	7	Now	$32.00
1998	7	Now	$31.00
1999	6	Now	$26.00
2000	6	Now	$25.00

MOORILLA ESTATE GEWURZTRAMINER ★★★★

1988	5	Now	$32.00
1989	6	Prior	
1990	7	Now	$42.00
1991	7	Now	$41.00
1992	6	Prior	
1993	6	Prior	
1994	7	Now	$37.00

1995	6	Now	$31.00
1996	6	Now	$30.00
1997	7	Now	$34.00
1998	6	Now	$28.00
1999	6	Now	$28.00
2000	7	Now	$31.00
2001	7	2004	$30.00

MOORILLA ESTATE PINOT NOIR ★★★★★

before 1989		Prior	
1989	5	Now	$35.00
1990	5	Now	$34.00
1991	6	Now	$40.00
1992	4	Now	$26.00
1993	3	Now	$19.00
1994	7	Now	$43.00
1995	6	Now	$36.00
1996	6	Now	$34.00
1997	7	Now	$39.00
1998	7	Now	$38.00
1999	6	Now	$31.00
2000	6	2004	$31.00
2001	7	2005	$35.00

MOORILLA ESTATE RIESLING ★★★★

before 1988		Prior	
1988	7	Now	$37.00
1989	7	Now	$36.00
1990	7	Now	$35.00
1991	6	Now	$29.00
1992	6	Now	$28.00
1993	6	Now	$27.00
1994	7	Now	$31.00
1995	6	Now	$26.00
1996	7	Now	$29.00
1997	7	Now	$28.00
1998	6	Now	$23.00
1999	7	Now	$27.00
2000	6	Now	$22.00
2001	7	Now	$25.00

Mooroodoc Estate *is a high quality Mornington Peninsula maker. Winemaker: Richard McIntyre.*

MOOROODUC ESTATE CABERNET SAUVIGNON ★★★★★

before 1990		Prior	
1990	5	Now	$42.00
1991	6	Now	$49.00
1992	6	Now	$48.00
1993	6	Now	$47.00

1994	7	2004	$52.00
1995	6	2004	$44.00
1996	4	Now	$28.00
1997	6	2008	$41.00
1998	6	2006	$40.00
1999	Not made		
2000	7	2010	$44.00
2001	5	2007	$30.00

MOOROODUC ESTATE CHARDONNAY ★★★★★

before 1993		Prior	
1993	6	Now	$38.00
1994	7	Now	$43.00
1995	6	Now	$36.00
1996	5	2004	$29.00
1997	5	Now	$28.00
1998	7	2004	$38.00
1999	6	2004	$32.00
2000	6	2005	$31.00
2001	7	2006	$35.00

MOOROODUC ESTATE PINOT NOIR ★★★★

before 1991		Prior	
1991	6	Now	$52.00
1992	5	Now	$42.00
1993	5	Now	$41.00
1994	5	2004	$40.00
1995	6	2004	$46.00
1996	6	2004	$45.00
1997	7	2006	$50.00
1998	6	2005	$42.00
1999	Not made		
2000	7	2010	$47.00
2001	7	2007	$45.00

***Morris** is one of the most respected Rutherglen wineries, now under the aegis of Orlando Wyndham. Their table wines are big and powerful, and their muscats are arguably the world's best. Winemaker: David Morris.*

MORRIS BLUE IMPERIAL ★★★

1984	5	Prior	
1985	6	Now	$26.00
1986	5	Now	$21.00
1987	5	Now	$21.00
1988	5	Now	$20.00
1989	7	Now	$27.00
1990	5	Now	$19.00
1991	Not made		
1996	5	2004	$18.00

1997	Not made		
1998	7	2010	$24.00
1999	6	2006	$20.00
2000	5	2006	$16.00

MORRIS CABERNET SAUVIGNON ★★★

before 1982		Prior	
1982	6	Now	$27.00
1983	6	Now	$26.00
1984	5	Now	$21.00
1985	5	Now	$21.00
1986	5	Now	$20.00
1987	6	Now	$23.00
1988	6	Now	$23.00
1989	6	Now	$22.00
1990	5	Now	$18.00
1991	6	Now	$21.00
1992	6	2004	$20.00
1993	5	2004	$16.50
1994	5	2004	$16.00
1995	6	2006	$18.50
1996	5	2005	$15.00
1997	5	2006	$14.50
1998	6	2007	$17.00
1999	6	2009	$16.50
2000	5	2009	$13.50

MORRIS CHARDONNAY ★★★

before 1990		Prior	
1990	6	Now	$19.50
1991	5	Prior	
1992	Not made		
1993	Not made		
1994	5	Now	$14.50
1995	5	Now	$14.00
1996	6	Now	$16.50
1997	6	Now	$16.00
1998	5	2004	$13.00
1999	5	2004	$12.50
2000	5	2005	$12.00
2001	6	2006	$14.00

MORRIS DURIF ★★★★

before 1977		Prior	
1977	7	Now	$48.00
1978	6	Prior	
1979	5	Prior	
1980	6	Now	$38.00
1981	5	Now	$30.00
1982	6	Now	$36.00
1983	6	Now	$35.00

1984	5	Now	$28.00
1985	6	Now	$32.00
1986	7	Now	$37.00
1987	5	Now	$25.00
1988	5	Now	$25.00
1989	6	Now	$29.00
1990	6	2005	$28.00
1991	6	2005	$27.00
1992	6	2006	$26.00
1993	5	2005	$21.00
1994	6	2006	$25.00
1995	6	2007	$24.00
1996	5	2007	$19.50
1997	5	2008	$19.00
1998	6	2009	$22.00
1999	6	2010	$21.00
2000	6	2012	$21.00

MORRIS SEMILLON ★★★

before 1990		Prior	
1990	6	Now	$19.00
1991	Not made		
1992	Not made		
1993	Not made		
1994	6	Now	$16.50
1995	5	Now	$13.50
1996	7	Now	$18.50
1997	6	Now	$15.00
1998	6	Now	$15.00
1999	5	2004	$12.00
2000	5	2006	$11.50
2001	5	2007	$11.00

MORRIS SHIRAZ ★★★★

before 1985		Prior	
1985	6	Now	$25.00
1986	7	Now	$28.00
1987	5	Now	$19.50
1988	6	Now	$23.00
1989	5	Now	$18.50
1990	5	Now	$18.00
1991	5	2004	$17.50
1992	7	2004	$23.00
1993	5	2004	$16.50
1994	6	2005	$19.00
1995	5	2006	$15.50
1996	6	20054	$18.00
1997	5	2005	$14.50
1998	6	2007	$17.00
1999	5	2007	$13.50
2000	5	2008	$13.00

Moss Brothers *(not to be confused with its near neighbour Moss Wood) is a Margaret River vineyard. Winemakers: David and Jane Moss.*

MOSS BROTHERS CABERNET /MERLOT ★★★

before 1999		Prior	
1999	7	2010	$36.00
2000	7	2005	$35.00
2001	7	2011	N/R

MOSS BROTHERS CHARDONNAY ★★★

before 1998		Prior	
1998	6	Now	$25.00
1999	6	Now	$25.00
2000	Not made		
2001	7	2004	$27.00
2002	7	2006	$26.00

MOSS BROTHERS PINOT NOIR ★★★

before 1997		Prior	
1997	7	Now	$27.00
1998	7	2004	$26.00
1999	7	2004	$26.00
2000	6	2006	$21.00
2001	Not made		

MOSS BROTHERS SEMILLON ★★★

before 2000		Prior	
2000	7	2005	$19.00
2001	7	2008	$18.50
2002	7	2008	$18.00

MOSS BROTHERS SHIRAZ ★★★★

1998	7	2005	$32.00
1999	7	2006	$31.00
2000	7	2010	$30.00
2001	7	2005	$30.00

MOSS BROTHERS VERDELHO ★★★

1998	6	Prior	
1999	No data		
2000	6	Now	$18.00
2001	6	Now	$17.50
2002	7	2004	$20.00

Moss Wood *is one of Australia's best wineries. The wines are deep, full and complex, with superb fruit and balance. Winemaker: Keith Mugford.*

MOSS WOOD CABERNET SAUVIGNON ★★★★★

1973	4	Now	$120.00
1974	4	Now	$115.00
1975	6	Now	$170.00

1976	6	Now	$165.00
1977	6	Now	$160.00
1978	Not made		
1979	4	Now	$100.00
1980	6	Now	$145.00
1981	5	Now	$115.00
1982	4	Now	$92.00
1983	6	Now	$130.00
1984	4	Now	$86.00
1985	7	Now	$145.00
1986	6	Now	$120.00
1987	7	Now	$140.00
1988	5	Now	$96.00
1989	6	2006	$110.00
1990	7	2005	$125.00
1991	7	2006	$120.00
1992	5	2005	$86.00
1993	6	2008	$100.00
1994	7	2007	$110.00
1995	7	2009	$110.00
1996	7	2010	$105.00
1997	6	2011	$88.00
1998	6	2012	$86.00
1999	7	2014	$98.00
2000	7	2015	$94.00

MOSS WOOD CHARDONNAY ★★★★

1980	3	Prior	
1981	Not made		
1982	Not made		
1983	4	Now	$70.00
1984	5	Now	$86.00
1985	5	Now	$84.00
1986	5	Now	$80.00
1987	5	Now	$78.00
1988	5	Now	$76.00
1989	5	Now	$74.00
1990	7	Now	$100.00
1991	6	Now	$84.00
1992	6	2004	$82.00
1993	7	2005	$92.00
1994	7	2005	$90.00
1995	7	2006	$86.00
1997	6	2007	$72.00
1997	5	2007	$58.00
1998	6	2008	$68.00
1999	7	2009	$78.00
2000	6	2010	$64.00
2001	7	2008	$72.00

MOSS WOOD PINOT NOIR ★★★★

1977	3	Prior	
1978	Not made		
1979	3	Now	$36.00
1980	3	Now	$35.00
1981	6	Now	$68.00
1982	4	Now	$44.00
1983	5	Now	$54.00
1984	5	Now	$52.00
1985	6	Now	$60.00
1986	6	Now	$58.00
1987	5	Now	$48.00
1988	6	Now	$54.00
1989	4	Now	$36.00
1990	6	Now	$52.00
1991	6	Now	$50.00
1992	6	2004	$49.00
1993	6	2005	$48.00
1994	5	Now	$39.00
1995	6	2004	$45.00
1996	6	2008	$44.00
1997	6	2008	$42.00
1998	7	2010	$48.00
1999	7	2011	$47.00
2000	6	2010	$39.00

MOSS WOOD SEMILLON ★★★★

before 1987		Prior	
1987	6	Now	$36.00
1988	5	Now	$29.00
1989	4	Now	$22.00
1990	7	2005	$39.00
1991	4	Now	$21.00
1992	6	2006	$31.00
1993	7	2008	$35.00
1994	7	Now	$34.00
1995	6	Now	$28.00
1996	7	Now	$32.00
1997	7	2007	$31.00
1998	6	2010	$26.00
1999	7	2010	$29.00
2000	7	2010	$29.00
2001	7	2010	$28.00

***Mountadam Vineyard** is a stylish and high quality maker at High Eden in the Eden Valley. Winemaker: Adam Wynn.*

MOUNTADAM CABERNET SAUVIGNON ★★★★★

before 1994		Prior	
1994	6	Now	$49.00
1995	5	Now	$39.00

1996	7	Now	$52.00
1997	6	Now	$44.00
1998	7	Now	$50.00

MOUNTADAM CHARDONNAY ★★★★★

before 1992		Prior	
1992	6	Now	$43.00
1993	6	Now	$42.00
1994	5	Now	$34.00
1995	6	Now	$39.00
1996	7	Now	$45.00
1997	6	Now	$37.00
1998	7	Now	$42.00
1999	6	2004	$35.00
2000	6	2005	$34.00

MOUNTADAM PINOT NOIR ★★★★

before 1991		Prior	
1991	7	Now	$52.00
1992	6	Prior	
1993	7	Now	$49.00
1994	5	Prior	
1995	5	Now	$33.00
1996	7	Now	$45.00
1997	5	Now	$31.00
1998	7	Now	$43.00
1999	6	Now	$35.00
2000	7	Now	$40.00

MOUNTADAM "THE RED"
(CABERNET/MERLOT) ★★★★★

before 1992		Prior	
1992	7	Now	$64.00
1993	Not made		
1994	6	Now	$52.00
1995	6	Now	$50.00
1996	7	Now	$58.00
1997	7	Now	$56.00
1998	7	2004	$54.00

Mount Anakie *(Zambelli Wine Estates) is a Geelong maker on the vineyard originally established by Tom Maltby, and later developed by Stephen Hickinbotham. The reds were gloriously intense, but little has been heard or seen of recent wines. Winemaker: Otto Zambelli.*

MOUNT ANAKIE CHARDONNAY ★★★

before 1992		Prior	
1992	7	Now	$28.00
1993	7	Now	$27.00
1994	5	Now	$19.00
1995	5	Now	$18.50

1996	6	Now	$21.00
1997	6	Now	$21.00
1998	5	Now	$17.00

MOUNT ANAKIE CABERNET SAUVIGNON ★★★★

1987	7	Prior	
1988	6	Now	$21.00
1989	7	Now	$24.00
1990	6	Now	$20.00
1991	5	Now	$16.50
1992	6	Now	$19.00
1993	7	Now	$21.00
1994	6	Now	$18.00
1995	5	Now	$14.50

MOUNT ANAKIE DOLCETTO ★★★

before 1992		Prior	
1992	6	Now	$17.00
1993	6	Now	$16.50
1994	5	Now	$13.00
1995	6	Now	$15.50

MOUNT ANAKIE RIESLING ★★

before 1990		Prior	
1989	6	Now	$13.50
1990	7	Prior	
1991	6	Now	$13.00
1992	7	Now	$14.50
1993	7	Now	$14.00
1994	6	Now	$11.50
1995	6	Now	$11.50
1996	6	Now	$11.00

MOUNT ANAKIE SHIRAZ ★★★★

before 1989		Prior	
1989	5	Now	$19.50
1990	7	Now	$26.00
1991	7	Now	$25.00
1992	6	Now	$21.00
1993	7	Now	$24.00
1994	5	Now	$16.50
1995	5	Now	$16.00

Mount Avoca *is a Victorian producer whose range of substantial and emphatic wines are of considerable elegance. Winemaker: Matthew Barry.*

MOUNT AVOCA CABERNET SAUVIGNON ★★★★

before 1990		Prior	
1990	6	Now	$28.00
1991	7	Now	$32.00

1992	6	Now	$26.00
1993	6	Now	$25.00
1994	6	2005	$25.00
1995	6	Now	$24.00
1996	6	2005	$23.00
1997	6	2007	$22.00
1998	7	2009	$26.00
1999	6	2008	$21.00
2000	7	2010	$24.00

MOUNT AVOCA CHARDONNAY ★★★★

before 1994		Prior	
1994	5	2004	$22.00
1995	5	2004	$22.00
1996	5	2005	$21.00
1997	6	2006	$25.00
1998	6	2009	$24.00
1999	6	2008	$23.00
2000	6	2007	$23.00
2001	6	2009	$22.00

MOUNT AVOCA RESERVE NOBLE SEMILLON (375ml) ★★★★

1999	6	2006	$19.00
2000	7	2011	$21.00

MOUNT AVOCA RESERVE SHIRAZ ★★★★★

1997	7	2005	$37.00
1998	7	2007	$36.00
1999	7	2008	$35.00

MOUNT AVOCA RHAPSODY (TREBBIANO/SAUVIGNON BLANC) ★★

before 1996		Prior	
1996	6	Now	$15.00
1997	6	Now	$14.50
1998	6	Now	$14.00
1999	6	Now	$13.50
2000	6	Now	$13.00
2001	6	Now	$13.00

MOUNT AVOCA SAUVIGNON BLANC ★★★★

before 1996		Prior	
1996	6	Now	$23.00
1997	6	2004	$23.00
1998	7	2005	$26.00
1999	6	2005	$21.00
2000	7	2008	$24.00
2001	7	2008	$24.00
2002	7	2010	$23.00

MOUNT AVOCA SHIRAZ ★★★★

before 1996		Prior	
1996	6	Now	$24.00
1997	6	Now	$23.00
1998	6	2005	$22.00
1999	6	2004	$22.00
2000	7	2008	$25.00
2001	7	2008	$24.00

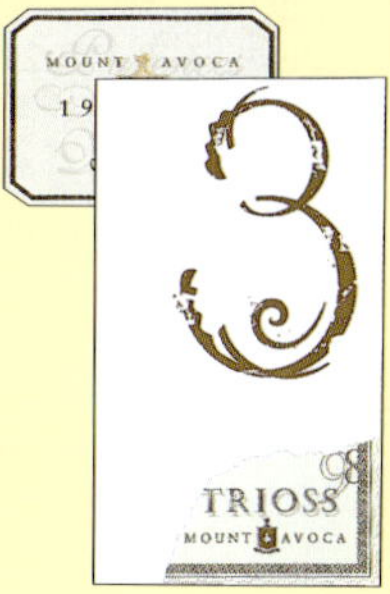

MOUNT AVOCA TRIOSS (SAUVIGNON BLANC/ CHARDONNAY/SEMILLON) ★★

before 1998		Prior	
1998	7	Now	$14.50
1999	7	Now	$14.00
2000	7	Now	$13.50
2001	7	Now	$13.00
2002	7	Now	$13.00

***Mount Helen** vineyard in Victoria's Strathbogie Ranges produces some of the State's better wines. It is now part of Beringer Blass. Winemaker: Matt Steel.*

MOUNT HELEN CABERNET/MERLOT ★★★★

before 1988		Prior	
1988	5	Now	$33.00
1989	Not made		
1990	5	Now	$31.00
1991	4	Prior	
1992	Not made		
1993	4	Now	$22.00
1994	6	Now	$33.00
1995	6	Now	$32.00
1996	7	Now	$36.00
1997	7	2004	$35.00
1998	7	2010	$34.00

MOUNT HELEN CHARDONNAY ★★★★

before 1994		Prior	
1994	5	Now	$26.00
1995	5	Now	$25.00
1996	5	Now	$24.00
1997	5	Now	$24.00
1998	7	Now	$32.00
1999	5	2004	$22.00
2000	6	2004	$26.00

***Mount Horrocks** Wines are Clare Valley producers of some remarkably good wines. Winemaker: Stephanie Toole.*

MOUNT HORROCKS CABERNET SAUVIGNON/MERLOT ★★★★

before 1990		Prior	
1990	5	Now	$41.00
1991	5	Now	$40.00

1992	5	Now	$39.00
1993	5	Now	$38.00
1994	5	Now	$37.00
1995	5	2004	$36.00
1996	5	2005	$35.00
1997	5	2005	$34.00
1998	6	2008	$39.00
1999	7	2008	$44.00
2000	7	2010	$43.00

MOUNT HORROCKS CHARDONNAY ★★★★

before 1997		Prior	
1997	4	Now	$22.00
1998	4	Now	$21.00
1999	5	Now	$26.00
2000	6	2004	$30.00
2001	6	2005	$30.00

MOUNT HORROCKS CORDON CUT RIESLING (375ml) ★★★★

before 1993		Prior	
1993	5	Now	$25.00
1994	5	Now	$25.00
1995	5	Now	$24.00
1996	7	Now	$33.00
1997	6	Now	$27.00
1998	6	2005	$26.00
1999	7	2005	$30.00
2000	7	2008	$29.00
2001	7	2008	$28.00

MOUNT HORROCKS SEMILLON (/SAUVIGNON BLANC from 1995) ★★★★

before 1996		Prior	
1996	4	Now	$22.00
1997	4	2005	$21.00
1998	4	2006	$20.00
1999	5	2008	$25.00
2000	6	2010	$29.00
2001	6	2010	$28.00

MOUNT HORROCKS SHIRAZ ★★★★★

1996	7	2010	$45.00
1997	5	2008	$31.00
1998	6	2010	$36.00
1999	6	2010	$35.00
2000	7	2012	$40.00

MOUNT HORROCKS WATERVALE RIESLING ★★★★

before 1990		Prior	
1990	6	Now	$30.00
1991	5	Now	$24.00
1992	5	Now	$23.00
1993	4	Now	$18.50

1994	6	Now	$27.00
1995	6	Now	$26.00
1996	6	2005	$25.00
1997	7	2006	$28.00
1998	6	2005	$24.00
1999	7	2010	$27.00
2000	7	2012	$26.00
2001	7	2012	$25.00

Mount Hurtle *is the McLaren Vale winery of Geoff Merrill. Wine made under this label is distributed solely through one liquor chain. Winemaker: Geoff Merrill.*

MOUNT HURTLE CABERNET SAUVIGNON/MERLOT ★★★★

1985	5	Now	$26.00
1986	5	Now	$26.00
1987	4	Now	$20.00
1988	Not made		
1989	Not made		
1990	6	Now	$27.00
1991	6	Now	$26.00
1992	5	Now	$21.00
1993	6	Now	$25.00
1994	6	Now	$24.00
1995	6	Now	$23.00
1996	7	2004	$27.00
1997	6	2004	$22.00
1998	7	2006	$25.00

MOUNT HURTLE SAUVIGNON BLANC ★★★

before 1997		Prior	
1997	6	Now	$16.50
1998	7	Now	$18.50
1999	7	Now	$18.00
2000	6	Now	$15.00

MOUNT HURTLE SHIRAZ ★★★

1990	6	Now	$26.00
1991	5	Now	$21.00
1992	5	Now	$20.00
1993	6	Now	$23.00
1994	7	Now	$27.00
1995	6	Now	$22.00
1996	7	2004	$25.00
1997	6	2004	$21.00
1998	7	2006	$24.00

***Mount Ida**, like Mount Helen, is now owned by Beringer Blass. The wine is vintaged in the Heathcote area. Winemaker: Matt Steel.*

MOUNT IDA SHIRAZ ★★★★★

1992	7	Now	$56.00
1993	Not made		
1994	7	Now	$52.00
1995	5	Now	$36.00
1996	7	2008	$49.00
1997	6	2008	$41.00
1998	7	2009	$47.00
1999	7	2012	$45.00
2000	7	2009	$44.00
2001	7	2010	$43.00

***Mount Langi Ghiran** is a Great Western district producer with a growing range of respected wines. Winemaker: Trevor Mast.*

MOUNT LANGI GHIRAN CABERNET SAUVIGNON BLEND ★★★★

before 1985		Prior	
1985	5	Now	$36.00
1986	7	2005	$49.00
1987	5	Now	$34.00
1988	6	Now	$39.00
1989	6	Now	$38.00
1990	7	Now	$43.00
1991	6	Now	$36.00
1992	6	Now	$35.00
1993	7	Now	$39.00
1994	7	2004	$38.00
1995	No data		
1996	7	2005	$36.00
1997	7	2007	$35.00
1998	6	2008	$29.00

***Mount Majura Vineyard** is a small Canberra District vineyard recently having undergone some modest expansion. Winemaker: Frank van de Loo.*

MOUNT MAJURA CABERNET FRANC/MERLOT ★★★

1993	4	Prior	
1994	4	2004	$22.00
1995	3	Prior	
1996	6	2004	$31.00
1997	4	Now	$20.00
1998	3	Prior	

1999	5	2005	$23.00
2000	5	2008	$23.00
2001	6	2009	$27.00

MOUNT MAJURA CHARDONNAY ★★★★

1995	4	Prior	
1996	4	Now	$26.00
1997	3	Prior	
1998	3	Prior	
1999	5	2004	$30.00
2000	6	2005	$35.00
2001	5	2005	$28.00
2002	6	2006	$33.00

MOUNT MAJURA PINOT NOIR ★★★★

1991	5	Prior	
1992	6	Now	$35.00
1993	Not made		
1994	4	2004	$22.00
1995	Not made		
1999	4	2005	$21.00
2000	6	2007	$30.00
2001	Not made		
2002	6	2009	$29.00

***Mount Mary** is an extreme quality small vineyard in the Yarra Valley. Their wines are among Australia's best. Winemakers: John Middleton and Rob Hall.*

MOUNT MARY QUINTET (CABERNETS) ★★★★★

1975	5	Now	$215.00
1976	6	Now	$250.00
1977	7	Now	$280.00
1978	7	Now	$270.00
1979	7	Now	$270.00
1980	7	Now	$260.00
1981	7	Now	$250.00
1982	6	Now	$210.00
1983	5	Prior	
1984	7	Now	$230.00
1985	6	Now	$190.00
1986	7	Now	$215.00
1987	6	Now	$180.00
1988	7	2004	$205.00
1989	5	Now	$140.00
1990	7	2005	$190.00
1991	7	2006	$185.00
1992	7	2007	$180.00
1993	7	2008	$175.00
1994	7	2009	$170.00
1995	7	2010	$165.00
1996	7	2011	$160.00

1997	7	2011	$155.00
1998	7	2012	$150.00
1999	7	2012	$145.00
2000	7	2014	$140.00
2001	7	2015	$140.00
2002	7	2016	$135.00

MOUNT MARY CHARDONNAY ★★★★★

before 1980		Prior	
1980	6	Now	$120.00
1981	6	Now	$115.00
1982	6	Now	$110.00
1983	6	Now	$110.00
1984	7	Prior	
1985	7	Now	$120.00
1986	6	Now	$100.00
1987	6	Now	$98.00
1988	7	Now	$110.00
1989	7	Now	$105.00
1990	6	Now	$90.00
1991	6	Now	$86.00
1992	7	Now	$98.00
1993	7	2004	$96.00
1994	7	2005	$92.00
1995	7	2006	$90.00
1996	7	2007	$88.00
1997	6	2008	$72.00
1998	7	2009	$82.00
1999	7	2010	$80.00
2000	7	2010	$78.00
2001	7	2012	$76.00
2002	7	2013	$74.00

MOUNT MARY PINOT NOIR ★★★★★

1976	6	Now	$250.00
1977	6	Now	$245.00
1978	6	Now	$235.00
1979	5	Prior	
1980	7	Now	$260.00
1981	7	Now	$250.00
1982	7	Now	$245.00
1983	6	Now	$205.00
1984	6	Now	$200.00
1985	6	Now	$190.00
1986	7	Now	$220.00
1987	7	Now	$210.00
1988	7	Now	$205.00
1989	6	Now	$170.00
1990	7	Now	$190.00
1991	7	Now	$190.00
1992	7	2004	$180.00

1993	7	2005	$175.00
1994	6	2005	$145.00
1995	7	2007	$165.00
1996	7	2008	$160.00
1997	7	2009	$155.00
1998	7	2010	$150.00
1999	7	2011	$145.00
2000	7	2012	$140.00
2001	7	2013	$140.00
2002	7	2014	$135.00

MOUNT MARY TRIOLET (SAUVIGNON BLANC/SEMILLON/MUSCADELLE) ★★★★★

1986	6	Now	$105.00
1987	5	Now	$86.00
1988	6	Now	$100.00
1989	7	Now	$110.00
1990	7	Now	$110.00
1991	7	Now	$105.00
1992	7	Now	$100.00
1993	7	2004	$100.00
1994	7	2005	$98.00
1995	7	2006	$94.00
1996	7	2007	$92.00
1997	7	2008	$88.00
1998	7	2009	$86.00
1999	7	2010	$84.00
2000	7	2010	$82.00
2001	7	2011	$78.00
2002	7	2012	$76.00

***Mount Pleasant** is a very famous Hunter Valley vineyard once owned and operated by Maurice O'Shea. For decades it has been the premier vineyard and label of McWilliams. Winemaker: Philip Ryan.*

MOUNT PLEASANT CHARDONNAY ★★★

before 1998		Prior	
1998	7	Now	$15.00
1999	7	Now	$14.50
2000	7	2004	$14.00
2001	7	2004	$14.00

MOUNT PLEASANT ELIZABETH SEMILLON ★★★

before 1990		Prior	
1990	6	Now	$21.00
1991	5	Now	$17.00
1992	7	Now	$23.00
1993	7	Now	$22.00

1994	7	Now	$22.00
1995	7	2004	$21.00
1996	7	2005	$21.00
1997	7	2006	$20.00
1998	7	2007	$19.50
1999	7	2008	$19.00
2000	7	2009	$18.50
2001	7	2010	N/R

MOUNT PLEASANT LOVEDALE SEMILLON

★★★★★

1984	7	Prior	
1985	Not made		
1986	7	Prior	
1987	Not made		
1995	7	2005	$50.00
1996	7	2006	$49.00
1997	7	2007	$47.00
1998	7	2008	$46.00
1999	7	2009	$45.00
2000	7	2010	N/R
2001	7	2011	N/R

MOUNT PLEASANT MAURICE O'SHEA CHARDONNAY

★★★★★

before 1997		Prior	
1997	Not made		
1998	7	Now	$35.00
1999	7	Now	$33.00
2000	7	2004	$33.00
2001	Not made		

MOUNT PLEASANT MAURICE O'SHEA SHIRAZ

★★★★★

1987	7	Now	$52.00
1988	7	Now	$50.00
1989	Not made		
1990	Not made		
1991	7	Now	$46.00
1992	Not made		
1993	6	Now	$37.00
1994	7	Now	$42.00
1995	7	Now	$41.00
1996	7	2004	$39.00
1997	7	2005	$38.00
1998	7	2006	$37.00
1999	7	2007	$36.00
2000	7	2008	$35.00
2001	Not made		

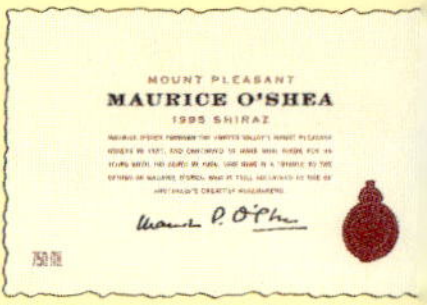

MOUNT PLEASANT MERLOT ★★★★

1991	7	Now	$22.00
1992	Not made		
1996	6	Prior	
1997	6	Now	$17.00
1998	7	2006	$19.50
1999	7	2006	$19.00
2000	7	2007	$18.50
2001	6	2007	$15.50

MOUNT PLEASANT PHILIP SHIRAZ ★★★

before 1991		Prior	
1991	7	Now	$24.00
1992	6	Now	$20.00
1993	6	Now	$20.00
1994	6	Now	$19.00
1995	7	Now	$22.00
1996	7	Now	$21.00
1997	7	2004	$20.00
1998	7	2005	$20.00
1999	7	2006	$19.50
2000	7	2007	$18.50
2001	6	2008	N/R

MOUNT PLEASANT OLD PADDOCK AND OLD HILL SHIRAZ ★★★★★

before 1985		Prior	
1985	7	Now	$43.00
1986	7	Now	$42.00
1987	7	Now	$41.00
1988	Not made		
1989	6	Now	$33.00
1990	6	Now	$32.00
1991	Not made		
1992	Not made		
1993	6	Now	$29.00
1994	7	Now	$33.00
1995	7	Now	$32.00
1996	7	2004	$31.00
1997	7	2005	$30.00
1998	7	2006	$29.00
1999	7	2007	$28.00
2000	7	2008	$28.00
2001	Not made		

MOUNT PLEASANT ROSEHILL SHIRAZ ★★★★★

1984	7	Now	$50.00
1985	7	Now	$50.00
1986	Not made		

1987	7	Now	$47.00
1988	6	Now	$39.00
1989	6	Now	$38.00
1990	5	Prior	
1991	7	Now	$42.00
1992	Not made		
1993	Not made		
1994	Not made		
1995	7	Now	$37.00
1996	7	2004	$36.00
1997	7	2005	$35.00
1998	7	2006	$34.00
1999	7	2007	$33.00
2000	7	2008	$32.00
2001	7	2009	$31.00

***Mount View Estate** is a small terraced vineyard near Cessnock in the Hunter Valley. Unusually for the area, their range includes some very fine fortified wines. Winemaker: Keith Tulloch.*

MOUNT VIEW ESTATE CABERNET SAUVIGNON ★★★

before 1983		Prior	
1983	7	Now	$36.00
1984	Not made		
1985	5	Prior	
1986	6	Prior	
1987	6	Prior	
1988	6	Prior	
1989	5	Prior	
1990	6	Prior	
1991	6	Now	$24.00
1992	Not made		
1993	5	Now	$19.00
1994	7	Now	$26.00
1995	Not made		
1996	5	Now	$17.50
1997	6	Now	$20.00
1998	No data		
1999	No data		
2000	5	2007	$15.50

MOUNT VIEW ESTATE CHARDONNAY ★★★

before 1993		Prior	
1993	6	Now	$17.00
1994	6	Now	$16.50
1995	5	Now	$13.50

1996	No data		$13.50
2000	6	Now	$15.00
2001	7	2004	$17.50

MOUNT VIEW ESTATE SHIRAZ ★★★★

before 1986		Prior	
1986	7	Now	$29.00
1987	6	Prior	
1988	Not made		
1989	Not made		
1990	6	Prior	
1991	7	Now	$25.00
1992	5	Prior	
1993	6	Now	$20.00
1994	7	Now	$22.00
1995	6	Now	$19.00
1996	5	Now	$15.00
1997	6	Now	$18.00
1998	No data		
1999	No data		
2000	7	2007	$19.00

MOUNT VIEW ESTATE VERDELHO (LIQUEUR) ★★★★

1986	6	Now	$25.00
1987	7	Now	$29.00
1988	6	Now	$24.00
1989	6	Now	$23.00
1990	5	Now	$19.00
1991	7	Now	$25.00
1992	5	Now	$17.50
1993	6	Now	$20.00
1994	7	2004	$23.00
1995	6	2004	$19.50

MOUNT VIEW ESTATE VERDELHO (TRADITIONAL) ★★★

before 1988		Prior	
1988	7	Now	$30.00
1989	6	Prior	
1990	6	Prior	
1991	7	Now	$28.00
1992	6	Prior	
1993	7	Now	$26.00
1994	5	Now	$18.00
1995	6	Now	$21.00
1996	7	Now	$24.00
1997	7	Now	$23.00
1998	No data		
2000	5	2004	$15.50

Nepenthe Vineyards *are innovative Lenswood (Adelaide Hills) makers whose range includes an admirable Zinfandel. Winemaker: Peter Leske.*

NEPENTHE CHARDONNAY ★★★★

1997	7	Now	$35.00
1998	5	Now	$24.00
1999	6	Now	$28.00
2000	6	2004	$27.00
2001	6	2005	$27.00

NEPENTHE PINOT NOIR ★★★★

1997	4	Prior	
1998	6	Now	$35.00
1999	6	Now	$34.00
2000	6	2005	$33.00
2001	6	2005	$32.00

NEPENTHE RIESLING ★★★★

1998	7	Now	$24.00
1999	6	Now	$20.00
2000	6	2004	$19.50
2001	6	2006	$19.00

NEPENTHE SAUVIGNON BLANC ★★★

before 2001		Prior	
2001	6	Now	$18.00

NEPENTHE SEMILLON ★★★★

1997	6	Now	$27.00
1998	7	2005	$30.00
1999	6	Now	$25.00
2000	5	Now	$20.00
2001	6	2006	$24.00

NEPENTHE "THE FUGUE" (CABERNET/MERLOT) ★★★★

1997	7	2005	$42.00
1998	6	Now	$35.00
1999	6	2005	$34.00
2000	6	2007	$33.00

NEPENTHE UNWOODED CHARDONNAY ★★★

before 2000		Prior	
2000	6	Now,	
2001	6	Now	$16.00

NEPENTHE ZINFANDEL ★★★★★

1997	7	Now	$58.00
1998	4	Prior	
1999	6	Now	$47.00
2000	6	Now	$46.00
2001	7	2004	$52.00

***Nicholson River Winery** in Victoria's Gippsland area produces, among other wines, a Chardonnay whose quality in its best years is little short of supreme. Winemaker: Ken Eckersley.*

NICHOLSON RIVER CHARDONNAY ★★★★★

before 1997		Prior	
1997	7	Now	$60.00
1998	5	Now	$42.00
1999	6	2004	$49.00
2000	6	2005	$47.00
2001	5	2005	$38.00

NICHOLSON RIVER PINOT NOIR ★★★★★

before 1990		Prior	
1990	6	Now	$46.00
1991	5	Now	$37.00
1992	7	Now	$50.00
1993	6	Now	$42.00
1994	Not made		
1995	Not made		
1996	7	Now	$45.00
1997	Not made		
1998	5	Now	$30.00
1999	6	2005	$35.00
2000	7	2006	$40.00
2001	7	2007	$39.00

***Normans Wines** are substantial McLaren Vale based producers of a large, reliable range including the flagship "Chais Clarendon" wines. Winemakers: Peter Fraser and Rebecca Kennedy.*

NORMANS ADELAIDE HILLS CHARDONNAY ★★★★

1998	6	204	$26.00
1999	5	2004	$21.00
2000	7	2006	$29.00

NORMANS BOTRYTIS (375ml) ★★★★

1995	5	Now	$24.00
1996	6	Now	$28.00
1997	6	Now	$27.00
1998	Not made		
1999	6	Now	$26.00

NORMANS CHAIS CLARENDON CABERNET SAUVIGNON ★★★★

before 1988		Prior	
1988	6	Now	$52.00
1989	5	Now	$42.00
1990	7	Now	$56.00
1991	5	Now	$39.00

1992	6	Now	$46.00
1993	Not made		
1994	6	2005	$43.00
1995	6	2006	$42.00
1996	7	2008	$47.00
1997	Not made		
1998	7	2010	$45.00
1999	7	2010	N/R

NORMANS CHAIS CLARENDON CHARDONNAY ★★★★

before 1990		Prior	
1990	7	Now	$32.00
1991	5	Now	$22.00
1992	Not made		
1993	Not made		
1994	6	Now	$24.00
1995	5	Now	$20.00
1996	5	Now	$19.50
1997	6	Now	$22.00
1998	Not made		
1999	7	2005	$25.00

NORMANS CHAIS CLARENDON SHIRAZ ★★★★

before 1989		Prior	
1989	6	Now	$48.00
1990	7	Now	$54.00
1991	Not made		
1992	6	Now	$44.00
1993	6	Now	$43.00
1994	6	Now	$42.00
1995	6	Now	$40.00
1996	7	Now	$46.00
1997	6	Now	$38.00
1998	7	2010	$43.00
1999	7	2010	N/R

NORMANS ENCOUNTER BAY CABERNET SAUVIGNON ★★★

1997	6	2008	$16.00
1998	7	2005	$18.00
1999	6	2006	$15.00

NORMANS ENCOUNTER BAY CHARDONNAY ★★★

1998	6	2005	$14.50
1999	6	2005	$14.00
2000	6	2006	$14.00

NORMANS ENCOUNTER BAY MERLOT ★★★

1997	6	Now	$16.00
1998	7	2005	$18.00
1999	6	2006	$15.00

NORMANS ENCOUNTER BAY SHIRAZ ★★★

1997	6	Now	$16.00
1998	6	2005	$15.50
1999	7	2006	$17.50

NORMANS LANGHORNE CREEK CABERNET SAUVIGNON /FRANC ★★★★

1997	5	Now	$22.00
1998	7	2008	$30.00
1999	6	2008	$25.00

NORMANS OLD VINE SHIRAZ ★★★★

1997	6	Now	$23.00
1998	7	2005	$27.00
1999	7	2008	$26.00

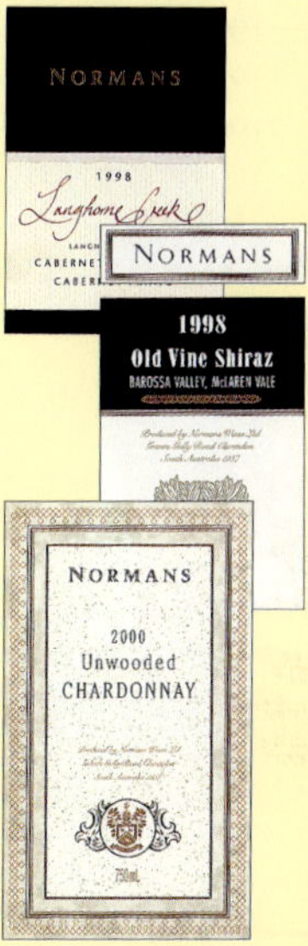

NORMANS UNWOODED CHARDONNAY ★★★

1996	7	Now	$15.50
1997	6	Now	$12.50
1998	7	Now	$14.50
1999	6	Now	$12.00
2000	7	Now	$13.50

NORMANS WHITE LABEL CABERNET SAUVIGNON ★★★

before 1990		Prior	
1990	5	Now	$15.00
1991	6	Now	$17.50
1992	6	Now	$17.00
1993	5	Now	$13.50
1994	6	Now	$16.00
1995	6	Now	$15.50
1996	7	Now	$17.50
1997	6	2004	$14.50
1998	6	2008	$14.00
1999	6	2008	N/R

NORMANS WHITE LABEL CHARDONNAY ★★★

before 1990		Prior	
1990	6	Now	$18.50
1991	5	Now	$15.00
1992	5	Now	$14.50
1993	6	Now	$17.00
1994	5	Now	$13.50
1995	6	Now	$16.00
1996	7	Now	$18.00

1997	6	Now	$15.00
1998	6	Now	$14.50
1999	7	2004	$16.50

NORMANS WHITE LABEL MERLOT ★★★

1995	6	Now	$14.50
1996	7	Now	$16.50
1997	6	Now	$13.50
1998	6	Now	$13.50
1999	7	Now	$15.00

NORMANS WHITE LABEL PINOT NOIR ★★★

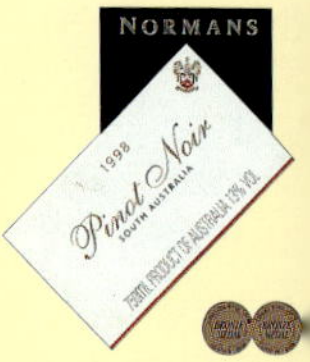

1996	5	Now	$13.50
1997	5	Now	$13.50
1998	6	Now	$15.50
1999	6	Now	$15.00

***Oakridge Estate** is a Yarra Valley (Coldstream) maker of a remarkably powerful yet graceful Reserve Cabernet (produced only in outstanding years). Winemaker: Steve Warne.*

OAKRIDGE ESTATE CABERNET SAUVIGNON /MERLOT ★★★★

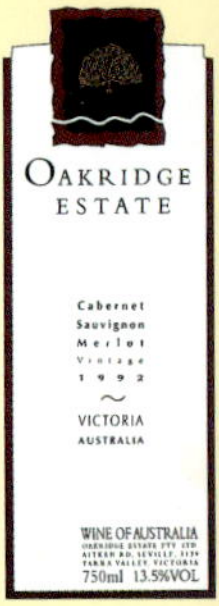

before 1991		Prior	
1991	7	Now	$30.00
1992	6	Now	$25.00
1993	5	Prior	
1994	6	Now	$24.00
1995	6	Now	$23.00
1996	5	Prior	
1997	6	Now	$22.00
1998	6	Now	$21.00
1999	6	Now	$20.00
2000	6	2005	$20.00

OAKRIDGE ESTATE CHARDONNAY ★★★★

1993	5	Prior	
1994	6	Now	$22.00
1995	5	Now	$18.50
1996	4	Prior	
1997	7	Now	$24.00
1998	6	Now	$20.00
1999	6	Now	$19.50
2000	6	2004	$19.00

OAKRIDGE RESERVE CABERNET SAUVIGNON ★★★★★

1986	5	Prior	
1987	Not made		
1988	Not made		
1989	Not made		
1990	5	Now	$50.00
1991	7	Now	$68.00
1992	Not made		
1993	Not made		
1994	6	Now	$52.00
1995	5	Now	$43.00
1996	Not made		
1997	7	2005	$56.00
1998	Not made		
1999	Not made		
2000	7	2008	$52.00

***Oakvale** is an historic winery in the Hunter Valley's Pokolbin area, established in 1893. It's recent purchase by its new proprietors has been accompanied by a substantial upgrade to the winery facilities. Winemaker: Richard Owens.*

OAKVALE CLASSIC SHIRAZ ★★★

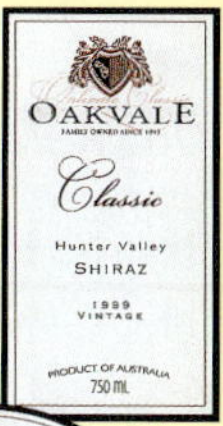

1998	No data		
1999	7	2004	$20.00
2000	7	2005	$20.00

OAKVALE PEACH TREE RESERVE CHARDONNAY ★★★★

before 1994		Prior	
1994	6	Now	$33.00
1995	7	Now	$38.00
1996	6	Now	$31.00
1997	6	Now	$31.00
1998	No data		
1999	6	Now	$29.00
2000	7	2007	$33.00

OAKVALE PEACH TREE RESERVE SEMILLON ★★★★

1986	5	Prior	
1987	7	Now	$49.00
1988	7	Now	$48.00
1989	5	Now	$33.00
1990	6	Now	$38.00
1991	6	Now	$37.00
1992	6	Now	$36.00
1993	5	Now	$29.00
1994	6	Now	$34.00

1995	7	Now	$39.00
1996	6	Now	$32.00
1997	7	Now	$36.00
1998	No data		
1999	7	2010	$34.00
2000	7	2010	$33.00

OAKVALE RESERVE PEPPERCORN SHIRAZ ★★★★

1985	6	Prior	
1986	Not made		
1987	7	Now	$49.00
1988	5	Prior	
1989	6	Now	$39.00
1990	6	Prior	
1991	7	Now	$43.00
1992	Not made		
1993	6	Now	$35.00
1994	6	Now	$34.00
1995	7	Now	$39.00
1996	6	Now	$32.00
1997	6	Now	$31.00
1998	No data		
1999	6	2006	$29.00
2000	7	2008	$33.00

***Orlando** (Orlando Wyndham) is a large producer with a comprehensive range of well respected wines. Winemaker: Philip Laffer.*

ORLANDO CENTENARY HILL BAROSSA SHIRAZ ★★★★★

1994	6	Now	$54.00
1995	5	Now	$44.00
1996	7	2006	$60.00
1997	6	2007	$50.00
1998	7	2013	$56.00
1999	6	2009	$47.00
2000	Not made		
2001	Not made		
2002	7	2020	N/R

ORLANDO GRAMPS BAROSSA VALLEY GRENACHE ★★★★

before 1999		Prior	
1999	6	Now	$16.00
2000	Not made		
2001	Not made		
2002	7	2004	$17.00

ORLANDO GRAMPS BOTRYTIS SEMILLON ★★★

before 1996		Prior	
1996	7	Now	$20.00
1997	7	Now	$19.00
1998	7	Now	$18.50
1999	5	Now	$13.00
2000	Not made		
2001	7	Now	$17.00
2002	7	2004	$16.50

ORLANDO GRAMPS CABERNET/MERLOT ★★★★

before 1995		Prior	
1995	5	Now	$15.50
1996	6	Now	$18.50
1997	5	Now	$15.00
1998	7	2004	$20.00
1999	6	2007	$16.50
2000	6	2008	$16.00
2001	7	2009	$18.50

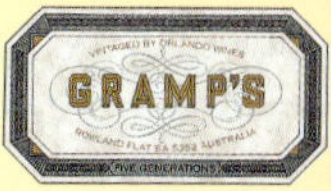

ORLANDO GRAMPS CHARDONNAY ★★★

before 1996		Prior	
1996	7	Now	$20.00
1997	6	Now	$16.50
1998	7	Now	$19.00
1999	7	Now	$18.50
2000	5	Now	$12.50
2001	7	Now	$17.50
2002	7	Now	$17.00

ORLANDO JACARANDA RIDGE COONAWARRA CABERNET ★★★★★

1982	7	Now	$105.00
1983	Not made		
1984	Not made		
1985	Not made		
1986	6	Now	$80.00
1987	5	Now	$66.00
1988	6	Now	$76.00
1989	5	Now	$62.00
1990	Not made		
1991	7	Now	$82.00
1992	5	Now	$56.00
1993	Not made		
1994	5	Now	$52.00
1995	Not made		
1996	7	2008	$70.00
1997	5	2005	$49.00
1998	7	2012	$66.00

1999	6	2009	$54.00
2000	6	2010	N/R
2001	Not made		

ORLANDO JACOBS CREEK CHABLIS SEMILLON/SAUVIGNON BLANC) ★★

before 1997		Prior	
1997	6	Now	$7.75
1998	7	Now	$8.75
1999	7	Now	$8.50
2000	7	Now	$8.25

ORLANDO JACOBS CREEK CHARDONNAY ★★★

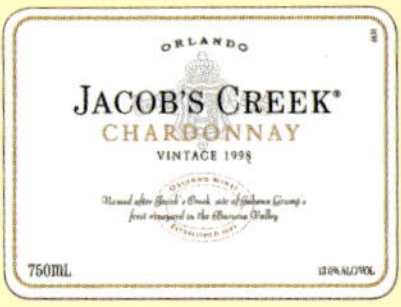

before 1996		Prior	
1996	7	Now	$18.00
1997	7	Now	$17.50
1998	7	Now	$17.00
1999	7	Now	$16.50
2000	6	Now	$13.50
2001	7	Now	$15.50
2002	7	Now	$15.00

ORLANDO JACOBS CREEK GRENACHE/SHIRAZ ★★

before 2002		Prior	
2002	7	Now	
2003	5	Now	$8.00

ORLANDO JACOBS CREEK LIMITED RELEASE SHIRAZ/CABERNET ★★★★★

1994	6	Now	$64.00
1995	5	Now	$52.00
1996	7	2005	$70.00
1997	5	2005	$49.00
1998	7	2013	$66.00
1999	7	2009	$64.00
2000	7	2012	N/R
2002	7	2015	N/R

ORLANDO JACOBS CREEK MERLOT ★★

2000	5	Prior	
2001	5	Now	
2002	5	Now	$8.00

ORLANDO JACOBS CREEK RESERVE CABERNET SAUVIGNON ★★★★

1998	7	2006	$19.50
1999	5	2004	$13.50
2000	6	2004	$15.50
2001	6	2005	$15.00
2002	7	2010	N/R

ORLANDO JACOBS CREEK RESERVE SHIRAZ ★★★★

1998	6	2006	$15.50
1999	7	2009	$18.00
2000	7	2008	$17.00
2001	6	2006	$14.50
2002	7	2010	N/R

ORLANDO JACOBS CREEK RIESLING ★★

before 1995		Prior	
1995	7	Now	$18.50
1996	7	Now	$18.00
1997	7	Now	$17.50
1998	7	Now	$17.00
1999	7	Now	$16.50
2000	7	Now	$16.00
2001	6	Now	$13.00
2002	7	Now	$15.00

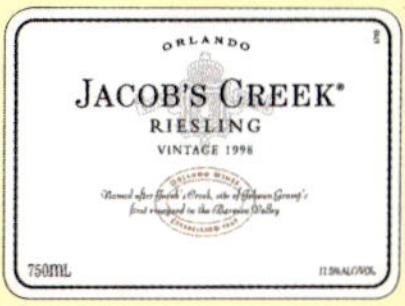

ORLANDO JACOBS CREEK SEMILLON/CHARDONNAY ★★

1998	7	Now	$11.00
1999	6	Now	$9.00
2000	5	Now	$7.25
2001	7	Now	$10.00
2002	7	Now	$9.75

ORLANDO JACOBS CREEK SEMILLON/SAUVIGNON BLANC ★★

1996	6	Prior	
1997	6	Now	$8.25
1998	7	Now	$9.25
1999	7	Now	$9.00
2000	7	Now	$8.75
2001	6	Now	$7.25

ORLANDO JACOBS CREEK SHIRAZ/CABERNET ★★

before 1998		Prior	
1998	7	Now	$9.50
1999	6	Now	$7.75
2000	6	Now	$7.50
2001	7	2004	$8.50
2002	7	2005	$8.25

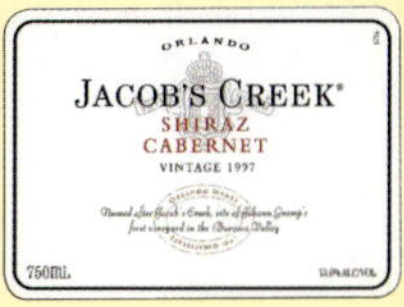

ORLANDO LAWSONS PADTHAWAY SHIRAZ ★★★★

before 1988		Prior	
1988	7	Now	$92.00
1989	6	Now	$78.00

1990	6	Now	$74.00
1991	7	2004	$84.00
1992	5	Now	$58.00
1993	6	2005	$68.00
1994	7	2010	$78.00
1995	Not made		
1996	7	2014	$74.00
1997	6	2010	$60.00
1998	7	2016	$68.00
1999	6	2009	$58.00
2000	6	2010	$56.00
2001	Not made		
2002	7	2020	N/R

ORLANDO RUSSET RIDGE CABERNET/SHIRAZ/MERLOT ★★★★

1991	6	Now	$21.00
1992	5	Prior	
1993	5	Prior	
1994	6	Now	$19.50
1995	4	Prior	
1996	7	2004	$21.00
1997	5	Now	$14.50
1998	7	2006	$20.00
1999	6	2004	$16.50
2000	Not made		
2001	Not made		

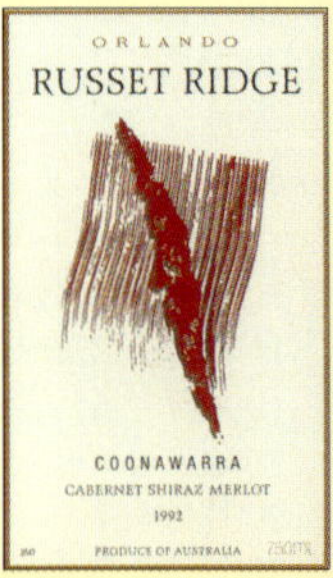

ORLANDO RUSSET RIDGE CHARDONNAY ★★★

1996	6	Now	$14.00
1997	7	Now	$16.00
1998	7	Now	$15.50

ORLANDO STEINGARTEN RIESLING ★★★★★

before 1987		Prior	
1987	7	Now	$40.00
1988	7	Now	$39.00
1989	6	Now	$32.00
1990	7	Now	$36.00
1991	6	Now	$30.00
1992	6	Now	$29.00
1993	Not made		
1994	7	Now	$32.00
1995	7	Now	$31.00
1996	7	Now	$30.00
1997	7	Now	$29.00
1998	7	Now	$29.00
1999	7	Now	$28.00
2000	Not made		
2001	7	2004	$26.00
2002	7	2004	$25.00

ORLANDO ST HELGA EDEN VALLEY RIESLING ★★★★

before 1986		Prior	
1986	7	Now	$27.00
1987	6	Prior	
1988	6	Now	$22.00
1989	6	Now	$21.00
1990	7	Now	$24.00
1991	5	Prior	
1992	7	Now	$23.00
1993	6	Now	$19.00
1994	7	Now	$21.00
1995	7	Now	$21.00
1996	7	Now	$20.00
1997	6	Now	$17.00
1998	7	Now	$19.00
1999	7	Now	$18.50
2000	5	Now	$13.00
2001	7	Now	$17.50
2002	7	2004	$17.00

ORLANDO ST HILARY CHARDONNAY ★★★★

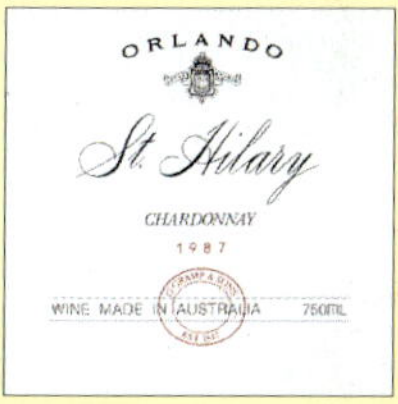

before 1992		Prior	
1992	7	Now	$25.00
1993	6	Now	$21.00
1994	6	Now	$20.00
1995	6	Now	$20.00
1996	7	Now	$22.00
1997	7	Now	$22.00
1998	7	Now	$21.00
1999	7	Now	$20.00
2000	6	Now	$17.00
2001	7	Now	$19.50
2002	7	2004	$18.50

ORLANDO ST HUGO COONAWARRA CABERNET SAUVIGNON ★★★★

before 1982		Prior	
1982	7	Now	$54.00
1983	Prior		$54.00
1990	6	Now	$43.00
1991	7	Now	$49.00
1992	5	2005	$34.00
1993	5	Now	$33.00
1994	6	2005	$38.00
1995	Not made		
1996	7	2008	$42.00
1997	5	2008	$29.00
1998	7	2012	$40.00

1999	6	2008	$33.00
2000	6	2010	$32.00
2001	6	2011	$31.00

ORLANDO TRILOGY CABERNET SAUVIGNON/FRANC/MERLOT ★★★

1998	7	Now	$16.50
1999	5	Now	$11.50
2000	6	Now	$13.50
2001	7	2004	$15.00
2002	7	2006	N/R

Parker Estate *is a Coonawarra vineyard producing Bordeaux style reds of remarkable quality. The flagship wine, Terra Rossa First Growth, is an extraordinary achievement. Winemaker: Chris Cameron.*

PARKER ESTATE TERRA ROSSA FIRST GROWTH ★★★★★

1988	6	Now	$110.00
1989	5	Now	$92.00
1990	7	Now	$125.00
1991	7	2004	$120.00
1992	Not made		
1993	5	Now	$82.00
1994	6	2004	$96.00
1995	Not made		
1996	6	2008	$90.00
1997	Not made		
1998	7	2012	$100.00
1999	6	2010	$82.00

Passing Clouds *is a Bendigo district maker with very individual wines of grace and power. Winemaker: Graeme Leith.*

PASSING CLOUDS "ANGEL BLEND" (CABERNETS) ★★★★

1982	6	Now	$60.00
1983	Not made		
1984	6	Now	$56.00
1985	6	Now	$56.00
1986	Not made		
1987	6	Now	$52.00
1988	Not made		
1989	Not made		
1990	6	2005	$48.00
1991	6	2006	$47.00
1992	6	2007	$45.00
1993	Not made		
1994	6	2009	$43.00
1995	6	2010	$41.00

1996	6	Now	$40.00
1997	6	Now	$39.00
1998	6	2004	$38.00
1999	6	2005	$37.00
2000	6	2006	$36.00
2001	6	2008	$35.00

PASSING CLOUDS SHIRAZ/CABERNET SAUVIGNON ★★★★

1980	6	Now	$58.00
1981	6	Now	$56.00
1982	6	Now	$54.00
1983	6	Now	$52.00
1984	6	Now	$50.00
1985	5	Now	$41.00
1986	6	Now	$48.00
1987	4	Prior	
1988	5	Prior	
1989	5	Prior	
1990	6	Prior	
1991	6	Now	$41.00
1992	6	Now	$40.00
1993	Not made		
1994	6	Now	$38.00
1995	6	Now	$37.00
1996	6	Now	$36.00
1997	6	Now	$35.00
1998	6	Now	$34.00
1999	6	2004	$33.00
2000	6	2005	$32.00
2001	6	2008	$31.00

PASSING CLOUDS PINOT NOIR ★★★★

before 1994		Prior	
1994	7	Now	$31.00
1995	6	Now	$26.00
1996	6	Now	$25.00
1997	6	Now	$24.00
1998	6	Now	$24.00
1999	5	Now	$19.00
2000	6	Now	$22.00
2001	6	2004	$22.00

PASSING CLOUDS SHIRAZ ★★★★

1994	5	Now	$36.00
1995	Not made		
1996	6	Now	$41.00
1997	6	Now	$40.00
1998	6	Now	$39.00
1999	Not made		
2000	6	Now	$37.00
2001	6	2004	$36.00

***Pauletts Polish Hill River Wines** is a Clare area producer of finely crafted wines. Winemaker: Neil Paulett.*

PAULETTS POLISH HILL RIVER RIESLING ★★★★

before 1990		Prior	
1990	7	Now	$28.00
1991	6	Now	$23.00
1992	6	Now	$23.00
1993	7	Now	$26.00
1994	6	Now	$21.00
1995	7	2005	$24.00
1996	6	Now	$20.00
1997	6	2005	$20.00
1998	6	2008	$19.50
1999	5	2009	$15.50
2000	6	2010	$18.00
2001	6	2011	$17.50
2002	7	2012	$20.00

PAULETTS POLISH HILL RIVER SHIRAZ ★★★★

1984	7	Prior	
1985	4	Now	$21.00
1986	6	Now	$31.00
1987	6	Now	$30.00
1988	5	Now	$24.00
1989	7	Now	$33.00
1990	5	Now	$23.00
1991	6	Now	$27.00
1992	5	Now	$21.00
1993	6	Now	$25.00
1994	6	Now	$24.00
1995	6	Now	$24.00
1996	5	Now	$19.50
1997	5	Now	$18.50
1998	7	2005	$25.00
1999	6	2005	$21.00
200	6	2008	$20.00

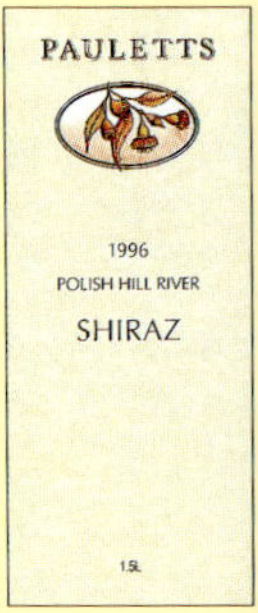

***Peel Estate** is a South West Coastal (W.A.) producer of stylish and elegant wines. Winemaker: Will Nairn.*

PEEL ESTATE CABERNET SAUVIGNON ★★★★

1983	5	Prior	
1984	7	Now	$60.00
1985	7	Now	$58.00
1986	5	Prior	
1987	4	Prior	
1988	Not made		
1989	5	Now	$37.00
1990	6	Now	$43.00
1991	5	Now	$35.00
1992	6	Now	$41.00

1993	6	Now	$40.00
1994	6	2004	$38.00
1995	5	Now	$31.00
1996	6	2006	$36.00
1997	6	2007	$35.00
1998	7	2008	$40.00
1999	7	2009	$39.00
2000	7	2010	$38.00

PEEL ESTATE CHARDONNAY ★★★★

before 1990		Prior	
1990	7	Now	$31.00
1991	5	Now	$22.00
1992	6	Now	$25.00
1993	5	Now	$20.00
1994	6	2004	$24.00
1995	5	Now	$19.50
1996	6	2004	$22.00
1997	6	2005	$22.00
1998	6	2006	$21.00
1999	7	2007	$24.00
2000	7	2008	$23.00
2001	7	2009	$23.00

PEEL ESTATE CHENIN BLANC (WOOD-AGED) ★★★★

before 1986		Prior	
1986	6	Now	$33.00
1987	5	Now	$27.00
1988	7	Now	$37.00
1989	5	Now	$25.00
1990	6	Now	$29.00
1991	5	Now	$24.00
1992	6	Now	$28.00
1993	6	Now	$27.00
1994	7	2004	$30.00
1995	6	2006	$25.00
1996	5	2006	$20.00
1997	6	2009	$24.00
1998	7	2010	$27.00
1999	6	2010	$22.00
2000	6	2010	$22.00

PEEL ESTATE SHIRAZ ★★★★

before 1986		Prior	
1986	7	Now	$62.00
1987	5	Prior	
1988	7	Now	$58.00
1989	5	Now	$40.00
1990	7	Now	$54.00
1991	5	Prior	

1992	6	Now	$44.00
1993	6	Now	$43.00
1994	7	2010	$49.00
1995	6	2005	$40.00
1996	7	2011	$46.00
1997	6	2010	$38.00
1998	7	2012	$43.00
1999	7	2012	$42.00

Pendarves Estate *at Belford in the Hunter Valley is a 20 hectare vineyard with a range of varieties prime among which is Verdelho. Winemaker: Greg Silkman.*

PENDARVES ESTATE CHAMBOURCIN ★★★

1997	5	Now	$18.00
1998	7	2006	$24.00
1999	6	2005	$20.00
2000	6	2005	$20.00

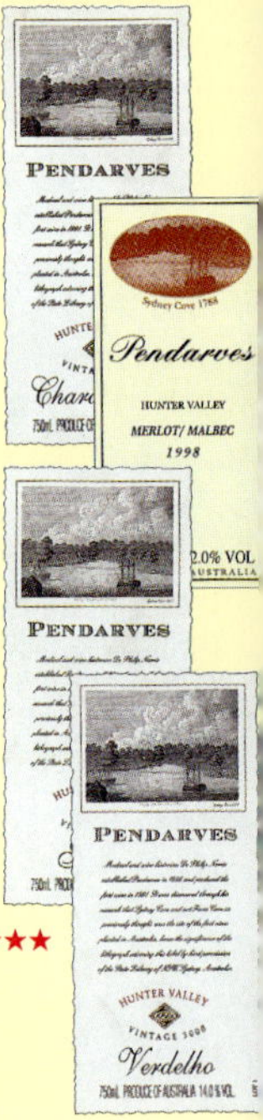

PENDARVES ESTATE CHARDONNAY ★★★★

1998	6	Now	$22.00
1999	5	Now	$18.00
2000	6	2005	$21.00

PENDARVES ESTATE MERLOT BLEND ★★★★

1997	4	Now	$24.00
1998	5	2005	$29.00
1999	4	2004	$22.00
2000	5	2005	$27.00

PENDARVES ESTATE SHIRAZ ★★★★

1998	6	Now	$28.00
1999	5	Now	$22.00
2000	6	2005	$26.00

PENDARVES ESTATE VERDELHO ★★★★

1998	5	Now	$19.00
1999	4	Now	$14.50
2000	6	Now	$21.00

Penfolds *is the flagship label of the huge Southcorp Wine Group. They have a richly warranted reputation, particularly for red wines. Winemakers: Peter Gago et al.*

PENFOLDS ADELAIDE HILLS CHARDONNAY ★★★★

1995	6	Now	$32.00
1996	7	Now	$37.00
1997	6	Now	$30.00
1998	7	Now	$34.00
1999	6	Now	$29.00

No longer made

PENFOLDS AGED RIESLING ★★★★

before 1997		Prior	
1997	5	Now	$15.50
1998	6	2004	$18.50
1999	7	2006	$21.00

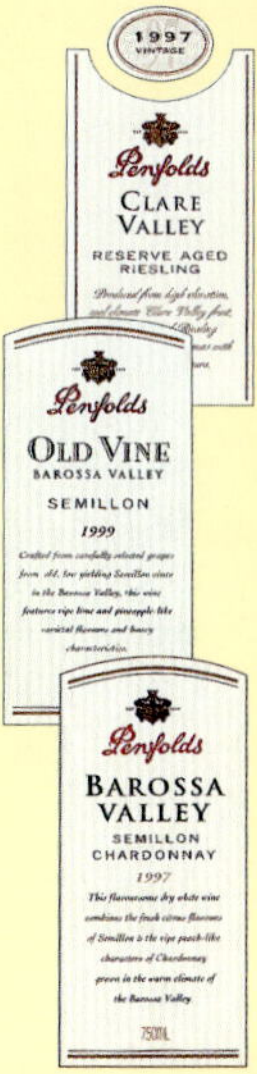

PENFOLDS BAROSSA VALLEY OLD VINES SEMILLON ★★★★

1995	6	Now	$20.00
1996	5	Now	$16.50
1997	6	Now	$19.00
1998	6	Now	$18.50

No longer made

PENFOLDS BAROSSA VALLEY SEMILLON/CHARDONNAY ★★★

before 1996		Prior	
1996	6	Now	$13.00
1997	6	Now	$12.50
1998	7	Now	$14.00
1999	5	Now	$10.00

No longer made

PENFOLDS BIN 28 KALIMNA SHIRAZ ★★★★

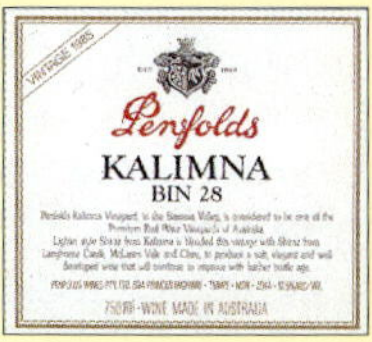

before 1986		Prior	
1986	7	Now	$43.00
1987	5	Prior	
1988	6	Now	$35.00
1989	5	Prior	
1990	7	Now	$38.00
1991	7	Now	$37.00
1992	5	Now	$26.00
1993	5	Now	$25.00
1994	5	Now	$24.00
1995	4	Prior	
1996	7	Now	$32.00
1997	5	Now	$22.00
1998	7	2005	$30.00
1999	5	Now	$21.00
2000	5	2005	$20.00
2001	7	2008	$28.00

PENFOLDS BIN 128 COONAWARRA SHIRAZ ★★★★

before 1990		Prior	
1990	6	Now	$33.00
1991	7	Now	$38.00
1992	4	Prior	
1993	6	Now	$30.00
1994	5	Now	$24.00
1995	4	Now	$19.00

1996	7	2004	$32.00
1997	6	Now	$27.00
1998	7	2005	$31.00
1999	5	Now	$21.00
2000	5	2005	$20.00
2001	6	2006	$24.00

PENFOLDS BIN 389 CABERNET SAUVIGNON/SHIRAZ ★★★★

before 1982		Prior	
1982	7	Now	$70.00
1983	7	Now	$68.00
1984	4	Prior	
1985	6	Prior	
1986	6	Now	$52.00
1987	6	Now	$50.00
1988	6	Now	$50.00
1989	6	Now	$48.00
1990	7	Now	$54.00
1991	7	Now	$52.00
1992	5	Now	$37.00
1993	7	Now	$50.00
1994	6	Now	$42.00
1995	4	Now	$27.00
1996	7	2005	$46.00
1997	5	2004	$32.00
1998	7	2007	$43.00
1999	5	2006	$30.00
2000	5	2007	$29.00

PENFOLDS BIN 407 CABERNET SAUVIGNON ★★★★

1990	7	Now	$40.00
1991	7	Now	$39.00
1992	5	Prior	
1993	5	Now	$26.00
1994	7	2004	$36.00
1995	4	Prior	
1996	7	2004	$34.00
1997	5	Now	$23.00
1998	7	2006	$32.00
1999	5	2004	$22.00
2000	5	2005	$21.00
2001	7	2009	$29.00

PENFOLDS BIN 707 CABERNET SAUVIGNON ★★★★★

1976	6	Now	$160.00
1977	5	Prior	
1978	6	Prior	
1979	5	Prior	

1980	6	Prior	
1981	Not made		
1982	6	Prior	
1983	7	Now	$150.00
1984	5	Prior	
1985	6	Prior	
1986	7	Now	$135.00
1987	5	Now	$96.00
1988	6	Now	$110.00
1989	5	Now	$90.00
1990	7	Now	$120.00
1991	7	Now	$120.00
1992	5	Now	$82.00
1993	6	Now	$96.00
1994	6	2004	$94.00
1995	Not made		
1996	7	2007	$100.00
1997	5	2005	$70.00
1998	7	2009	$96.00
1999	5	2007	$66.00
2000	Not made		

PENFOLDS CHARDONNAY "THE VALLEYS"

★★★★

before 1994		Prior	
1994	7	Now	$20.00
1995	6	Prior	
1996	6	Now	$16.00
1997	7	Now	$18.50
1998	6	Now	$15.50
1999	6	Now	$15.00
2000	5	2004	$12.00

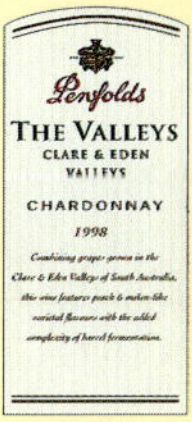

PENFOLDS EDEN VALLEY RESERVE RIESLING

★★★★

1999	7	Now	$30.00
2000	Not made		
2001	5	Now	$20.00
2002	7	2008	$27.00

PENFOLDS GRANGE

★★★★★

***Please note:** Many of the older years of this wine listed below should probably be shown as "Prior". However the extreme desirability to collectors of Grange coupled with the fact that the cellaring conditions of such a wine are likely to be of a high standard, justify a "Now" classification and the concomitant value calculation. Speaking of which, however, it must be said that both the retail and the auction prices paid for Grange vintages are wildly illogical, collector-driven values which grossly inflate the prices of rarer vintages* *(rare often because no one bothered to keep the lesser years) and undervalue the years in which collectors acquired and kept good quantities of the wines.*

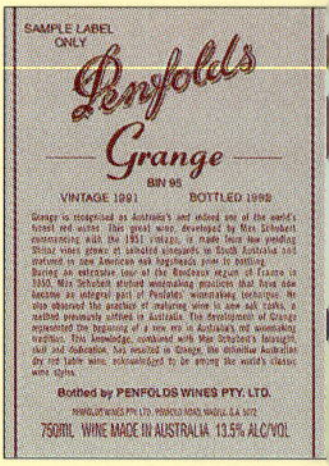

1951	5	Now	$1080.00
1952	6	Now	$1260.00
1953	7	Now	$1440.00
1954	3	Now	$600.00
1955	7	Now	$1360.00
1956	6	Now	$1120.00
1957	4	Now	$720.00
1958	3	Now	$520.00
1959	4	Now	$680.00
1960	5	Now	$820.00
1961	4	Now	$640.00
1962	6	Now	$940.00
1963	5	Now	$760.00
1964	4	Now	$580.00
1965	7	Now	$1000.00
1966	6	Now	$840.00
1967	5	Now	$680.00
1968	4	Now	$520.00
1969	4	Now	$500.00
1970	6	Now	$740.00
1971	7	Now	$840.00
1972	5	Now	$580.00
1973	5	Now	$560.00
1974	5	Now	$540.00
1975	6	Now	$640.00
1976	7	Now	$720.00
1977	6	Now	$600.00
1978	5	Now	$490.00
1979	5	Now	$470.00
1980	6	Now	$540.00
1981	6	Now	$540.00
1982	6	Now	$520.00
1983	7	Now	$580.00
1984	4	Now	$330.00
1985	5	Now	$400.00
1986	7	2005	$540.00
1987	6	Now	$450.00
1988	6	Now	$430.00
1989	5	Now	$350.00
1990	7	2006	$480.00
1991	7	2006	$460.00
1992	5	Now	$320.00
1993	5	2005	$310.00
1994	6	2007	$360.00
1995	5	2006	$290.00

1996	7	2012	$400.00
1997	5	2008	$280.00
1998	7	2014	$380.00

PENFOLDS KOONUNGA HILL CHARDONNAY ★★

before 2001		Prior	
2001	7	2004	
2002	5	2004	
2003	5	2005	$11.00

PENFOLDS KOONUNGA HILL SEMILLON/CHARDONNAY ★★

2001	6	204,	
2002,	5	2004	
2003	5	2005	$11.00

PENFOLDS KOONUNGA HILL SEMILLON/SAUVIGNON BLANC ★★

1995	6	Prior	
1996	6	Now	$12.00
1997	5	Now	$9.75
1998	6	Now	$11.00

No longer made

PENFOLDS KOONUNGA HILL SHIRAZ/CABERNET ★★★

1990	7	Now	$19.50
1991	7	Now	$19.00
1992	5	Now	$13.00
1993	6	Now	$15.50
1994	5	Now	$12.50
1995	6	Now	$14.50
1996	7	Now	$16.50
1997	5	Now	$11.50
1998	7	2005	$15.50
1999	5	2004	$10.50
2000	5	2004	$10.50
2001	7	2006	$14.00
2002	6	2006	$12.00

PENFOLDS MAGILL ESTATE SHIRAZ ★★★★★

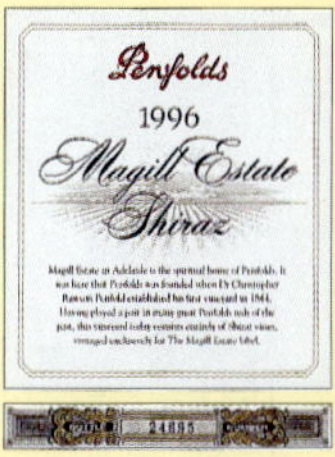

before 1990		Prior	
1990	6	Now	$56.00
1991	7	Now	$62.00
1992	5	Prior	
1993	5	Now	$42.00
1994	6	Now	$50.00
1995	6	2004	$48.00
1996	6	2005	$47.00
1997	5	2005	$38.00

1998	7	2008	$50.00
1999	5	2006	$35.00
2000	5	2007	$34.00

PENFOLDS OLD VINES BAROSSA VALLEY RED ★★★

1992	7	Now	$28.00
1993	5	Now	$19.50
1994	6	Now	$22.00
1995	6	Now	$22.00
1996	7	Now	$25.00
1997	6	Now	$20.00

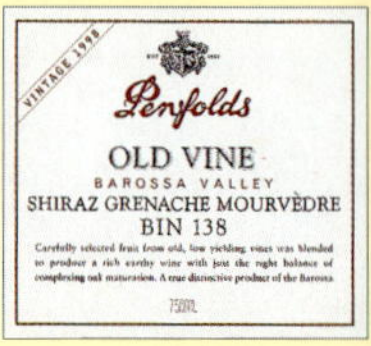

PENFOLDS RAWSONS RETREAT CHARDONNAY ★★

2001	5	Prior	
2002	5	Now	
2003	5	2004	$10.00

PENFOLDS RAWSONS RETREAT SEMILLON/CHARDONNAY ★★

before 2002		Prior	
2002	6	Now	
2003	5	2004	$10.00

PENFOLDS RAWSONS RETREAT SHIRAZ/CABERNET ★★

1995	5	Prior	
1996	6	Now	$12.50
1997	5	Prior	
1998	6	Now	$12.00
1999	6	Now	$11.50
2000	5	Now	$9.25
2001	6	2004	$10.50
2002	6	2004	$10.50

PENFOLDS RWT SHIRAZ ★★★★★

1997	5	2005	$100.00
1998	7	2009	$135.00
1999	6	2007	$110.00
2000	6	2007	$110.00

PENFOLDS ST HENRI ★★★★★

before 1986		Prior	
1986	7	Now	$86.00
1987	5	Now	$60.00
1988	5	Now	$58.00
1989	5	Now	$56.00
1990	7	Now	$76.00
1991	6	Now	$64.00
1992	5	Now	$52.00
1993	5	Now	$50.00
1994	6	Now	$58.00
1995	6	Now	$56.00

1996	7	2006	$64.00
1997	5	2005	$45.00
1998	7	2010	$60.00
1999	6	2008	$50.00

PENFOLDS "THE CLARE ESTATE" CHARDONNAY ★★★

before 1996		Prior	
1996	6	Now	$13.00
1997	7	Now	$15.00

No longer made

PENFOLDS "THE CLARE ESTATE" RED BLEND ★★★

before 1990		Prior	
1990	6	Now	$16.50
1991	7	Now	$18.50
1992	5	Now	$13.00
1993	6	Now	$15.00
1994	6	Now	$14.50
1995	6	Now	$14.00
1996	6	Now	$14.00

No longer made

PENFOLDS THOMAS HYLAND CHARDONNAY ★★★

2001	5	2004	
2002	6	2006	
2003	5	2006	$16.00

PENFOLDS THOMAS HYLAND SHIRAZ ★★★

2000	5	2004	
2001	6	2006	$18.00
2002	5	2006	N/R

PENFOLDS YATTARNA CHARDONNAY ★★★★★

1995	5	Prior	
1996	7	2005	$125.00
1997	6	2004	$105.00
1998	7	2005	$120.00
1999	6	2006	$100.00
2000	6	2007	$96.00

***Penley Estate** is a recently established 67 hectare vineyard in Coonawarra producing four fine reds and an admirable sparkling wine. Winemaker: Kym Tolley.*

PENLEY ESTATE HYLAND SHIRAZ ★★★★

before 1997		Prior	
1997	5	Now	$18.50
1998	6	2005	$21.00

1999	6	2006	$21.00
2000	7	2008	$24.00
2001	6	2008	$20.00

PENLEY ESTATE MERLOT ★★★★

before 1998		Prior	
1998	5	Now	$29.00
1999	5	2004	$28.00
2000	6	2005	$33.00

PENLEY ESTATE PHOENIX (CABERNET SAUVIGNON) ★★★★

before 1997		Prior	
1997	5	Now	$20.00
1998	6	2004	$24.00
1999	7	2006	$27.00
2000	7	2008	$26.00
2001	6	2008	$22.00

PENLEY ESTATE RESERVE CABERNET SAUVIGNON ★★★★★

1989	6	Now	$82.00
1990	7	Now	$94.00
1991	7	2006	$92.00
1992	6	2004	$76.00
1993	7	2007	$86.00
1994	7	2008	$84.00
1995	5	2004	$58.00
1996	6	2008	$68.00
1997	7	2009	$76.00
1998	7	2013	$74.00
1999	7	2014	$72.00

PENLEY ESTATE SHIRAZ/CABERNET ★★★★

1989	4	Prior	
1990	5	Now	$36.00
1991	7	Now	$50.00
1992	6	Now	$41.00
1993	6	Now	$40.00
1994	6	Now	$39.00
1995	6	Now	$38.00
1996	6	2004	$37.00
1997	6	2005	$36.00
1998	7	2008	$40.00
1999	7	2009	$39.00

PENLEY ESTATE TRADITIONAL METHOD

★★★★★

1989	4	Now	$30.00
1990	6	Now	$44.00
1991	7	Now	$49.00
1992	Not made		
1993	Not made		
1994	7	2005	$45.00
1995	Not made		
1996	Not made		
1997	7	2007	$41.00

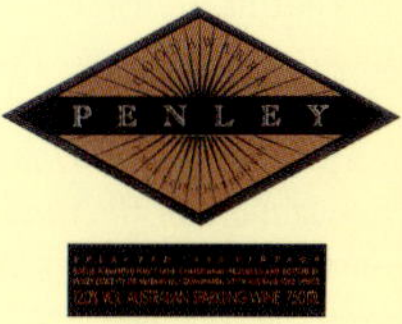

***Pertaringa Wines** are McLaren Vale based makers using fruit from their 33 hectare vineyard acquired in 1980 and redeveloped by Geoff Hardy. Winemakers: Geoff Hardy and Ben Riggs.*

PERTARINGA MCLAREN VALE CABERNET SAUVIGNON

★★★★

1990	6	Now	$31.00
1991	6	Now	$30.00
1992	Not made		
1993	Not made		
1994	6	Now	$27.00
1995	Not made		
1996	5	Now	$21.00
1997	6	Now	$25.00
1998	7	2005	$28.00
1999	6	2006	$24.00

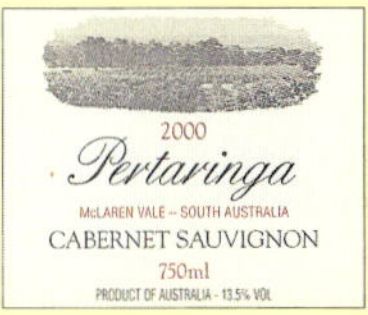

PERTARINGA MCLAREN VALE SHIRAZ

★★★★

1994	5	Now	$25.00
1995	Not made		
1996	6	Now	$29.00
1997	7	2004	$32.00
1998	7	2005	$31.00
1999	7	2006	$31.00
2000	7	2008	$30.00

PERTARINGA MCLAREN VALE SEMILLON

★★★★

1994	6	Now	$21.00
1995	Not made		
1996	5	Now	$16.50
1997	6	2004	$19.50
1998	5	2005	$15.50
1999	7	2007	$21.00
2000	7	2008	$21.00

***Petaluma** is a label under which some fine wines are released, grapes coming from the producer's vineyards in Clare, Piccadilly Valley and Coonawarra, but all vinified at the Petaluma winery at Piccadilly in the Mount Lofty Ranges. (Please note: some of these winemaker's ratings may appear surprisingly low. This is purely because this winemaker prefers to use more of the range of 1 to 7 in comparing his wines with themselves in other years. Would that more others would do the same.) Winemaker: Brian Croser.*

PETALUMA CHARDONNAY ★★★★★

before 1986		Prior	
1986	4	Now	$46.00
1987	4	Now	$45.00
1988	4	Now	$44.00
1989	4	Now	$42.00
1990	5	Now	$50.00
1991	5	Now	$50.00
1992	7	Now	$68.00
1993	4	Now	$38.00
1994	4	Now	$36.00
1995	6	Now	$52.00
1996	6	2004	$52.00
1997	7	2005	$58.00
1998	5	2004	$41.00
1999	6	2004	$47.00
2000	5	2005	$38.00
2001	5	2004	$37.00

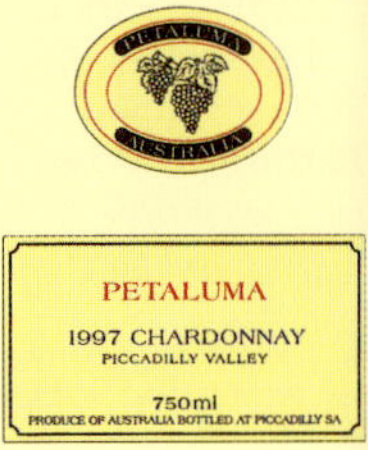

PETALUMA COONAWARRA REDS ★★★★★

1979	4	Now	$88.00
1980	3	Now	$64.00
1981	3	Now	$62.00
1982	4	Now	$82.00
1983	Not made		
1984	2	Prior	
1985	3	Prior	
1986	5	Now	$90.00
1987	5	Now	$88.00
1988	6	Now	$100.00
1989	Not made		
1990	6	2005	$96.00
1991	5	2005	$78.00
1992	7	2010	$105.00
1993	5	2005	$74.00
1994	6	2010	$86.00
1995	6	2010	$84.00
1996	4	2005	$54.00
1997	5	2005	$66.00
1998	7	2010	$88.00
1999	5	2008	$62.00
2000	5	2008	$60.00

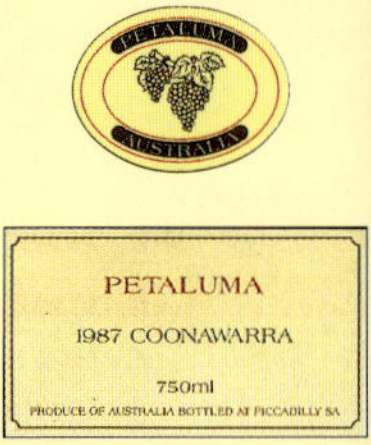

PETALUMA RIESLING ★★★★★

before 1981		Prior	
1981	4	Now	$35.00
1982	4	Now	$34.00
1983	2	Prior	
1984	4	Now	$32.00
1985	5	Now	$39.00
1986	5	Now	$38.00
1987	6	Now	$45.00
1988	4	Now	$29.00
1989	3	Now	$21.00
1990	4	Now	$27.00
1991	4	Now	$26.00
1992	6	Now	$38.00
1993	5	Now	$31.00
1994	5	Now	$30.00
1995	4	Now	$23.00
1996	7	2005	$40.00
1997	5	2005	$27.00
1998	No data		
1999	7	2005	$36.00
2000	5	2004	$25.00
2001	5	2005	$24.00
2002	6	2007	$28.00

***Peter Lehmann Wines** is a greatly respected Barossa winemaker with a reliable range of pleasantly underpriced fine wines. Winemakers: Andrew Wigan, Ian Hongell and Leonie Lange.*

PETER LEHMANN CABERNET SAUVIGNON ★★★★

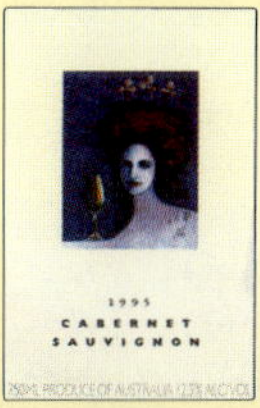

before 1989		Prior	
1989	6	Now	$27.00
1990	7	Now	$30.00
1991	6	Now	$25.00
1992	7	Now	$28.00
1993	7	2004	$28.00
1994	6	Now	$23.00
1995	5	Now	$18.50
1996	7	2006	$25.00
1997	5	Now	$17.50
1998	6	2005	$20.00
1999	6	2007	$20.00
2000	7	2008	$22.00
2001	7	2009	$22.00

PETER LEHMANN CHARDONNAY ★★★★

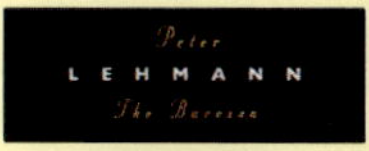

before 1997		Prior	
1997	6	Now	$16.00
1998	7	2008	$18.00
1999	6	2005	$15.00

2000	6	2007	$14.50
2001	7	2009	$16.50
2002	7	2010	$16.00

PETER LEHMANN CLANCY'S (SHIRAZ BLEND) ★★★★

before 1992		Prior	
1992	7	Now	$19.00
1993	6	Now	$15.50
1994	6	Now	$15.50
1995	5	Prior	
1996	7	2004	$17.00
1997	7	2005	$16.50
1998	7	2005	$16.00
1999	5	2004	$11.00
2000	6	2006	$13.00
2001	7	2008	$14.50
2002	7	2009	$14.00

PETER LEHMANN MENTOR (CABERNET/MALBEC/SHIRAZ/MERLOT) ★★★★★

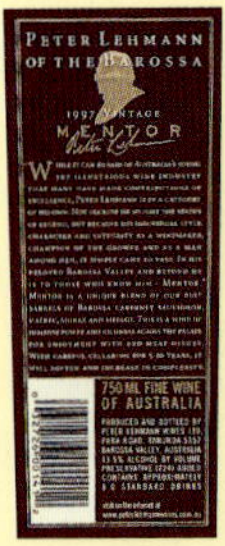

1991	6	Now	$45.00
1992	7	Now	$50.00
1993	7	Now	$49.00
1994	6	2004	$41.00
1995	6	2005	$40.00
1996	7	2006	$45.00
1997	6	2007	$38.00
1998	7	2010	$43.00

PETER LEHMANN NOBLE (BOTRYTIS) SEMILLON (375ml) ★★★★

1981	5	Prior	
1982	7	Now	$31.00
1983	Not made		
1984	6	Now	$25.00
1985	7	Now	$28.00
1986	5	Prior	
1987	6	Prior	
1988	6	Now	$22.00
1989	6	Now	$21.00
1990	6	Now	$21.00
1991	Not made		
1992	7	2004	$23.00
1993	Not made		
1994	6	2004	$18.50
1995	5	2005	$15.00
1996	6	2006	$17.50
1997	5	2006	$14.00
1998	6	2008	$16.50
1999	7	2009	$19.00
2000	7	2010	$18.00

PETER LEHMANN RIESLING ★★★★

before 1992		Prior	
1992	5	Now	$12.00
1993	7	Now	$16.50
1994	6	Now	$14.00
1995	6	Now	$13.50
1996	6	2006	$13.00
1997	7	2007	$15.00
1998	7	2008	$14.50
1999	6	2004	$12.00
2000	7	2008	$13.50
2001	7	2007	$13.00
2002	7	2010	$13.00

PETER LEHMANN SEMILLON ★★★

before 1992		Prior	
1992	6	Now	$14.50
1993	6	Prior	
1994	7	Now	$16.00
1995	7	Now	$15.50
1996	6	Now	$12.50
1997	6	2004	$12.50
1998	7	2005	$14.00
1999	7	2004	$13.50
2000	7	2006	$13.00
2001	7	2007	$13.00
2002	7	2008	$12.50

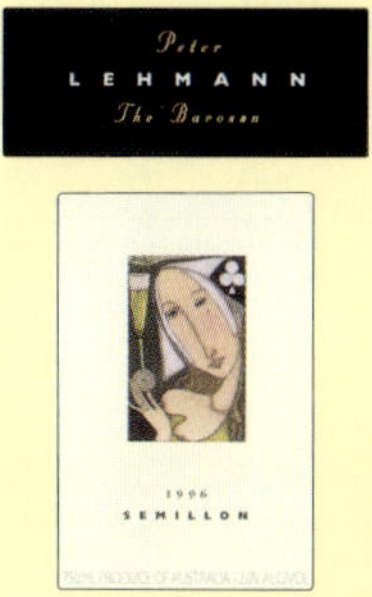

PETER LEHMANN SHIRAZ ★★★

before 1992		Prior	
1992	7	Now	$26.00
1993	7	Now	$26.00
1994	7	Now	$25.00
1995	6	Now	$21.00
1996	7	Now	$23.00
1997	7	2005	$23.00
1998	7	2006	$22.00
1999	6	2007	$18.50
2000	7	2008	$21.00
2001	7	2009	$20.00

PETER LEHMANN STONEWELL SHIRAZ ★★★★★

1987	6	Prior	
1988	6	Now	$84.00
1989	7	Now	$96.00
1990	7	Now	$94.00
1991	7	Now	$90.00
1992	6	Now	$76.00
1993	7	2004	$86.00
1994	7	2005	$82.00
1995	6	2005	$68.00
1996	7	2007	$78.00
1997	6	2010	$64.00
1998	7	2012	$74.00

__Pewsey Vale__ is a very fine vineyard in the cooler heights (480 metres) of the Eden Valley. The owners are S. Smith and Sons of Yalumba fame. Winemaker: Louisa Rose.

PEWSEY VALE CABERNET SAUVIGNON ★★★

before 1997		Prior	
1997	5	Now	$15.50
1998	6	Now	$18.50

No longer made.

PEWSEY VALE CONTOURS RIESLING ★★★★★

1995	6	Now	$24.00
1996	6	Now	$24.00
1997	7	Now	$27.00
1998	7	2004	N/R
1999	6	2005	N/R
2000	6	2006	N/R
2001	6	2007	N/R
2002	7	2008	N/R

PEWSEY VALE RIESLING ★★★★

before 1997		Prior	
1997	7	Now	$21.00
1998	6	Now	$18.00
1999	5	2004	$14.50
2000	7	2004	$19.50
2001	6	2006	$16.50
2002	7	2007	$18.50

__Pfeiffer Wines__ is a North East Victorian fortified wine specialist, but produces as well a small range of attractive and inexpensive table wines. Cellar door sales only. Winemaker: Chris Pfeiffer.

PFEIFFER AUSLESE TOKAY (375ml) ★★★★

before 1987		Prior	
1987	5	Now	$20.00
1988	7	Now	$27.00
1989	6	Now	$23.00
1990	6	Now	$22.00
1991	5	Prior	
1992	5	Prior	
1993	6	Now	$20.00
1994	7	2004	$23.00
1995	6	Now	$19.00
1996	5	Now	$15.50
1997	5	Now	$15.00
1998	6	2005	$17.50
1999	Not made		

2000	7	2008	$19.50
2001	6	2008	$16.00
2002	5	2008	$13.00

PFEIFFER CABERNET SAUVIGNON ★★★

1985	3	Prior	
1986	6	Now	$26.00
1987	5	Prior	
1988	6	Now	$24.00
1989	6	Now	$24.00
1990	5	Now	$19.50
1991	7	Now	$26.00
1992	7	2005	$25.00
1993	6	2005	$21.00
1994	6	2005	$20.00
1995	6	2006	$20.00
1996	7	2008	$22.00
1997	7	2008	$22.00
1998	5	2005	$15.00
1999	7	2010	$21.00
2000	6	2010	$17.50
2001	6	2010	N/R
2002	7	2012	N/R

PFEIFFER CHARDONNAY ★★★

before 1988		Prior	
1988	7	Now	$26.00
1989	4	Now	$14.00
1990	5	Now	$17.50
1991	5	Prior	
1992	7	2004	$23.00
1993	6	2004	$19.00
1994	7	2004	$21.00
1995	6	Now	$18.00
1996	7	2006	$20.00
1997	5	2004	$14.00
1998	5	2006	$13.50
1999	7	2010	$18.50
2000	6	2008	N/R
2001	5	2008	N/R
2002	Not made		

PFEIFFER PINOT NOIR ★★★

before 1998		Prior	
1988	7	Now	$28.00
1989	6	Now	$23.00
1990	6	Now	$23.00
1991	6	Now	$22.00
1992	7	Now	$25.00
1993	Not made		
1994	7	2006	$24.00

1995	5	Now	$16.50
1996	6	2006	$19.00
1997	6	2007	$18.50
1998	7	2010	$21.00
1999	6	2010	$17.50
2000	6	2010	$17.00
2001	5	2010	N/R
2002	5	2010	N/R

***Phillip Island Vineyard** and Winery is an intriguing development of David and Cathy Lance of Diamond Valley Estate fame. Winemakers: David Lance and James Lance.*

PHILLIP ISLAND CABERNET SAUVIGNON

★★★

1997	5	Now	$29.00
1998	6	Now	$33.00
1999	6	Now	$32.00
2000	7	2004	$37.00
2001	6	2005	$31.00

PHILLIP ISLAND CHARDONNAY

★★★★

1997	7	Prior	
1998	6	Now	$32.00
1999	Not made		
2000	6	Now	$30.00
2001	6	2004	$29.00

PHILLIP ISLAND MERLOT

★★★★

1997	6	Now	$42.00
1998	6	Now	$41.00
1999	5	Now	$33.00
2000	6	2004	$39.00
2001	7	2006	$44.00

PHILLIP ISLAND SAUVIGNON BLANC

★★★

1997	6	Prior	
1998	7	Now	$39.00
1999	6	Now	$32.00
2000	6	Now	$31.00
2001	5	Now	$25.00
2002	7	2004	$35.00

PHILLIP ISLAND "THE NOBBIES" PINOT NOIR

★★★★

1996	7	Prior	
1997	6	Now	$29.00
1998	7	Now	$33.00
1999	5	Now	$23.00
2000	6	Now	$27.00
2001	6	2004	$26.00

***Picardy** is a 7 hectare vineyard in the Pemberton area of Western Australia. It was established by Bill Pannell who created Moss Wood. Winemakers: Bill and Dan Pannell.*

PICARDY CHARDONNAY ★★★

1999	5	Now	$26.00
2000	5	2004	$25.00
2001	5	2005	$25.00

PICARDY MERLOT/CABERNET ★★★★★

1997	7	2004	$35.00
1998	5	2006	$24.00
1999	7	2007	$33.00

PICARDY PINOT NOIR ★★★★

1996	6	Now	$32.00
1997	6	Now	$31.00
1998	5	2004	$25.00
1999	7	2005	$35.00

PICARDY SHIRAZ ★★★★★

1997	6	2007	$30.00
1998	6	2008	$29.00
1999	7	2009	$33.00

***Pierro Vineyards** is a Margaret River maker with 10 hectares of vines. The range includes a superb Chardonnay. Winemaker: Michael Peterkin.*

PIERRO CABERNETS ★★★★★

1994	4	Now	$49.00
1995	4	Now	$47.00
1996	5	Now	$56.00
1997	4	Now	$44.00
1998	6	2004	$64.00
1999	7	2008	$74.00

PIERRO CHARDONNAY ★★★★★

1985	4	Prior	
1986	6	Now	$56.00
1987	5	Now	$45.00
1988	5	Prior	
1989	6	Now	$50.00
1990	6	Now	$50.00
1991	5	Now	$40.00
1992	5	Now	$39.00
1993	6	Now	$45.00
1994	6	Now	$44.00
1995	5	Now	$36.00
1996	6	Now	$42.00
1997	6	Now	$40.00
1998	6	Now	$39.00
1999	6	2004	$38.00
2000	7	2005	$43.00

PIERRO PINOT NOIR ★★★★

before 1990		Prior	
1990	5	Now	$40.00
1991	Not made		
1992	5	Now	$38.00
1993	5	Now	$37.00
1994	5	Now	$36.00
1995	6	Now	$42.00
1996	6	Now	$41.00
1997	6	Now	$39.00
1998	5	Now	$32.00
1999	6	2004	$37.00
2000	5	2005	$30.00

PIERRO SEMILLON/SAUVIGNON BLANC ★★★★

before 1992		Prior	
1992	6	Now	$29.00
1993	6	Now	$29.00
1994	5	1996	$23.00
1995	5	Now	$22.00
1996	5	Now	$22.00
1997	6	Now	$25.00
1998	No data		
1999	6	Now	$24.00
2000	No data		
2001	7	2004	$26.00

Pike's Wines *is a Clare area vineyard making limited quantities of very fine wines. Winemaker: Neil Pike.*

PIKE'S CABERNET SAUVIGNON ★★★★

1984	5	Now	$33.00
1985	6	Now	$38.00
1986	6	Now	$37.00
1987	6	Now	$36.00
1988	5	Now	$29.00
1989	6	Now	$34.00
1990	6	Now	$33.00
1991	7	Now	$38.00
1992	6	2005	$31.00
1993	5	2005	$25.00
1994	5	2005	$24.00
1995	6	2006	$28.00
1996	6	2007	$28.00
1997	5	2008	$22.00
1998	6	2009	$26.00
1999	6	2008	$25.00
2000	6	2010	$24.00

PIKE'S RIESLING ★★★★

1985	6	Now	$30.00
1986	6	Now	$29.00
1987	6	Now	$28.00
1988	5	Now	$23.00
1989	5	Now	$22.00
1990	7	Now	$30.00
1991	6	Now	$25.00
1992	6	Now	$24.00
1993	6	Now	$24.00
1994	5	Now	$19.00
1995	7	2004	$26.00
1996	5	2004	$18.00
1997	7	2005	$24.00
1998	7	2007	$24.00
1999	6	2007	$20.00
2000	5	2007	$16.00
2001	7	2010	$22.00

PIKE'S POLISH HILL RIVER SHIRAZ ★★★★

1987	6	Now	$34.00
1988	6	Now	$33.00
1989	5	Now	$27.00
1990	7	Now	$37.00
1991	7	Now	$36.00
1992	5	2004	$25.00
1993	6	2005	$29.00
1994	6	2005	$28.00
1995	6	2006	$27.00
1996	7	2007	$31.00
1997	5	2007	$21.00
1998	7	2010	$29.00
1999	6	2008	$24.00
2000	6	2010	$23.00

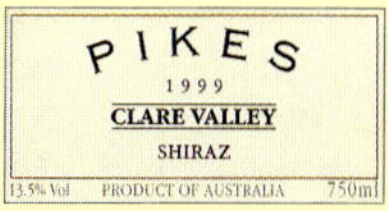

***Pipers Brook Vineyard** is a viticulturally exemplary vineyard in the Launceston area. The wines are among the country's finest. Winemaker: Dr Andrew Pirie.*

PIPERS BROOK VINEYARD
CABERNET SAUVIGNON ★★★★★

1981	6	Prior	
1982	7	Now	$70.00
1983	5	Now	$48.00
1984	5	Now	$47.00
1985	4	Now	$36.00
1986	5	Prior	
1987	4	Prior	
1988	6	2005	$50.00
1989	5	Now	$41.00

1990	Not made		
1991	6	Now	$46.00
1992	6	Now	$45.00
1993	Not made		
1994	Not made		
1995	7	2005	$48.00
1996	Not made		
1997	6	2006	$38.00
1998	7	2014	$44.00
1999	7	2014	$42.00

PIPERS BROOK VINEYARD CHARDONNAY ★★★★★

before 1986		Prior	
1986	7	Now	$58.00
1987	5	Now	$41.00
1988	5	Prior	
1989	5	Now	$39.00
1990	5	Now	$37.00
1991	7	2005	$50.00
1992	7	2005	$50.00
1993	6	Now	$41.00
1994	6	Now	$40.00
1995	7	Now	$45.00
1996	5	2005	$31.00
1997	7	Now	$43.00
1998	7	2005	$41.00
1999	7	Now	$40.00
2000	7	2005	$39.00

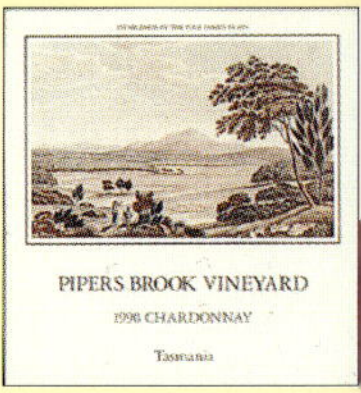

PIPERS BROOK VINEYARD GEWURZTRAMINER ★★★★

1987	6	Now	$39.00
1988	7	Now	$44.00
1989	5	Now	$31.00
1990	6	Now	$36.00
1991	7	Now	$40.00
1992	6	Now	$34.00
1993	6	Now	$33.00
1994	Not made		
1995	7	2005	$36.00
1996	6	Now	$30.00
1997	7	Now	$34.00
1998	6	Now	$28.00
1999	7	Now	$32.00
2000	7	2004	$31.00
2001	7	2005	$30.00

PIPERS BROOK VINEYARD PINOT NOIR ★★★★★

before 1988		Prior	
1988	6	Now	$49.00
1989	Not made		

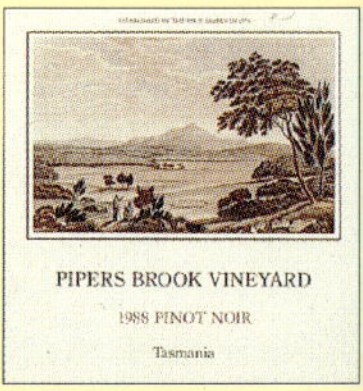

1990	6	Now	$47.00
1991	6	Now	$45.00
1992	7	Now	$50.00
1993	3	Prior	
1994	7	Now	$48.00
1995	6	Now	$40.00
1996	6	2005	$39.00
1997	6	Now	$38.00
1998	5	2006	$30.00
1999	7	2008	$42.00
2000	7	2006	$40.00

PIPERS BROOK VINEYARD RIESLING ★★★★

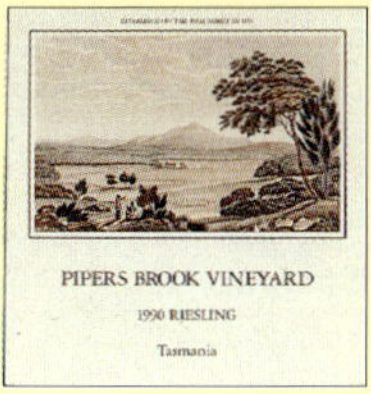

before 1986		Prior	
1986	5	Now	$28.00
1987	5	Now	$27.00
1988	5	Now	$26.00
1989	6	Now	$31.00
1990	6	Now	$30.00
1991	7	Now	$34.00
1992	7	Now	$33.00
1993	7	Now	$32.00
1994	7	2005	$31.00
1995	7	Now	$30.00
1996	6	Now	$25.00
1997	7	2010	$28.00
1998	7	2010	$27.00
1999	7	2008	$27.00
2000	7	2006	$26.00

PIPERS BROOK VINEYARD SUMMIT CHARDONNAY ★★★★★

1990	5	Now	$52.00
1991	7	2008	$72.00
1992	7	2005	$70.00
1993	Not made		
1994	7	2005	$66.00
1995	Not made		
1996	Not made		
1997	7	2010	$60.00
1998	7	2004	$58.00
1999	7	2010	$56.00

***Plantagenet** is the longest established vineyard in the Mount Barker area of Western Australia. Winemaker: Gavin Berry.*

PLANTAGENET CABERNET SAUVIGNON (MOUNT BARKER) ★★★★

before 1987		Prior	
1987	5	Now	$31.00
1988	7	Now	$42.00

1989	5	Now	$29.00
1990	6	Now	$34.00
1991	7	2005	$38.00
1992	6	2006	$32.00
1993	7	2008	$36.00
1994	7	2010	$35.00
1995	6	2005	$29.00
1996	6	2009	$28.00
1997	7	2015	$32.00
1998	7	2020	$31.00
1999	7	2020	$30.00

PLANTAGENET CHARDONNAY (MT BARKER) ★★★★

before 1987		Prior	
1987	5	Now	$29.00
1988	5	Now	$28.00
1989	5	Now	$27.00
1990	6	Now	$32.00
1991	5	Now	$25.00
1992	5	Now	$25.00
1993	5	Now	$24.00
1994	6	Now	$28.00
1995	5	Now	$23.00
1996	6	Now	$26.00
1997	7	Now	$30.00
1998	7	2004	$29.00
1999	7	2006	$28.00
2000	7	2007	$27.00

PLANTAGENET CHARDONNAY (OMRAH) ★★★

before 1998		Prior	
1998	6	Now	$16.50
1999	7	Now	$18.50
2000	7	Now	$18.00
2001	7	Now	$17.50

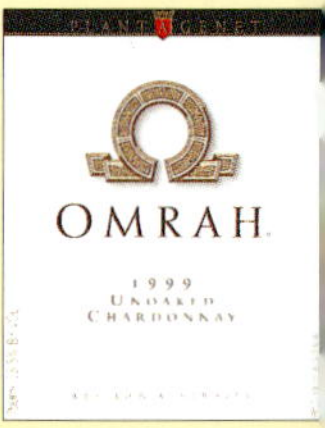

PLANTAGENET MERLOT/CABERNET (OMRAH) ★★★

before 1996		Prior	
1996	6	Now	$20.00
1997	7	Now	$23.00
1998	7	2004	$22.00
1999	7	2005	$21.00
2000	7	2006	$21.00

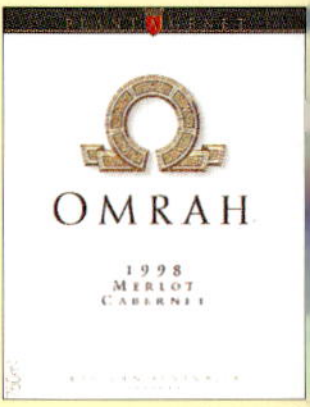

PLANTAGENET PINOT NOIR (MOUNT BARKER) ★★★★

1985	6	Now	$37.00
1986	6	Now	$36.00
1987	4	Now	$23.00

1988	6	Now	$34.00
1989	5	Now	$27.00
1990	6	Now	$32.00
1991	6	Now	$31.00
1992	6	Now	$30.00
1993	6	Now	$29.00
1994	7	2004	$33.00
1995	7	Now	$32.00
1996	7	Now	$31.00
1997	7	2004	$30.00
1998	7	2004	$29.00
1999	7	2005	$28.00
2000	7	2005	$28.00

PLANTAGENET RIESLING (MOUNT BARKER) ★★★

1985	7	Now	$29.00
1986	7	Now	$28.00
1987	6	Now	$23.00
1988	6	Now	$22.00
1989	5	Now	$18.50
1990	6	Now	$21.00
1991	6	Now	$20.00
1992	6	2005	$20.00
1993	7	2005	$23.00
1994	5	Now	$15.50
1995	6	2005	$18.50
1996	6	2005	$18.00
1997	7	2010	$20.00
1998	7	2010	$19.50
1999	7	2010	$19.00
2000	7	2010	$18.50
2001	7	2012	$18.00

PLANTAGENET SAUVIGNON BLANC (OMRAH) ★★★

1996	5	Prior	
1997	5	Now	$15.50
1998	5	Now	$15.00
1999	7	Now	$21.00
2000	7	Now	$20.00
2001	7	Now	$19.50

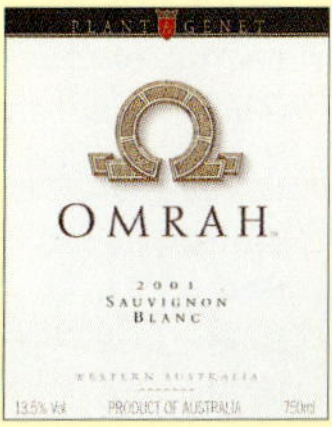

PLANTAGENET SHIRAZ (MOUNT BARKER) ★★★★

before 1983		Prior	
1983	7	Now	$62.00
1984	6	Now	$52.00
1985	6	Now	$50.00
1986	6	Now	$49.00
1987	5	Now	$40.00
1988	6	Now	$47.00

1989	6	Now	$45.00
1990	6	Now	$44.00
1991	7	2005	$50.00
1992	Not made		
1993	7	2010	$47.00
1994	7	2015	$46.00
1995	6	2010	$38.00
1996	6	2010	$37.00
1997	7	2012	$42.00
1998	7	2015	$40.00
1999	7	2015	$39.00
2000	6	2012	$33.00

PLANTAGENET SHIRAZ (OMRAH) ★★★

1997	6	Now	$17.00
1998	7	2005	$19.50
1999	7	2006	$19.00
2000	7	2006	$18.50

***Plunkett Wines** have a 100 hectare vineyard at Avenel in Victoria's Strathbogie Ranges wine region. Among their range of very agreeable wines is a fine Reserve Shiraz. Winemaker: Sam Plunkett.*

PLUNKETT STRATHBOGIE RANGES RESERVE SHIRAZ ★★★★

1997	5	Now	$39.00
1998	5	2004	$38.00
1999	5	2005	$37.00
2000	5	2006	$35.00
2001	5	2007	$34.00
2002	6	2009	$40.00

***Poet's Corner Wines** is an offshoot of the Mudgee producer Montrose, but now a label in its own right. It is part of the Orlando Wyndham group. Winemaker: James Manners.*

POET'S CORNER HENRY LAWSON CABERNET SAUVIGNON ★★★

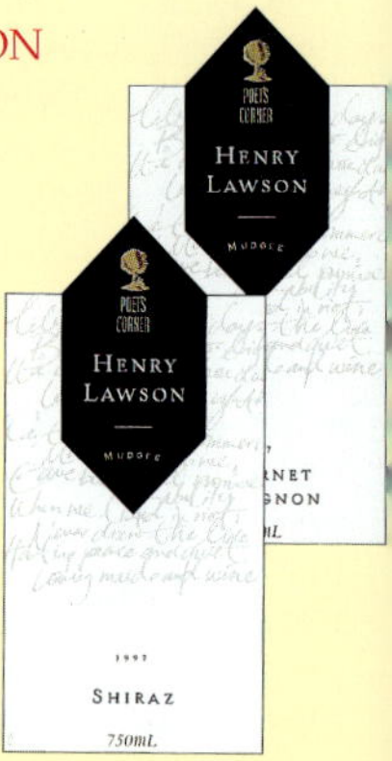

1997	6	Now	$18.50
1998	6	2004	$18.00
1999	6	2007	$17.50
2000	Not made		
2001	5	2006	$13.50

POET'S CORNER HENRY LAWSON SHIRAZ ★★★

1997	6	Now	$17.00
1998	6	2004	$16.50
1999	7	2007	$19.00
2000	Not made		
2001	6	2008	$15.00

POET'S CORNER SEMILLON ★★★

2000	7	2004	
2001	6	2004	
2002	5	2004	$14.00

POET'S CORNER SHIRAZ/CABERNET/ CABERNET FRANC ★★

before 1998		Prior	
1998	5	Now	$9.00
1999	6	Now	$10.00
2000	No data		
2001	7	2004	$11.50
2002	7	2005	$11.00

POET'S CORNER SEMILLON/ SAUVIGNON BLANC/CHARDONNAY ★★

before 1999		Prior	
1999	7	Now	$11.00
2000	7	Now	$11.00
2001	7	Now	$10.50
2002	6	2004	$8.75

POET'S CORNER UNWOODED CHARDONNAY ★★

before 1999		Prior	
1999	6	Now	$10.00
2000	7	Now	$11.00
2001	7	Now	$11.00
2002	6	2004	$9.00

***Poole's Rock** is a 5 hectare vineyard at Broke in the Hunter Valley owned by Harbridge Fine Wines who also own the neighbouring Cockfighter's Ghost vineyard. Winemaker: Phil Ryan.*

POOLE'S ROCK CHARDONNAY ★★★★

1996	6	Now	$27.00
1997	6	Now	$26.00
1998	6	Now	$25.00
1999	7	Now	$29.00

***Port Phillip Estate** in the Mornington Peninsula was established by a Melbourne QC, but sold to the Gjergja family in early 2000. Winemaker: Lindsay McCall.*

PORT PHILLIP ESTATE CHARDONNAY ★★★★

before 1999		Prior	
1999	6	Now	$22.00
2000	4	Prior	
2001	5	2004	$18.00

PORT PHILLIP ESTATE PINOT NOIR ★★★★

before 1997		Prior	
1997	7	Now	$36.00
1998	6	Now	$30.00
1999	6	Now	$29.00
2000	7	2006	$33.00
2001	6	2007	$28.00

PORT PHILLIP ESTATE SHIRAZ ★★★★

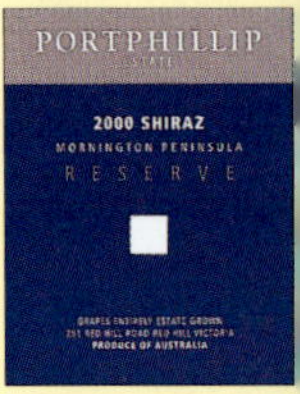

before 1997		Prior	
1997	7	Now	$37.00
1998	6	2004	$31.00
1999	Not made		
2000	7	2008	$34.00
2001	5	2008	$24.00

***Portree Vineyard** in Victoria's Macedon region produce a fine, lemony, seemingly fragile but long-lived Chardonnay. Winemaker: Ken Murchison.*

PORTREE CHARDONNAY ★★★★★

1995	6	2004	$33.00
1996	Not made		
1997	6	2005	$31.00
1998	5	2004	$25.00
1999	5	2004	$24.00
2000	5	2005	N/R
2001	7	2006	N/R

***Preece** is the label under which Mitchelton Wines release two well-distributed and reliable wines which honour the great maker Colin Preece, who was consultant in the establishment of the Mitchelton vineyards. Winemaker: Don Lewis.*

PREECE CABERNET SAUVIGNON ★★★★

before 1995		Prior	
1995	6	Now	$18.50
1996	6	Now	$18.00
1997	5	Now	$14.50
1998	6	2006	$17.00
1999	6	Now	$16.50
2000	5	2006	$13.50
2001	6	2006	$15.50

PREECE CHARDONNAY ★★★★

before 1996		Prior	
1996	6	Now	$17.00
1997	6	Now	$16.50

1998	7	Now	$18.50
1999	6	Now	$15.50
2000	7	Now	$17.50
2001	6	Now	$14.50
2002	6	Now	$14.00

***Primo Estate** is a family-owned Adelaide Plains producer with a brilliant and innovative maker with extreme quality aspirations. Winemaker: Joe Grilli.*

PRIMO ESTATE COLOMBARD

★★★

before 2001		Prior	
2001	6	Now	$15.00

PRIMO ESTATE JOSEPH "LA MAGIA" BOTRYTIS RIESLING (375ml)

★★★★

before 1991		Prior	
1991	6	Now	$39.00
1992	Not made		
1993	6	Now	$37.00
1994	6	Now	$36.00
1995	5	Now	$29.00
1996	5	Now	$28.00
1997	Not made		
1998	6	Now	$32.00
1999	Not made		
2000	Not made		
2001	6	2005	$29.00

PRIMO ESTATE JOSEPH CABERNET/MERLOT

★★★★

before 1990		Prior	
1990	6	Now	$64.00
1991	6	Now	$62.00
1992	6	Now	$60.00
1993	5	2005	$49.00
1994	6	2006	$56.00
1995	5	2006	$46.00
1996	6	2009	$52.00
1997	5	2009	$43.00
1998	6	2010	$50.00
1999	6	2009	$49.00
2000	5	2010	$39.00

***Prince Albert** is a very small Geelong area vineyard planted solely to Pinot Noir. Winemaker: Bruce Hyett.*

PRINCE ALBERT PINOT NOIR

★★★★

1978	7	Now	$70.00
1979	3	Prior	
1980	Not made		

1981	3	Prior	
1982	7	Now	$62.00
1983	5	Now	$43.00
1984	6	Now	$50.00
1985	6	Now	$48.00
1986	6	Now	$47.00
1987	5	Now	$38.00
1988	5	Now	$37.00
1989	6	Now	$43.00
1990	6	Now	$42.00
1991	6	Now	$40.00
1992	7	Now	$46.00
1993	6	Now	$38.00
1994	6	Now	$37.00
1995	7	Now	$42.00
1996	6	Now	$35.00
1997	7	Now	$39.00
1998	7	2004	$38.00
1999	6	Now	$32.00
2000	7	2005	$36.00
2001	6	2004	$30.00

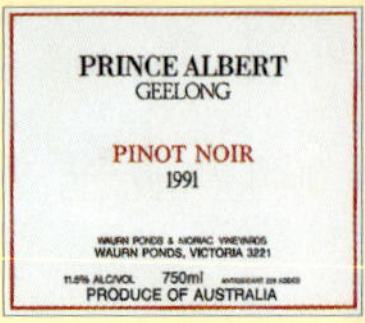

***Pyrenees Wines** - see Warrenmang.*

***Redbank** is a very fine Victorian maker of tight, powerful and long-lived red wines. Winemaker: Neill Robb.*

REDBANK "NEILL ROBB PRIVATE BIN" CABERNET ★★★★★

1984	6	Now	$210.00
1985	7	Now	$240.00
1986	7	Now	$235.00
1987	5	Now	$160.00
1988	7	Now	$220.00
1989	6	2004	$180.00
1990	7	2006	$210.00
1991	7	2010	$200.00
1992	7	2012	$195.00
1993	Not made		
1994	Not made		
1995	7	2020	$180.00
1996	Not made		
1997	7	2025	$170.00
1998	7	2026	$160.00
1999	7	2022	$160.00
2000	7	2020	$155.00

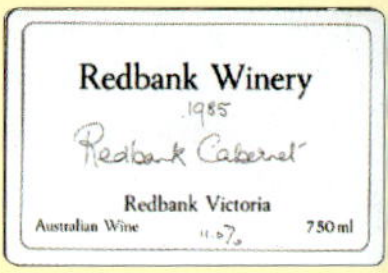

REDBANK LONG PADDOCK ★★★★

1985	6	Now	$17.50
1986	7	Now	$19.50
1987	6	Now	$16.50

1988	7	Now	$18.50
1989	6	Now	$15.50
1990	7	Now	$17.50
1991	6	Now	$14.50
1992	6	Now	$14.00
1993	6	Now	$13.50
1994	6	Now	$13.00
1995	6	Now	$13.00
1996	7	Now	$14.50
1997	6	Now	$12.00
1998	7	Now	$13.50
1999	7	2005	$13.50
2000	6	2005	$11.00

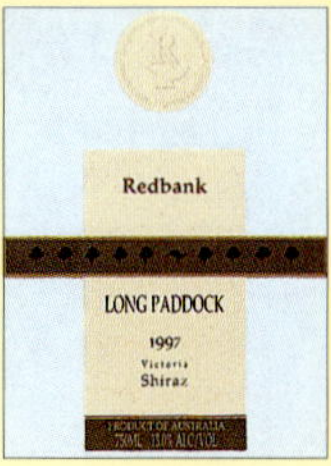

REDBANK SALLY'S PADDOCK ★★★★★

1979	6	Now	$82.00
1980	7	Now	$94.00
1981	7	2010	$90.00
1982	6	Now	$76.00
1983	7	Now	$86.00
1984	6	Now	$72.00
1985	6	Now	$68.00
1986	7	Now	$78.00
1987	5	Now	$54.00
1988	7	Now	$74.00
1989	6	Now	$62.00
1990	7	2010	$70.00
1991	7	2020	$68.00
1992	6	2007	$56.00
1993	6	2008	$54.00
1994	6	2005	$52.00
1995	7	2009	$60.00
1996	7	2010	$58.00
1997	7	2015	$56.00
1998	7	2016	$54.00
1999	7	2016	$52.00
2000	7	2017	$52.00

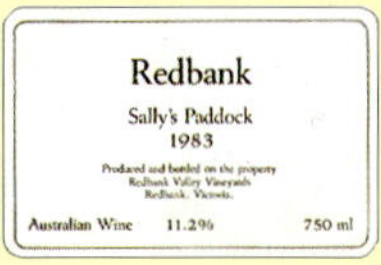

***Redbrook** - see Evans and Tate Margaret River wines.*

***Redgate** is a Margaret River producer owned and operated by the Ullinger family. Winemaker: Andrew Forsell.*

REDGATE CABERNET FRANC ★★★★

before 1995		Prior	
1995	7	Now	$58.00
1996	6	Now	$48.00
1997	5	Now	$39.00
1998	5	2004	$38.00
1999	7	2008	$52.00
2000	5	2005	$36.00
2001	7	2010	$49.00

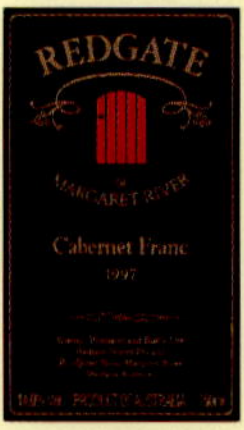

REDGATE CABERNET SAUVIGNON (/MERLOT from 1999) ★★★★

before 1995		Prior	
1995	7	Now	$45.00
1996	6	Now	$38.00
1997	5	Prior	
1998	5	2005	$30.00
1999	7	2007	$40.00
2000	5	2005	$28.00
2001	7	2005	$38.00

REDGATE CHARDONNAY ★★★★

before 1995		Prior	
1995	6	Now	$26.00
1996	6	Now	$25.00
1997	Not made		
1998	6	Now	$24.00
1999	6	Now	$23.00
2000	Not made		
2001	6	2004	$22.00
2002	7	2006	$24.00

REDGATE SAUVIGNON BLANC RESERVE ★★★★

before 1996		Prior	
1996	6	Now	$24.00
1997	7	Now	$27.00
1998	3	Prior	
1999	6	Now	$22.00
2000	5	Now	$18.00
2001	7	2005	$24.00
2002	7	2007	$23.00

REDGATE SAUVIGNON BLANC/SEMILLON ★★★

1999	7	Prior	
2000	7	Now	$20.00
2001	7	Now	$19.50
2002	7	2004	$19.00

REDGATE SEMILLON ★★★★

1997	7	Now	$29.00
1998	3	Prior	
1999	5	Now	$20.00
2000	7	Now	$27.00
2001	7	Now	$26.00
2002	7	Now	$25.00

REDGATE SHIRAZ ★★★★

1995	7	Now	$34.00
1996	5	Now	$24.00
1997	5	Now	$23.00

1998	6	2004	$27.00
1999	7	2008	$30.00
2000	5	2005	$21.00
2001	7	2009	$29.00

***Red Hill Estate** is a Mornington Peninsula vineyard producing a most agreeable Methode Champenoise as well as some finely crafted Burgundian styles. Winemaker: Michael Kyberd.*

RED HILL ESTATE BLANC DE BLANC

★★★★

1998	6	Now	$26.00
1999	Not made		$26.00
2000	7	Now	$29.00
2001	6	Now	$24.00

RED HILL ESTATE BLANC DE NOIRS

★★★★★

1998	5	Now	$36.00
1999	6	Now	$42.00
2000	7	Now	$48.00
2001	6	Now	$40.00

RED HILL ESTATE CHARDONNAY

★★★★

1994	5	Now	$21.00
1995	5	Now	$20.00
1996	4	Prior	
1997	6	Now	$23.00
1998	7	Now	$26.00
1999	6	Now	$22.00
2000	6	2004	$21.00
2001	7	2006	$24.00

RED HILL ESTATE METHODE CHAMPENOISE

★★★★

1991	6	Now	$31.00
1992	5	Now	$25.00
1993	7	Now	$34.00
1994	5	Now	$23.00
1995	5	Now	$23.00
1996	6	Now	$27.00
1997	6	Now	$26.00

Not made since 1997

RED HILL ESTATE PINOT NOIR

★★★★

before 1996		Prior	
1996	6	Now	$25.00
1997	6	Now	$24.00
1998	6	Now	$23.00
1999	6	Now	$23.00
2000	7	2005	$26.00
2001	6	2005	$21.00

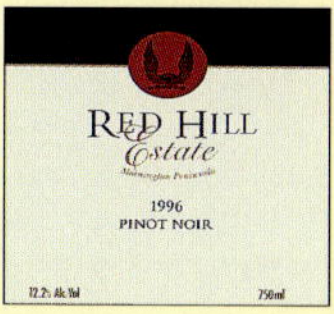

***Redman** is one of the most respected names amongst the catalogue of established Coonawarra producers. Winemaker: Bruce Redman.*

REDMAN CABERNET SAUVIGNON ★★★★

1975	6	Prior	
1976	7	Now	$58.00
1977	6	Prior	
1978	6	Prior	
1979	6	Now	$46.00
1980	7	Now	$52.00
1981	6	Now	$43.00
1982	6	Now	$42.00
1983	4	Prior	
1984	7	Now	$46.00
1985	5	Now	$32.00
1986	6	Now	$37.00
1987	7	Now	$42.00
1988	7	Now	$41.00
1989	5	Now	$28.00
1990	7	Now	$39.00
1991	6	Now	$32.00
1992	7	Now	$36.00
1993	7	Now	$35.00
1994	6	2004	$29.00
1995	5	2005	$24.00
1996	6	2006	$28.00
1997	5	2005	$22.00
1998	7	2008	$30.00
1999	7	2008	$30.00
2000	7	2010	$29.00
2001	6	2010	$24.00

REDMAN CABERNET/MERLOT ★★★★

1990	6	Now	$39.00
1991	6	Now	$37.00
1992	6	Now	$36.00
1993	7	2005	$41.00
1994	6	2005	$34.00
1995	6	2005	$33.00
1996	6	2006	$32.00
1997	5	2004	$26.00
1998	7	2008	$35.00
1999	6	2009	$29.00
2000	7	2010	$33.00
2001	6	2010	$28.00

REDMAN SHIRAZ ★★★

1975	4	Prior	
1976	7	Now	$46.00
1977	5	Prior	

1978	4	Prior	
1979	4	Prior	
1980	6	Now	$35.00
1981	6	Now	$34.00
1982	6	Now	$33.00
1983	4	Prior	
1984	7	Now	$36.00
1985	5	Now	$25.00
1986	6	Now	$29.00
1987	5	Now	$23.00
1988	7	Now	$32.00
1989	6	Now	$26.00
1990	7	Now	$30.00
1991	6	Now	$25.00
1992	6	Now	$24.00
1993	7	Now	$27.00
1994	6	Now	$23.00
1995	4	Now	$15.00
1996	6	2004	$21.00
1997	5	2005	$17.50
1998	7	2008	$24.00
1999	6	2009	$20.00
2000	7	2010	$22.00
2001	5	2009	$15.50

Reynella *- see Chateau Reynella.*

The Reynolds Wine Company *is near Muswellbrook in the Upper Hunter Valley. The wines are vinified in a rebuilt 1837 sandstone winery. Winemaker: Jon Reynolds.*

REYNOLDS CABERNET SAUVIGNON (ORANGE) ★★★

1994	5	Now	$24.00
1995	6	Now	$28.00
1996	6	Now	$27.00
1997	6	2004	$26.00
1998	7	Now	$30.00
1999	6	2004	$25.00
2000	5	2004	$20.00

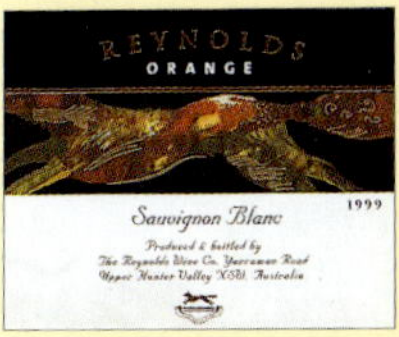

REYNOLDS CHARDONNAY (ORANGE) ★★★

1995	5	Now	$18.50
1996	5	Now	$18.00
1997	6	Now	$21.00
1998	5	Now	$17.00
1999	6	Now	$20.00
2000	6	Now	$19.50

REYNOLDS MERLOT (ORANGE) ★★★★

1988	7	Now	$42.00
1989	6	Now	$35.00
1990	Not made		
1991	5	Now	$27.00

1992	5	Now	$26.00
1993	5	Now	$26.00
1994	5	Now	$25.00
1995	6	Now	$29.00
1996	6	Now	$28.00
1997	5	Now	$23.00
1998	7	Now	$31.00
1999	6	2004	$26.00
2000	5	2004	$21.00

REYNOLDS SEMILLON ★★★★

1989	6	Now	$21.00
1990	Not made		
1991	7	Now	$23.00
1992	7	Now	$23.00
1993	5	Now	$16.00
1994	4	Now	$12.50
1995	5	Now	$15.00
1996	6	Now	$17.50
1997	6	Now	$17.00
1998	5	Now	$13.50
1999	6	2004	$16.00
2000	6	2004	$15.50

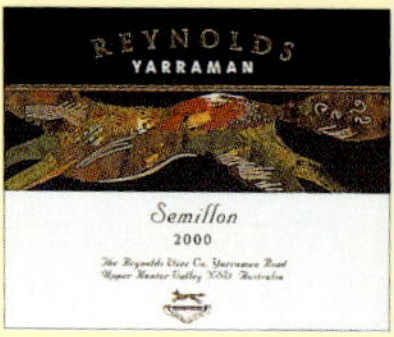

REYNOLDS SHIRAZ ★★★

1993	5	Now	$18.00
1994	6	Now	$21.00
1995	7	Now	$23.00
1996	6	Now	$19.50
1997	6	Now	$19.00
1998	7	Now	$21.00
1999	7	Now	$21.00

***Ribbon Vale Estate**, a very long, very narrow vineyard at Margaret River, has a small range of emphatic wines. Now owned by Moss Wood, the range is being rationalised. The entries below refer to the pre Moss Wood wines. Winemaker: Jan Davies.*

RIBBON VALE CABERNET/MERLOT ★★★

1986	5	Now	$41.00
1987	5	Now	$40.00
1988	6	Now	$47.00
1989	Not made		
1990	6	Now	$44.00
1991	6	Now	$43.00
1992	Not made		
1993	7	Now	$47.00
1994	7	Now	$46.00
1995	7	Now	$45.00
1996	7	Now	$43.00

1997	7	Now	$42.00
1998	6	2008	$35.00
1999	6	2009	$34.00
2000	7	2010	$38.00

RIBBON VALE MERLOT ★★★

before 1991		Prior	
1991	6	Now	$42.00
1992	5	Now	$33.00
1993	6	Now	$39.00
1994	7	Now	$44.00
1995	6	Now	$37.00
1996	7	Now	$42.00
1997	6	Now	$35.00
1998	7	2005	$39.00
1999	7	2005	$38.00

RIBBON VALE SAUVIGNON BLANC ★★★

before 1996		Prior	
1996	6	Now	$27.00
1997	7	Now	$31.00
1998	7	Now	$30.00
1999	6	Now	$25.00

RIBBON VALE SEMILLON ★★★★

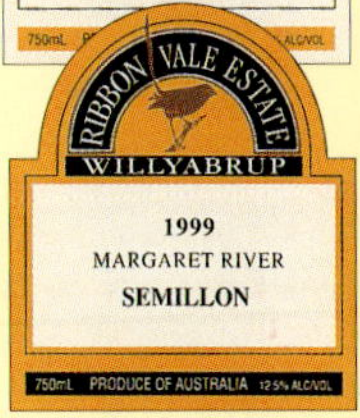

before 1997		Prior	
1997	7	Now	$20.00
1998	6	Now	$17.00
1999	7	Now	$19.00

RIBBON VALE WOOD MATURED SEMILLON ★★★★

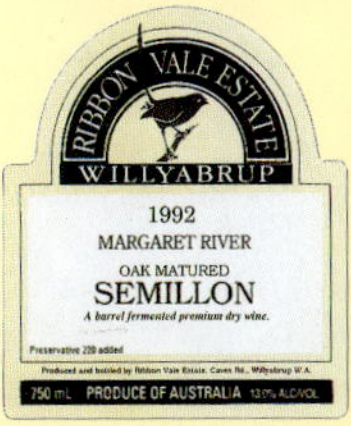

1988	5	Now	$20.00
1989	5	Now	$19.50
1990	5	Now	$19.00
1991	Not made		
1992	6	Now	$21.00
1993	Not made		
1994	6	Now	$20.00
1995	6	Now	$19.50
1996	7	Now	$22.00
1997	6	Now	$18.50

Discontinued.

***Richard Hamilton** is a growing McLaren Vale label owned by the Hamilton wine Group with 50 hectares under vine. Winemakers: Pip Treadwell and Tim Bailey.*

RICHARD HAMILTON CABERNET SAUVIGNON "HUT BLOCK" ★★★★

before 1990		Prior	
1990	6	Now	$26.00
1991	6	Now	$25.00
1992	5	Now	$20.00

1993	5	Now	$20.00
1994	6	Now	$23.00
1995	5	Now	$19.00
1996	7	Now	$25.00
1997	6	Now	$21.00
1998	7	2008	$24.00
1999	6	2008	$20.00

RICHARD HAMILTON CHARDONNAY ★★★★

before 1993		Prior	
1993	5	Now	$17.00
1994	6	Now	$20.00
1995	6	Now	$19.50
1996	7	Now	$22.00
1997	7	2004	$21.00
1998	5	Now	$15.00
1999	6	2005	$17.50
2000	6	2005	$17.00

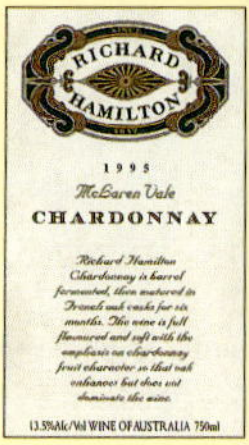

RICHARD HAMILTON MERLOT ★★★

before 1994		Prior	
1994	5	Now	$18.00
1995	5	Now	$17.50
1996	6	Now	$20.00
1997	7	2005	$23.00
1998	7	2005	$22.00
1999	6	2006	$19.00

RICHARD HAMILTON GRENACHE/SHIRAZ ★★★★

before 1994		Prior	
1994	4	Now	$23.00
1995	5	Now	$28.00
1996	6	Now	$32.00
1997	6	2005	$32.00
1998	7	2006	$36.00

RICHARD HAMILTON OLD VINE SHIRAZ ★★★★★

before 1993		Prior	
1993	6	Now	$50.00
1994	6	Now	$49.00
1995	5	Now	$39.00
1996	7	2016	$54.00
1997	6	2010	$45.00
1998	7	2020	$50.00

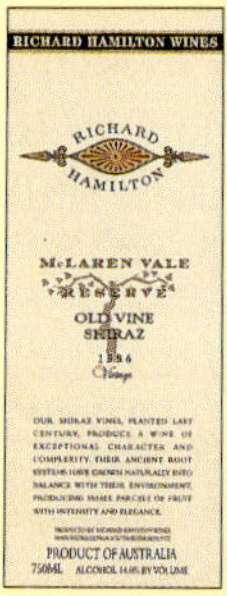

RICHARD HAMILTON SHIRAZ ★★★

before 1995		Prior	
1995	5	Now	$19.00
1996	6	2006	$22.00
1997	5	2005	$17.50
1998	7	2008	$24.00

RICHARD HAMILTON SHIRAZ/GRENACHE "BURTON'S VINEYARD" ★★★★★

before 1995		Prior	
1995	6	2005	$48.00
1996	4	Now	$31.00
1997	4	Now	$30.00
1998	7	2008	$52.00

***Richmond Grove** is a Barossa Valley based operation within the giant Orlando Wyndham group. The Rieslings are admirable. Winemaker: John Vickery.*

RICHMOND GROVE BAROSSA RIESLING ★★★★★

1994	7	Now	$18.00
1995	6	Now	$15.00
1996	7	Now	$17.00
1997	7	Now	$16.50
1998	7	Now	$16.00
1999	7	2004	$15.50
2000	7	2005	$15.00
2001	Not made		

RICHMOND GROVE BAROSSA SHIRAZ ★★★

1993	6	Now	$18.50
1994	7	Now	$21.00
1995	7	Now	$20.00
1996	7	Now	$20.00
1997	7	2004	$19.00
1998	7	2005	$18.50
1999	7	2008	$18.00

RICHMOND GROVE CABERNET/ SHIRAZ/MERLOT ★★★

1989	4	Now	$10.00
1990	4	Now	$9.75
1991	7	Now	$16.50
1992	6	Now	$13.50
1993	6	Now	$13.50
1994	6	Now	$13.00
1995	7	Now	$14.50
1996	7	Now	$14.00
1997	7	Now	$14.00
1998	7	Now	$13.50
1999	7	Now	$13.00
2000	7	Now	$12.50

RICHMOND GROVE COONAWARRA CABERNET SAUVIGNON ★★★

1992	6	Now	$20.00
1993	6	Now	$19.00
1994	7	Now	$22.00
1995	6	Now	$18.00
1996	7	Now	$20.00
1997	7	Now	$20.00
1998	7	2005	$19.50
1999	7	2007	$19.00

RICHMOND GROVE COONAWARRA SHIRAZ ★★★

1997	7	Now	$19.00
1998	Not made		
1999	7	2006	$18.00

RICHMOND GROVE COWRA CHARDONNAY ★★

1992	6	Now	$14.00
1993	6	Now	$14.00
1994	6	Now	$13.50
1995	7	Now	$15.00
1996	6	Now	$12.50
1997	7	Now	$14.50
1998	7	Now	$14.00
1999	7	Now	$13.50
2000	7	Now	$13.00

RICHMOND GROVE COWRA VERDELHO ★★

1992	5	Now	$10.00
1993	6	Now	$11.50
1994	7	Now	$13.00
1995	6	Now	$11.00
1996	7	Now	$12.50
1998	7	Now	$12.00
1999	7	Now	$11.50

RICHMOND GROVE FRENCH CASK CHARDONNAY ★★★

1988	3	Now	$9.25
1989	4	Now	$12.00
1990	5	Now	$14.50
1991	6	Now	$17.00
1992	5	Now	$13.50
1993	6	Now	$16.00
1994	7	Now	$18.00
1995	5	Now	$12.50
1996	6	Now	$14.50
1997	7	Now	$16.50
1998	7	Now	$16.00

1999	7	Now	$15.50
2000	7	Now	$15.00
2001	7	Now	$14.50

RICHMOND GROVE HUNTER VALLEY SEMILLON ★★★

1987	4	Now	$16.00
1988	4	Now	$15.50
1989	3	Now	$11.50
1990	4	Now	$14.50
1991	4	Now	$14.50
1992	4	Now	$14.00
1993	5	Now	$17.00
1994	6	Now	$19.50
1995	7	Now	$22.00
1996	6	Now	$18.50
1997	7	Now	$21.00
1998	7	Now	$20.00
1999	7	Now	$20.00

RICHMOND GROVE HUNTER VALLEY SEMILLON/CHARDONNAY ★★

1987	4	Now	$9.75
1988	4	Now	$9.50
1989	3	Now	$6.75
1990	4	Now	$8.75
1991	4	Now	$8.50
1992	4	Now	$8.25
1993	5	Now	$10.00
1994	6	Now	$11.50
1995	7	Now	$13.50
1996	6	Now	$11.00
1997	7	Now	$12.50
1998	7	Now	$12.00
1999	7	Now	$12.00

RICHMOND GROVE VERDELHO ★★★

1992	5	Now	$11.00
1993	6	Now	$13.00
1994	7	Now	$15.00
1995	6	Now	$12.50
1996	7	Now	$14.00
1997	Not made		
1998	7	Now	$13.00
1999	7	Now	$13.00
2000	7	Now	$12.50
2001	7	Now	$12.00

RICHMOND GROVE WATERVALE RIESLING ★★★★★

1994	6	Now	$16.00
1995	7	Now	$18.00
1996	7	Now	$17.50

1997	7	Now	$17.00
1998	7	Now	$16.50
1999	7	2004	$16.00
2000	7	2005	$15.50
2001	7	2006	$15.00

***Riddoch Estate** is part of the Wingara Group who also own Katnook, Deakin Estate and Sunnycliff. Since 1990 all Riddoch wines have been from Coonawarra fruit. No ratings have been forthcoming for some years. Winemaker: Wayne Stehbens.*

RIDDOCH CABERNET SAUVIGNON (/MERLOT) ★★★★

RIDDOCH CABERNET/SHIRAZ ★★★

RIDDOCH CHARDONNAY ★★★★

RIDDOCH SHIRAZ ★★★★

***Robertson's Well** is a label used by Beringer Blass for two Coonawarra red wines. Winemaker: Andrew Hales.*

ROBERTSON'S WELL COONAWARRA CABERNET ★★★★

1992	7	Now	$30.00
1993	6	Now	$25.00
1994	7	Now	$28.00
1995	6	Now	$23.00
1996	7	2004	$26.00
1997	6	Now	$22.00
1998	7	2005	$25.00
1999	6	2007	$21.00
2000	6	2008	$20.00

ROBERTSON'S WELL SHIRAZ ★★★★

1996	7	Now	$27.00
1997	6	Now	$22.00
1998	7	2004	$25.00
1999	6	2005	$21.00
2000	6	2008	$20.00

***The Robson Vineyard** - see Murray Robson Wines.*

***The Rochford Winery** is a very small producer in Victoria's Macedon region. Winemaker: David Creed.*

ROCHFORD CABERNET SAUVIGNON ★★★★

before 1994		Prior	
1994	5	Now	$37.00
1995	4	Now	$29.00
1996	5	Now	$35.00
1997	3	Now	$20.00
1998	5	2005	$33.00
1999	6	2006	$39.00
2000	5	2007	$31.00

ROCHFORD CHARDONNAY ★★★★

1995	5	Now	$37.00
1996	3	Now	$22.00
1997	6	Now	$42.00
1998	Not made		
1999	4	Now	$26.00
2000	5	2004	$32.00

ROCHFORD PINOT NOIR ★★★★

before 1994		Prior	
1994	7	Now	$58.00
1995	3	Now	$24.00
1996	4	Now	$31.00
1997	5	Now	$38.00
1998	5	Now	$37.00
1999	5	2005	$36.00
2000	6	2005	$42.00

***Rockford Wines** are Barossa Valley makers of a range of improbably generous wines from unirrigated vineyards. The makers apparently prefer not to supply vintage ratings. Winemaker: Robert O'Callaghan.*

ROCKFORD BASKET PRESS SHIRAZ ★★★★

ROCKFORD CABERNET SAUVIGNON ★★★★

***Romany Rye** - see Eppalock Ridge.*

***Rosemount**, now acquired by Southcorp, is a moderately large Upper Hunter producer of a large and eminently successful range of wines. Their Chardonnays are particularly popular. Winemaker: Philip Shaw.*

ROSEMOUNT BALMORAL SYRAH ★★★★★

1991	7	2010	$88.00
1992	7	2015	$86.00
1993	6	2010	$72.00
1994	7	2015	$80.00
1995	7	2020	$78.00
1996	7	2025	$76.00
1997	6	2020	$64.00
1998	7	2020	$72.00

ROSEMOUNT ESTATE CABERNET SAUVIGNON (DIAMOND LABEL) ★★★

before 1990		Prior	
1990	7	Now	$24.00
1991	6	Now	$20.00
1992	6	Now	$19.50
1993	5	Now	$15.50
1994	6	Now	$18.00

1995	6	2006	$17.50
1996	6	2007	$17.00
1997	7	2020	$19.50
1998	7	2010	$19.00

ROSEMOUNT ESTATE CHARDONNAY (DIAMOND LABEL) ★★★

1986	6	Prior	
1987	7	Now	$28.00
1988	6	Prior	
1989	5	Now	$19.00
1990	6	Now	$22.00
1991	6	Now	$21.00
1992	6	Now	$21.00
1993	6	Now	$20.00
1994	6	2005	$19.50
1995	5	Now	$16.00
1996	6	Now	$18.50
1997	6	2007	$18.00
1998	5	Now	$14.50
1999	7	2005	$20.00

ROSEMOUNT ESTATE SHIRAZ (DIAMOND LABEL) ★★★

1986	6	Now	$24.00
1987	6	Prior	
1988	5	Prior	
1989	5	Prior	
1990	6	Prior	
1991	6	Now	$21.00
1992	6	Now	$20.00
1993	7	Now	$23.00
1994	6	Now	$19.50
1995	5	Now	$15.50
1996	7	2005	$21.00
1997	6	2007	$18.00
1998	7	2009	$20.00
1999	6	2010	$17.00

ROSEMOUNT GIANTS CREEK (HUNTER VALLEY CHARDONNAY) ★★★★

1987	7	Now	$34.00
1988	6	Now	$28.00
1989	6	Now	$27.00
1990	6	2005	$27.00
1991	5	Now	$21.00
1992	5	Now	$21.00
1993	6	Now	$24.00
1994	7	2010	$28.00

1995	6	2020	$23.00
1996	7	2015	$26.00
1997	5	2010	$18.00
1998	6	2010	$21.00
1999	7	2010	$24.00

ROSEMOUNT GSM (GRENACHE/SHIRAZ/MOURVEDRE) ★★★★

1994	7	Now	$37.00
1995	6	Now	$30.00
1996	7	Now	$35.00
1997	6	2008	$29.00
1998	6	2008	$28.00
1999	6	2008	$27.00

ROSEMOUNT ORANGE VINEYARD CABERNET SAUVIGNON ★★★★

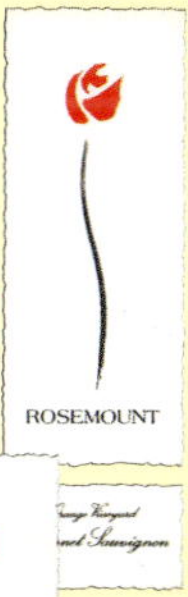

1993	6	Now	$30.00
1994	6	Now	$29.00
1995	7	2005	$33.00
1996	5	2010	$23.00
1997	6	2010	$27.00
1998	6	2010	$26.00
1999	5	2009	$21.00

ROSEMOUNT ORANGE VINEYARD CHARDONNAY ★★★★

1992	6	Prior	
1993	6	2007	$30.00
1994	6	2008	$29.00
1995	7	2009	$33.00
1996	7	2012	$32.00
1997	7	2008	$31.00
1998	5	2005	$22.00
1999	6	2006	$25.00
2000	6	2006	$24.00
2001	6	2007	$24.00

ROSEMOUNT ROXBURGH CHARDONNAY ★★★★★

1982	7	Now	$105.00
1983	6	Prior	
1984	7	Now	$100.00
1985	6	Now	$84.00
1986	6	Now	$82.00
1987	7	2010	$92.00
1988	4	Now	$50.00
1989	5	Now	$62.00
1990	7	2006	$84.00
1991	6	2007	$70.00
1992	6	2009	$68.00
1993	6	Now	$66.00

1994	5	Now	$54.00
1995	5	2005	$52.00
1996	7	2010	$70.00
1997	7	2012	$68.00
1998	6	2008	$56.00
1999	5	2006	$46.00

ROSEMOUNT SHOW RESERVE CHARDONNAY

★★★★

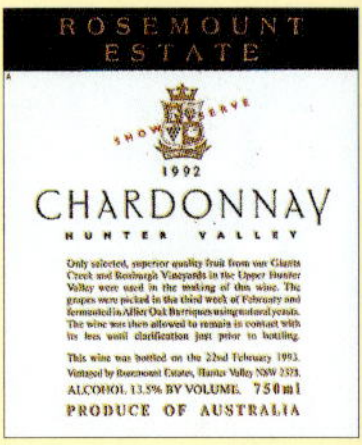

1980	6	Prior	
1981	7	Now	$50.00
1982	7	2008	$50.00
1983	5	Prior	
1984	6	2004	$40.00
1985	7	Now	$46.00
1986	6	Now	$38.00
1987	7	2012	$43.00
1988	6	Now	$36.00
1989	6	Now	$35.00
1990	5	2004	$28.00
1991	6	Now	$33.00
1992	6	2007	$32.00
1993	7	2005	$36.00
1994	5	Now	$25.00
1995	5	2006	$24.00
1996	7	2010	$33.00
1997	7	2015	$32.00
1998	6	2005	$26.00
1999	7	2008	$30.00
2000	6	2007	N/R
2001	6	2008	$27.00

ROSEMOUNT SHOW RESERVE COONAWARRA CABERNET SAUVIGNON

★★★★★

1981	5	Now	$38.00
1982	7	Now	$52.00
1983	5	Now	$36.00
1984	5	Prior	
1985	7	2004	$48.00
1986	6	2005	$40.00
1987	5	2006	$32.00
1988	6	Now	$38.00
1989	7	2010	$43.00
1990	7	Now	$41.00
1991	7	2009	$40.00
1992	6	2011	$33.00
1993	5	2004	$27.00

1994	7	2015	$37.00
1995	5	2015	$25.00
1996	6	2015	$30.00
1997	6	2015	$29.00
1998	5	2010	$23.00
1999	5	2009	$22.00

ROSEMOUNT SHOW RESERVE HUNTER VALLEY SEMILLON ★★★★

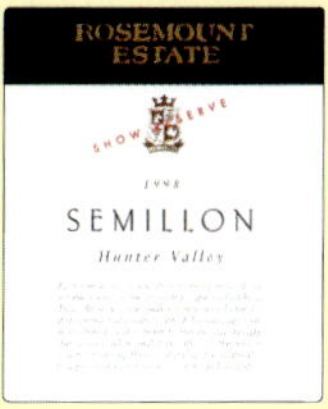

1981	7	Now	$50.00
1982	7	Now	$49.00
1983	Not made		
1984	Not made		
1985	Not made		
1986	7	Now	$43.00
1987	7	Now	$42.00
1988	5	Now	$29.00
1989	7	2004	$40.00
1990	6	2006	$33.00
1991	6	2011	$32.00
1992	Not made		
1993	Not made		
1994	Not made		
1995	5	2010	$23.00
1996	7	2016	$32.00
1997	Not made		
1998	7	2015	$30.00
1999	7	2015	$29.00
2000	7	2012	$28.00

ROSEMOUNT SHOW RESERVE MCLAREN VALE SHIRAZ ★★★★

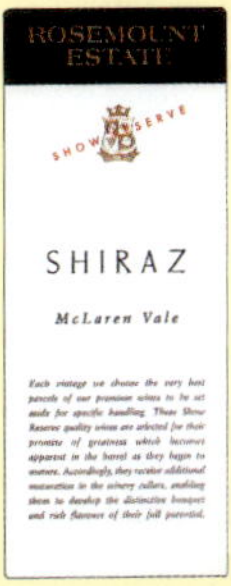

1989	6	2008	$36.00
1990	5	2010	$29.00
1991	7	2015	$39.00
1992	Not made		
1993	Not made		
1994	7	2010	$36.00
1995	6	2008	$30.00
1996	7	2015	$34.00
1997	6	2010	$28.00
1998	6	2010	$27.00
1999	6	2009	$26.00
2000	6	2006	$26.00

ROSEMOUNT TRADITIONAL (CABERNET/MERLOT/PETIT VERDOT) ★★★★

1988	6	Now	$34.00
1989	5	Now	$27.00
1990	6	Now	$32.00
1991	5	Now	$26.00
1992	7	2006	$35.00
1993	6	2006	$29.00
1994	6	2012	$28.00
1995	6	2005	$28.00

1996	7	2010	$31.00
1997	7	2010	$30.00
1998	6	2008	$25.00
1999	5	2007	$20.00

***The Rothbury Estate**, begun as a purist Pokolbin producer of consistently reliable wines, expanded to be owners of Baileys, Saltram and St Huberts. They are now part of Beringer Blass. Winemaker: Neil McGuigan.*

The ROTHBURY ESTATE BROKENBACK CHARDONNAY ★★★★

before 1991		Prior	
1991	6	Now	$27.00
1992	7	Now	$30.00
1993	6	Now	$25.00
1994	7	Now	$29.00
1995	Not made		
1996	6	Now	$23.00
1997	6	Now	$22.00
1998	7	Now	$25.00
1999	Not made		
2000	6	2005	$20.00
2001	7	2007	$23.00
2002	6	2008	$19.50

The ROTHBURY ESTATE BROKENBACK SEMILLON ★★★★

before 1984		Prior	
1984	7	Now	$41.00
1985	4	Now	$23.00
1986	7	Now	$39.00
1987	5	Now	$27.00
1988	4	Now	$21.00
1989	6	Now	$30.00
1990	6	2010	$29.00
1991	5	Now	$24.00
1992	7	2010	$32.00
1993	5	Now	$22.00
1994	6	2020	$26.00
1995	5	Now	$21.00
1996	6	Now	$25.00
1997	7	2005	$28.00
1998	7	2005	$27.00
1999	6	2004	$22.00
2000	7	2008	$25.00
2001	7	2008	$25.00
2002	7	2009	$24.00

The ROTHBURY ESTATE BROKENBACK SHIRAZ ★★★★

before 1983		Prior	
1983	7	Now	$56.00
1984	4	Prior	

1985	6	Prior	
1986	7	Now	$52.00
1987	7	Now	$50.00
1988	5	Now	$35.00
1989	5	Now	$34.00
1990	5	Now	$33.00
1991	7	2010	$45.00
1992	No data		
1993	5	Now	$30.00
1994	6	2005	$35.00
1995	7	2005	$40.00
1996	7	2005	$38.00
1997	Not made		
1998	7	2006	$36.00
1999	6	2009	$30.00
2000	6	2007	$29.00

The ROTHBURY ESTATE COWRA CHARDONNAY ★★★

before 2000		Prior	
2000	6	Now	$14.00
2001	6	2004	
2002	6	2005	$12.00

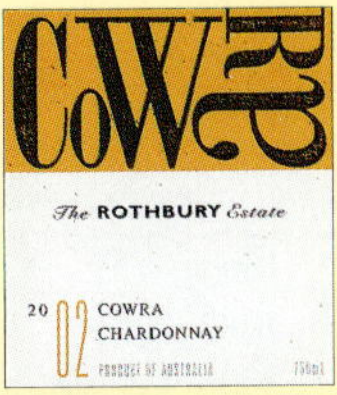

The ROTHBURY ESTATE MUDGEE SHIRAZ ★★★

before 1991		Prior	
1991	7	2010	$23.00
1992	Not made		
1993	5	Now	$15.50
1994	6	Now	$18.00
1995	7	Now	$20.00
1996	6	2004	$17.00
1997	6	Now	$16.50
1998	7	2004	$19.00
1999	No data		
2000	6	2004	$15.00

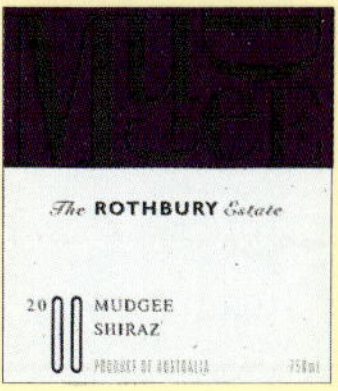

***Rouge Homme** is a long established and respected Coonawarra based maker owned by Southcorp. Winemaker: Brett Sharpe.*

ROUGE HOMME CABERNET SAUVIGNON ★★★

before 1990		Prior	
1990	7	Now	$25.00
1991	7	Now	$24.00
1992	6	Now	$20.00
1993	6	Now	$19.50
1994	7	Now	$22.00
1995	5	Now	$15.50
1996	7	Now	$21.00
1997	6	Now	$17.50
1998	7	2004	$19.50
1999	7	2004	$19.00

No longer made.

ROUGE HOMME CABERNET/MERLOT ★★★★

1992	5	Now	$19.00
1993	7	Now	$26.00
1994	7	Now	$25.00
1995	5	Now	$17.50
1996	7	Now	$23.00
1997	6	Now	$19.50
1998	7	Now	$22.00
1999	7	Now	$21.00
2000	7	2005	$21.00
2001	Not made		
2002	5	2005	$14.00
2003	6	2007	N/R

ROUGE HOMME CHARDONNAY ★★★

before 1996		Prior	
1996	7	Now	$23.00
1997	7	Now	$22.00
1998	7	Now	$21.00
1999	7	Now	$21.00
2000	6	Now	$17.50
2000	Not made		
2002	Not made		
2003	6	Now	$16.00

ROUGE HOMME PINOT NOIR ★★★

1983	6	Now	$29.00
1984	4	Prior	
1985	6	Prior	
1986	5	Prior	
1987	5	Now	$22.00
1988	5	Prior	
1989	5	Prior	
1990	5	Now	$20.00
1991	6	Now	$23.00
1992	5	Now	$19.00
1993	6	Now	$22.00
1994	7	Now	$25.00
1995	6	Now	$20.00
1996	6	Now	$20.00
1997	7	Now	$22.00
1998	6	Now	$19.00
1999	6	Now	$18.50
2000	6	Now	$18.00

No longer made.

ROUGE HOMME RICHARDSON'S WHITE BLOCK CHARDONNAY ★★★

before 1991		Prior	
1991	6	Now	$17.00
1992	5	Now	$14.00

1993	6	Now	$16.00
1994	6	Now	$15.50
1995	6	Now	$15.00
1996	7	Now	$17.50
1997	7	Now	$16.50
1998	7	Now	$16.50
1999	7	Now	$16.00
2000	6	Now	$13.00

ROUGE HOMME RICHARDSON'S RED (CABERNET/MERLOT/MALBEC/FRANC) ★★★

1992	5	Now	$15.00
1993	7	Now	$20.00
1994	7	Now	$20.00
1995	6	Now	$16.50
1996	7	Now	$18.50
1997	7	Now	$18.00

ROUGE HOMME SHIRAZ/CABERNET ★★★

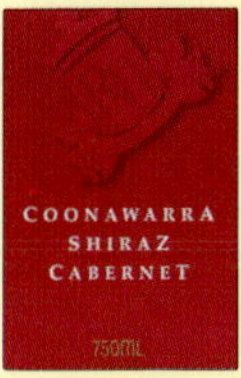

1980	7	Now	$39.00
1981	5	Prior	
1982	5	Prior	
1983	Not made		
1984	5	Prior	
1985	6	Now	$29.00
1986	6	Now	$28.00
1987	5	Prior	
1988	5	Prior	
1989	4	Prior	
1990	7	Now	$29.00
1991	7	Now	$28.00
1992	6	Now	$24.00
1993	6	Now	$23.00
1994	7	Now	$26.00
1995	6	Now	$21.00
1996	7	Now	$24.00
1997	7	Now	$24.00
1998	7	Now	$23.00
1999	7	Now	$22.00
2000	7	2005	$22.00
2001	Not made		
2002	5	2006	$14.50
2003	6	2007	N/R

***Rymill** is a painstakingly operated Coonawarra vineyard who, in addition to supplying grapes to other makers, produce an increasing quantity of their own wine. Winemakers: John Innes and Clemence Dournois.*

RYMILL CABERNET SAUVIGNON ★★★★

1995	5	2004	$25.00
1996	7	2005	$34.00
1997	6	2005	$28.00
1998	7	2006	$32.00
1999	6	2007	$27.00

RYMILL MERLOT/CABERNET FRANC/ CABERNET SAUVIGNON ★★★★

1998	7	2004	$22.00
1999	6	2004	$18.50
2000	6	2005	$18.00

RYMILL SHIRAZ ★★★★

1995	5	2004	$22.00
1996	7	2005	$30.00
1997	6	2005	$25.00
1998	6	2006	$24.00
1999	7	2006	$27.00
2000	5	2005	$19.00

***St Hallett** is an old Barossa Valley producer whose rebuilt vineyards and new winery equipment have achieved for it an esteemed position as one of the valley's best makers. Winemaker: Stuart Blackwell.*

ST HALLETT BLACKWELL SHIRAZ ★★★★

1994	6	Prior	
1995	5	Now	$31.00
1996	6	2006	$36.00
1997	4	Now	$23.00
1998	7	2010	$39.00
1999	5	2007	$27.00
2000	6	2009	$32.00

ST HALLETT CABERNET/ MERLOT ★★★★

before 1991		Prior	
1991	6	Now	$22.00
1992	7	Now	$25.00
1993	6	Now	$21.00
1994	5	Now	$17.00
1995	5	Now	$16.50
1996	7	Now	$22.00
1997	5	Now	$15.50
1998	7	2005	$21.00
1999	6	2006	$18.00

ST HALLETT CHARDONNAY ★★★

before 1989		Prior	
1989	6	Now	$24.00
1990	6	Now	$23.00
1991	6	Now	$23.00
1992	5	Now	$18.50
1993	6	Now	$21.00
1994	6	Now	$21.00
1995	5	Now	$17.00
1996	6	Now	$19.50
1997	6	2004	$19.00
1998	7	2006	$21.00
1999	6	2006	$18.00

ST HALLETT EDEN VALLEY RIESLING ★★★★★

1996	5	Now	$16.00
1997	6	2006	$19.00
1998	5	Now	$15.00
1999	Not made		
2000	6	2008	$17.00
2001	6	2007	$16.50
2002	7	2012	$19.00

ST HALLETT FAITH SHIRAZ ★★★

1994	6	Now	$28.00
1995	5	Now	$23.00
1996	5	Now	$22.00
1997	Not made		
1998	5	Now	$21.00
1999	5	Now	$20.00
2000	7	2005	$27.00
2001	6	2006	$23.00

ST HALLETT OLD BLOCK SHIRAZ ★★★★★

1980	3	Prior	
1981	Not made		
1982	5	Now	$88.00
1983	6	Now	$100.00
1984	6	Now	$98.00
1985	6	Now	$96.00
1986	7	Now	$105.00
1987	5	Now	$74.00
1988	6	Now	$88.00
1989	5	Now	$70.00
1990	6	Now	$82.00
1991	7	Now	$94.00
1992	5	Now	$64.00
1993	6	2004	$76.00
1994	6	2005	$74.00
1995	6	2005	$70.00
1996	7	2010	$80.00
1997	5	2008	$56.00
1998	7	2015	$76.00
1999	6	2012	$62.00
2000	6	2013	$62.00

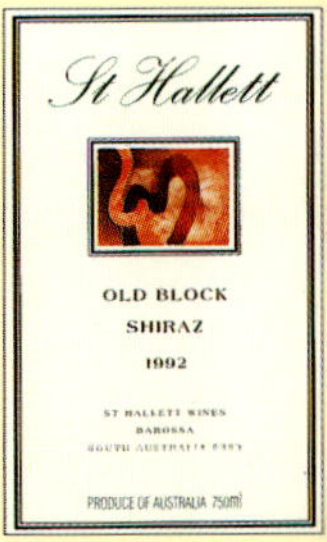

***St Huberts** (owned by Beringer Blass) is a small vineyard in the Yarra Valley renowned for the quality of its Cabernet fruit. Winemaker: Matt Steel.*

ST HUBERTS CABERNET SAUVIGNON ★★★★

before 1979		Prior	
1979	7	Now	$54.00
1980	6	Now	$45.00

1981	6	Now	$44.00
1982	7	Now	$49.00
1983	Not made		
1984	6	Prior	
1985	5	Prior	
1986	5	Prior	
1987	Not made		
1988	6	Now	$35.00
1989	Not made		
1990	7	Now	$39.00
1991	6	2004	$32.00
1992	6	2005	$31.00
1993	6	2006	$30.00
1994	7	2008	$34.00
1995	5	2006	$24.00
1996	6	2006	$28.00
1997	7	2008	$32.00
1998	7	2008	$31.00
1999	7	2010	$30.00
2000	6	2010	$25.00

ST HUBERTS CHARDONNAY ★★★★

before 1993		Prior	
1993	6	Now	$26.00
1994	7	Now	$30.00
1995	7	Now	$29.00
1996	6	Now	$24.00
1997	7	Now	$27.00
1998	7	2004	$26.00
1999	7	2004	$26.00
2000	6	2005	$21.00
2001	6	2006	$21.00

ST HUBERTS PINOT NOIR ★★★★

before 1989		Prior	
1989	7	Now	$42.00
1990	7	Now	$40.00
1991	5	Now	$28.00
1992	5	Now	$27.00
1993	5	Now	$26.00
1994	5	Now	$25.00
1995	6	Now	$30.00
1996	6	Now	$29.00
1997	6	Now	$28.00
1998	7	Now	$32.00
1999	7	Now	$31.00
2000	7	2006	$30.00
2001	7	2008	$29.00

St Leonards, part of All Saints Estate, is the label under which the best of the Estate's wines are released. Winemaker: Peter Brown.

ST LEONARDS CHARDONNAY ★★★★

1993	Not made		
1994	7	Prior	
1995	6	Now	$20.00
1996	5	Now	$16.50
1997	5	Now	$16.00
1998	6	Now	$19.00
1999	5	Now	$15.00
2000	5	Now	$14.50
2001	5	2004	$14.50

ST LEONARDS CHENIN BLANC ★★★

before 1996		Prior	
1996	6	Now	$18.00
1997	6	Now	$17.50
1998	6	2004	$17.00
1999	6	2005	$16.50
2000	6	2004	$16.00
2001	5	2006	$13.00
2002	5	2006	$12.50

St Matthias *is a 8 hectare vineyard in Tasmania's West Tamar Valley, now owned and operated by Moorilla Estate, where the wine is now made. Winemaker: Alain Rousseau.*

ST MATTHIAS CHARDONNAY ★★★

1996	6	Now	$19.00
1997	7	Now	$21.00
1998	7	Now	$21.00
1999	6	Now	$17.50

ST MATTHIAS RIESLING ★★★

1996	6	Now	$19.00
1997	7	Now	$21.00
1998	7	Now	$21.00
1999	6	Now	$17.50
2000	6	Now	$17.00
2001	7	2004	$19.00

Saddlers Creek Wines *are Hunter Valley producers of a sizable range of wines of substantial body and agreeable palate. Winemaker: John Johnstone.*

SADDLERS CREEK BLUEGRASS CABERNET ★★★★

1995	7	Now	$29.00
1996	6	Now	$24.00
1997	4	Prior	

1998	6	Now	$23.00
1999	6	2005	$22.00
2000	7	2005	$25.00

SADDLERS CREEK CLASSIC HUNTER SEMILLON ★★★

1998	5	2005	$17.00
1999	6	2006	$20.00
2000	7	2007	$23.00
2001	7	2007	$22.00

SADDLERS CREEK EQUUS HUNTER SHIRAZ ★★★★

1996	5	Now	$21.00
1997	4	Now	$16.50
1998	7	2004	$28.00
1999	6	2004	$24.00

SADDLERS CREEK EQUUS McLAREN SHIRAZ (RESERVE) ★★★★★

1996	5	Now	$41.00
1997	6	Now	$48.00
1998	7	2005	$54.00
1999	7	2005	$52.00

SADDLERS CREEK MARROWBONE CHARDONNAY ★★★★

before 1997		Prior	
1997	6	Now	$22.00
1998	5	Now	$18.00
1999	6	Now	$21.00
2000	7	Now	$23.00

***Salitage** is an impressive maker from the Pemberton region of Western Australia. The name is derived from the first two letters of each of the names of the Horgan family's four children Sarah, Lisa, Tamara and Gerard. Winemaker: Patrick Coutts.*

SALITAGE CABERNET BLEND ★★★★

1995	5	Now	$39.00
1996	5	Now	$38.00
1997	Not made		
1998	5	Now	$35.00
1999	6	2006	$41.00
2000	5	2005	$33.00
2001	6	2008	$39.00

SALITAGE CHARDONNAY ★★★★

before 1999		Prior	
1999	6	Now	$34.00
2000	6	Now	$33.00
2001	6	2004	$32.00
2002	6	2005	$32.00

SALITAGE PINOT NOIR ★★★★★

1993	5	Prior	
1994	5	Now	$41.00
1995	4	Now	$32.00
1996	5	Prior	
1997	5	Now	$38.00
1998	5	Now	$37.00
1999	6	2004	$43.00
2000	6	2004	$42.00
2001	6	2005	$40.00
2002	6	2005	$39.00

***Sally's Paddock** - see Redbank*

***Saltram**, an historic name in Australian wine, had been perhaps a little torpid for a decade or so. The operation is now owned by Beringer Blass, we can expect a higher profile to be shown. The famous "Mamre Brook" label has now split into two wines - a Cabernet and a Shiraz. Winemaker: Nigel Dolan.*

SALTRAM MAMRE BROOK BAROSSA VALLEY CABERNET ★★★★

1996	7	2004	$26.00
1997	6	2004	$21.00
1998	7	2005	$24.00
1999	7	2007	$24.00
2000	6	2007	$20.00

SALTRAM MAMRE BROOK BAROSSA VALLEY SHIRAZ ★★★

1996	7	Now	$25.00
1997	6	Now	$21.00
1998	7	2005	$24.00
1999	7	2007	$23.00
2000	7	2009	$22.00

SALTRAM MAMRE BROOK CABERNET SAUVIGNON/ SHIRAZ ★★★

1980	5	Now	$22.00
1981	5	Now	$21.00
1982	6	Now	$24.00
1983	6	Now	$24.00
1984	6	Now	$23.00
1985	7	Now	$26.00
1986	7	Now	$25.00
1987	7	Now	$25.00
1988	5	Now	$17.00
1989	7	Now	$23.00
1990	5	Now	$16.00
1991	Not made		

1992	Not made		
1993	6	Now	$18.00
1994	6	Now	$17.50
1995	6	Now	$17.00

Not made as a blend after 1995.

SALTRAM MAMRE BROOK CHARDONNAY ★★★

before 1994		Prior	
1994	7	Now	$23.00
1995	6	Prior	
1996	7	Prior	
1997	5	Now	$15.00
1998	7	Now	$20.00
1999	6	Now	$17.00
2000	7	2005	$19.50

SALTRAM NUMBER ONE SHIRAZ ★★★★★

1994	7	2004	$68.00
1995	6	2005	$56.00
1996	7	2008	$64.00
1997	6	2008	$52.00
1998	7	2011	$60.00
1999	7	2013	$58.00
2000	7	2015	$56.00

***Sandalford** is one of the Swan Valley's bigger producers. They have recently undergone a complete re-organisation of their range, which now consists of two labels - the Premium and the Element ranges. Winemaker: Paul Boulden.*

SANDALFORD CABERNET SAUVIGNON ★★★★

1997	4	Prior	
1998	6	Now	$37.00
1999	6	Now	$35.00
2000	5	2005	$29.00
2001	7	2012	$39.00
2002	7	2015	$38.00

SANDALFORD CHARDONNAY ★★★★

1998	5	Prior	
1999	4	Now	$26.00
2000	5	Now	$32.00
2001	6	2008	$38.00
2002	6	2010	$36.00

SANDALFORD ELEMENT CHARDONNAY ★★

2000	5	Prior	
2001	6	Now	
2002	7	2004	$12.50

SANDALFORD ELEMENT CHENIN BLANC/VERDELHO ★★

2000	5	Prior	
2001	6	Prior	
2002	7	Now	$12.50

SANDALFORD ELEMENT LATE HARVEST ★★

2000	5	Prior	
2001	6	Prior	
2002	7	Now	$12.50

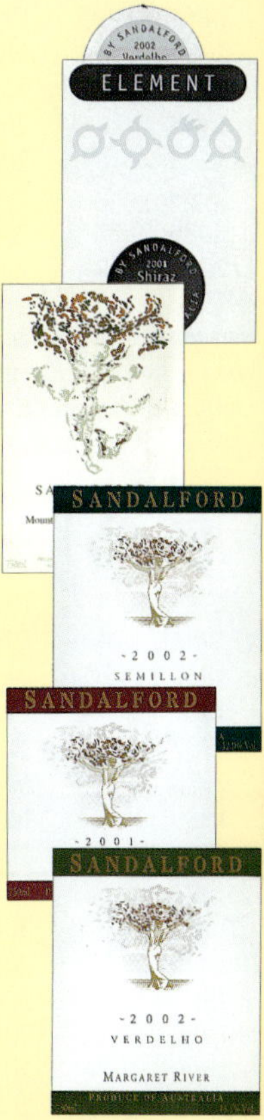

SANDALFORD ELEMENT SHIRAZ/CABERNET ★★

before 2001		Prior	
2001	6	Now	$13.00
2002	7	2004	$15.00

SANDALFORD RIESLING ★★★

before 2001		Prior	
2001	7	2010	$27.00
2002	7	2012	$26.00

SANDALFORD SEMILLON ★★★

1999	5	Prior	
2000	5	Now	$19.50
2001	Not made		
2002	6	2010	$22.00

SANDALFORD SHIRAZ ★★★

1997	4	Prior	
1998	5	Now	$28.00
1999	6	Now	$32.00
2000	Not made		
2001	6	2006	$30.00
2002	7	2010	$35.00

SANDALFORD VERDELHO ★★★

before 2001		Prior	
2001	5	Now	$18.50
2002	6	2004	$21.00

__Sandstone Wines__ is the label established by Margaret River based winemaking consultants Mike and Jan Davies.
Winemakers: Jan and Mike Davies.

SANDSTONE CABERNET SAUVIGNON ★★★

before 1991		Prior	
1991	6	Now	$37.00
1992	7	2005	$42.00
1993	6	Now	$35.00
1994	5	Prior	
1995	7	2005	$39.00
1996	7	2006	$38.00

1997	6	2005	$31.00
1998	7	2006	$35.00
1999	7	2008	$34.00
2000	7	2009	$33.00

SANDSTONE SEMILLON ★★★★

before 1995		Prior	
1995	5	Now	$19.50
1996	6	Now	$22.00
1997	7	2004	$25.00
1998	6	2004	$21.00
1999	7	2005	$24.00
2000	7	2006	$23.00
2001	7	2007	$22.00

***Scarpantoni Estates** are McLaren Flat producers with a good range of sensitively made wines. Winemakers: Domenico Scarpantoni and Michael Filippo.*

SCARPANTONI BLOCK 3 SHIRAZ ★★★

1980	5	Now	$32.00
1981	4	Now	$25.00
1982	5	Prior	
1983	5	Prior	
1984	4	Prior	
1985	5	Now	$28.00
1986	4	Prior	
1987	5	Now	$26.00
1988	6	Now	$30.00
1989	5	Now	$25.00
1990	7	2005	$34.00
1991	6	2005	$28.00
1992	6	2006	$27.00
1993	5	2005	$22.00
1994	6	2007	$25.00
1995	5	2007	$20.00
1996	7	2011	$28.00
1997	6	2008	$23.00
1998	7	2006	$26.00
1999	7	2005	$26.00
2000	6	2008	$21.00

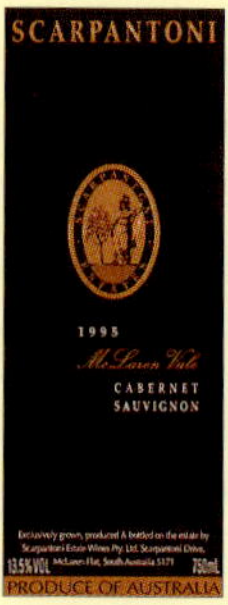

SCARPANTONI CABERNET SAUVIGNON ★★★

before 1983		Prior	
1983	5	Now	$28.00
1984	5	Now	$27.00
1985	5	Now	$26.00
1986	6	Now	$31.00
1987	5	Now	$25.00
1988	6	Now	$29.00

1989	5	Now	$23.00
1990	6	Now	$27.00
1992	6	Now	$26.00
1993	5	2005	$21.00
1994	7	2006	$29.00
1995	6	2005	$24.00
1996	7	2006	$27.00
1997	No data		
1998	No data		
1999	6	2006	$21.00
2000	5	2006	$17.50

SCARPANTONI CHARDONNAY ★★★

before 1991		Prior	
1991	4	Now	$11.00
1992	5	Now	$13.50
1993	4	Now	$10.00
1994	4	Now	$10.00
1995	6	Now	$14.50
1996	7	Now	$16.50

No data since 1996.

Scotchmans Hill *on the Bellarine Peninsula (Geelong area) is a 24 hectare vineyard planted with Cabernet Franc, Chardonnay, Riesling and Pinot Noir. Winemaker: Robin Brockett.*

SCOTCHMANS HILL CABERNET/MERLOT ★★★★

1990	6	Now	$42.00
1991	5	Prior	
1992	7	Now	$46.00
1993	4	Prior	
1994	7	2004	$43.00
1995	4	Prior	
1996	4	Prior	
1997	7	2007	$40.00
1998	6	Now	$33.00
1999	5	2006	$27.00
2000	5	2007	$26.00
2001	6	2009	$30.00

SCOTCHMANS HILL CHARDONNAY ★★★★

before 1997		Prior	
1997	6	Now	$33.00
1998	5	Now	$26.00
1999	5	Now	$26.00
2000	5	2004	$25.00
2001	6	2005	$29.00

SCOTCHMANS HILL PINOT NOIR ★★★

before 1994		Prior	
1994	7	Now	$31.00
1995	5	Now	$21.00

1996	5	Now	$21.00
1997	7	Now	$28.00
1998	7	Now	$27.00
1999	5	Prior	
2000	6	Prior	
2001	6	Now	$21.00
2002	7	2004	$24.00

SCOTCHMANS HILL RIESLING ★★★★

1989	7	Now	$44.00
1990	6	Now	$36.00
1991	6	Now	$35.00
1992	5	Prior	
1993	Not made		
1994	6	Now	$32.00
1995	Not made		
1996	4	Prior	
1997	6	2006	$29.00
1998	6	2006	$29.00
1999	7	2007	$32.00
2000	5	2004	$22.00

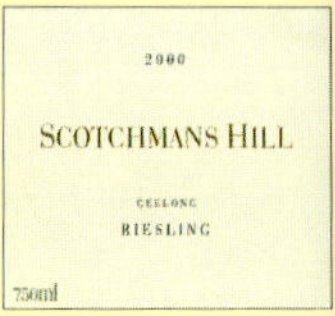

SCOTCHMANS HILL SAUVIGNON BLANC ★★★

before 2001		Prior	
2001	5	Now	
2002	7	Now	$22.50

***Seaview** (part of the Southcorp group) owns a clutch of McLaren Vale vineyards producing what has been a markedly popular range of wines. Now the label is used only for sparkling wines. Winemaker: Steve Goodwin.*

SEAVIEW CABERNET SAUVIGNON ★★★

before 1990		Prior	
1990	6	Now	$16.00
1991	7	Now	$18.00
1992	6	Now	$15.00
1993	7	Now	$17.00
1994	6	Now	$14.00
1995	6	Now	$13.50
1996	7	Now	$15.50
1997	6	Now	$13.00

No longer made.

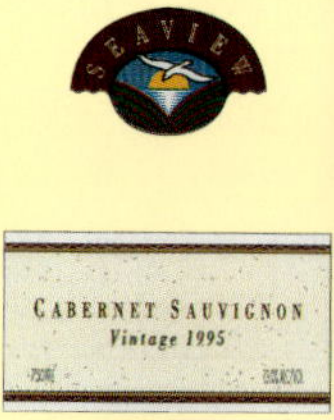

SEAVIEW CHARDONNAY ★★

before 1998		Prior	
1998	6	Now	$9.75
1999	6	Now	$9.50

No longer made.

SEAVIEW CHARDONNAY BLANC DE BLANCS ★★★

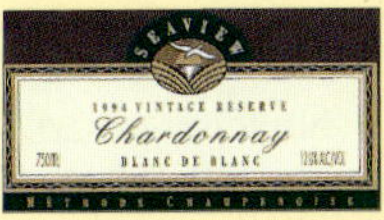

before 1995		Prior	
1995	No data		
1996	No data		
1997	No data		
1998	7	Now	$18.00
1999	7	Now	$17.50

SEAVIEW PINOT NOIR/CHARDONNAY BRUT ★★★

1991	6	Prior	
1992	7	Now	$22.00
1993	7	Now	$21.00
1994	7	Prior	
1995	6	Now	$17.50
1996	7	Now	$19.50
1997	6	Now	$16.50
1998	6	Now	$16.00
1999	7	Now	$18.00

SEAVIEW RIESLING ★★★

1993	6	Now	$10.50
1994	6	Now	$10.50
1995	Not made		
1996	7	Now	$11.50
1997	Not made		
1998	6	Now	$9.25
1999	6	Now	$9.00

No longer made.

SEAVIEW SAUVIGNON BLANC ★★

before 1998		Prior	
1998	6	Now	$13.00

No longer made.

SEAVIEW SEMILLON/ SAUVIGNON BLANC ★★

before 1997		Prior	
1997	6	Now	$12.00
1998	5	Now	$10.00

No longer made.

SEAVIEW SHIRAZ ★★★

1993	6	Now	$14.50
1994	7	Now	$16.50
1995	6	Now	$13.50
1996	7	Now	$15.50
1997	6	Now	$13.00

No longer made.

SEAVIEW VERDELHO ★★

1994	6	Now	$10.50
1995	6	Now	$10.00
1996	6	Now	$10.00

1997	Not made		
1998	7	Now	$11.00
1999	6	Now	$9.00

No longer made.

***Seppelt**, part of Southcorp Wines, is a large Adelaide based company with vineyards in three states: Barossa Valley, Padthaway and Adelaide Hills in South Australia, Great Western and Drumborg in Victoria and Barooga and Tumbarumba in New South Wales. Wines span the gamut from volume-selling to limited edition. Winemaker: Steve Goodwin.*

SEPPELT BLACK LABEL (TERRAIN SERIES) CABERNET SAUVIGNON ★★

before 1993		Prior	
1993	5	Now	$11.00
1994	6	Now	$12.50
1995	6	Now	$12.50
1996	7	Now	$14.00
1997	7	Now	$13.50
1998	7	2004	$13.00
1999	7	2005	$13.00

No longer made.

SEPPELT CHALAMBAR SHIRAZ ★★★

1991	7	Now	$25.00
1992	6	Now	$21.00
1993	7	2005	$24.00
1994	7	2010	$23.00
1995	7	2010	$22.00
1996	7	2010	$22.00
1997	7	2010	$21.00
1998	7	2008	$20.00
1999	7	Now	$20.00

SEPPELT CORELLA RIDGE CHARDONNAY ★★★

before 1995		Prior	
1995	6	Now	$13.50
1996	7	Prior	
1997	7	Now	$14.50
1998	7	Now	$14.50

No longer made.

SEPPELT DORRIEN CABERNET SAUVIGNON ★★★★★

before 1982		Prior	
1982	6	Now	$66.00
1983	Not made		
1984	6	Now	$62.00
1985	Not made		

1986	5	Now	$50.00
1987	6	Now	$58.00
1988	7	Now	$66.00
1989	6	Prior	
1990	7	Now	$62.00
1991	7	Now	$60.00
1992	6	Now	$50.00
1993	7	2005	$56.00
1994	7	2005	$54.00
1995	Not made		
1996	7	2008	$52.00

No longer made.

SEPPELT DRUMBORG RIESLING ★★★★

1993	7	2005	$29.00
1994	Not made		
1995	Not made		
1996	7	Now	$27.00
1997	7	Now	$26.00
1998	7	Now	$25.00
1999	7	Now	$25.00

No longer made.

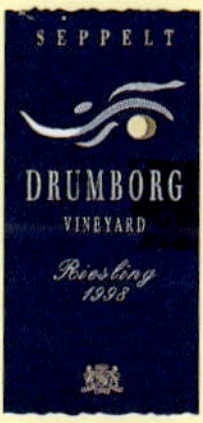

SEPPELT HARPERS RANGE CABERNET SAUVIGNON ★★★

1991	7	Now	$23.00
1992	6	Now	$19.50
1993	5	Now	$16.00
1994	7	Now	$21.00
1995	6	Now	$18.00
1996	7	Now	$20.00
1997	7	2005	$19.50
1998	7	2005	$19.00

No longer made.

SEPPELT SALINGER METHODE CHAMPENOISE ★★★★

before 1990		Prior	
1990	7	Now	$36.00
1991	7	Now	$35.00
1992	7	Now	$34.00
1993	7	Now	$33.00
1994	7	Now	$32.00
1995	6	Now	$26.00
1996	6	Now	$26.00
1997	7	Now	$29.00
1998	7	Now	$28.00
1999	6	Now	$23.00
2000	7	Now	$27.00

SEPPELT SUNDAY CREEK PINOT NOIR ★★★★

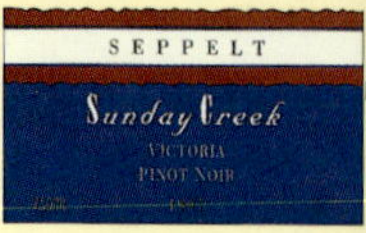

before 1995		Prior	
1995	7	Now	$19.50
1996	7	Now	$19.00
1997	7	Now	$18.50
1998	7	Now	$18.00

No longer made.

SEPPELT TERRAIN CHARDONNAY ★★★

1996	5	Now	$10.50
1997	6	Now	$12.50
1998	6	Now	$12.00
1999	7	Now	$14.00

No longer made.

SEPPELT TERRAIN SHIRAZ ★★

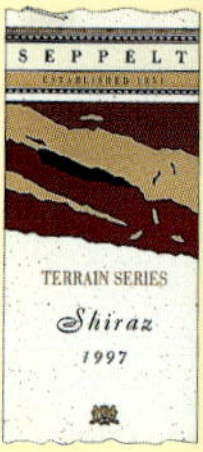

1995	6	Now	$12.00
1996	6	Now	$11.50
1997	7	Now	$13.50
1998	7	2004	$13.00
1999	7	2005	$12.50

No longer made.

***Sevenhill** is a Jesuit winery established in the Clare Valley in 1851, and renowned for some magnificent long-lived reds. Winemakers: Brother John May and John Monten.*

SEVENHILL CABERNET SAUVIGNON ★★★★

before 1989		Prior	
1989	5	Now	$32.00
1990	6	Now	$37.00
1991	5	Now	$30.00
1992	5	Now	$29.00
1993	5	Now	$28.00
1994	5	2006	$27.00
1995	4	2006	$21.00
1996	4	2007	$21.00
1997	6	2004	$30.00
1998	4	2008	$19.50
1999	5	2007	$24.00
2000	5	2008	$23.00
2001	4	2011	$18.00

SEVENHILL SHIRAZ/TOURIGA/MALBEC (formerly DRY RED) ★★★

before 1991		Prior	
1991	5	Now	$20.00
1992	5	Now	$19.50
1993	6	Now	$23.00
1994	5	Now	$18.50
1995	5	Now	$18.00
1996	5	Now	$17.50

1997	7	Now	$24.00
1998	4	Now	$13.00
1999	4	2004	$12.50
2000	4	2005	$12.50
2001	4	2006	$12.00

SEVENHILL RIESLING

★★★★

before 1991		Prior	
1991	5	Now	$26.00
1992	5	Now	$25.00
1993	6	Now	$29.00
1994	5	2004	$24.00
1995	4	2006	$18.50
1996	5	2004	$22.00
1997	6	Now	$26.00
1998	5	2004	$21.00
1999	5	2004	$20.00
2000	5	2009	$20.00
2001	5	2011	$19.50
2002	4	2012	$15.00

SEVENHILL SHIRAZ

★★★★

before 1989		Prior	
1989	6	Now	$38.00
1990	6	Now	$37.00
1991	5	Now	$30.00
1992	5	Now	$29.00
1993	6	Now	$34.00
1994	5	Now	$27.00
1995	4	2004	$21.00
1996	4	2004	$21.00
1997	7	Now	$35.00
1998	3	Now	$14.50
1999	4	2007	$19.00
2000	4	2006	$18.50
2001	4	2007	$18.00

SEVENHILL ST IGNATIUS

★★★★★

1990	5	Now	$33.00
1991	6	Now	$39.00
1992	5	Now	$31.00
1993	6	Now	$36.00
1994	5	Now	$29.00
1995	5	Now	$28.00
1996	5	2004	$28.00
1997	7	Prior	
1998	4	Now	$21.00
1999	5	2006	$25.00
2000	5	2007	$24.00
2001	4	2008	$19.00

Seville Estate is a leading Yarra Valley small vineyard whose wines are difficult to find but well worth the effort. The vineyard has now been acquired by Brokenwood. Winemaker: Iain Riggs.

SEVILLE ESTATE CHARDONNAY ★★★★★

before 1986		Prior	
1986	6	Now	$32.00
1987	6	Now	$31.00
1988	6	Now	$31.00
1989	6	Now	$30.00
1990	7	Now	$34.00
1991	7	Now	$33.00
1992	7	Now	$32.00
1993	6	Now	$26.00
1994	7	Now	$30.00
1995	7	Now	$29.00
1996	7	Now	$28.00
1997	No data		
1998	No data		
1999	7	2004	$26.00
2000	7	2005	$25.00

SEVILLE ESTATE PINOT NOIR ★★★★

before 1987		Prior	
1987	6	Now	$33.00
1988	7	Now	$37.00
1989	6	Now	$31.00
1990	Not made		
1991	7	Now	$34.00
1992	6	Now	$28.00
1993	6	Now	$27.00
1994	7	Now	$31.00
1995	6	Now	$26.00
1996	7	Now	$29.00
1997	No data		
1998	No data		
1999	5	Now	$19.00
2000	7	2005	$26.00

SEVILLE ESTATE RIESLING BOTRYTIS AFFECTED (375ml) ★★★★

1979	6	Now	$37.00
1980	7	Now	$42.00
1981	5	Now	$29.00
1982	6	Now	$34.00
1983	3	Now	$16.50
1984	6	Now	$32.00
1985	6	Now	$31.00
1986	Not made		
1987	6	Now	$29.00

1988	Not made		
1989	Not made		
1990	Not made		
1991	7	Now	$30.00
1992	7	Now	$30.00
1993	7	Now	$29.00
Not made after 1993			

SEVILLE ESTATE SHIRAZ ★★★★

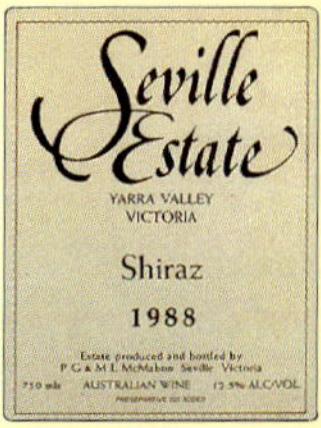

before 1983		Prior	
1983	6	Now	$37.00
1984	Not made		
1985	6	Now	$35.00
1986	7	Now	$39.00
1987	6	Now	$33.00
1988	7	Now	$37.00
1989	6	Now	$31.00
1990	7	Now	$35.00
1991	7	Now	$34.00
1992	7	Now	$33.00
1993	7	Now	$32.00
1994	6	Now	$26.00
1995	6	Now	$26.00
1996	6	Now	$25.00
1997	7	2006	$28.00
1998	Not made		
1999	6	2006	$23.00
2000	5	2004	$18.50

***Shaw & Smith** is a stylish and perfectionist winemaking partnership between Martin Shaw and Michael Hill Smith MW. The renown earned by their releases to date goes well beyond the shores of this continent. Winemaker: Martin Shaw.*

SHAW & SMITH M3 CHARDONNAY ★★★★★

before 1992		Prior	
1992	6	Now	$54.00
1993	4	Prior	
1994	5	Now	$43.00
1995	4	Prior	
1996	5	Now	$41.00
1997	4	Now	$31.00
1998	6	Now	$46.00
1999	6	Now	$45.00
2000	6	2005	$43.00
2001	6	2006	$42.00
2002	6	2007	$41.00

SHAW & SMITH UNOAKED CHARDONNAY ★★★★

before 2000		Prior	
2000	5	Now	
2001	5	Now	$21.00
2002	7	Now	
2003	6	Now	$22.00

SHAW & SMITH SAUVIGNON BLANC ★★★★★

before 2000		Prior	
2000	5	Now	
2001	5	Now	$22.00
2002	6	Now	
2003	6	2004	$22.00

***Spring Vale** is a fine vineyard on Tasmania's East Coast, producing a superb Pinot Noir. Winemaker: Andrew Hood.*

SPRING VALE PINOT NOIR ★★★★★

before 1992		Prior	
1992	6	Now	$48.00
1993	6	Now	$47.00
1994	6	Now	$45.00
1995	5	Now	$37.00
1996	4	Prior	
1997	6	Now	$42.00
1998	6	2002	$40.00
1999	5	Now	$33.00
2000	6	Now	$38.00

***Stanley** - see Leasingham.*

***Stanton and Killeen** make good honest Rutherglen wines worthy of considerable respect. Winemaker: Chris Killeen.*

STANTON AND KILLEEN MOODEMERE DURIF ★★★★

before 1992		Prior	
1992	7	Now	$37.00
1993	Not made		
1994	6	2004	$30.00
1995	6	2005	$29.00
1996	6	Now	$28.00
1997	7	Now	$32.00
1998	7	Now	$31.00
1999	5	2005	$21.00
2000	7	2006	$29.00
2001	6	2007	$24.00
2002	6	2008	$23.00

STANTON AND KILLEEN MOODEMERE SHIRAZ

★★★★

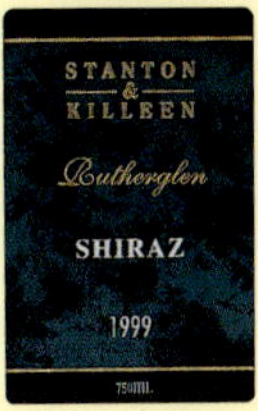

before 1995		Prior	
1995	5	Now	$23.00
1996	5	Now	$23.00
1997	Not made		
1998	Not made		
1999	5	Now	$21.00
2000	6	2005	$24.00
2001	5	2004	$19.50
2002	5	2005	$19.00

STANTON AND KILLEEN VINTAGE PORT

★★★★

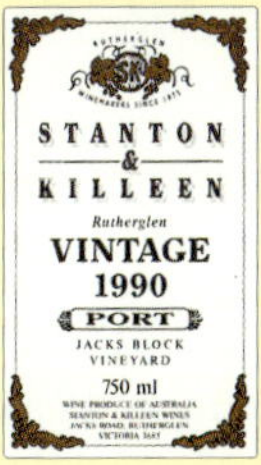

1971	5	Prior	
1972	7	Now	$82.00
1973	3	Prior	
1974	4	Prior	
1975	7	Now	$74.00
1976	6	Now	$62.00
1977	6	Now	$60.00
1978	5	Now	$49.00
1979	5	Now	$47.00
1980	5	Now	$46.00
1981	3	Now	$27.00
1982	6	Now	$52.00
1983	7	2005	$58.00
1984	5	Now	$41.00
1985	6	Now	$48.00
1986	7	2005	$54.00
1987	5	Now	$37.00
1988	7	2005	$50.00
1989	4	Now	$28.00
1990	7	2010	$48.00
1991	6	2006	$40.00
1992	7	2010	$45.00
1993	7	2010	$44.00
1994	5	2005	$30.00
1995	6	2010	$35.00
1996	5	2010	$28.00
1997	7	2017	$39.00
1998	6	2015	$32.00
1999	5	2015	$26.00
2000	5	2015	N/R
2001	5	2015	N/R
2002	7	2020	N/R

Stefano Lubiana Wines *are producers in Tasmania's Derwent Valley, with 8 hectares of vines. Winemaker: Stefano Lubiana.*

STEFANO LUBIANA CHARDONNAY ★★★★

1998	6	Now	$45.00
1999	6	2005	$44.00
2000	7	2008	$49.00
2001	7	2010	$48.00

STEFANO LUBIANA PINOT NOIR ★★★★

1998	7	2008	$52.00
1999	6	2006	$44.00
2000	7	2010	$49.00
2001	6	2010	$41.00

STEFANO LUBIANA RIESLING ★★★★

1997	6	Now	$30.00
1998	7	2006	$34.00
1999	6	2004	$28.00
2000	6	2007	$27.00
2001	6	2010	$26.00
2002	5	2008	$21.00

Stoney Vineyard *in Tasmania's Coal River Valley is a perfectionist operation producing some superb wines, the best of which are released as "Domaine A" (q.v.). Winemaker: Peter Althaus.*

STONEY VINEYARD AURORA ★★★★

before 1998		Prior	
1998	7	Now	$26.00
1999	7	Now	$25.00
2000	Not made		
2001	Not made		

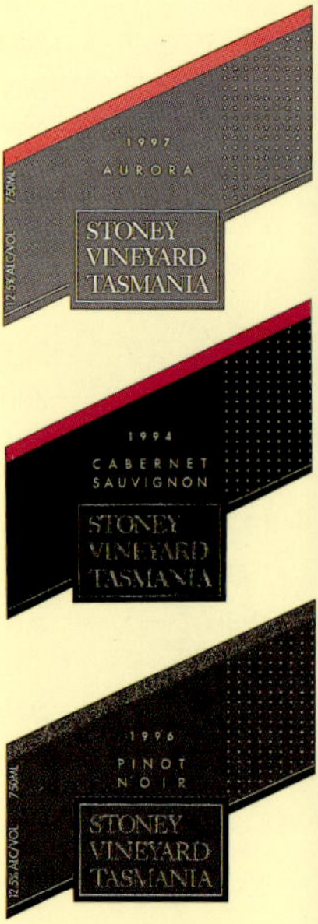

STONEY VINEYARD CABERNET SAUVIGNON ★★★★

1993	5	Now	$30.00
1994	7	Now	$41.00
1995	6	Now	$34.00
1996	4	Prior	
1997	Not made		
1998	7	2004	$36.00
1999	7	Now	$35.00
2000	7	2005	$34.00
2001	7	2008	N/R
2002	5	2009	N/R

STONEY VINEYARD PINOT NOIR ★★★★

1995	4	Now	$32.00
1995	4	Now	$31.00
1996	5	Now	$38.00

1997	Not made		
2001	7	2005	$50.00
2002	5	2008	N/R

STONEY VINEYARD SAUVIGNON BLANC ★★★★

before 1996		Prior	
1996	5	2004	$26.00
1997	7	2010	$35.00
1998	7	Now	$34.00
1999	6	Now	$28.00
2000	6	Now	$27.00
2001	7	Now	$31.00
2002	7	2004	$30.00

***Stonier Wines** is the largest of the Mornington Peninsula vineyards and perhaps the best exemplar of the area's extreme promise. As well as the premium Reserve wines there is a range of lower priced wines. Winemaker: Tod Dexter.*

STONIER CABERNET ★★★★

before 1998		Prior	
1998	7	Now	$24.00
1999	6	Now	$20.00
2000	7	Now	$23.00
2001	7	2005	$22.00

STONIER CHARDONNAY ★★★★

before 1998		Prior	
1998	5	Now	$22.00
1999	6	Now	$26.00
2000	7	Now	$29.00
2001	7	2004	$28.00
2002	5	2005	$20.00

STONIER PINOT NOIR ★★★★

before 1998		Prior	
1998	6	Now	$27.00
1999	5	Now	$22.00
2000	7	Now	$30.00
2001	6	Now	$25.00
2002	5	Now	$20.00

STONIER RESERVE CHARDONNAY ★★★★★

before 1998		Prior	
1998	6	Now	$40.00
1999	6	Now	$39.00
2000	7	Now	$45.00
2001	7	2004	$43.00
2002	7	2005	$42.00

STONIER RESERVE PINOT NOIR ★★★★★

before 1998		Prior	
1998	6	Now	$50.00
1999	5	Now	$41.00
2000	6	Now	$48.00
2001	6	Now	$46.00
2002	Not made		

***Tahbilk** has been producing wine in the Goulburn Valley since the mid 19th century. The historic vineyard and beautiful winery are still family owned and operated. Winemaker: Alister Purbrick.*

TAHBILK CABERNET SAUVIGNON ★★★★

before 1962		Prior	
1962	7	Now	$74.00
1963	5	Prior	
1964	7	Now	$70.00
1965	6	Now	$58.00
1966	6	Now	$56.00
1967	5	Now	$46.00
1968	7	Now	$62.00
1969	4	Prior	
1970	4	Prior	
1971	7	2005	$58.00
1972	5	Prior	
1973	4	Prior	
1974	4	Prior	
1975	3	Prior	
1976	6	Now	$43.00
1977	5	Now	$34.00
1978	6	Now	$40.00
1979	6	Now	$39.00
1980	6	Now	$38.00
1981	7	2005	$43.00
1982	6	Now	$36.00
1983	6	Now	$35.00
1984	6	2005	$33.00
1985	6	Now	$32.00
1986	7	2008	$37.00
1987	5	Now	$25.00
1988	5	Now	$25.00
1989	4	Now	$19.50
1990	6	Now	$28.00
1991	7	2010	$32.00
1992	6	2007	$26.00
1993	5	Now	$21.00
1994	5	2010	$21.00
1995	6	2013	$24.00
1996	6	2010	$23.00

1997	7	2015	$26.00
1998	7	2015	$26.00
1999	5	2011	$18.00
2000	6	2013	$21.00

TAHBILK CHARDONNAY ★★★

before 1994		Prior	
1994	5	Now	$21.00
1995	6	Now	$24.00
1996	5	Now	$20.00
1997	Not made		
1998	5	2004	$18.50
1999	6	2004	$22.00
2000	6	2006	$21.00

TAHBILK MARSANNE ★★★★

before 1985		Prior	
1985	5	Now	$19.50
1986	5	Now	$19.00
1987	7	Now	$25.00
1988	6	Now	$21.00
1989	7	Now	$24.00
1990	6	Now	$20.00
1991	6	Now	$19.50
1992	7	2005	$22.00
1993	6	Now	$18.50
1994	6	2005	$18.00
1995	6	2005	$17.50
1996	6	Now	$17.00
1997	6	2005	$16.50
1998	6	2007	$16.00
1999	6	2007	$15.50
2000	7	2010	$17.50
2001	6	2008	$14.50

TAHBILK RESERVE CABERNET SAUVIGNON (SHIRAZ IN '71, '72 AND '74) ★★★★★

before 1976		Prior	
1976	6	Now	$130.00
1977	5	Prior	
1978	5	Now	$100.00
1979	6	Now	$120.00
1980	6	Now	$115.00
1981	7	2005	$130.00
1982	7	Now	$125.00
1983	7	2005	$125.00
1984	7	Now	$120.00
1985	6	2005	$100.00
1986	6	2010	$98.00
1987	Not made		
1988	Not made		

1989	Not made		
1990	Not made		
1991	7	2015	$98.00
1992	6	2010	$82.00
1993	6	2007	$80.00
1994	6	2009	$78.00
1995	Not made		
1996	7	2015	$84.00
1997	7	2020	$82.00

TAHBILK RIESLING ★★★★

before 1989		Prior	
1989	6	Now	$24.00
1990	7	Now	$27.00
1991	5	Prior	
1992	6	Now	$22.00
1993	5	Now	$18.00
1994	7	Now	$24.00
1995	6	Now	$20.00
1996	6	2005	$20.00
1997	6	2006	$19.00
1998	6	2005	$18.50
1999	6	2009	$18.00
2000	7	2012	$20.00
2001	6	2006	$17.00
2002	6	2008	$16.50

TAHBILK RESERVE SHIRAZ ★★★★★

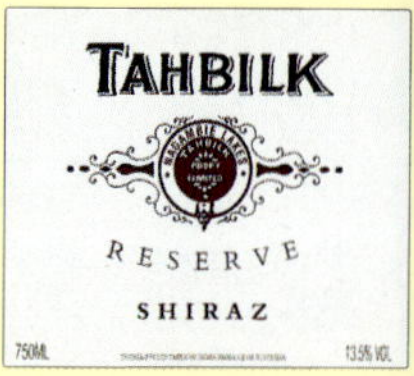

1994	6	2012	$76.00
1995	Not made		
1996	7	2015	$84.00
1997	6	2012	$70.00

TAHBILK SHIRAZ ★★★★

before 1976		Prior	
1976	6	Now	$39.00
1977	5	Prior	
1978	5	2004	$31.00
1979	6	2004	$36.00
1980	6	Now	$35.00
1981	7	2005	$39.00
1982	6	Now	$33.00
1983	Not made		
1984	6	2005	$31.00
1985	5	Now	$25.00
1986	7	2005	$34.00
1987	5	Now	$23.00
1988	6	Now	$27.00
1989	4	Now	$18.00
1990	5	Now	$21.00
1991	7	2005	$29.00

1992	6	Now	$24.00
1993	5	2004	$20.00
1994	6	2006	$23.00
1995	6	2008	$22.00
1996	6	2007	$21.00
1997	7	2014	$24.00
1998	7	2015	$24.00
1999	5	2008	$16.50
2000	6	2011	$19.50

TAHBILK SHIRAZ 1860 VINES ★★★★★

1979	5	Prior	
1980	Not made		
1981	6	2005	$180.00
1982	6	2005	$175.00
1983	Not made		
1984	7	2010	$190.00
1985	6	2005	$160.00
1986	7	2010	$180.00
1987	6	Now	$150.00
1988	6	Now	$145.00
1989	5	Now	$120.00
1990	6	Now	$140.00
1991	7	2015	$155.00
1992	7	2010	$150.00
1993	Not made		
1994	7	2010	$140.00
1995	7	2010	$140.00
1996	6	2010	$115.00
1997	7	2000	$130.00

***Taltarni** is a Central Victorian medium-sized company producing high quality wines, much of which is exported to England and the U. S. Winemaker: Peter Steer.*

TALTARNI CABERNET SAUVIGNON ★★★★

1977	6	Now	$56.00
1978	6	Now	$54.00
1979	6	Now	$52.00
1980	5	Now	$43.00
1981	6	Now	$50.00
1982	6	Now	$48.00
1983	5	Now	$39.00
1984	6	Now	$45.00
1985	5	Now	$37.00
1986	6	Now	$43.00
1987	6	Now	$41.00
1988	7	Now	$47.00
1989	6	Now	$39.00
1990	7	Now	$44.00
1991	7	Now	$43.00

1992	6	Now	$36.00
1993	5	Now	$29.00
1994	7	Now	$39.00
1995	6	2004	$33.00
1996	6	2004	$32.00
1997	7	2006	$36.00
1998	7	2005	$35.00
1999	Not made		
2000	6	2009	$28.00

TALTARNI FUME BLANC ★★★★

before 1996		Prior	
1996	7	Now	$19.00
1997	6	Now	$16.00

No data since 1997

TALTARNI MERLOT(/CABERNET FRANC) ★★★★

1984	5	Now	$35.00
1985	5	Now	$34.00
1986	6	Now	$40.00
1987	Not made		
1988	6	Now	$37.00
1989	6	Now	$36.00
1990	7	Now	$41.00
1991	7	Now	$40.00
1992	6	Now	$33.00
1993	6	Now	$32.00
1994	6	Now	$31.00
1995	6	Now	$30.00
1996	6	Now	$29.00
1997	6	2005	$29.00

TALTARNI SHIRAZ ★★★★

1977	6	Now	$56.00
1978	6	Now	$54.00
1979	5	Now	$45.00
1980	6	Now	$52.00
1981	6	Now	$50.00
1982	6	Now	$49.00
1983	5	Now	$40.00
1984	6	Now	$46.00
1985	6	Now	$45.00
1986	6	Now	$44.00
1987	6	Now	$42.00
1988	7	Now	$48.00
1989	6	Now	$40.00
1990	6	Now	$39.00
1991	7	Now	$44.00
1992	6	Now	$36.00
1993	6	Now	$35.00
1994	7	Now	$40.00

1995	6	Now	$33.00
1996	6	Now	$32.00
1997	6	2004	$31.00
1998	7	2004	$36.00
1999	6	Now	$29.00
2000	7	2006	$33.00
2001	7	2008	$32.00

***Tamburlaine** is a Hunter Valley producer whose wines have grown in both quantity and quality over the last eight years. Wine sales are exclusively from the cellar door. Winemaker: Mark Davidson.*

TAMBURLAINE MERLOT/CABERNET ★★★★

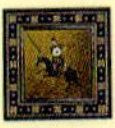

before 1993		Prior	
1993	6	Now	$29.00
1994	5	Now	$23.00
1995	7	Now	$32.00
1996	7	2004	$31.00
1997	7	2005	$30.00
1998	7	2006	$29.00
1999	6	2007	$24.00
2000	7	2008	$27.00
2001	5	2008	$19.00
2002	7	2010	$26.00

TAMBURLAINE CHARDONNAY "THE CHAPEL" ★★★★

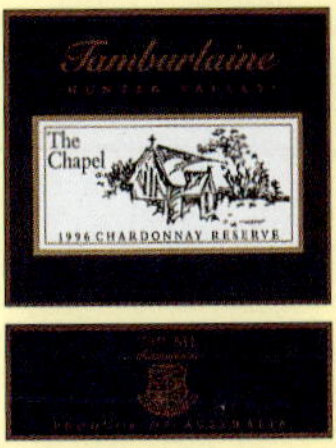

before 1994		Prior	
1994	7	Now	$32.00
1995	7	Now	$31.00
1996	6	Now	$26.00
1997	7	2004	$29.00
1998	7	2005	$28.00
1999	7	2007	$28.00
2000	7	2008	$27.00
2001	5	2007	$18.50
2002	6	2008	$21.00

TAMBURLAINE SEMILLON ★★★

before 1988		Prior	
1988	5	Now	$22.00
1989	6	Now	$26.00
1990	5	Now	$21.00
1991	6	2004	$24.00
1992	5	2005	$20.00
1993	7	2006	$27.00
1994	6	2007	$22.00
1995	6	2008	$22.00
1996	6	2009	$21.00
1997	7	2010	$24.00
1998	7	2011	$23.00

1999	7	2012	$22.00
2000	7	2009	$22.00
2001	5	2009	$15.00
2002	5	2010	$15.00

TAMBURLAINE "THE CHAPEL" RESERVE RED ★★★★

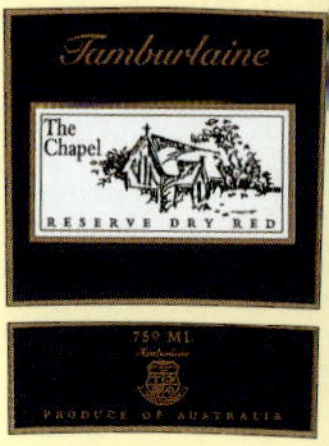

before 1993		Prior	
1993	6	2004	$29.00
1994	6	2005	$28.00
1995	5	2006	$23.00
1996	7	2007	$31.00
1997	7	2008	$30.00
1998	7	2009	$29.00
1999	7	2010	$28.00
2000	7	2011	$27.00
2001	5	2011	$19.00
2002	7	2012	$26.00

TAMBURLAINE VERDELHO ★★★

1991	6	Now	$23.00
1992	7	Now	$26.00
1993	6	Now	$22.00
1994	7	Now	$25.00
1995	6	Now	$20.00
1996	7	Now	$23.00
1997	5	Now	$16.00
1998	7	2005	$22.00
1999	6	2008	$18.50
2000	7	2009	$21.00
2001	6	2010	$17.50
2002	6	2010	$17.00

***Tapestry** is the label applied to wines made at the old Merrivale winery in McLaren Vale. The operation is owned by Brian Light. Winemaker: Jonathan Ketley.*

TAPESTRY CABERNET SAUVIGNON ★★★

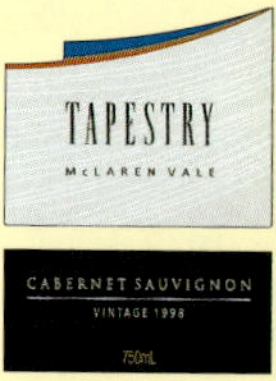

1993	5	Now	$23.00
1994	6	Now	$27.00
1995	5	Now	$22.00
1996	7	Now	$30.00
1997	6	Now	$24.00
1998	7	2004	$28.00
1999	5	Now	$19.50

TAPESTRY CHARDONNAY ★★★

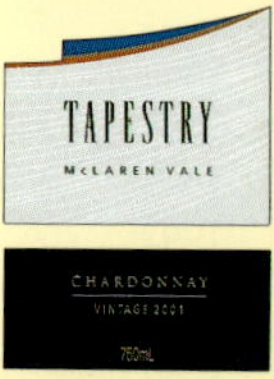

1996	5	Now	$22.00
1997	4	Now	$17.00
1998	6	Now	$25.00
1999	6	Now	$24.00
2000	No data		
2001	5	Now	$19.00

TAPESTRY SHIRAZ ★★★

1993	5	Now	$24.00
1994	6	Now	$27.00
1995	6	Now	$27.00
1996	7	Now	$30.00
1997	5	Now	$21.00
1998	6	2004	$24.00
1999	5	2004	$20.00

***Tarrawarra** is a high prestige Yarra Valley producer with a notable but individually styled Chardonnay. Winemaker: Clare Halloran.*

TARRAWARRA CHARDONNAY ★★★★

1986	4	Prior	
1987	6	Now	$70.00
1988	7	Prior	
1989	5	Prior	
1990	6	Now	$64.00
1991	6	Now	$62.00
1992	6	Prior	
1993	5	Now	$49.00
1994	6	Now	$56.00
1995	6	Now	$56.00
1996	7	Now	$62.00
1997	6	2005	$52.00
1998	7	2008	$60.00
1999	6	2005	$49.00
2000	6	2006	$48.00

TARRAWARRA PINOT NOIR ★★★★

before 1994		Prior	
1994	6	Now	$56.00
1995	7	Now	$64.00
1996	7	Now	$62.00
1997	6	Now	$52.00
1998	7	2004	$58.00
1999	5	2004	$40.00
2000	6	2005	$47.00

***Tatachilla**, an historic name in South Australian wine, had its renascence in 1995 with the re-opening of the superb winery, and has since produced some very impressive wines. Winemakers: Michael Fragos and Justin McNamee.*

TATACHILLA "1901" CABERNET SAUVIGNON ★★★★★

1998	6	2006	$40.00
1999	7	2006	$45.00
2000	7	2008	$44.00

TATACHILLA CLARENDON MERLOT ★★★★★

1997	6	2004	$44.00
1998	7	2004	$49.00
1999	6	2006	$41.00
2000	6	2007	$40.00

TATACHILLA FOUNDATION SHIRAZ ★★★★★

1994	5	Now	$48.00
1995	6	2005	$56.00
1996	7	2006	$64.00
1997	6	2006	$52.00
1998	7	2008	$60.00
1999	6	2008	$50.00
2000	6	2008	$48.00

TATACHILLA KEYSTONE GRENACHE/SHIRAZ ★★★

before 1996		Prior	
1996	7	Now	$25.00
1997	6	Now	$21.00
1998	7	2004	$24.00
1999	5	2004	$16.50
2000	5	2004	$16.00
2001	6	2005	$18.50
2002	6	2006	$18.00

TATACHILLA MCLAREN VALE CABERNET SAUVIGNON ★★★★

1994	5	Now	$23.00
1995	6	2004	$27.00
1996	7	2004	$31.00
1997	6	2005	$25.00
1998	7	2007	$29.00
1999	6	2007	$24.00
2000	5	2005	$19.50
2001	6	2006	$23.00

TATACHILLA MCLAREN VALE CHARDONNAY ★★★★

1997	5	Now	$17.00
1998	6	Now	$20.00
1999	6	2004	$19.50
2000	5	2005	$15.50
2001	6	2006	$18.50
2002	6	2007	$18.00

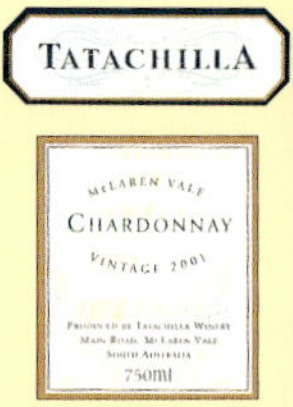

TATACHILLA MCLAREN VALE SHIRAZ ★★★★

1997	6	Now	$25.00
1998	7	2004	$29.00
1999	6	2005	$24.00
2000	5	2005	$19.50
2001	6	2007	$23.00

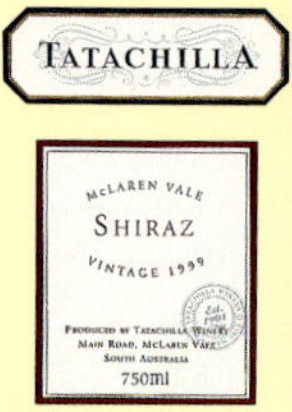

***Taylors of Clare** are medium-sized makers of a small range of popular and reliable wines. Winemakers: Adam Eggins and Craig Grafton.*

TAYLORS CABERNET SAUVIGNON ★★★

before 1986		Prior	
1986	6	Now	$24.00
1987	6	Now	$24.00
1988	5	Now	$19.00
1989	6	Now	$22.00
1990	6	Now	$21.00
1991	5	Now	$17.50
1992	7	Now	$24.00
1993	6	Now	$20.00
1994	7	Now	$22.00
1995	4	Now	$12.50
1996	6	Now	$18.00
1997	5	Now	$14.50
1998	7	Now	$20.00
1999	6	2004	$16.50
2000	6	2005	$16.00

TAYLORS CHARDONNAY ★★★

before 1992		Prior	
1992	7	Now	$22.00
1993	6	Now	$19.00
1995	5	Now	$15.00
1996	4	Now	$12.00
1997	5	Now	$14.50
1998	5	Now	$14.00
1999	7	Now	$19.00
2000	6	2004	$16.00

TAYLORS MERLOT ★★★

1998	4	Now	$12.00
1999	6	Now	$17.50
2000	6	2004	$17.00
2001	7	2006	$19.00

TAYLORS PINOT NOIR ★★★

before 1998		Prior	
1998	5	Now	$16.00
1999	3	Now	$9.50
2000	6	Now	$18.50
2001	6	2004	$18.00

TAYLORS RIESLING ★★

1989	7	Now	$25.00
1990	5	Now	$17.50
1991	3	Now	$10.00
1992	6	Now	$20.00
1993	2	Now	$6.50
1994	7	Now	$22.00
1995	Not made		

1996	6	Now	$17.50
1997	5	Now	$14.50
1998	7	2005	$19.50
1999	4	2007	$10.50
2000	7	2009	$18.50
2001	6	2010	$15.50

TAYLORS SHIRAZ ★★★

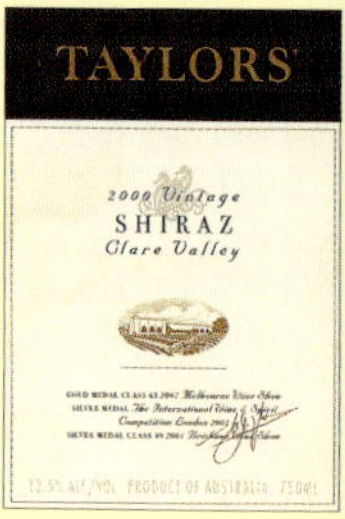

before 1986		Prior	
1986	6	Now	$24.00
1987	4	Now	$15.50
1988	5	Now	$19.00
1989	6	Now	$22.00
1990	7	Now	$25.00
1991	5	Now	$17.50
1992	4	Now	$13.50
1993	6	Now	$19.50
1994	7	Now	$22.00
1995	7	Now	$21.00
1996	4	Now	$12.00
1997	6	Now	$17.50
1998	6	2004	$17.00
1999	5	2004	$13.50
2000	7	2006	$18.50
2001	7	2007	$18.00

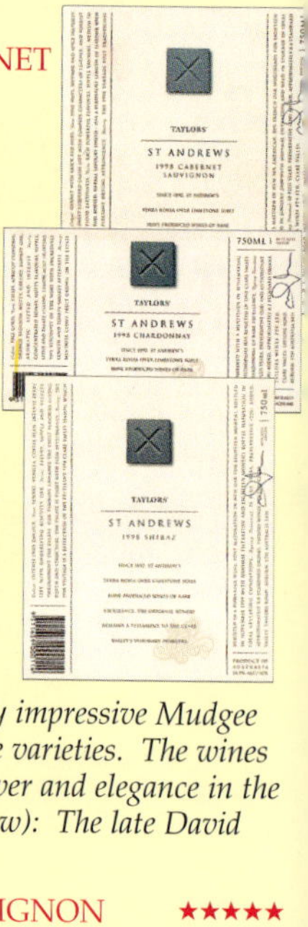

TAYLORS ST ANDREWS CABERNET SAUVIGNON ★★★★

1996	5	2005	$46.00
1997	5	2008	$45.00
1998	7	2010	$60.00

TAYLORS ST ANDREWS CHARDONNAY ★★★★

1996	4	Now	$24.00
1997	5	Now	$29.00
1998	7	2004	$40.00
1999	Not made		
2000	6	2007	$32.00

TAYLORS ST ANDREWS SHIRAZ ★★★★

1996	5	2004	$46.00
1997	5	2009	$45.00
1998	7	2010	$60.00

***Thistle Hill Vineyard** is an extremely impressive Mudgee maker with a limited range of the noble varieties. The wines are all notably generous, with both power and elegance in the fruit. Winemaker (for the vintages below): The late David Robertson.*

THISTLE HILL CABERNET SAUVIGNON ★★★★★

1984	5	Now	$28.00
1985	6	Now	$33.00
1986	7	Prior	

1987	6	Now	$31.00
1988	7	Now	$35.00
1989	6	Now	$29.00
1990	6	Now	$28.00
1991	5	Now	$23.00
1992	6	Now	$27.00
1993	6	Now	$26.00
1994	6	2004	$25.00
1995	5	Now	$20.00
1996	6	2004	$24.00
1997	6	2004	$23.00
1998	4	2005	$15.00
1999	6	2006	$22.00
2000	4	2007	N/R

THISTLE HILL CHARDONNAY

★★★★

1984	6	Now	$35.00
1985	5	Prior	
1986	6	Now	$33.00
1987	5	Prior	
1988	6	Now	$31.00
1989	4	Prior	
1990	6	Now	$30.00
1991	5	Now	$24.00
1992	6	Now	$28.00
1993	5	Now	$22.00
1994	6	Now	$26.00
1995	4	Prior	
1996	5	Now	$21.00
1997	6	Now	$24.00
1998	4	Now	$15.50
1999	6	Now	$23.00
2000	6	2004	$22.00

THISTLE HILL PINOT NOIR

★★★★★

1985	6	Now	$47.00
1986	6	Prior	
1987	5	Prior	
1988	6	Now	$43.00
1989	6	Now	$42.00
1990	7	Now	$47.00
1991	5	Prior	
1992	5	Now	$32.00
1993	5	Now	$31.00
1994	7	Now	$42.00
1995	5	Now	$29.00
1996	6	Now	$34.00
1997	5	Now	$27.00
1998	4	Now	$21.00
1999	5	Now	$26.00
2000	5	2004	$25.00

THISTLE HILL RIESLING ★★★★

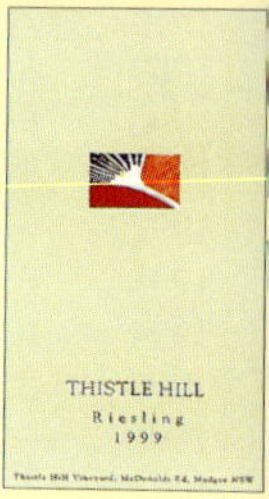

1989	5	Prior	
1990	6	Now	$21.00
1991	5	Now	$17.50
1992	5	Now	$17.00
1993	6	Now	$20.00
1994	6	Now	$19.00
1995	5	Now	$15.50
1996	5	Now	$15.00
1997	5	Now	$14.50
1998	Not made		
1999	6	2004	N/R
2000	Not made		

***Tim Adams Wines** is a winemaking operation in the Clare Valley, using fruit sourced from local growers. These generously flavoured wines are unfortunately not rated by the winemaker for this edition, so star rankings only are given. Winemaker: Tim Adams.*

TIM ADAMS ABERFELDY SHIRAZ ★★★★

TIM ADAMS CABERNET ★★★★

TIM ADAMS FERGUS GRENACHE ★★★

TIM ADAMS SEMILLON ★★★★

***Tin Cows** (formerly Tunnel Hill) Tin Cows is the second label of the Yarra Valley's Tarrawarra. The wines are both reasonably priced and of commendable quality. Winemaker: Clare Halloran.*

TIN COWS CHARDONNAY ★★★

before 1999		Prior	
1999	5	Now	$21.00
2000	5	Now	$20.00
2001	7	2004	$28.00

TIN COWS PINOT NOIR ★★★★

before 1999		Prior	
1999	5	Now	$22.00
2000	6	Now	$25.00
2001	7	2004	$29.00

***Tingle-Wood Wines** is a small maker in the Denmark area. Winemaker: Brenden Smith.*

TINGLE-WOOD RED TINGLE (CABERNET/SHIRAZ) ★★★

1998	6	Now	$18.50
1999	Not made		
2000	6	Now	$17.50
2001	7	Now	$19.50

TINGLE-WOOD YELLOW TINGLE (RIESLING) ★★★

before 1993		Prior	
1993	7	Now	$23.00
1994	Not made		
1995	No data		
1996	No data		
1997	5	Now	$14.50
1998	7	Now	$20.00
1999	Not made		
2000	6	Now	$16.00
2001	7	Now	$18.50

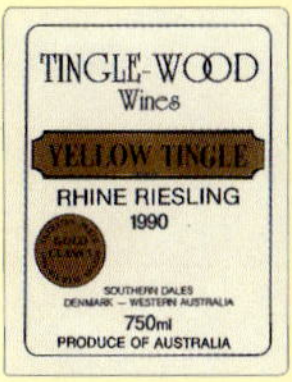

***Tisdall Wines** produce a range of reliable and inexpensive wines of agreeable quality. The winery changed hands in 1999, and the star rankings are for vintages from then on. Winemaker: Don Buchanan.*

TISDALL CABERNET/MERLOT ★★★

before 1991		Prior	
1991	7	Now	$21.00
1992	5	Now	$15.00
1993	4	Now	$11.50
1994	5	Now	$14.00
1995	6	Now	$16.50
1996	6	Now	$16.00
1997	No data		
1998	No data		
1999	6	Now	$14.50
2000	6	Now	$14.00

TISDALL CHARDONNAY ★★★

before 1988		Prior	
1988	3	Now	$12.00
1989	4	Now	$16.00
1990	5	Now	$19.00
1991	4	Now	$15.00
1992	5	Now	$18.00
1993	4	Now	$14.00
1994	6	Now	$20.00
1995	4	Now	$13.00
1996	5	Now	$16.00
1997	6	Now	$18.50
1998	No data		
1999	5	Now	$14.50
2000	5	Now	$14.00

***Tollana**, owned by Southcorp, is a traditional Eden Valley label with a range of popular wines. Recently Adelaide Hills fruit was also sourced. Apparently, the label has now been withdrawn. Winemaker: Neville Falkenberg.*

TOLLANA BOTRYTIS RIESLING (375ml) ★★★

before 1995		Prior	
1995	7	Now	$21.00
1996	5	Prior	
1997	6	Now	$16.50
1998	6	Now	$16.00
1999	6	Now	$16.00

No longer made.

TOLLANA CABERNET SAUVIGNON BIN 222 ★★★

before 1991		Prior	
1991	7	Now	$30.00
1992	5	Now	$21.00
1993	7	Now	$28.00
1994	5	Now	$20.00
1995	5	Now	$19.00
1996	7	2004	$26.00
1997	6	Now	$22.00
1998	5	204	$17.50
1999	5	2004	$17.00

No longer made.

TOLLANA EDEN VALLEY CHARDONNAY ★★★

before 1997		Prior	
1997	6	Now	$16.50
1998	6	Now	$16.00
1999	6	202	$15.50
2000	7	Now	$17.50

No longer made.

TOLLANA EDEN VALLEY SHIRAZ TR16 ★★★

before 1991		Prior	
1991	7	Now	$29.00
1992	6	Now	$24.00
1993	7	Now	$27.00
1994	5	Now	$19.00
1995	5	Now	$18.50
1996	6	Now	$21.00
1997	6	Now	$21.00
1998	7	2004	$24.00
2000	5	Now	$16.50

No longer made.

TOLLANA EDEN VALLEY RIESLING ★★★

before 1990		Prior	
1990	6	Now	$19.00
1991	6	Now	$18.50

1992	6	Now	$18.00
1993	5	Prior	
1994	6	Now	$17.00
1995	5	Now	$13.50
1996	Not made		
1997	Not made		
1998	6	Now	$15.00
1999	6	Now	$14.50
2000	7	2005	$16.50

No longer made.

TOLLANA EDEN VALLEY/ADELAIDE HILLS SAUVIGNON BLANC ★★

before 1999		Prior	
1999	5	Now	$14.00
2000	6	Now	$16.00

No longer made.

TOLLANA SHOW RESERVE SHIRAZ ★★★★

1991	6	Now	$25.00
1992	Not made		
1993	6	Now	$23.00
1994	Not made		
1995	5	Now	$18.50

Not made since 1995.

Treehouse *is the second label of the fine Pemberton maker Salitage. Winemaker: Patrick Coutts.*

TREEHOUSE CHARDONNAY/VERDELHO ★★★

before 1999		Prior	
1999	5	Now	$18.00
2000	5	Now	$17.50
2001	6	Now	$20.00
2002	6	2004	$19.50

TREEHOUSE CABERNET/MERLOT ★★★

1998	4	Prior	
1999	5	2004	$22.00
2000	5	2004	$22.00
2001	5	2005	$21.00
2002	5	2006	$20.00

TREEHOUSE PINOT NOIR ★★★

1998	4	Prior	
1999	6	Now	$25.00
2000	5	Now	$20.00
2001	5	Now	$19.50
2002	6	2004	$23.00

TREEHOUSE SHIRAZ ★★★

1997	6	Now	$26.00
1998	3	Prior	
1999	6	2004	$24.00

2000	5	2004	$19.50
2001	6	2005	$23.00
2002	6	2006	$22.00

Trentham Estate *is just across the Murray from Mildura, but produces wines of much higher quality than expectable from the area. Winemaker: Tony Murphy.*

TRENTHAM ESTATE CABERNET/MERLOT ★★

before 1992		Prior	
1992	5	Now	$19.00
1993	4	Prior	
1994	4	Prior	
1995	5	Now	$17.50
1996	6	Now	$20.00
1997	4	Prior	
1998	5	Now	$16.00
1999	6	Now	$18.50
2000	6	Now	$18.00
2001	6	Now	$17.50
2001	6	2004	$17.00

TRENTHAM ESTATE CHARDONNAY ★★★

before 1996		Prior	
1996	5	Now	$16.50
1997	5	Prior	
1998	5	Now	$15.50
1999	4	Now	$12.00
2000	5	Now	$15.00
2001	6	2004	$17.50
2002	7	Now	$19.50

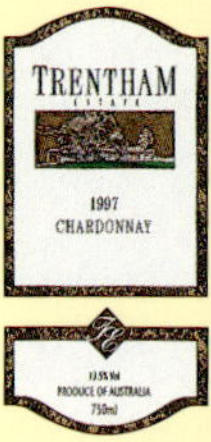

TRENTHAM ESTATE MERLOT ★★★

before 1996		Prior	
1996	5	Now	$16.50
1997	4	Prior	
1998	5	Now	$15.50
1999	5	Now	$15.00
2000	6	Now	$17.50
2001	6	2004	$17.00

TRENTHAM ESTATE SHIRAZ ★★★

1991	7	Prior	
1992	7	Now	$28.00
1993	4	Prior	
1994	5	Now	$18.50
1995	4	Prior	
1996	5	Now	$17.50
1997	4	Prior	
1998	4	Now	$13.00

1999	5	2004	$16.00
2000	6	2005	$19.00
2001	6	2006	$18.50

***Tulloch** is a famous maker in the Hunter Valley, established in 1895. Winemaker: J Y Tulloch.*

TULLOCH HECTOR OF GLEN ELGIN DRY RED ★★★★

before 1991		Prior	
1991	4	Now	$30.00
1992	Not made		
1993	Not made		
1994	6	Now	$42.00
1995	4	Prior	
1996	5	2005	$33.00
1997	7	2007	$45.00
1998	Not made		
1999	6	2010	N/R
2000	6	2010	N/R

TULLOCH VERDELHO ★★★

before 1995		Prior	
1995	5	Now	$16.00
1996	5	Now	$15.50
1997	6	Now	$18.50
1998	6	Now	$18.00
1999	6	Now	$17.00
2000	5	2004	$14.00
2001	6	2005	$16.00
2002	6	2006	$16.00

***Tunnel Hill** - see Tin Cows*

***Tyrrells** is a thriving Pokolbin family-owned company with a dedicated following. Winemaker: Bruce Tyrrell.*

TYRRELLS CHARDONNAY VAT 47 ★★★★★

1972	4	Prior	
1973	7	Now	$120.00
1974	5	Prior	
1975	5	Prior	
1976	6	Now	$98.00
1977	7	Now	$110.00
1978	5	Prior	
1979	7	Now	$100.00
1980	7	Now	$100.00
1981	5	Prior	
1982	6	Now	$82.00
1983	6	Prior	
1984	7	Now	$90.00
1985	6	Now	$74.00

1986	7	Now	$84.00
1987	6	Now	$70.00
1988	6	Prior	
1989	7	Now	$78.00
1990	6	Now	$64.00
1991	7	Now	$72.00
1992	6	Now	$60.00
1993	6	Now	$58.00
1994	6	Now	$56.00
1995	7	Now	$64.00
1996	6	Now	$54.00
1997	5	Now	$44.00
1998	5	2004	$42.00
1999	6	2006	$49.00
2000	6	2008	$48.00
2001	5	2008	$39.00

TYRRELLS DRY RED VAT 5 (SHIRAZ) ★★★

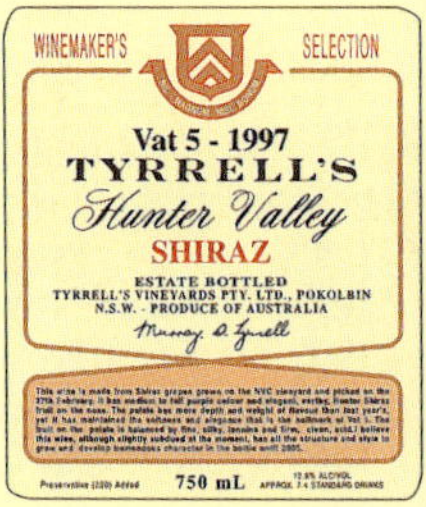

before 1975		Prior	
1975	7	Now	$80.00
1976	5	Prior	
1977	6	Now	$64.00
1978	5	Prior	
1979	6	Prior	
1980	6	Now	$58.00
1981	5	Now	$48.00
1982	5	Prior	
1983	6	Now	$54.00
1984	5	Prior	
1985	7	Now	$58.00
1986	5	Now	$41.00
1987	6	Now	$48.00
1988	5	Prior	
1989	6	Now	$45.00
1990	5	Now	$36.00
1991	7	Now	$50.00
1992	5	Now	$34.00
1993	5	Now	$33.00
1994	5	Now	$32.00
1995	7	2005	$44.00
1996	6	2005	$37.00
1997	6	2007	$35.00
1998	6	2007	$34.00
1999	5	2006	$28.00
2000	5	2008	$27.00
2001	5	2009	$26.00

TYRRELLS DRY RED VAT 9 (SHIRAZ) ★★★★★

before 1975		Prior	
1975	7	Now	$115.00
1976	6	Prior	

1977	7	Now	$110.00
1978	5	Prior	
1979	7	Now	$100.00
1980	6	Now	$86.00
1981	5	Now	$68.00
1982	5	Prior	
1983	6	Now	$78.00
1984	5	Prior	
1985	7	Now	$86.00
1986	5	Now	$60.00
1987	7	Now	$80.00
1988	6	Prior	
1989	6	Now	$66.00
1990	5	Now	$52.00
1991	7	Now	$72.00
1992	7	Now	$70.00
1993	5	Now	$48.00
1994	5	Now	$47.00
1995	6	2005	$54.00
1996	6	2005	$52.00
1997	6	2007	$52.00
1998	6	2007	$50.00
1999	5	2006	$41.00
2000	5	2009	N/R
2001	5	2008	N/R

TYRRELLS HUNTER/COONAWARRA SHIRAZ/CABERNET VAT 8 ★★★★

1990	5	Now	$54.00
1991	7	Now	$74.00
1992	5	Now	$52.00
1993	7	Now	$70.00
1994	6	Now	$58.00
1995	6	2005	$56.00
1996	6	2006	$54.00
1997	5	2004	$44.00
1998	6	2006	$52.00
1999	5	2006	$42.00
2000	5	2008	N/R
2001	5	2008	N/R

TYRRELLS HUNTER RIVER SEMILLON VAT 1 ★★★★★

before 1972		Prior	
1972	7	Now	$115.00
1973	6	Now	$98.00
1974	7	Prior	
1975	6	Prior	
1976	7	Now	$105.00
1977	6	Now	$88.00
1978	5	Now	$70.00

1979	5	Now	$68.00
1980	4	Now	$52.00
1981	5	Prior	
1982	5	Now	$62.00
1983	6	Now	$74.00
1984	5	Now	$58.00
1985	5	Now	$58.00
1986	7	Now	$78.00
1987	6	Now	$64.00
1988	5	Now	$52.00
1989	7	Now	$72.00
1990	6	Now	$60.00
1991	7	Now	$68.00
1992	6	Now	$56.00
1993	6	Now	$54.00
1994	7	2004	$62.00
1995	5	Now	$43.00
1996	6	2006	$50.00
1997	6	2007	$48.00
1998	5	2007	$39.00
1999	7	2005	N/R
2000	7	2010	N/R
2001	6	2011	N/R

TYRRELLS MOON MOUNTAIN CHARDONNAY ★★★★

1995	5	Now	$20.00
1996	7	Now	$28.00
1997	6	Now	$23.00
1998	5	Now	$19.00
1999	6	Now	$22.00
2000	5	2006	$18.00
2001	6	2007	$21.00

TYRRELLS PINOT NOIR VAT 6 ★★★★★

1974	5	Prior	
1975	5	Now	$84.00
1976	7	Now	$110.00
1977	4	Prior	
1978	4	Prior	
1979	5	Now	$74.00
1980	6	Now	$86.00
1981	7	Now	$98.00
1982	5	Now	$68.00
1983	6	Now	$80.00
1984	5	Now	$64.00
1985	6	Now	$74.00
1986	6	Now	$72.00
1987	6	Now	$70.00
1988	5	Now	$56.00

1989	7	Now	$78.00
1990	6	Now	$64.00
1991	7	Now	$74.00
1992	7	Now	$70.00
1993	6	Now	$58.00
1994	5	Now	$48.00
1995	Not made		
1996	6	2004	$54.00
1997	7	2008	$62.00
1998	6	2006	$50.00
1999	5	2006	$41.00
2000	5	2009	N/R
2001	6	2010	N/R

***Vasse Felix** is a very fine Margaret River maker with a small range of convincing wines including a sumptuously elegant Cabernet and one of the finer Shiraz wines in the country. Winemakers: Clive Otto and Will Shields.*

VASSE FELIX CABERNET SAUVIGNON ★★★★★

before 1985		Prior	
1985	7	Now	$54.00
1986	6	Now	$46.00
1987	4	Prior	
1988	6	Now	$43.00
1989	5	Prior	
1990	6	Now	$41.00
1991	7	Now	$46.00
1992	6	Now	$38.00
1993	5	Now	$31.00
1994	6	Now	$36.00
1995	7	Now	$41.00
1996	6	Now	$34.00
1997	6	Now	$33.00
1998	6	Now	$32.00
1999	7	2004	$36.00
2000	6	2004	$30.00
2001	7	2006	$34.00

VASSE FELIX CHARDONNAY (HEYTESBURY) ★★★★★

1998	5	Now	$31.00
1999	6	Now	$37.00
2000	6	Now	$36.00
2001	7	2005	$40.00

VASSE FELIX CLASSIC DRY WHITE ★★★★

before 1993		Prior	
1993	6	Now	$25.00
1994	5	Now	$20.00
1995	7	Now	$27.00

1996	6	Now	$23.00
1997	5	Now	$18.50
1998	6	Now	$21.00
1999	5	Now	$17.50
2000	6	Now	$20.00
2001	7	Now	$23.00
2001	6	Now	$19.00

VASSE FELIX HEYTESBURY (CABERNET) ★★★★★

1995	7	2004	$86.00
1996	6	2004	$70.00
1997	7	2006	$80.00
1998	6	2005	$66.00
1999	7	2008	$76.00
2000	5	2006	$52.00
2001	6	2009	$62.00

VASSE FELIX SEMILLON ★★★★

1998	5	Now	$19.50
1999	6	2004	$23.00
2000	7	2004	$26.00
2001	6	2005	$21.00
2002	7	2006	$24.00

VASSE FELIX SHIRAZ ★★★★★

before 1991		Prior	
1991	7	Now	$60.00
1992	4	Prior	
1993	6	Now	$48.00
1994	7	Now	$54.00
1995	6	Now	$46.00
1996	7	Now	$52.00
1997	6	Now	$43.00
1998	4	Prior	
1999	7	2004	$47.00
2000	6	2004	$39.00
2001	5	2005	$32.00

***Virgin Hills** is a high country, cool climate vineyard near Kyneton in Victoria. Winemaker: Peter Howland.*

VIRGIN HILLS (DRY RED) ★★★★★

1974	7	Now	$130.00
1975	6	Now	$110.00
1976	6	Prior	
1977	3	Prior	
1978	6	Now	$100.00
1979	6	Now	$96.00
1980	6	Now	$94.00
1981	5	Now	$76.00

1982	7	Now	$100.00
1983	7	2005	$100.00
1984	4	Now	$56.00
1985	7	2005	$94.00
1986	4	Now	$52.00
1987	3	Now	$38.00
1988	7	2008	$86.00
1989	Not made		
1990	6	Now	$70.00
1991	7	2008	$80.00
1992	7	2010	$76.00
1993	6	2004	$64.00
1994	7	2004	$72.00
1995	6	2010	$60.00
1996	No data		
1997	6	2010	$56.00
1998	7	2008	$64.00

***Wantirna Estate** is a Yarra Valley vineyard of extremely small size and extremely high quality. Winemakers: Maryann and Reg Egan.*

WANTIRNA ESTATE CABERNET SAUVIGNON/MERLOT ★★★★★

before 1986		Prior	
1986	7	Now	$94.00
1987	6	Now	$78.00
1988	7	Now	$88.00
1989	6	Now	$74.00
1990	6	Now	$72.00
1991	7	Now	$82.00
1992	7	Now	$78.00
1993	6	Now	$66.00
1994	7	Now	$74.00
1995	7	2004	$72.00
1996	6	2005	$60.00
1997	7	2006	$68.00
1998	7	2006	$66.00
1999	7	2007	$64.00
2000	7	2008	$62.00

WANTIRNA ESTATE CHARDONNAY ★★★★★

before 1994		Prior	
1994	7	Now	$62.00
1995	7	Now	$60.00
1996	7	Now	$58.00
1997	6	Now	$48.00
1998	7	Now	$54.00
1999	6	Now	$46.00
2000	7	Now	$52.00

WANTIRNA ESTATE PINOT NOIR ★★★★★

before 1991		Prior	
1991	6	Now	$72.00
1992	7	Now	$82.00
1993	6	Now	$68.00
1994	6	Now	$66.00
1995	7	Now	$74.00
1996	7	Now	$72.00
1997	7	Now	$70.00
1998	6	Now	$58.00
1999	7	2004	$66.00
2000	7	2004	$64.00
2001	7	2005	$62.00

Warramate *is a small, low key Yarra Valley vineyard with hand-crafted wines. Winemakers: Jack and David Church.*

WARRAMATE CABERNET SAUVIGNON ★★★

before 1990		Prior	
1990	6	Now	$36.00
1991	7	Now	$40.00
1992	6	Now	$33.00
1993	6	Now	$32.00
1994	6	Now	$31.00
1995	7	Now	$36.00
1996	6	Now	$30.00
1997	7	2004	$34.00
1998	6	2005	$28.00

WARRAMATE RIESLING ★★★★

before 1994		Prior	
1994	7	Now	$21.00
1995	7	Now	$20.00
1996	7	Now	$20.00
1997	7	Now	$19.50
1998	7	Now	$19.00
1999	7	Now	$18.50
2000	7	Now	$18.00

WARRAMATE SHIRAZ ★★★★

before 1991		Prior	
1991	6	Now	$39.00
1992	7	Now	$45.00
1993	6	Now	$37.00
1994	6	Now	$36.00
1995	7	Now	$41.00
1996	6	Now	$34.00
1997	7	2004	$38.00
1998	7	2004	$37.00

***Warrenmang** is a ten hectare vineyard in the Moonambel district of Central Victoria. Winemaker: Allen Hart.*

WARRENMANG GRAND PYRENEES ★★★★

before 1996		Prior	
1996	6	Now	$39.00
1997	6	2004	$38.00
1998	7	2005	$43.00
1999	6	2006	$36.00

WARRENMANG SHIRAZ ★★★★

before 1996		Prior	
1996	6	Now	$46.00
1997	7	2004	$52.00
1998	7	2005	$50.00
1999	6	2006	$42.00
2000	7	2007	$47.00

***Water Wheel Vineyards** have completely changed their wine styles since new owners took over. The following ratings apply to the new wines. Winemaker: Bill Trevaskis.*

WATER WHEEL CABERNET SAUVIGNON ★★★★

before 1993		Prior	
1993	7	Now	$23.00
1994	6	Now	$19.00
1995	6	Now	$18.50
1996	7	Now	$21.00
1997	7	Now	$20.00
1998	6	Now	$17.00
1999	5	2004	$14.00
200	6	2006	$16.00

WATER WHEEL CHARDONNAY ★★★

before 1995		Prior	
1995	5	Now	$13.50
1996	6	Now	$15.50
1997	7	Now	$17.50
1998	7	Now	$17.00
1999	7	Now	$16.50
2000	5	Now	$11.50
2001	6	2004	$13.50

WATER WHEEL SHIRAZ ★★★

before 1993		Prior	
1993	7	Now	$22.00
1994	5	Prior	
1995	6	Now	$17.50
1996	7	Now	$20.00
1997	7	Now	$19.50
1998	7	Now	$19.00
1999	6	2004	$15.50

Wendouree *(formerly Birks Wendouree) is a Clare Valley maker of some of the most powerful, long living red wines Australia has produced. Since 1980 the style has changed to present a much greater elegance, without sacrificing the depth of these remarkable wines. Unfortunately the proprietors do not believe in rating their own wines, so the wines are simply named and "star ranked" as follows. Winemaker: Tony Brady.*

WENDOUREE CABERNET SAUVIGNON ★★★★

WENDOUREE SHIRAZ ★★★★

Wignalls Wines *in the Albany region of Western Australia produce wines of marked elegance and power including a justly renowned Pinot Noir. Winemaker: Bill Wignall.*

WIGNALLS CABERNET SAUVIGNON ★★★★

1994	7	Now	$41.00
1995	Not made		
1996	5	Prior	
1997	4	Prior	
1998	6	Now	$31.00
1999	7	2006	$36.00
2000	7	2006	$35.00

WIGNALLS CHARDONNAY ★★★★

1985	7	Now	$50.00
1986	6	Now	$42.00
1987	5	Prior	
1988	6	Now	$40.00
1989	5	Prior	
1990	6	Now	$37.00
1991	6	Now	$36.00
1992	5	Prior	
1993	6	Now	$34.00
1994	5	Prior	
1995	5	Prior	
1996	7	2005	$37.00
1997	6	2005	$30.00
1998	5	2004	$24.00
1999	4	Now	$19.00
2000	4	Now	$18.50
2001	5	2005	$22.00

WIGNALLS PINOT NOIR ★★★★★

before 1993		Prior	
1993	7	Now	$50.00
1994	3	Prior	
1995	5	Now	$33.00
1996	3	Prior	
1997	6	2004	$38.00
1998	5	Now	$30.00

1999	6	2004	$35.00
2000	6	2005	$34.00
2001	7	2006	$39.00

WIGNALLS SAUVIGNON BLANC

★★★★

before 1999		Prior	
1999	7	Now	$19.50
2000	6	Now	$16.50

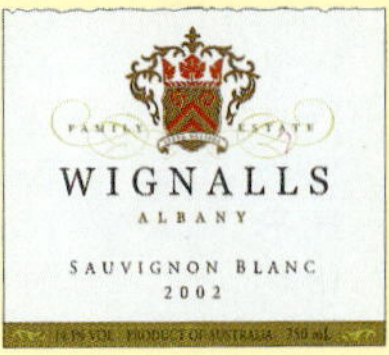

***Wildwood** is a small maker in Victoria's Sunbury region. The wines to date are of impressive style and elegance. Winemaker: Wayne Stott.*

WILDWOOD CABERNETS

★★★★

before 1993		Prior	
1993	7	Now	$46.00
1994	6	Now	$38.00
1995	4	Now	$24.00
1996	5	Now	$30.00
1997	6	2004	$35.00
1998	5	2004	$28.00
1999	6	2005	$33.00
2000	5	2005	$26.00
2001	6	2005	$31.00

WILDWOOD CHARDONNAY

★★★★

before 1996		Prior	
1996	5	Now	$23.00
1997	6	Now	$27.00
1998	5	Now	$22.00
1999	5	Now	$21.00
2000	6	2004	$25.00
2001	5	2005	$20.00

WILDWOOD "THE DUNALISTER" (MERLOT/CABERNET FRANC)

★★★★★

before 1995		Prior	
1996	5	Now	$36.00
1997	6	2004	$42.00
1998	Not made		
1999	5	2004	$33.00
2000	6	2004	$38.00
2001	5	2005	$31.00

WILDWOOD PINOT NOIR

★★★★

before 1996		Prior	
1996	6	Now	$30.00
1997	5	Now	$24.00
1998	7	Now	$33.00
1999	6	Now	$28.00
2000	4	Now	$18.00
2001	6	2005	$26.00

WILDWOOD SHIRAZ ★★★★

before 1993		Prior	
1993	7	Now	$47.00
1994	Not made		
1995	5	Now	$32.00
1996	6	Now	$37.00
1997	7	Now	$42.00
1998	6	2004	$35.00
1999	7	2005	$39.00
2000	Not made		
2001	5	2004	$26.00

***Willespie** are Margaret River producers of a range of densely flavoured and convincing wines. Winemaker: Kevin Squance.*

WILLESPIE CABERNET SAUVIGNON ★★★★

before 1984		Prior	
1984	5	Now	$41.00
1985	5	Now	$40.00
1986	5	Now	$38.00
1987	7	2005	$52.00
1988	6	Now	$44.00
1989	7	Now	$49.00
1990	7	Now	$48.00
1991	7	Now	$47.00
1992	6	Now	$39.00
1993	7	Now	$44.00
1994	7	Now	$43.00
1995	7	Now	$41.00
1996	6	Now	$34.00
1997	7	2004	$39.00
1998	7	2005	$38.00

WILLESPIE CABERNET SAUVIGNON RESERVE ★★★★★

1995	7	2006	$62.00
1996	7	2006	$60.00
1997	7	2007	$60.00

WILLESPIE SAUVIGNON BLANC ★★★★

before 1997		Prior	
1997	7	Now	$23.00
1998	7	Now	$22.00
1999	7	Now	$22.00
2000	No data		
2001	7	2004	$21.00

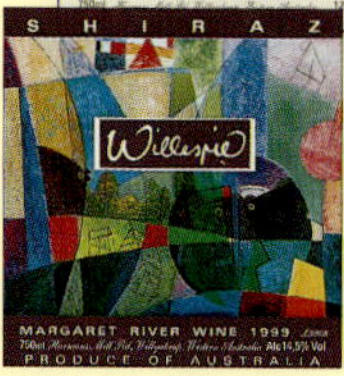

WILLESPIE SHIRAZ ★★★★

1997	7	2004	$31.00
1998	7	2005	$30.00
1999	7	2006	$30.00

WILLESPIE VERDELHO ★★★★

before 1990		Prior	
1990	7	Now	$25.00
1991	7	Now	$25.00
1992	6	Now	$20.00
1993	7	Now	$23.00
1994	6	Now	$19.50
1995	7	Now	$22.00
1996	6	Now	$18.50
1997	7	Now	$21.00
1998	7	Now	$20.00

***Willow Creek** is a new Mornington Peninsula producer with 15 hectares of Chardonnay, Cabernet and Pinot Noir. Winemaker: Simon Black.*

WILLOW CREEK CABERNET SAUVIGNON ★★★★

1993	6	Now	$36.00
1994	5	Now	$29.00
1995	5	Now	$29.00
1996	Not made		
1997	Not made		
1998	5	2004	$26.00
1999	4	2004	$20.00
2000	5	2005	$25.00
2001	6	2006	$29.00

WILLOW CREEK PINOT NOIR ★★★

before 1997		Prior	
1997	5	Now	$29.00
1998	4	Now	$22.00
1999	5	Now	$27.00
2000	5	2004	$26.00
2001	5	2005	$26.00

WILLOW CREEK TULUM CHARDONNAY ★★★

1993	4	Prior	
1994	4	Now	$26.00
1995	5	Now	$31.00
1996	Not made		
1997	Not made		
1998	5	Now	$28.00
1999	4	Now	$22.00
2000	5	Now	$27.00
2001	6	2004	$31.00

WILLOW CREEK UNOAKED CHARDONNAY ★★★★

1994	5	Now	$19.50
1995	5	Now	$19.00
1996	5	Now	$18.50

1997	6	Now	$21.00
1998	4	Now	$13.50
1999	4	Now	$13.50
2000	5	Now	$16.00

***The Wilson Vineyard** is a Polish Hill River region (Clare Valley) producer who has done a great deal to promote the high quality of the area. Winemaker: John Wilson.*

The WILSON VINEYARD CABERNET SAUVIGNON ★★★★

1982	4	Prior	
1983	Not made		
1984	5	Prior	
1985	6	Prior	
1986	6	Now	$31.00
1987	6	Now	$30.00
1988	7	Now	$34.00
1989	5	Now	$23.00
1990	7	Now	$32.00
1991	5	Prior	
1992	7	Now	$30.00
1993	Not made		
1994	7	Now	$28.00
1995	5	Now	$19.50
1996	5	Now	$19.00
1997	6	Now	$22.00
1998	6	2004	$21.00
1999	6	2005	$21.00
2000	6	2008	$20.00

The WILSON VINEYARD CHARDONNAY ★★★

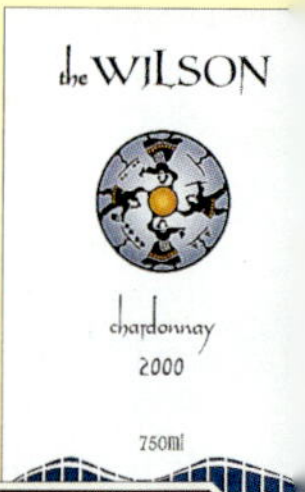

before 1998		Prior	
1998	5	Now	$14.50
1999	5	Prior	
2000	6	2004	$16.50
2001	6	2005	$16.00

The WILSON VINEYARD HIPPOCRENE (SPARKLING RED) ★★★★

1990	6	Now	$34.00
1991	7	Now	$38.00
1992	4	Prior	
1993	4	Prior	
1994	6	Now	$30.00
1995	5	2004	$24.00
1996	6	2006	$28.00

The WILSON VINEYARD RIESLING ★★★★

1985	7	Now	$32.00
1986	7	Now	$32.00
1987	4	Prior	

1988	7	Now	$30.00
1989	6	Now	$25.00
1990	6	Now	$24.00
1991	7	Now	$27.00
1992	7	Now	$26.00
1993	6	Now	$22.00
1994	7	Now	$25.00
1995	7	Now	$24.00
1996	7	Now	$23.00
1997	7	2006	$23.00
1998	7	2008	$22.00
1999	6	2008	$18.50
2000	5	2005	$15.00
2001	7	2010	$20.00

The WILSON VINEYARD
ZINFANDEL (375 ml) ★★★

1986	5	Now	$29.00
1987	4	Prior	
1988	6	Now	$32.00
1989	Not made		
1990	6	Now	$31.00
1991	6	Now	$30.00
1992	Not made		
1993	Not made		
1994	6	Now	$27.00
1995	Not made		
1996	Not made		
1997	7	2005	$29.00
1998	Not made		
1999	6	2006	$23.00
2000	Not made		
2001	7	2008	$26.00

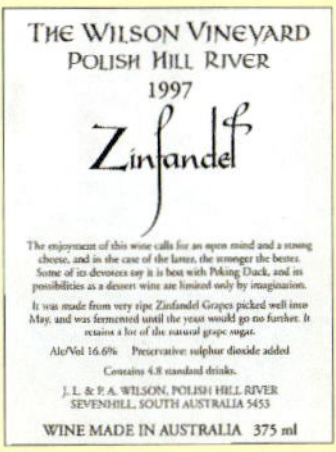

***The Wilton Estate** is the premium brand of St Peters Distillery and Winery. Winemaker: Not stated.*

WILTON ESTATE BOTRYTIS SEMILLON ★★★★

before 1992		Prior	
1992	7	Now	$27.00
1993	5	Prior	
1994	6	Prior	
1995	5	Prior	
1996	6	Now	$20.00
1997	6	Now	$20.00
1998	Not made		
1999	Not made		
2000	6	Now	$18.00
2001	Not made		
2002	Not made		

WILTON ESTATE CABERNET MERLOT ★★

before 1997		Prior	
1997	6	Now	$14.50
1998	Not made		
1999	Not made		
2000	6	Now	$13.50
2001	Not made		
2002	Not made		

WILTON ESTATE CHARDONNAY ★★

before 1996		Prior	
1996	6	Now	$11.50
1997	6	Now	$11.00
1998	Not made		
1999	Not made		
2000	Not made		
2001	6	Now	$10.00
2002	Not made		

WILTON ESTATE SEMILLON CHARDONNAY ★★

before 1998		Prior	
1998	5	Now	$7.50
1999	6	Now	$8.75
2000	5	Now	$7.00
2001	6	Now	$8.25
2002	6	Now	$8.00

WILTON ESTATE SHIRAZ/ CABERNET/MERLOT ★★

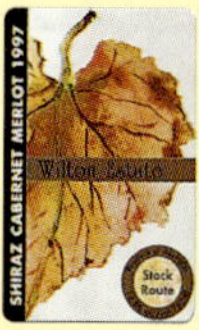

before 1997		Prior	
1997	6	Now	$11.00
1998	Not made		
1999	6	Now	$10.50
2000	Not made		
2001	6	Now	$10.00

WILTON ESTATE SHIRAZ/ MOURVEDRE ★★

1996	6	Prior	
1997	5	Now	$7.50
1998	5	Now	$7.50

***Windy Ridge Vineyard and Winery** in South Gippsland is the southernmost vineyard on the Australian mainland. Its owner would also probably lay claim to it's being the windiest. Winemaker: Graeme Wilson.*

WINDY RIDGE CABERNET/MALBEC ★★★★

1988	4	Now	$34.00
1989	5	Prior	
1990	7	Now	$56.00

1991	6	Now	$46.00
1992	Not made		
1993	Not made		
1994	6	2004	$42.00
1995	7	2005	$48.00
1996	4	Now	$26.00
1997	7	2007	$45.00
1998	6	2008	$38.00
1999	5	2009	$30.00
2000	7	2012	$41.00
2001	6	2010	N/R
2001	6	2012	N/R

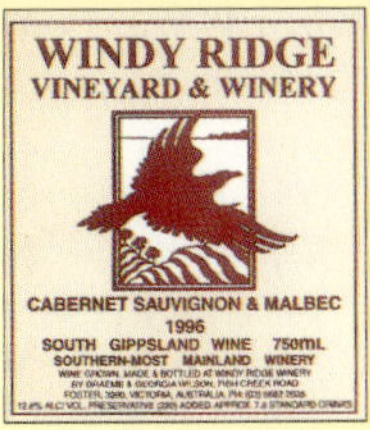

WINDY RIDGE PINOT NOIR ★★★★★

1988	5	Prior	
1989	7	Now	$66.00
1990	5	Prior	
1991	5	Prior	
1992	Not made		
1993	Not made		
1994	6	Now	$49.00
1995	7	Now	$56.00
1996	5	Now	$39.00
1997	6	2004	$45.00
1998	7	2007	$50.00
1999	5	2005	$35.00
2000	7	2010	$48.00
2001	6	2010	$40.00
2001	6	2010	N/R

***Winstead** is a tiny (1.2 ha) vineyard in Tasmania's Bagdad region. The wines are admirable. Winemaker: Andrew Hood.*

WINSTEAD PINOT NOIR ★★★★

1994	7	2005	$40.00
1995	6	Now	$33.00
1996	5	Now	$27.00
1997	6	2005	$32.00
1998	6	Now	$31.00
1999	6	2005	$30.00
2000	7	2006	$34.00

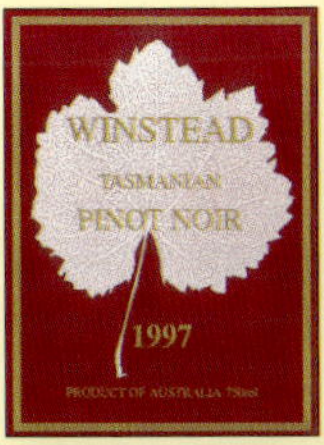

WINSTEAD RIESLING ★★★★★

1994	6	Now	$22.00
1995	7	Now	$25.00
1996	5	Now	$17.50
1997	7	Now	$24.00
1998	6	2005	$20.00
1999	5	2005	$16.00
2000	5	Now	$15.50
2001	6	2004	$18.00

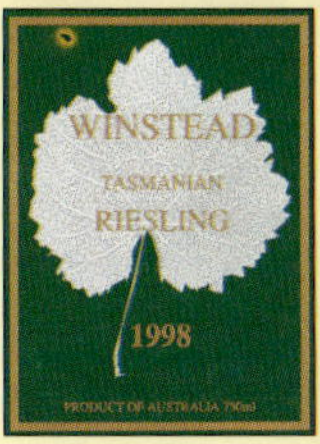

Wirra Wirra *is a McLaren Vale producer of a range of very stylish and elegant wines. Winemaker: Ben Riggs.*

WIRRA WIRRA "THE ANGELUS" CABERNET SAUVIGNON ★★★★★

before 1984		Prior	
1984	6	Now	$84.00
1985	5	Now	$68.00
1986	Not made		
1987	5	Now	$64.00
1988	5	Now	$62.00
1989	5	Now	$60.00
1990	6	Now	$70.00
1991	6	Now	$68.00
1992	6	2005	$66.00
1993	6	2005	$64.00
1994	6	2004	$62.00
1995	6	2005	$60.00
1996	6	2006	$58.00
1997	5	2004	$47.00
1998	7	2005	$64.00
1999	6	2008	$54.00
2000	6	2008	$52.00
2001	6	2008	$50.00

WIRRA WIRRA CHARDONNAY ★★★★

before 1990		Prior	
1990	6	Now	$33.00
1991	7	Now	$37.00
1992	6	Now	$31.00
1993	5	Now	$25.00
1994	5	2004	$24.00
1995	6	2004	$28.00
1996	6	2004	$27.00
1997	No data		
1998	No data		
1999	6	Now	$25.00

WIRRA WIRRA CHURCH BLOCK ★★★★

before 1982		Prior	
1982	6	Now	$38.00
1983	5	Prior	
1984	5	Now	$30.00
1985	5	Now	$29.00
1986	7	Now	$39.00
1987	5	Now	$27.00
1988	6	Now	$32.00
1989	6	Now	$31.00
1990	6	Now	$30.00
1991	6	Now	$29.00
1992	6	Now	$28.00

1993	5	Now	$23.00
1994	6	Now	$26.00
1995	5	Now	$21.00
1996	5	Now	$21.00
1997	6	Now	$24.00
1998	7	2005	$27.00
1999	6	2005	$23.00
2000	6	2006	$22.00
2001	6	2007	$21.00

WIRRA WIRRA HAND PICKED RIESLING ★★★★

before 1986		Prior	
1986	6	Now	$30.00
1987	5	Now	$24.00
1988	5	Now	$23.00
1989	5	Now	$23.00
1990	6	Now	$26.00
1991	6	2004	$26.00
1992	6	2004	$25.00
1993	5	Now	$20.00
1994	6	Now	$23.00
1995	5	Now	$19.00
1996	6	Now	$22.00
1997	6	Now	$21.00
1998	6	2004	$21.00
1999	6	2004	$20.00
2000	7	2004	$23.00
2001	5	2004	$16.00
2002	6	2006	$18.50

WIRRA WIRRA MCLAREN VALE SHIRAZ ★★★★

1999	5	2005	$29.00
2000	6	2007	$34.00
2001	5	2006	$28.00

WIRRA WIRRA ORIGINAL BLEND ★★★

1997	6	Now	$18.00
1998	7	2004	$20.00
1999	7	2005	$19.50

No longer made.

WIRRA WIRRA SCRUBBY RISE ★★★

1998	5	Now	$17.00
1999	6	2004	$19.50
2000	5	2004	$16.00
2001	6	2005	$18.50
2002	6	2008	$18.00

WIRRA WIRRA SAUVIGNON BLANC ★★★

before 1998		Prior	
1998	6	Now	$25.00
1999	5	Now	$20.00

2000	6	Now	$24.00
2001	No data		
2002	6	Now	$22.00

WIRRA WIRRA SEMILLON/SAUVIGNON BLANC ★★★

before 1990		Prior	
1990	6	Now	$21.00
1991	5	Now	$17.50
1992	5	Now	$17.00
1993	5	Now	$16.50
1994	6	Now	$19.50
1995	4	Now	$12.50
1996	6	Now	$18.00
1997	6	Now	$17.50

No longer made.

WIRRA WIRRA SHIRAZ ★★★★

1989	5	Now	$58.00
1990	6	Now	$66.00
1991	7	2005	$76.00
1992	6	2010	$62.00
1993	5	Now	$50.00
1994	7	2004	$70.00
1995	6	2005	$58.00
1996	6	2006	$56.00
1997	5	Now	$45.00
1998	7	2008	$62.00
1999	6	2008	$50.00
2000	6	2009	$50.00
2001	6	2009	$49.00

***Witchmount Estate** in the Sunbury region of Victoria is a recently established vineyard with a range of varieties, some of which (yet to appear as wines) will not have been seen before in Australia. The Chardonnay is both good and underpriced. Winemaker: Tony Ramunno.*

WITCHMOUNT ESTATE CHARDONNAY ★★★★

2000	5	Now	
2001	5	Now	$16.00
2002	6	2005	N/R

***Wolf Blass** wines have generated an immense reputation in the last decade - a reputation for both quality and reliability. Winemakers: Chris Hatcher, Caroline Dunn, John Glaetzer and Wendy Stuckey.*

WOLF BLASS CABERNET SAUVIGNON/SHIRAZ/MERLOT (BLACK LABEL) ★★★★★

1973	6	Now	$270.00
1974	6	Now	$260.00
1975	7	Now	$290.00
1976	6	Now	$245.00

1977	6	Now	$240.00
1978	6	Now	$230.00
1979	6	Now	$225.00
1980	7	Now	$250.00
1981	6	Now	$210.00
1982	7	Now	$240.00
1983	6	Now	$200.00
1984	6	Now	$190.00
1985	6	Now	$185.00
1986	6	Now	$180.00
1987	6	Now	$175.00
1988	6	2005	$170.00
1989	6	Now	$165.00
1990	6	2005	$160.00
1991	7	2010	$180.00
1992	6	2008	$150.00
1993	6	2010	$145.00
1994	7	2010	$165.00
1995	6	2006	$140.00
1996	6	2010	$135.00
1997	6	2010	$130.00
1998	7	2015	$150.00
1999	6	2015	$120.00

WOLF BLASS CABERNET SAUVIGNON/SHIRAZ (GREY LABEL) ★★★

before 1976		Prior	
1976	5	Now	$70.00
1977	5	Now	$68.00
1978	6	Now	$80.00
1979	6	Now	$76.00
1980	5	Now	$62.00
1981	6	Now	$72.00
1982	5	Now	$58.00
1983	5	Now	$56.00
1984	6	Now	$66.00
1985	6	Now	$64.00
1986	5	Now	$52.00
1987	5	Now	$50.00
1988	6	Now	$58.00
1989	5	Now	$48.00
1990	7	Now	$64.00
1991	5	2004	$45.00
1992	6	2005	$52.00
1993	6	2004	$50.00
1994	7	2007	$58.00
1995	6	2008	$48.00
1996	6	2010	$47.00
1997	6	2008	$45.00
1998	7	2012	$50.00

1999	6	2010	$43.00
2000	6	2012	$41.00
2001	6	2014	$40.00

WOLF BLASS CABERNET SAUVIGNON/SHIRAZ (YELLOW LABEL) ★★★

before 1985		Prior	
1985	5	Now	$21.00
1986	5	Now	$20.00
1987	5	Now	$19.50
1988	6	Now	$23.00
1989	5	Now	$18.50
1990	6	Now	$21.00
1991	5	Now	$17.50
1992	6	Now	$20.00
1993	6	Now	$19.50
1994	5	Now	$16.00
1995	5	Now	$15.50
1996	7	2004	$21.00
1997	6	Now	$17.50
1998	7	2004	$20.00
1999	6	Now	$16.50
2000	6	2004	$16.00
2001	6	2005	$15.50

WOLF BLASS CLASSIC DRY WHITE ★★★

before 1993		Prior	
1993	6	Now	$15.00
1994	6	Now	$14.50
1995	7	Now	$16.50
1996	6	Now	$14.00
1997	6	Now	$13.50
1998	7	Now	$15.00
1999	6	Now	$12.50
2000	5	Now	$10.00
2001	6	Now	$12.00
2002	6	2004	$11.50

WOLF BLASS CLASSIC SHIRAZ (BROWN LABEL) ★★★★

before 1984		Prior	
1984	6	Now	$49.00
1985	6	Now	$48.00
1986	6	Now	$46.00
1987	7	Now	$52.00
1988	6	Now	$44.00
1989	6	Now	$42.00
1990	7	Now	$48.00
1991	6	Now	$40.00
1992	6	Now	$39.00
1993	7	Now	$44.00

1994	6	Now	$36.00
1995	6	2004	$35.00
1996	6	2010	$34.00
1997	6	2008	$33.00
1998	7	2012	$38.00
1999	7	2012	$37.00
2000	7	2012	$36.00
2001	7	2011	$35.00

WOLF BLASS PINOT NOIR/ CHARDONNAY CUVEE ★★★

before 1991		Prior	
1991	6	Now	$24.00
1992	5	Now	$19.50
1993	6	Now	$23.00
1994	7	Now	$26.00
1995	7	Now	$25.00
1996	7	Now	$24.00
1997	6	Now	$20.00
1998	6	2004	$19.50
1999	7	2004	$22.00
2000	7	2005	$21.00

WOLF BLASS RIESLING (GOLD LABEL) ★★★★

before 1989		Prior	
1989	5	Now	$21.00
1990	6	Now	$25.00
1991	7	Now	$28.00
1992	7	Now	$27.00
1993	6	Now	$22.00
1994	6	Now	$22.00
1995	6	Now	$21.00
1996	7	Now	$24.00
1997	7	Now	$23.00
1998	7	Now	$23.00
1999	7	Now	$22.00
2000	7	2008	$21.00
2001	6	2008	$18.00
2002	7	2010	$20.00

WOLF BLASS RIESLING (YELLOW LABEL) ★★★

before 1989		Prior	
1989	5	Now	$13.50
1990	6	Now	$16.00
1991	6	Now	$15.50
1992	Not made		
1993	7	Now	$17.00
1994	6	Now	$14.00
1995	7	Now	$16.00
1996	6	Now	$13.50
1997	6	Now	$13.00

1998	7	Now	$14.50
1999	7	Now	$14.50
2000	7	Now	$14.00
2001	6	Now	$11.50
2002	6	2004	$11.00

WOLF BLASS SHOW CHARDONNAY ★★★★

before 1988		Prior	
1988	7	Now	$34.00
1989	6	Now	$28.00
1990	6	Now	$28.00
1991	Not made		
1994	7	Now	$30.00
1995	6	Now	$25.00
1996	6	Now	$24.00
1997	6	Now	$24.00
1998	7	Now	$27.00

No longer made.

***Woodstock** are McLaren Flat producers whose wines have rapidly been afforded prominence throughout Australia. Winemaker: Scott Collett.*

WOODSTOCK BOTRYTIS SWEET WHITE (375ml) ★★★★

1984	6	Now	$21.00
1985	7	Now	$24.00
1986	6	Now	$20.00
1987	7	Now	$23.00
1988	Not made		
1989	Not made		
1990	6	Now	$18.00
1991	7	Now	$20.00
1992	6	Now	$17.00
1993	6	Now	$16.50
1994	6	Now	$16.00
1995	5	Now	$12.50
1996	6	Now	$15.00
1997	7	Now	$17.00
1999	7	Now	$16.50

WOODSTOCK CABERNET SAUVIGNON ★★★★

1981	6	Prior	
1982	7	Now	$35.00
1983	6	Now	$29.00
1984	7	Now	$33.00
1985	5	Now	$22.00
1986	6	Now	$26.00
1987	7	Now	$30.00
1988	7	Now	$29.00
1989	6	Now	$24.00

1990	6	Now	$23.00
1991	6	Now	$23.00
1992	7	2006	$26.00
1993	6	Now	$21.00
1994	7	Now	$24.00
1995	6	2006	$20.00
1996	7	2008	$23.00
1997	7	2008	$22.00
1998	6	2005	$18.50

WOODSTOCK CHARDONNAY ★★★

before 1996		Prior	
1996	5	Now	$15.00
1997	6	Now	$17.00
1998	7	Now	$19.50
1999	No data		
2000	6	2004	$16.00

WOODSTOCK SAUVIGNON BLANC/SEMILLON ★★★

before 1990		Prior	
1990	6	Now	$19.00
1991	6	Now	$18.50
1992	6	Now	$18.00
1993	Not made		
1994	6	Now	$17.00
1995	6	Now	$16.50
1996	6	Now	$16.00
1997	Not made		
1998	6	Now	$15.00
1999	No data		
2000	No data		
2001	6	2004	$14.00

WOODSTOCK SHIRAZ ★★★

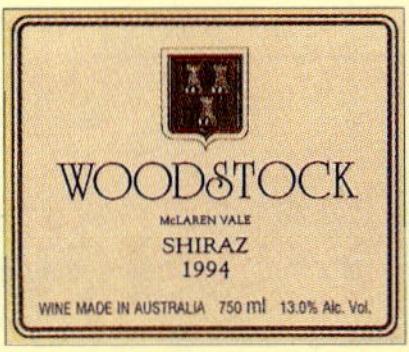

1982	6	Now	$26.00
1983	5	Now	$21.00
1984	7	Now	$28.00
1985	Not made		
1986	6	Now	$23.00
1987	6	Now	$22.00
1988	7	Now	$25.00
1989	6	Now	$21.00
1990	6	Now	$20.00
1991	6	Now	$20.00
1992	6	Now	$19.00
1993	6	2004	$18.50
1994	7	2006	$21.00
1995	6	2005	$17.50
1996	6	2005	$17.00

1997	6	2005	$16.50
1998	6	2006	$16.00
1999	5	2006	$13.00

WOODSTOCK "THE STOCKS" SHIRAZ (CABERNET IN 1993) ★★★★

1991	6	2006	$34.00
1992	Not made		
1994	7	2006	$37.00
1994	6	2004	$31.00
1995	7	2008	$35.00
1996	7	2010	$34.00
1997	No data		
1998	6	2010	$27.00

***Wyndham Estate** in the Hunter Valley has been one of the most successful marketers in the Australian wine world, and is now part of Orlando Wyndham. Winemaker: Brett McKinnon.*

WYNDHAM ESTATE CABERNET/MERLOT BIN 888 ★★★

before 1995		Prior	
1995	6	Now	$14.00
1996	7	Now	$16.00
1997	6	Now	$13.50
1998	7	Now	$15.00
1999	7	Now	$14.50

WYNDHAM ESTATE CABERNET SAUVIGNON BIN 444 ★★★

before 1996		Prior	
1996	7	Now	$15.00
1997	7	Now	$14.50
1998	7	Now	$14.00
1999	7	Now	$14.00

WYNDHAM ESTATE CABERNET/ SHIRAZ/RUBY CABERNET ★★

1998	7	Prior	
1999	7	Now	$9.50
2000	7	Now	$9.25
2001	7	Now	$9.00

WYNDHAM ESTATE CHARDONNAY BIN 222 ★★

before 1998		Prior	
1998	7	Now	$15.00
1999	7	Now	$14.50
2000	7	Now	$14.00
2001	7	Now	$14.00

WYNDHAM ESTATE MERLOT BIN 999 ★★

1998	7	Prior	
1999	6	Now	$12.00
2000	7	Now	$13.50

WYNDHAM ESTATE PINOT NOIR BIN 333 ★★★

before 1998		Prior	
1998	7	Now	$14.50
1999	7	Now	$14.00
2000	7	Now	$14.00

WYNDHAM ESTATE OAK CASK CHARDONNAY ★★

before 1998		Prior	
1998	6	Now	$13.00
1999	6	Now	$12.50
2000	7	Now	$14.00

WYNDHAM ESTATE SEMILLON BIN 777 ★★

1998	6	Prior	
1999	7	Now	$14.00
2000	7	Now	$13.50

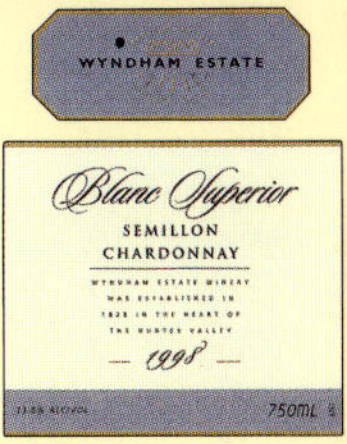

WYNDHAM ESTATE SEMILLON/ CHARDONNAY ★★

before 1999		Prior	
1999	7	Now	$8.00
2000	7	Now	$8.00
2001	7	Now	N/R

WYNDHAM ESTATE SEMILLON/ SAUVIGNON BLANC ★★

before 1999		Prior	
1999	7	Now	$9.50
2000	7	Now	$9.25
2001	7	Now	$9.00

WYNDHAM ESTATE SHOW RESERVE CABERNET/MERLOT ★★★

1996	7	Now	$25.00
1997	7	Now	$24.00
1998	7	2004	$24.00

WYNDHAM ESTATE SHOW RESERVE CHARDONNAY ★★★

1997	7	Now	$20.00
1998	7	Now	$19.50
1999	7	Now	$19.00

WYNDHAM ESTATE SHOW RESERVE MUDGEE CABERNET SAUVIGNON ★★★★

1996	7	2006	$49.00
1997	Not made		
1998	Not made		
1999	7	2008	$45.00

WYNDHAM ESTATE SHOW RESERVE SEMILLON ★★★

1991	7	Now	$26.00
1992	Not made		
1993	Not made		
1994	7	Now	$24.00
1995	7	2004	$23.00
1996	Not made		
1997	7	2006	$22.00

WYNDHAM ESTATE SHOW RESERVE SHIRAZ ★★★

1991	7	Now	$30.00
1992	Not made		
1993	7	Now	$29.00
1994	Not made		
1995	6	Now	$23.00
1996	Not made		
1997	7	2005	$25.00

WYNDHAM ESTATE SHIRAZ BIN 555 ★★

before 1997		Prior	
1997	7	Now	$15.00
1998	7	Now	$14.50
1999	7	Now	$14.00
2000	7	Now	$14.00

WYNDHAM ESTATE UNWOODED CHARDONNAY ★★

1998	7	Prior	
1999	7	Now	$9.50
2000	7	Now	$9.25
2001	7	Now	$9.00

WYNDHAM ESTATE VERDELHO ★★

before 1999		Prior	
1999	6	Now	$8.50
2000	7	Now	$9.50
2001	7	Now	$9.25

WYNDHAM ESTATE VINTAGE BRUT ★★★

1998	6	Prior	
1999	7	Now	$19.00
2000	7	Now	$18.50

WYNDHAM ESTATE VINTAGE CHARDONNAY BRUT ★★★

1997	6	Prior	
1998	Not made		
1999	7	Now	$19.00
2000	7	Now	$18.50

__Wynn's Coonawarra Estate__ are leading red wine makers whose confidence in Coonawarra once saved the area as a vignoble. They are now in the immense Southcorp stable. Winemakers: Sue Hodder and Sarah Pidgeon.

WYNNS COONAWARRA ESTATE
CABERNET SAUVIGNON ★★★★

before 1982		Prior	
1982	7	Now	$70.00
1983	3	Prior	
1984	4	Now	$38.00
1985	5	Now	$46.00
1986	7	Now	$62.00
1987	4	Now	$35.00
1988	5	Now	$42.00
1989	4	Prior	
1990	7	2010	$56.00
1991	6	2005	$47.00
1992	5	Now	$38.00
1993	6	2005	$44.00
1994	6	2005	$43.00
1995	5	Now	$34.00
1996	5	2005	$33.00
1997	4	2005	$26.00
1998	7	2008	$44.00
1999	5	2005	$31.00
2000	6	2008	$36.00

WYNNS COONAWARRA ESTATE
CABERNET/SHIRAZ/MERLOT ★★★★

before 1982		Prior	
1982	6	Now	$37.00
1983	4	Prior	
1984	5	Prior	
1985	5	Now	$28.00
1986	7	Now	$39.00
1987	4	Now	$21.00
1988	5	Now	$26.00
1989	4	Prior	
1990	6	2005	$29.00
1991	6	Now	$28.00
1992	4	Now	$18.50
1993	5	Now	$22.00
1994	5	2005	$21.00
1995	4	Now	$17.00
1996	5	2005	$20.00
1997	5	Now	$20.00
1998	7	2005	$27.00
1999	6	2005	$22.00
2000	5	2005	$18.00

WYNNS COONAWARRA ESTATE CHARDONNAY

★★★

before 1992		Prior	
1992	5	Now	$28.00
1993	4	Now	$22.00
1994	5	Now	$27.00
1995	6	Now	$31.00
1996	5	Now	$25.00
1997	5	Now	$24.00
1998	6	Now	$28.00
1999	5	Now	$23.00
2000	6	Now	$27.00
2001	6	2004	$26.00
2002	6	2005	$25.00

WYNNS JOHN RIDDOCH CABERNET SAUVIGNON

★★★★★

1982	7	Now	$180.00
1983	Not made		
1984	5	Now	$120.00
1985	4	Now	$96.00
1986	6	2005	$135.00
1987	5	Now	$110.00
1988	5	2005	$105.00
1989	Not made		
1990	7	2010	$140.00
1991	7	2010	$140.00
1992	5	2005	$96.00
1993	6	2010	$110.00
1994	6	2010	$110.00
1995	Not made		
1996	5	2008	$86.00
1997	4	2005	$66.00
1998	7	2010	$110.00
1999	6	2010	$94.00
2000	Not made		

WYNNS COONAWARRA ESTATE MICHAEL SHIRAZ

★★★★★

1990	7	2005	$135.00
1991	6	Now	$110.00
1992	Not made		
1993	6	2010	$105.00
1994	6	2010	$100.00
1995	Not made		
1996	5	2010	$80.00
1997	5	2005	$78.00
1998	6	2005	$92.00
1999	Not made		
2000	Not made		

WYNNS COONAWARRA ESTATE RIESLING ★★★

before 1996		Prior	
1996	5	Now	$12.50
1997	5	Now	$12.00
1998	6	Now	$14.00
1999	6	Now	$13.50
2000	6	Now	$13.00
2001	5	2005	$10.50
2002	7	2006	$14.50

WYNNS COONAWARRA ESTATE SHIRAZ ★★★★

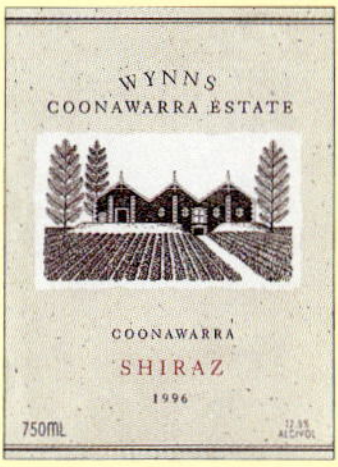

1982	6	Now	$35.00
1983	4	Prior	
1984	5	Now	$27.00
1985	5	Now	$26.00
1986	7	Now	$36.00
1987	4	Now	$20.00
1988	5	Now	$24.00
1989	4	Now	$19.00
1990	7	Now	$32.00
1991	6	Now	$26.00
1992	4	Now	$17.00
1993	7	2005	$29.00
1994	5	Now	$20.00
1995	4	Now	$15.50
1996	5	Now	$19.00
1997	5	Now	$18.50
1998	7	2005	$25.00
1999	6	2005	$21.00
2000	6	2006	$20.00
2001	6	2010	$20.00

***Xanadu** is a Margaret River winery whose wines show markedly generous fruit. Winemaker: Jurg Muggli.*

XANADU CABERNET SAUVIGNON ★★★

before 1989		Prior	
1989	5	Now	$40.00
1990	6	Now	$47.00
1991	6	2005	$45.00
1992	6	Now	$44.00
1993	5	Now	$35.00
1994	7	2005	$48.00
1995	7	2010	$47.00
1996	7	2007	$45.00
1997	6	2010	$38.00
1998	6	2009	$37.00
1999	6	2009	$36.00
2000	5	2008	$29.00

XANADU CABERNET SAUVIGNON RESERVE ★★★★★

1989	5	Now	$62.00
1990	6	Now	$72.00
1991	7	2010	$80.00
1992	6	2008	$68.00
1993	5	Now	$54.00
1994	6	2010	$64.00
1995	7	2015	$72.00
1996	7	2015	$70.00
1997	7	2015	$68.00
1998	7	2012	$66.00

XANADU CHARDONNAY ★★★★

before 1991		Prior	
1991	6	Now	$30.00
1992	6	Now	$29.00
1993	6	Now	$28.00
1994	6	2005	$27.00
1995	4	Now	$18.00
1996	6	2005	$26.00
1997	7	2005	$29.00
1998	6	Now	$24.00
1999	5	Now	$20.00
2000	7	2004	$27.00

XANADU SEMILLON ★★★

before 1989		Prior	
1989	5	Now	$21.00
1990	5	Now	$20.00
1991	6	Now	$23.00
1992	6	Now	$23.00
1993	5	Now	$18.50
1994	6	Now	$21.00
1995	6	Now	$21.00
1996	7	2005	$23.00
1997	7	2005	$23.00
1998	No data		
1999	6	Now	$18.50
2000	6	Now	$18.00

***Yaldara** is a long-established (1947) Barossa maker whose large range of wines is undergoing a transformation, part of which involves the creation of the premium "Farms" label. Winemaker: Matt Tydeman.*

YALDARA FARMS MERLOT/CABERNET ★★★★

1991	6	Now	$47.00
1992	5	Prior	
1993	Not made		

1994	Not made		
1995	6	Now	$42.00
1996	7	Now	$47.00
1997	7	2005	$46.00
1998	7	2006	$44.00
1999	7	2007	$43.00

YALDARA FARMS SHIRAZ ★★★★

1997	6	2004	$45.00
1998	7	2006	$50.00
1999	6	2007	$42.00

YALDARA JULIANS CABERNET/MERLOT ★★★

1996	7	Now	$23.00
1997	6	Now	$19.50
1998	7	Now	$22.00
1999	6	Now	$18.00

YALDARA JULIANS SHIRAZ ★★★

1996	7	Now	$22.00
1997	Not made		
1998	7	Now	$21.00
1999	6	Now	$18.00

***Yalumba** is the best known brand in the S. Smith and Sons empire, which includes Pewsey Vale and Heggies. Wines from this fine family firm are honest, reliable and sometimes very good indeed. Winemakers: Louisa Rose and Kevin Glastonbury.*

YALUMBA BAROSSA CABERNET/SHIRAZ ★★★

1998	6	Now	$16.00
1999	5	Now	$13.00
2000	6	2004	$15.00
2001	6	2005	$15.00
2002	7	2006	N/R

YALUMBA BAROSSA CHARDONNAY ★★★

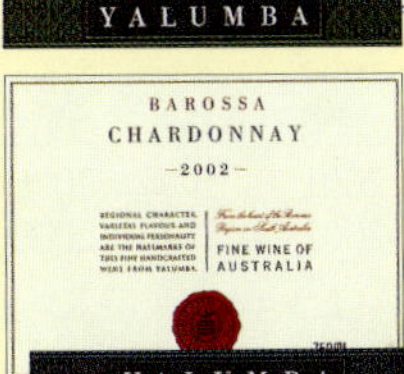

1999	6	Prior	
2000	6	Now	$16.50
2001	6	Now	$16.00
2002	7	2004	$18.00

YALUMBA BAROSSA SHIRAZ ★★★★

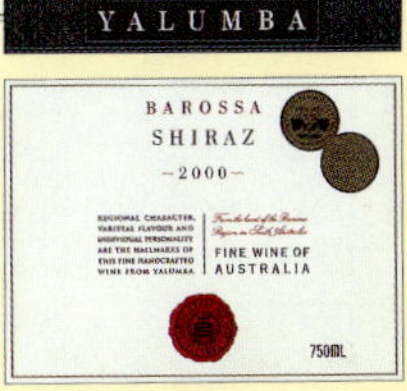

before 1998		Prior	
1998	6	Now	$19.00
1999	5	Now	$15.00
2000	6	2004	$17.50
2001	7	2005	$20.00
2002	7	2006	N/R

YALUMBA BUSH VINE GRENACHE ★★★★

before 2000		Prior	
2000	7	Now	$20.00
2001	7	2004	$18.00
2002	7	2005	$18.00

YALUMBA CHARDONNAY★★★

before 1999		Prior	
1999	6	Now	$17.00
2000	6	Now	$16.50
2001	7	Now	$18.50

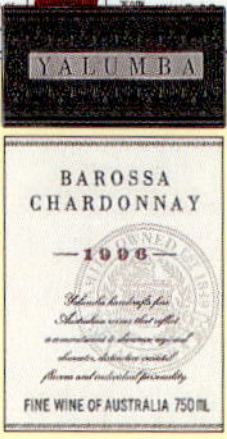

YALUMBA "D" METHODE CHAMPENOISE ★★★★★

before 1996		Prior	
1996	6	Now	$28.00
1997	6	Now	$27.00
1998	7	Now	$31.00
1999	7	Now	$30.00
2000	6	2004	N/R
2001	6	2005	N/R
2002	7	2006	N/R

YALUMBA EDEN VALLEY VIOGNIER ★★★

1999	6	Now	$22.00
2000	7	Now	$25.00
2001	7	Now	$24.00
2002	6	Now	$20.00

YALUMBA HAND-PICKED EDEN VALLEY RIESLING ★★★★

2000	7	2005	
2001	6	2006	
2002	7	2007	$25.00

YALUMBA MAWSONS (LIMESTONE COAST CAB/SHIRAZ/MERLOT) ★★★

1996	5	Now	$18.00
1997	6	Now	$21.00
1998	6	2004	$20.00
1999	5	Now	$16.50
2000	6	2005	$19.00
2001	5	2005	N/R
2002	6	2006	N/R

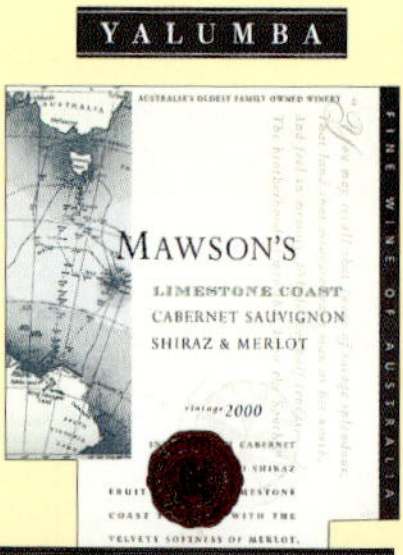

YALUMBA RESERVE CHARDONNAY ★★★★

before 1995		Prior	
1995	6	Now	$27.00
1996	6	Now	$27.00
1997	5	Now	$21.00
1998	6	Now	$25.00
1999	6	204	$24.00

No longer made

YALUMBA SHIRAZ/VIOGNIER ★★★★

1998	6	Now	$34.00
1999	5	Now	$28.00
2000	7	2004	$38.00
2001	7	2005	N/R
2002	7	2006	N/R

YALUMBA "THE MENZIES" CABERNET SAUVIGNON ★★★★

before 1994		Prior	
1994	7	Now	$50.00
1995	5	Now	$34.00
1996	7	Now	$47.00
1997	6	Now	$39.00
1998	6	2004	$38.00
1999	5	2004	$30.00
2000	7	2006	$42.00
2001	6	2006	N/R
2002	5	2007	N/R

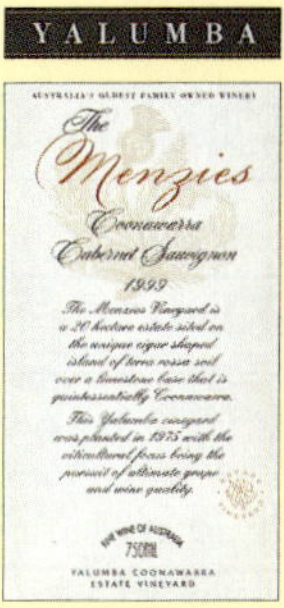

YALUMBA "THE OCTAVIUS" (SHIRAZ) ★★★★★

before 1993		Prior	
1993	7	Now	$120.00
1994	7	2005	$115.00
1995	6	2004	$98.00
1996	6	2006	$94.00
1997	6	2006	$92.00
1998	7	2008	$100.00
1999	6	2012	$86.00
2000	6	2010	N/R
2001	7	2012	N/R
2002	7	2010	N/R

YALUMBA "THE RESERVE" (CABERNET/SHIRAZ) ★★★★★

1990	7	Now	$125.00
1991	Not made		
1992	7	Now	$120.00
1993	Not made		
1994	Not made		
1995	Not made		
1996	6	2006	$92.00
1997	Not made		
1998	7	2008	N/R
1999	6	2010	N/R
2000	6	2010	N/R
2001	7	2012	N/R
2002	6	2012	N/R

YALUMBA "THE SIGNATURE" RESERVE CABERNET SAUVIGNON/SHIRAZ ★★★★★

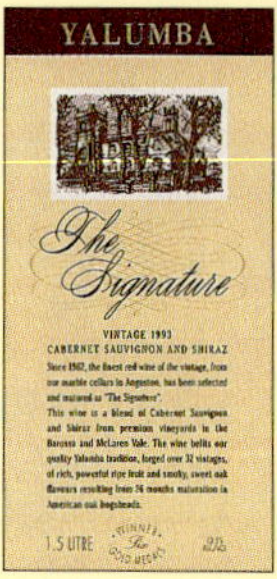

before 1992		Prior	
1992	7	2005	$56.00
1993	5	Prior	
1994	6	2005	$45.00
1995	5	2005	$36.00
1996	6	2006	$43.00
1997	5	2006	$34.00
1998	7	2008	$47.00
1999	6	2010	$39.00
2000	6	2012	N/R
2001	7	2012	N/R
2002	7	2010	N/R

YALUMBA "THE VIRGILIUS" VIOGNIER ★★★★★

1998	6	Now	$44.00
1999	7	Now	$50.00
2000	7	Now	$49.00
2001	7	Now	$47.00
2002	7	Now	$46.00

YALUMBA TRICENTENARY GRENACHE ★★★★

1999	7	Now	$37.00
2000	7	2004	$36.00
2001	7	2005	$35.00
2002	7	2006	N/R

Yarra Burn*, yet another Yarra Valley maker specializing in the noble varieties, has been acquired by BRL Hardy. Winemaker: Steve Flamsteed.*

YARRA BURN CABERNETS ★★★

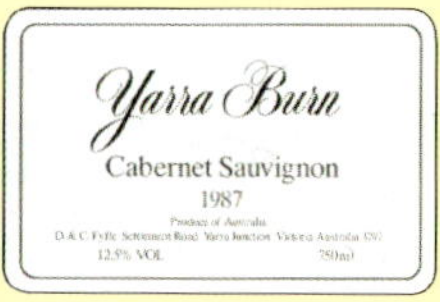

before 1984		Prior	
1984	7	Now	$47.00
1985	5	Now	$33.00
1986	6	Now	$38.00
1987	5	Now	$31.00
1988	6	Now	$36.00
1989	5	Now	$29.00
1990	6	Now	$34.00
1991	6	Now	$33.00
1992	7	Now	$37.00
1993	5	Now	$26.00
1994	6	Now	$30.00
1995	7	2005	$34.00
1996	5	2004	$23.00
1997	5	2005	$23.00
1998	6	2006	$26.00

1999	6	2004	$26.00
2000	6	2006	$25.00
2001	6	2007	$24.00

YARRA BURN CHARDONNAY ★★★★

before 1990		Prior	
1990	6	Now	$29.00
1991	5	Now	$23.00
1992	5	Now	$23.00
1993	5	Now	$22.00
1994	5	Now	$21.00
1995	7	Now	$29.00
1996	5	Now	$20.00
1997	6	Now	$23.00
1998	7	Now	$26.00
1999	6	Now	$22.00
2000	5	Now	$18.00
2001	6	2004	$21.00

YARRA BURN PINOT NOIR ★★★★

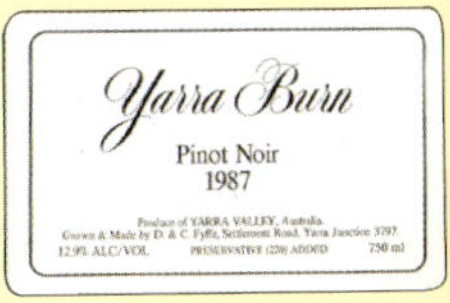

before 1988		Prior	
1988	7	Now	$46.00
1989	6	Now	$38.00
1990	5	Now	$31.00
1991	5	Now	$30.00
1992	5	Now	$29.00
1993	5	Now	$28.00
1994	4	Now	$22.00
1995	Not made		
1996	Not made		
1997	7	Now	$35.00
1998	5	Now	$24.00
1999	5	Now	$23.00
2000	6	Now	$27.00
2001	4	2004	$18.00

***Yarra Edge** are Yarra Valley makers with two very impressive wines, notable for concentrated flavours without sacrifice of elegance. Winemakers: Tom Carson and Dan Buckle.*

YARRA EDGE CABERNETS ★★★★

1990	6	Now	$44.00
1991	7	Now	$50.00
1992	6	Now	$42.00
1993	6	2005	$41.00
1994	5	Now	$33.00
1995	7	2005	$45.00
1996	5	2005	$31.00
1997	7	2010	$42.00
1998	7	2012	$41.00
1999	6	2005	$34.00
2000	7	2010	$39.00

YARRA EDGE CHARDONNAY ★★★★

1990	6	Now	$38.00
1991	7	Now	$43.00
1992	7	Now	$42.00
1993	6	Now	$35.00
1994	4	Now	$22.00
1995	6	Now	$33.00
1996	7	Now	$37.00
1997	6	Now	$31.00
1998	7	2005	$35.00
1999	7	2005	$34.00
2000	6	2005	$28.00

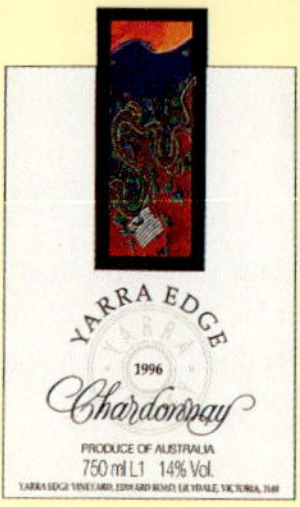

***Yarra Ridge**, the largest producer in the Yarra Valley, is part-owned by Beringer Blass. Winemaker: Matt Steel.*

YARRA RIDGE BOTRYTIS SEMILLON (375ml) ★★★★

1988	7	Now	$29.00
1989	Not made		
1990	6	Now	$24.00
1991	6	Now	$23.00
1992	6	Now	$22.00
1993	7	Prior	
1994	6	Now	$21.00
1995	6	Prior	
1996	6	Prior	
1997	Not made		
1998	7	Now	$22.00
1999	Not made		

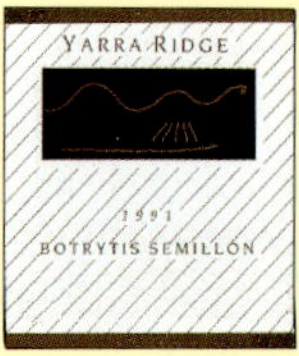

YARRA RIDGE CABERNET SAUVIGNON ★★★★

before 1990		Prior	
1990	7	Now	$33.00
1991	6	Now	$27.00
1992	6	Now	$26.00
1993	6	Now	$25.00
1994	6	Now	$25.00
1995	5	Now	$20.00
1996	6	Now	$23.00
1997	7	2005	$26.00
1998	7	2005	$26.00
1999	6	2007	$21.00

YARRA RIDGE CHARDONNAY ★★★

1992	7	Prior	
1993	6	Now	$24.00
1994	6	Now	$23.00
1995	6	Now	$23.00
1996	5	Now	$18.50

1997	6	Now	$21.00
1998	6	Now	$21.00
1999	6	Now	$20.00
2000	6	Now	$20.00

YARRA RIDGE MERLOT ★★★★

1995	7	Now	$24.00
1996	5	Now	$17.00
1997	7	Now	$23.00
1998	7	2005	$22.00
1999	6	2005	$18.50

YARRA RIDGE PINOT NOIR ★★★★

1992	6	Now	$28.00
1993	5	Now	$22.00
1994	5	Now	$22.00
1995	5	Now	$21.00
1996	7	Now	$29.00
1997	6	Now	$24.00
1998	6	Now	$23.00
1999	6	2004	$23.00
2000	7	2005	$26.00

YARRA RIDGE RESERVE PINOT NOIR ★★★★★

1992	7	Now	$50.00
1993	Not made		
1994	Not made		
1995	Not made		
1996	7	Now	$45.00
1997	7	Now	$43.00
1998	7	2004	$42.00
1999	Not made		
2000	7	2007	$40.00

YARRA RIDGE SAUVIGNON BLANC ★★★

before 1996		Prior	
1996	5	Now	$18.50
1997	6	Now	$21.00
1998	6	Now	$21.00
1999	7	Now	$24.00
2000	7	Now	$23.00
2001	6	Now	$19.00

YARRA RIDGE SHIRAZ ★★★★

1994	5	Now	$21.00
1995	6	Now	$24.00
1996	Not made		
1997	7	Now	$27.00
1998	7	2004	$26.00
1999	5	2005	$18.00

***Yarra Valley Hills** is essentially a grower supplying other wineries in the region, having some wines contract made for their own label. They are now controlled by Dromana Estate. Winemaker: Martin Williams.*

YARRA VALLEY HILLS CABERNET SAUVIGNON ★★★★

1997	7	2006	$25.00
1998	6	2005	$21.00
1999	Not made		
2000	7	2008	$23.00

YARRA VALLEY HILLS CHARDONNAY ★★★★

1998	6	Now	$19.00
1999	6	2004	$18.50
2000	7	2006	$21.00

YARRA VALLEY HILLS PINOT NOIR ★★★★

1997	6	2006	$23.00
1998	6	Now	$22.00
1999	6	2004	$22.00

YARRA VALLEY HILLS SAUVIGNON BLANC ★★★

1997	7	Now	$18.50
1998	6	Now	$15.50
1999	6	Now	$15.00
2000	7	Now	$17.00

***Yarra Yering** is a small, purist operation in the Yarra Valley whose wines were in the forefront of the movement towards greater elegance in Australian wines. The winemaker's ratings have been unavailable for recent years. Winemaker: Bailey Carrodus.*

YARRA YERING CHARDONNAY ★★★★

YARRA YERING DRY RED NUMBER 1 (CABERNETS) ★★★★★

YARRA YERING DRY RED NUMBER 2 (SHIRAZ BLEND) ★★★★★

YARRA YERING PINOT NOIR ★★★★★

YARRA YERING SEMILLON (DRY WHITE NUMBER 1) ★★★★

YARRA YERING UNDERHILL SHIRAZ ★★★★

***Yarrabank** is a Yering Station operation dedicated to the production of extreme quality sparkling wine. Winemaker: Claude Thibaud.*

YARRABANK CUVEE BRUT ★★★★★

1993	7	Now	$44.00
1994	7	Now	$43.00
1995	7	Now	$42.00

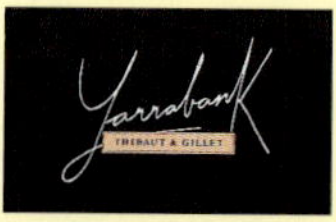

1996	6	2004	$35.00
1997	7	2005	$39.00
1998	7	2006	$38.00
1999	7	2008	$37.00
2000	7	2007	$36.00
2001	7	2008	N/R

***Yellowglen** was established in the Ballarat area as a specialist Champagne-style producer and have been resoundingly successful as such. It is part of the Beringer Blass group. Winemaker: Charles Hargrave.*

YELLOWGLEN CUVEE VICTORIA METHODE CHAMPENOISE ★★★★

before 1994		Prior	
1994	7	Now	$34.00
1995	7	Now	$33.00
1996	7	Now	$32.00
1997	6	Now	$27.00
1998	7	2005	$30.00

YELLOWGLEN VINTAGE BRUT ★★★

before 1992		Prior	
1992	7	Now	$38.00
1993	7	Now	$37.00
1994	5	Now	$25.00
1995	6	Now	$30.00
1996	No data		
1997	6	Now	$28.00
1998	7	2005	$32.00
1999	6	2005	$26.00

***Yeringberg** is a tiny (2 hectare) vineyard in the Yarra Valley which annually produces 800 cases of graceful, handmade wines. Winemaker: Guill de Pury.*

YERINGBERG
(Formerly CABERNET) ★★★★★

before 1976		Prior	
1976	7	Now	$130.00
1977	5	Now	$90.00
1978	2	Prior	
1979	6	Now	$100.00
1980	7	Now	$115.00
1981	7	Now	$110.00
1982	6	Now	$94.00
1983	4	Now	$60.00
1984	6	Now	$88.00
1985	5	Now	$70.00
1986	6	Now	$82.00
1987	4	Now	$54.00

1988	7	Now	$92.00
1989	4	Now	$50.00
1990	7	Now	$86.00
1991	7	Now	$84.00
1992	7	Now	$80.00
1993	6	Now	$68.00
1994	6	Now	$66.00
1995	6	Now	$64.00
1996	6	2004	$62.00
1997	5	2005	$50.00
1998	7	2006	$68.00
1999	6	2006	$56.00

YERINGBERG CHARDONNAY ★★★★★

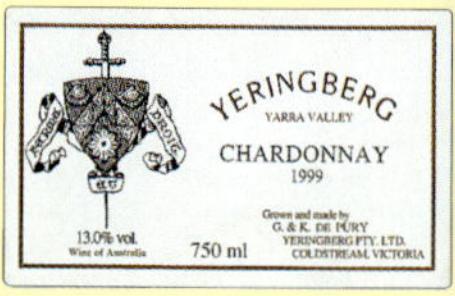

before 1980		Prior	
1980	5	Now	$66.00
1981	5	Now	$64.00
1982	4	Prior	
1983	4	Now	$49.00
1984	5	Now	$58.00
1985	7	Now	$80.00
1986	5	Now	$56.00
1987	5	Now	$54.00
1988	7	Prior	
1989	5	Now	$50.00
1990	6	Now	$58.00
1991	6	Prior	
1992	6	Now	$56.00
1993	7	Now	$62.00
1994	7	Now	$62.00
1995	5	Now	$43.00
1995	5	Now	$41.00
1996	5	Now	$40.00
1997	5	Now	$39.00
1998	6	Now	$45.00
1999	6	Now	$44.00
2000	6	2004	$43.00

YERINGBERG MARSANNE/ ROUSSANNE ★★★★

1979	5	Now	$70.00
1980	3	Now	$41.00
1981	5	Now	$66.00
1982	5	Now	$64.00
1983	2	Prior	
1984	7	Now	$84.00
1985	6	Now	$70.00
1986	2	Prior	
1987	7	Now	$78.00
1988	7	Now	$76.00

1989	3	Prior	
1990	6	Now	$60.00
1991	5	Prior	
1992	6	Now	$58.00
1993	6	Now	$56.00
1994	5	Now	$45.00
1995	5	Now	$44.00
1996	6	Now	$50.00
1997	6	Now	$50.00
1998	6	Now	$48.00
1999	6	Now	$47.00
2000	6	2004	$45.00

YERINGBERG PINOT NOIR ★★★★

before 1979		Prior	
1979	5	Now	$80.00
1980	7	Prior	
1981	7	Now	$105.00
1982	7	Now	$100.00
1983	5	Prior	
1984	4	Prior	
1985	6	Now	$80.00
1986	7	Now	$92.00
1987	5	Now	$62.00
1988	6	Now	$74.00
1989	6	Now	$72.00
1990	5	Now	$58.00
1991	6	Now	$68.00
1992	7	Now	$76.00
1993	6	Now	$64.00
1994	7	Now	$72.00
1995	6	Now	$60.00
1996	7	Now	$68.00
1997	7	Now	$66.00
1998	7	2004	$64.00
1999	6	Now	$52.00

***Yering Station** is a 1988 replanting of part of the first Victorian vineyard of Paul de Castella, originally established in the Yarra Valley in 1838. Winemakers: Tom Carson and Dan Buckle.*

YERING STATION CABERNET SAUVIGNON(/MERLOT) ★★★★

1991	7	Now	$34.00
1992	5	Now	$24.00
1993	5	Now	$23.00
1994	5	Now	$22.00
1995	6	Now	$26.00
1996	5	Now	$21.00

1997	6	2007	$24.00
1998	7	2009	$28.00
1999	7	2010	$27.00
2000	7	2010	$26.00
2001	6	2008	N/R
2002	5	2010	N/R

YERING STATION CHARDONNAY

★★★★

1991	7	Now	$37.00
1992	6	Now	$30.00
1993	7	Now	$35.00
1994	5	Now	$24.00
1995	5	Now	$23.00
1996	5	Now	$22.00
1997	6	Now	$26.00
1998	6	Now	$25.00
1999	7	2005	$29.00
2000	7	2005	$28.00
2001	7	2006	$27.00
2002	7	2008	$26.00

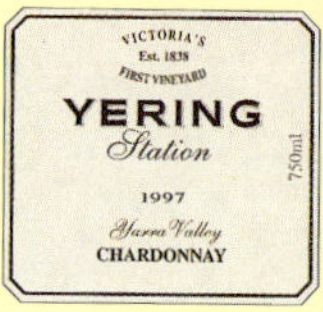

YERING STATION PINOT NOIR

★★★

1991	6	Now	$35.00
1992	4	Now	$22.00
1993	4	Now	$22.00
1994	5	Now	$26.00
1995	5	Now	$25.00
1996	7	Now	$35.00
1997	7	2004	$34.00
1998	7	2004	$33.00
1999	6	2004	$27.00
2000	7	2006	$31.00
2001	6	2006	$26.00
2002	7	2006	$29.00

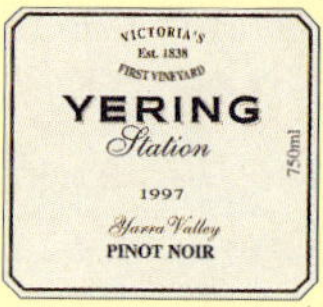

Zema Estate *is a painstakingly purist red wine vineyard in Coonawarra. Winemaker: Tom Simons.*

ZEMA ESTATE CABERNET SAUVIGNON

★★★★

before 1992		Prior	
1992	7	Now	$35.00
1993	7	Now	$34.00
1994	7	Now	$33.00
1995	5	Prior	
1996	7	2004	$31.00
1997	6	2004	$26.00
1998	7	2008	$30.00
1999	7	2006	$29.00

2000	7	2010	$28.00
2001	6	2010	$23.00
2002	6	2012	$22.00

ZEMA ESTATE CLUNY (CABERNET/MERLOT/MALBEC/CAB.FRANC)

★★★★

1993	5	Prior	
1994	6	Now	$29.00
1995	6	Now	$28.00
1996	7	Now	$32.00
1997	7	Now	$31.00
1998	7	2005	$30.00
1999	6	2005	$25.00
2000	7	2006	$29.00
2001	6	2006	$24.00
2002	7	2008	$27.00

ZEMA ESTATE FAMILY SELECTION CABERNET SAUVIGNON

★★★★★

1988	7	Prior	
1989	Not made		
1990	7	Prior	
1991	6	Now	$52.00
1992	7	Now	$60.00
1993	6	Now	$50.00
1994	7	2006	$56.00
1995	Not made		
1996	7	2010	$52.00
1997	Not made		
1998	7	2012	$50.00
1999	7	2010	$49.00
2000	7	2012	$47.00
2001	7	2012	$46.00

ZEMA ESTATE SHIRAZ

★★★★

before 1990		Prior	
1990	7	Now	$38.00
1991	6	Prior	
1992	7	Now	$36.00
1993	6	Now	$30.00
1994	7	Prior	
1995	5	Prior	
1996	7	2004	$32.00
1997	6	Now	$26.00
1998	7	2006	$30.00
1999	6	2006	$25.00
2000	7	2008	$28.00
2001	6	2008	$23.00
2002	7	2010	$27.00